The Heart of Every Marriage
– Real Stories by Real People

Mike and Connie Gilbride

Jesus is the ♡ of every marriage!

Mike   Connie

Mike
&
Connie
Gilbride

The Heart of Every Marriage –
Real Stories by Real People

Great Plains Ministry
2019

First Printing: 2019

ISBN: 978-0-359-81287-5

Ordering Information:
Special discounts are available on quantity purchases by corporations,
associations, educators, and others. For details, contact the publisher at
the address listed below.

U.S. trade bookstores and wholesalers please contact:

Great Plains Ministry
5907 W Wren Place
Sioux Falls, SD 57107
or email: www.greatplainsministry.org

Title page photo by Caleb Weerts
Cover design by Dale Weerts

Dedication

To our parents…

Gene & Delores Vilhauer

Francis (Bud) & Beth Gilbride

Dear Mom and Dad…You never pretended to be perfect, but you taught us more about commitment and teamwork by how you lived every day than by what you said.

Acknowledgments

We will be forever grateful our marriage fell apart! We thank Jesus for stepping in to rescue us from our 'perfectly fake' marriage. He revealed cracks and broken places, so He could heal them and rebuild us into partners nothing could destroy.

For the bravery and honesty in telling your stories, we thank each of you interviewed for this book. You opened your lives so others could be encouraged and find the hope to never give up.

To our son, Matthew: We are blessed God allowed us to be your parents - as imperfect as we were and are. You lived through many of the challenging, often painful, times in our marriage. We pray you see Jesus was always there every minute and never let us...or you...go!

Our gratitude for the numerous marriages placed in our lives as Godly examples. We pray we would also be a model of Christ's love to others in the same way they have been to us.

Our story began on October 17, 1970

Copyright © 2018 Kyla Briney Photography

Table of Contents

Why Stories?

Why not tell you ten easy steps to a better marriage? Couldn't we just cheer you up, pat you on the back and call it good?

It would have been much easier than traveling coast to coast with less than professional video equipment crammed into our car and thousands of miles of highway looming before us. Our task? Videotape interviews as over 60 individuals shared their marriage stories. Then once back home, figure out how to bring their stories to your hearts as if they were telling it themselves! Overwhelming? Yes, but…no ten steps to success nor an encouraging pat on the back could say what these real stories say about real life!

Why <u>their</u> stories? We had a miraculous story of rescue and renewal in our own marriage, but we aren't the only ones. God turned our eyes toward other couples all over the country, with stories only they could tell, with words that came from their own mouths.

We were invited into their lives and put face to face with an honest, unabridged look behind the walls of their homes where everyday life takes place. We laughed and cried along with them. Although this is not their whole story, what they share with you has no shortage of the unexpected…the trying…the challenging. There is also no drought of blessings.

Heart stories

On this journey, we witnessed hearts of all shapes and sizes. From a distance, we found many appeared undamaged…like the flawless ones we would expect on Sunday morning at church. When examined more closely, we discovered every heart had a few nicks and scratches. Some were even broken or shattered.

Someone once asked of our project, 'Did you go looking for people with the worst problems?' No…we did not stack the deck. We didn't intentionally seek out the most challenging situations to keep this book interesting. Most of the time, we had no idea what these couples faced in their lives until we hit the 'record' button on the camera.

We discovered no story was identical, but each one came with a heart filled hope. In a world so devoid of hope, that was the story that needed to be told.

A testimony

Revelation 12:11a says, 'They triumphed over him (the enemy) by the blood of the Lamb and by the word of their testimony…'. Every story with Jesus in it is a testimony and has the power to overcome the enemy.

Believe us when we say the enemy threw out roadblocks to the completion of this book! He would do anything (and tried) to stop these stories from being told because stories…testimonies…hold power to point to the One who can change, save and rebuild lives.

Go ahead…offend!

We believe every marriage that lasts, offends the enemy. So, go ahead and offend away! Shout it out loud! Here's something great to throw in Satan's face: 'We survived! God healed our marriage! No matter what happens, we are <u>never</u> going to leave or give up!'

STOP - STOP - STOP!!!

As you read these stories, we have two warnings:
1. If you find yourself comparing yourself or your marriage- STOP!!! Their marriage is <u>not</u> your marriage!
2. If you are tempted to use this book as a club to clobber your husband or your wife - STOP!

These life stories shared are meant to encourage and bless you. To inspire you and give you hope. Ok…now you can continue reading!!

His story

Each of us has a story. More importantly, each of us has a story where Jesus is the main character. Even if we didn't write Him into the plot, or even invite Him to be a part of it, His fingerprints are all over it! He created marriage, so every story is <u>His</u> story. As each page is turned, it points to the Author. We thank the Creator and Author for the new life He infused into our marriage…and is ready to infuse into yours!!

Mike and Connie

Josh & Crystal – Raw Honesty

MARRIED 15 YEARS

"I am the LORD, the God of all mankind. Is anything too hard for me?" Jeremiah 32:27

W e bicker more than pretty much anyone else we know!", Crystal tossed out with raw honesty.

Josh told us. "Early on, we felt lots of little conflicts that are well handled and well behaved are much better than a few big ones where people just go nuts and lose their cool. So, we have lots of little conflicts."

With her usual candor, Crystal continued, "We are both pretty antagonistic people. It goes back to 'He's passionate about what he thinks and I'm outspoken'."

Josh smiled, "And don't like to be wrong."

They both chuckled loudly as Crystal agreed, "And I <u>don't</u> like to be wrong. I remember when we were both doing youth ministry and the kids would just look at us and say, 'Are you two OK?' 'Oh yah...we're fine. This is normal'!"

Call the marriage counselor!

If you judged only on the bickering they seemed to accomplish on a regular basis, you would immediately dial the local chapter of 'Save-a-Marriage or Else'! But...Josh and Crystal told us their story with eyes intent on each other, as if we weren't even in the room. They have a bond tightly forged through separation, anticipation, pain, joy and yes...even bickering!

In the beginning...

'He's perfect for you!'...the exact comment from a friend trying to 'set up' a blind date! She had heard that story before but...Wait! This might be different. After all, it was an invitation to a Bible study...and...she accepted.

The perfect plan, except the first time she met him, he was with another girl! "So, I didn't really notice Crystal. Like any good guy, I was focused on the one I was with. Crystal didn't know the other relationship wasn't very serious." In fact, it was when this long-distance relationship fizzled out that Josh and Crystal finally started dating.

The attraction?

"I remember enjoying the fact that Crystal was outspoken...that she had opinions. A lot of girls that age were working really hard to be whatever they think you want them to be. I enjoyed the fact she seemed to know where she was going, and she seemed to have strong opinions and wasn't just waiting for someone to tell her who to be. And...I was drawn to the fact that she seemed just wholesome."

"He was definitely a person of his convictions. He wasn't easily swayed. So, he spoke passionately about anything he was talking about and he had a reason for everything he believed. I had grown up in a Christian home but there were times I just believed things because that was what I was taught to believe.

He was intriguing. I was used to guys wanting to make me happy and being what I wanted them to be and doting on me...and he did that to an extent, but he was very slow and methodical. He told me, 'I'm not saying anything until I mean it.' I remember telling him I loved him really early on and he was like..."

She put on a blank stare and barely moved her head up and down as Josh finished her thought, "...you'll hear it when you hear it."

They laughed as she said, "It was very different to not have some guy that hadn't been pining after me for a while and then was, 'I finally got her'!"

Their philosophy

"I had pretty well been programmed if I was going to date a girl, it needed to be an investigation if I wanted to marry her. I wasn't going to start talking about how I loved her and how amazing and how perfect she was. That was going to come after I decided she was the one I wanted to marry. Why build up all this emotion in front of the actual decision..."

Crystal smiled, "...And I was an 18-year-old girl who was emotional and didn't know what to do with this!"

He realized early on in their relationship, he didn't need or want anything more than Crystal. After finding her, he was not shopping around. "You just have to choose and stick with your choice. I felt good about it. It was a rational choice. It was an emotional choice and I have never regretted it."

Crystal looked intently at her husband, "...the first moment I was like, 'OK, there's something different about this relationship'." At the time, she was up to her neck in planning a huge youth camp and was over the top in the 'stressed-out' department. She tended to let everything pile on and most people around her would either say, 'It's not a big deal...you're fine...get over it' or 'That's awful' and commiserate with her. Josh approached her in a completely different way.

She was totally performance oriented and a people pleaser; he was more 'just the facts, Ma'am.' He would toss out questions such as: 'So, what if it's a complete failure?'

Crystal would quickly leap back with, 'That's not an option! It can't be a complete failure!'

Unrelenting in his probing, 'No...worst case scenario...what would happen?'

'We would have to return everyone's money and we'd have to...'

'Sooo?'

She moved her palm in a circle in front of Josh and giggled at her feelings at the time. 'Oh...there's a whole bunch of rational happening right here that I don't understand at all.'

"It was really good for me and he just supported me in ways other people never had been able to and that's continued through our marriage. When I'm going crazy, he has the ability to just 'right the ship' and so, it allows me to approach whatever we need to in life without being overwhelmed."

Break up?

How could they break up when they seemed perfect for each other? None the less, after dating about five months, there was a breakup. According to Josh, "It wasn't a bad break up. We both decided we needed to take some time apart, mature a little and get a better idea where we were going so that we were sure if we got back together, we would be a good match. I felt our relationship wasn't necessarily bringing us closer to God at that time and I felt like one of us needed to pull the plug before it got worse. I tried a couple of times...and she talked me out of it multiple times. Then a couple of weeks later she broke up with me!"

"I did!", she snickered. "We totally liked each other." However, her driving force was the fact she was moving to Boise and absolutely knew she wanted to pursue youth ministry and didn't want him to just enter into youth ministry because she was.

During that time of separation, they saw each other occasionally because they shared the same group of friends. When they eventually began talking again, they felt as if there was still something there.

The ultimatum

Josh was being deployed to Kuwait, so they made some major decisions about how they would communicate while he was gone. Crystal said, "We weren't going to talk the whole time he was gone. We weren't going to email. We were only going to write letters. We wanted to be really intentional about what we said and how we said it."

Josh said, "The whole time we were apart, I saw it as an opportunity for me to grow up a bit and for her to clarify what she wanted so we could be more intentional once we were back together. That was always my plan...to get back together." He felt they needed to pray about their relationship while separated and when he came back, both needed their minds made up about whether their relationship would end or continue. He gave her what he called 'the ultimatum'!

"He made it very clear he was definitely interested. He told me, 'Either we're going to pursue this relationship and I'm going to stay here and I'm going to go to school or...I'm going to leave you alone and I'll be gone'. So, I had to make a decision."

The parent problem

Pulling no punches, Crystal said, "I was 20 and old enough to be making some decisions on my own but I really respected my parents' opinion. I was in this spot where I really think this could be the person I want to marry, but my parents absolutely despised him."

Josh gulped back an obvious reaction as he said, "That's a strong word!"

Crystal gave him a look that she meant what she said. "My Dad called you 'the worm' over Thanksgiving dinner!"

Both convulsed in uncontrollable laughter, as Josh covered his eyes with his hands. At the end of the day, it came down to the fact that her Mom didn't want Crystal marrying somebody in the military.

She had another choice to make: Go against her parents or back away from her relationship with Josh. She had to be sure there was really something between them to take that monumental risk.

The return and THE answer

Josh returned from his deployment and Crystal grinned, "I knew what I was going to answer, but <u>he</u> didn't know my answer." Her huge smile might have given him a hint, but she held the answer close to her chest as long as she could. Then she gave him the, 'Yah! I'm in'!

Everyone was excited except, you guessed it...Crystal's parents.

That was a conversation Josh would rather have avoided! "They had been 'rid' of me for almost two years while we were not dating and then the year in Kuwait. Now I was back sitting in their living room telling them 'I am going to date your daughter again'." He was declaring his intent to not just date their daughter, but likely marry her someday.

Crystal didn't want to deal with her parents either but finally agreed to meet her Mom for dinner. "That ended with my Mother bawling in a hotel room and me feeling like a terrible human being." As if he could imagine being there that night, Josh tossed in, "Awkward dinner!"

As they were getting more and more serious, they were both very conscious her parents continued to hope and pray the relationship would fizzle out and fall apart.

She explained, "That should have made us fight a lot more than it did...but it didn't. We just kind of kept weathering all of the conversations." Whether it was roommate drama, things going on with his parents who were divorced or her Mom not liking Josh, their relationship wasn't the source of the drama in their lives. She felt it was always a stabilizing force.

Hard conversations

Every date included challenging conversations; diving into the hard issues of life. They grilled each other with all the difficult questions and set everything out on the table that might bring conflict to a marriage.

There was also an abundance of hard conversations in Crystal's head! "It was really hard because my parents had always given me good counsel and I felt like had been good advisors. It was just such a loud voice in my head...the voice of doubt for me."

Josh added, "It was hard because I respected them too, so to have them against our relationship was really a struggle. Our strategy was just to wait and to trust that God would change us or change them but if it was meant to be it would work out."

Opinion changed by tragedy

A sudden tragedy hit Crystal's family when her brother, Brian, was killed in a car accident. Prior to that, Josh wasn't around her family much. She felt all her parents knew about Josh could be summed up this way: 'He was this guy who was in the military and...and...he was just kind of this nuisance.'

"When this tragedy hit the family," Josh quietly commented, "I was around all the time and they got to see a different side of me."

Crystal lived about a 45-minute drive from her parents' home and there were many times, even late into the night, when she needed to be near them while dealing with the loss. Josh would drop everything and drive her to be with family. He cleaned out Brian's apartment, to spare her parents the pain.

As they were trying to decide where everyone was going to sit at the funeral, her Mom asked, 'Do you want Josh to sit with you?'

"She saw you leaning on me while you were grieving in a way that made her feel comfortable. I think that was the beginning of her seeing that I could be a good husband."

The garage epiphany

A few weeks later, Crystal and her Mom were talking when the subject of the wedding arose. Crystal responded, 'We're not talking about this until you guys are fine with Josh. I'm not having these conversations because it's too hard'.

'Oh, we're fine with him. We're happy about this'.

'Since when? This is new to me.' According to her Mom, they were fine with Josh for a few weeks.

'You coulda told me!' Crystal put her index finger up to her Mom: 'STOP!'. "I literally went out to the garage where Josh was working, and I said, 'You may now propose...whenever you like'!" How could they not crack up at <u>that</u> memory!

The proposal

Crystal had the biggest grin as Josh reiterated what he originally told her about proposals. "There's no way I'm going to propose to you before I actually know your answer because that's something they do in movies. That's not real life. You don't ask someone to marry you if you're not sure they actually will."

With that in mind, Josh was searching for a proposal that would be unique and kind of funny, but he said, "The surprise would be <u>when</u> and <u>how</u> and not that I was asking."

The ring

Crystal grinned and then chortled, "My credit was better than his, so we actually used my credit to buy my wedding ring. He paid for it...but it was kind of a joke at the time."

She knew exactly where the ring was...on a closet shelf in his apartment. "I would go over to his apartment to go somewhere with him and I would sneak into the closet to take a peak and he would be like: 'Get out! You DO NOT get to try on it on tonight'!"

'But, I want to! I know where's it's at!' That's when he hid it!

He kept the 'when' a mystery, as the proposal dangled in front of her nose like a carrot. The evening of her birthday dinner was filled with a dramatic roller coaster ride as she tried to guess if he would propose. His classic pauses and thoughtful remarks were followed by silence. Crystal finally gave up hope it would happen <u>that</u> night!

To close the evening, they parked on the top of a hill and sat in the truck bed to watch the sunset. That's when Josh told her he got her something. Could this be it?

With her eyes closed, he slipped something around her neck and instructed her not to look down.

"Then I looked at Josh and he had something orange coming out of his ears. 'Are those carrots?',"she quizzed him. "I finally figured out he had orange ear plugs because, I always said I was going to scream when he proposed. I looked down and the ring was on the necklace."

"After she quit screaming, I got down on my knee and asked her."

Difficult person tamed

At one point in wedding planning, her biological Dad asked to walk her down the aisle. That was not something she expected. In frustration, she firmly said, 'I'm done. I'm done with this relationship. It hurts too much. I don't care anymore'!

Josh's responded to her, 'That's not the right way to behave. You don't get to do that.' Then he softened and encouraged her to mend that relationship with her Dad. He also started stepping in and helping her set healthy boundaries with her Dad.

"There were times I would be on the phone and he could see me getting too emotional. He would walk over and take the phone and end the conversation." She was learning to trust his leadership and they were experiencing the gift of partnership.

Mine vs Ours

Crystal proudly reported, "I came out of high school and weathered all of college and had $2000 in my savings account. 'Whooo-Whooo...$2000!' At the time, it was a really big deal for me because it was my money. That was like my security."

They were now married, so Josh was thinking, 'These are OUR finances, so your savings is OUR savings. We are coming up on another semester where I need to buy a bunch of books and tuition. After I get that paid out, my income and GI bill will be coming in and we make that back.'

"He needed $1800 of my $2000 for SIX months." Her sweet, newlywed response to his request: 'NO! That's mine!'

Josh rolled his eyes, "It blew me away. 'What do you mean yours? All my stuff's yours...but all your stuff isn't mine'?"

"Looking back, it's funny, but I remember it was this huge moment for me. I said I trusted his judgment. I said that we're doing life together. It was just this moment where it was very tangible that I was having to let go of all of that and trust him."

She added, "In less than six months we had more money than we'd ever had. It set the stage for a lot of decisions in their future because he would ask, 'Do you trust me?' My answer, 'Yup! We've been here before'!"

Small decisions - Big trust

They came to the point where Josh began looking for a job after graduation. Crystal said, "I didn't want to leave Boise at all, under any circumstances."

He told her, 'I'm going to try to find a job here but there's going to be a point that might not be possible.'

She was now having to trust his intent. 'He knows I want to be here. He said that's what he was going to try to do and so I can trust that that's what he's really doing.'

Josh discovered his wife was one who worried more about the future than he realized. He looked over at Crystal and said, "The way you dealt with uncertainty about the future was to just not take risks and to hold things really close. I was more the kind of person who wanted to put together a good plan and then just execute it." They had to work together to develop a strategy for making big life decisions that respected both of their outlooks and opinions. They were learning how to compromise, and in the process, building trust.

Communication blocker

Communication? Josh piped up, "We argue!"

"Yah", Crystal continued, "because we approach life so differently. I tend to be pretty emotional and I didn't always fight fair." She spoke to Josh, "You're very rational and logical and straight forward, so it took us a little while. My inclination was if things got too heated, then I didn't want to continue the conversation. Your approach is always like, 'No, we have to get to the other side of this, so as uncomfortable as it is, we have to figure out how to make it through this and come up with a plan for how to do this better or how to address the situation'."

She admitted, "At first, it just made me mad. 'Just leave me alone'!" They looked at each other and light laughter came from their hearts as she reflected. "Now I feel like we really have good communication because it's like, we don't just let something sit and stew and bother us. We're going to work through it."

Josh added, "We never did any yelling, name calling...none of that kind of stuff that can really escalate. But...we would get into these funks where we'd been bickering <u>every</u> day about <u>everything</u>...for a couple of weeks. I always sensed when it was really going to be uncomfortable for a while. It was when we would start not thinking the best about the other person's intentions...like at every turn." Toss in a few mind games from both sides and he admitted, "Those were the tough times!"

Recognize the trap

Crystal stepped in, "I think part of it was just recognizing it. A lot of times we just wouldn't talk about it and hope it would go away." They soon discovered it wasn't always some concrete event or insurmountable hurt they could identify but a myriad of little things that had built up. Crystal's voice teased as she popped in with, "<u>Everything</u> you do annoys me! You brush your too teeth loud! You're driving me crazy!"

Once they recognized the trap they had fallen into, Crystal could say, 'You're not accusing me of being a terrible wife. We're just not getting along right now.' Her method of breaking that trend of communication blockage was to pull out the calendar and begin planning things she knew would 'reset' their relationship. It might include sleeping in a Saturday morning followed by cooking breakfast together and working on some household chores together. She would also add a little play time into the day. She needed the diversion of some activity that would break the tension.

Josh said, "Those activities are sort of like a salve that heals." He then shook his head slightly, "The thing that would wear on me the most is feeling like somebody is upset with me, disappointed in me." He didn't want it to accumulate, so he felt a strong need to get it out on the table. He admitted, "It may not get better right away but at least we both recognize it's happening, and we don't want it to keep happening."

Crystal laughed in agreement as he continued, "We don't want this to last forever and neither of us believes the end is near. Just having that out on the table always made me feel like, 'Whether we're in a funk for another 24 hours or 24 days, it WILL end, the clouds will part, and things will get back to normal'."

He said, "It's just better to go, 'You know what...this just happens sometimes. Yes, we can do better in the future and avoid the things that put us here but there is no sense trying to blame or be angry at this point'."

Crystal smiled at her husband, "As I work alongside you or am doing something with you, inevitably, you will do something that will make me laugh. That is going to make me have more positive feelings towards you again." She gently patted him on the leg as she snickered, "It's a really good thing you're a comedian!" That's when the real 'knee-slapping' began.

Hang on or give up?

Josh said, "I watched my parents divorce when I was about 10 or 12. Just watching that and seeing what that was like and being old enough to think about it..." He paused, "When we got married, we very much had this idea that we might not like each other 10 years from now but we're not going to get a divorce." They were determined to never even allow divorce to be on the table.

Crystal said, "My parents had been divorced, his parents had been divorced, tons of our friends' parents had been divorced. It was just a part of what we had grown up in and what was normal for us. We didn't like it...and didn't like all the complications it had added to our lives as kids."

Before marriage, they discussed numerous scenarios that could cause them to separate but agreed not one of them would give them reason to divorce. That gave Crystal stability in knowing even if she came home having to admit she spent too much money they really didn't have, he might groan loudly, roll his eyes at her and be upset, but he was not going to leave her.

It's really strong!

They wanted children and had been trying for a while without success. Even though it could be labeled a hardship, Josh said, "It's hard to call it a hardship for me because as difficult as it's been, it's been incredibly encouraging to be able to go through it. I feel closer to her than I have ever before in our marriage."

It wasn't, however, an easy road to walk. They suffered a failed adoption followed by the physical and emotional stress of fertility treatments. They finally got pregnant but then suffered a miscarriage. Josh said, "To get to what we thought was the end of the road and then see that plan sort of dashed, was really, really hard. Yet, within a week or two of that, I think I just felt so encouraged...there was this confidence...that we could stand up under anything. As hard as that was individually...together it was kind of like...piling the weight on top of something you build and seeing that it didn't buckle or crack. It's just that confidence that 'Wow...this thing we built (our marriage) ...it's really strong'!"

Crystal said, "There were definitely times I questioned myself and my ability to withstand what we were going through. While Josh always tended to handle everything better and I think it's the rational side of him. I'm also naturally really impatient about everything. Anyone who has known me for any length of time knows that I want what I want when I want it and I'm used to getting it!"

She dabbed at the corners of her eyes. Laughter and tears mingled as she said, "We will have waited almost seven years for a baby from the time we first started trying, so that was hard. But...our marriage was the thing I could always rely on."

One night to be mad

When going through the difficult challenges of infertility, failed adoption and miscarriage, she would often ask, 'How do you handle this'?

Since there was nothing they could do about it, Josh's response was: 'OK, we're going to pick one night and we're just going to be completely irresponsible and pout and be mad.'

She added, "We would order an obscene amount of greasy Chinese food and rent a comedy and we would kind of like just hole up in the house."

They had many people in their lives who knew and loved them, who would want to call and console them. However, that night, they turned off their phones. Crystal remembered their philosophy: 'The rest of the world can be a part of this later. Right now, it's just us.' "We would cry our way through it...usually me more than him and we'd eat all this food. You can say anything tonight and it doesn't get held against you. Tonight, is the selfish part of it and we can just respond and react and be angry and that's OK. When we woke up in the morning, we had to take one step forward."

Dreams dashed

After the miscarriage, they knew they needed to eventually, sooner or later, face their closest friends with their sad news. Tears continued to flow as Crystal shared, "I remember literally a moment where we stood up to leave our friends and I was just leaning on him physically...every part of me needed him to be able to stand up at the at moment. One of our friends from the group commented later about just watching that and how it was a picture of our marriage and just how we relied on each other. For that couple of weeks, I just remember knowing that this was going to be hard and there wasn't anything I was going to like about it but that he was going to be there in every way that I needed."

Sometimes she was OK when they went to bed but two hours later woke up struggling. He would get up with her and watch anything on TV to distract and make them laugh. "I remember thinking, 'I could not be getting through this now...but because he's here, I can'."

Josh quietly added, "We don't want to have to do it again or anything like it, but life has these moments. It's just good to know we're ready."

They both dabbed at their tears as Crystal softly spoke about their hopes being dashed by miscarriage, close calls, myriad disappointments and a drained bank account. "Early on it was easier because it was new and like a workout routine. You weren't quite as sore yet and things didn't hurt as badly. There was still hope and still all of these other options. It had only been a year...it had only been two years...it had only been three years. As time wore on it got harder and harder to believe." They had to begin to face the hard reality they might never have children.

Afraid to hope

Crystal continued, "We were doing fertility treatments."

Josh gave us the statistics. "It's supposed to work approximately 1 in 3 so after five tries it should have been 95% chance that it worked."

In the seventh month of treatments, they got pregnant only to lose their baby two months later. Crystal said, "We took three months off to let everything calm down and then we started up again. All the tests said, 'This should be easy. You got pregnant once so it's a great sign this should happen quickly'."

Sadness returned to her eyes. "We went through month after month after month after month. It got to about a year of trying again and the doctor basically sat us down and said, 'This isn't working. We basically have two options. We can stop what we've been doing, and we can try In Vitro, which is obviously more expensive'." (Their finances would limit them to one shot at In Vitro.)

She smiled, "It would have been like, 'We're taking basically everything we've got...and by the way, don't be stressed because that doesn't help'!" They both laughed as she said, "Yah...no stress!"

The doctor offered a second option, 'We can try putting you on some pretty aggressive hormonal medication treatments and we can try for three months but we'll only try it for three months.' They chose to use this option to take place during the summer when as a teacher, she would be off work.

She barely smiled, "We did the first round and it didn't work but there was a sense of hope. They upped the medications the second time around. Round two not working was devastating and really was the point where I just kind of lost it." Even so, they chose to go into round three.

The logical part of Josh kicked in as he said, 'Let's start talking now about what we're going to do when it doesn't work...so we can be surprised if it works! 'Do we go back and look at adoption again? How do you feel about In Vitro? Do we go pester the clinic and say, 'We know you said you were going to stop but we want to throw another $7000 at you.' Keep trying? or what?' "That conversation didn't go really well!"

Angry at everyone!

Crystal glanced down slightly before looking up to speak, "It came to a point that I was definitely angry. I was mad at God. I was mad at the clinic. I was mad at everybody and everything and the world wasn't fair, and I was really upset!"

She looked at her husband and confidently said, "...usually he likes me, and I know that." Josh looked over at her and couldn't hold in the laughter before she continued. "He approves of the decisions I'm making. He admires the way I handle situations...all of those things. We had a conversation that night where he said, my view of God offended him."

Her argument: "I had done all these things and I had now waited long enough. I had endured the trial and I was done! God needed to understand and needed to give me what I wanted because I was DONE!"

Risked confrontation

It had to finally be addressed. Normally, Josh would assume another woman, or a close friend should approach the subject, but he knew he was the one God was asking to lovingly confront his wife.

She hit her hand into her palm and looked over at Josh, "When we finally had to address it...I can't remember exactly what you said that night, but it was something like: 'You don't deserve anything good'!" That's when they looked at each other and howled out loud at her memory of his brutally honest comments!

"He wasn't angry, but he just flat out called me out for how I was acting and what I was saying. His sharp truth said, 'That's not how this works. We don't love God because of what He gives us! Is this really what you think? Because if it is...I don't even want to try next month because I don't want God to give us something if this is where you're at'!"

They might have joined in the hilarity now, but it wasn't all that funny at the time! "I felt the anger grow in me at everything he was saying. I remember going to bed and we didn't talk. When I finally started processing through it...I wasn't angry at him. I was angry because everything he said was true. I was angry I had put myself in that position. I had allowed myself to build up this attitude and I just didn't want to be challenged."

Crystal meekly continued, "I could see on the other side of it, but it was a life in which I didn't identify God as being good. I was going to have to settle for less. It would always be something I would be bitter about. We would survive, and we would be married, and life would go on, but it wouldn't be the life I was supposed to have. God would have robbed me of something. And that's what my husband saw in me that disturbed him."

Josh shook his head in agreement. He had to approach her with the truth. He was willing to live on the edge; willing to risk his wife's anger for her good. "When you're married, you start to feel closer to your spouse than any other person in your life. I understood her feelings, because I have had them myself. There are moments where you have to put your money where your mouth is, and act based on the faith you say you have."

Once I was blind

"By God's grace, the next morning (after Josh's challenge), I was like, 'No, that's not who I'm going to be and I'm not going to walk that road! If the choice is: 'Be childless and yet have a walk with God...or have a child but still have this view of God that He's going to give me what I think I deserve'. I have to choose my relationship with God. It still took a while to get there because I was working through the process of what it looks like that God is good even when He's not giving me good things."

The cloud was gone

They were on their last month of injections and she was very doubtful it worked. She said to Josh, 'Really...for the first time...I don't feel like there's this kind of cloud hanging over me.' Tears trickled down her cheeks as Josh smiled at her next comment. "Josh was like, 'Good...we are finally making some progress'."

On the way home from work, she thought about taking a pregnancy test, not necessarily to determine if she was pregnant but to prepare herself for the let-down to come. "We have wasted more money on pregnancy tests than anyone ever should!", she laughed.

She took the test and in shock, could hardly mouth the words, "It's....It's positive!" She didn't know what to do with herself. "I'm the only person in the world right know that knows that I'm pregnant...I can't even contain it. I'm laughing! I'm excited! I'm sitting there trying to rationalize...like maybe it's not true...a false positive test. This can't actually be happening!"

They were supposed to go over to her parents' home for dinner that night. She called Josh and asked if he could come home before going to her parents. Clueless, he said, 'I'm going to work a little bit late and then I'll swing by and pick you up.'

"Of all nights!" she exclaimed. "At first you were running a little bit late and then you were running so late because traffic was bad, and you told me you would just meet me at my parents' house." She remembered stumbling over words as she tried to convince him to come home first. By this time in the interview, they were almost rolling on the ground holding their stomachs!

"Josh walked through the door and I was standing right there...'I'm pregnant!' Of course, he was super excited...but said in a matter of fact tone said, 'I figured out you either needed me to load something into the car or you were pregnant'!"

From excitement to fear

Joy filled her face, "We were pregnant on the last try! The news was followed by sheer excitement for a few days...which was then followed by fear for a few months."

"My attitude: 'I've got to give her a couple of days to be happy and then I gotta start toughening her up. You know we have make sure we can survive another miscarriage because it could totally happen. I don't want to just have nothing but confetti and balloons until we crash into the wall. I need to start having conversations...so we did'."

She said, "It was this constant balance of excitement...and then trying to hold it loosely. 'It looks like I'm getting something good from God but that isn't what makes God good'." There were moments of doubt as to how she would survive if they lost another baby, but she came to the place where she could honestly say, 'He's in control and He's still good'.

A quiet sigh came from her heart, "God definitely has taught us a lot over the last few years." She wiped tears away, "Obviously not always what we want or what we are praying for but..."

No matter how much he mopped at the tears, Josh couldn't stop more from forming in his eyes as he completed her sentence with a simple, "Yah".

"The whole pregnancy has been a mix of absolute sheer excitement and…", followed by her whispered, "…is everything OK?"

Never struggle alone

They had a lot of friends but when they were struggling in their own relationship, they didn't want to uncover their struggles to them. Josh shared that they now know the importance of being open with other couples and having both friends and mentors with whom you can be transparent and honest about your marriage. "I think it just adds a level of accountability. Our hope is that if we aren't doing well it would be hard to hide."

Crystal feels she has people in her life that can help her address problem areas before they become huge issues. "It creates opportunities for each of us to be a better version of who we need to be, and we bring something better to our marriage than if we were just isolated and doing life alone."

Better together

Josh said, "I feel blessed I have someone in my life that makes me better. One thing we love about our relationship is just how much better we are together than apart. I'm constantly aware I have a tendency to procrastinate and I don't follow through on tasks. Left to my own devices, I would really struggle in a lot of areas. People don't even see me struggle because of her. When she's with me through life, it just covers over all of them and then people see a much more mature and responsible person than I would be otherwise."

She admitted, "I tend to take on too much. That's just like my natural inclination to say 'yes' to everything, to do everything and to just live a life that's completely unsustainable, in the long term. He came into my life and was 'No, that's not how we live'. That allowed me to say, 'OK...we need a little bit of space in our life'."

She looked at him and broke into a broad smile. "I don't feel I'm the type of person who laughs a lot, but he can make me laugh no matter what's going on in life. We can go out with people tonight…but 'why'? We'll have a ton more fun spending the weekend at home together, working on stupid projects or doing nothing. We just have more fun doing normal life together."

Josh grinned, "Sad but true!"

The truth

In all the raw honesty of their story - here is the truth! They don't have to be perfect to try to impress anyone. Together they have forged through mountains of tough stuff in their young marriage. Josh and Crystal realize they can't afford to be anything but real with you and with each other.

And then there were three!

The day after we completed our interview with Josh and Crystal, their little boy, Cooper, arrived safely into their world. This adventurous, inquisitive little man lights up their lives every day in ways they could only imagine while waiting those long seven years for him to arrive!

Bill & Bobbie – It Gets Better All the Time

MARRIED 58 YEARS

"May your fountain be blessed, and may you rejoice in the wife of your youth." Proverbs 5:18

Copyright © Tyler Ogburn Photography

My first recollection of Bobbie was this beautiful little-blond haired pony-tail, swishing back and forth, going down the hall of our high school. I saw her and said, 'I've GOT to meet her'!"

At this point, Bobbie smiled up at Bill, and we could almost imagine that little blond ponytail still swinging as she moved her head.

"Over the course of several months, we had some classes together, but I was dating other girls at the time. Bobbie and I would sit and talk about the relationships we were having...not with each other, but with others! We had some good conversations. I saw a very practical young lady that was fully engaged in life, as far as I could see."

That platonic relationship went on about two and a half years when Bill woke up! "I told my best friend, 'You know, I think I'm going to marry her.' We hadn't dated when all of a sudden, I'm thinkin'...'This is the one!' 'This is the one!' So, I asked her out. We were seventeen. A very mature seventeen!" Now they were both in an uproar of laughter at the absurdity of that statement!

They were good friends first, and Bill smiled as he proudly said, "And we still are! We had our first date, and probably six months later I asked her to marry me. Well, I really didn't ask her to marry me at first. We were sitting in the car in front of her house, talking about life. I made a comment about us having children. She said, 'Oh', I haven't heard you say anything about marriage yet'. That's when I said, 'Honey, would you marry me'!"

They marched down the aisle at age 18. Bobbie had graduated from high school and Bill had quit school in the tenth grade. School was not at the top of his life list. According to Bill, they were young and foolish. His Mom was vehemently opposed to the marriage and told him it would never last. Bobbie laughed as Bill said, "Yup, she said that many times!"

Bobbie said, "My parents were fine with it. Even when he was running around not knowing the Lord, my Mama said, 'He will make a good missionary. He'll be a preacher someday'." Bobbie told us Bill was extremely skeptical about those preacher and missionary remarks, "But," Bobbie nodded, "my Mama saw something in him."

No clue!

Premarital counseling? Nonexistent! On top of that, Bobbie snickered, "I had never been to a wedding!"

Bill snorted as he said, "Our wedding was kind of a joke!"

Bobbie actually held her chest to keep from exploding into laughter as she recounted, "We didn't even know that most people have a reception. We got married. They threw rice. And we took off! That was it! I know...it's hilarious!"

They were off on a short honeymoon. When they came back to church the next Sunday, they were approached with this: 'Now that you're married, how would you like to be leaders of MYF (Methodist Youth Fellowship)?'

They both gasped for air, so they could hardly speak. Bobbie caught her breath and said, "We had no clue what we were doing. We did it for a little while but that is just an example how little we knew and how little people helped us!"

Challenges piled on

Bobbie felt there were so many challenges in their marriage, it was hard to name them. Not understanding what marriage or love was. Getting used to each other. Finances. Raising children.

"My wife was not a difficult woman. She's never been difficult. For me, the difficulty was raising children. My parents didn't do a very good job of raising us. I don't think I ever remember, except in the later years of my Dad's life, him saying he loved us. Those words didn't come out. Emotion was very difficult for them to express and I did what I saw my parents do. I soon realized there was a need to express emotions, to show love and all those other things you use in helping to develop children."

Those would be enough challenges, but then, let's add 20 years of military life to the mix. Bill signed up for the Army, in October 1962, during the Cuban Missile Crisis, when they were married just over a year. "I surprised Bobbie by saying, 'Honey, I'm going down to the recruiting station in Atlanta'. I almost didn't tell her...almost just went."

"It was probably one of the best things that ever happened. I believe it drew us closer together. I believe the separations we had over all those years only made our marriage stronger, because we would come back together with an intensity and a strength in staying together. I'm glad I did what I did, but there were a lot of tough times."

Like a single Mom

Bobbie's voice sadly began, "He was not with me when either of the children were born and that was very hard."

Bill looked down and shook his head in agreement.

Her voice cracked as she spoke: "Chuck was eight months old before he saw his Daddy so, for 16 months, I had him by myself."

As she wiped away tears, she continued, "We had been in Germany and when we came back, I was pregnant with our daughter, Bretta. Bill went to an assignment in Virginia and I came home and stayed with my Mama. When Bretta was a week old, he came home and saw her. When she was a month old, we moved to Virginia to be with him. The first ten years of our marriage, we were apart more than we were together. I couldn't have done it without the Lord and a lot of family support."

Faith life

Taking a long look back at her life, at 14 years old, Bobbie had a realization of sin and forgiveness. That was when she asked the Lord into her heart. As Bobbie shared about her faith, Bill was wiping tears from his eyes. Bill was raised in church and felt that was one of things his Mom and Dad did right. "Every Sunday, without fail, we were in church. Every Sunday. Unfortunately, that was the only time there was reference to God or any sense of a spiritual relationship the rest of the week. So, I had been in church, and I knew about this God who was distant and far away, who may or may not hear anything you say."

"In 1961, when Bobbie and I were dating, we went to a church revival. The first couple of nights, it was 'just sit there and listen'. On that last night, the preacher really laid it on thick. He began to talk about a relationship with the Lord and the need for salvation. Nobody ever told me that. That night, the preacher was speaking to everybody, but he was speaking to me. He continued to tell 'me' I needed to accept

Christ into my heart, ask for forgiveness of sins and begin to commit my life to serving Him and following Him. I said, 'GOLLLY...I've never heard this before'. So, when the altar call came, I went to kneel and asked Jesus into my heart. I was 18 years old."

After they married, Bill said he tried to do all the 'churchy' stuff. "I made an attempt to read the King James Bible. Took the children to church every Sunday. Prayed at meals. I did the best I could, but there was still something just not there. I would go to church and listen to the message, but there was still not an overwhelming commitment and relationship I felt like I needed in my life. I wasn't really searching, but I knew that something wasn't where it needed to be."

Their hands entwined, Bobbie looked up at Bill with a hint of sadness in her eyes and recounted the next part of the story. She was on the women's ministry committee and Bill was the Sunday School Superintendent of their church. They both sighed at the thought of how differently they lived at home from what they did at church.

Had enough

They cruised along on autopilot but about 20 years into their marriage when Bill finally said he had enough. "I needed to find peace in my life, and I wasn't getting it at home. Bobbie did not have a clue. I was just restless inside. Our son, Chuck, had been into drugs and went into the military and our daughter, Bretta, was a rebellious teenager. I felt the only way I could get peace in my life was to divorce...separate myself from my family and search for the peace that I desperately wanted."

Bill thought his job in the military was enough stress on its own without having other stressors, like family. He made a decision on Friday night that on the following Monday morning, he was going to the legal office at the Army post to file for a divorce. He was done and ready to do something about it!

I needed that peace

God had something else in mind and was orchestrating the events in their lives. Wind back the story several months prior to Bill's desperate private divorce declaration. Bobbie went to a women's ministry planning meeting at church. Before she realized there was a problem in her own marriage, she said, 'I wish there was something we could do for the family and the home'. Her friend, Barbara, remembered a resource ministry that focused on reaching families and blurted out, 'Son Shine Ministries!' That was what led to the Valentine weekend that began the change of a lifetime in their family.

Bill got a huge smile on his face as he added, "I think she planned all that! Nice little banquet Friday night and then Son Shine Ministries was going to start their thing with one little session on Friday night..." We could just imagine the wheels turning in his head so many years ago...'Just a Friday night! Can't be any threat in that!'

Bobbie defended herself with, "My total reason was the children because they were so rebellious...nothing to do with our marriage. I was totally clueless that our marriage was in trouble!"

"So, on Friday night, my wife says, 'Honey, are you going to go with me?' 'Yeh – Yeh...I'll go with you', but inside I'm thinking, 'This is ridiculous! This is stupid!' I didn't sense any love for Bobbie anymore. I didn't hate her. I just didn't have anything there. I'm gonna go to this Valentine's banquet and pretend to love my wife and blah, blah, blah, blah. And I finally said, 'Yah, I'll go' cuz I didn't want her to look bad in front of all the ladies at church."

By then, their daughter, Bretta came downstairs and asked if she had to go to this 'thing'. Bill's honest answer was, 'If I gotta go...you gotta go!'

Smiling, she looked up at Bill as he continued, "That night we had a nice meal, candlelight...all that good stuff and then the main speaker, Lew Shaffer, spoke for an hour. I was intently listening to this man because he was making sense, and he was talking about Jesus. Chaplains I knew in our military chapel usually talked in big theoretical terms and didn't ever get down to the nuts and bolts. But this guy, at the very end, said this: 'I am more at peace in my life right now'." Bill had to take a minute to gather up his emotions as his voice began to crack and tears welled up in his eyes. He then finished the speaker's statement, "I am more at peace in my life right now...than I've ever been because Jesus is my best friend."

They both wiped tears from their eyes and we did, too. "That's what I had been looking for", Bill said as he was even more choked up. They grasped each other's hands as he continued, "I needed to know...I needed that peace."

He set our marriage free

Nothing was going to keep Bill from going to that program again the next day. "I needed to hear what this guy had to say, because what he'd said so far was just everything I needed."

Bill, then reached out his hand in front of his chest and closed his hand as if he was grasping and pulling that truth to his heart. "That weekend was amazing. I heard things about what I was supposed to be doing as a husband and a father that nobody had ever told me. It made sense because it was from the Word of God, and it was backed up by a relationship with Jesus that was never going to leave you. He was always going to be there to give you what you needed for every situation."

Both were trying to wipe tears from their eyes as Bill continued, "On Monday morning, it was amazing! I didn't want to go to work. I wanted to stay at home because...because God had taken my heart and knocked that wall down that kept me from seeing who Bobbie was and what God had given me in her. I was head over heels in love with her." Bobbie laughed softly and smiled as Bill continued, "Just like that! This wasn't something you spend months counseling and working out. Just like that He set me free and set our marriage free and gave us our daughter back. That was the point on February 1982 when God changed my life."

Wrong focus

Bobbie recalled, "My focus had been totally wrong. I learned at the seminar that I didn't have any clue what a wife's role was. I thought all of our problems were the kids, because I was focused on the kids instead of my husband where my focus needed to be." Her voice began to crack as she continued, "It totally changed how I looked at our marriage and our life, our kids, and Bill. I had no idea what a spiritual wife was, even though my Mom was one. I just wasn't taught. God revealed the truth to me.

The speaker's wife, Sandy, taught the women during that seminar. She is such a wonderful teacher. She told me, 'God is going to use you, and He is going to make such a difference in women's lives'." We could tell Bobbie was humbled by that statement as she looked up and placed her hand on her chest. The question she remembered asking, 'Who me?' came with tears and a breaking in her voice. "It's just been watching His faithfulness over the years as we've grown so much closer and helped so many people. It wasn't us. It was Jesus. I know now, my focus had to be on Jesus first and then my husband and then the kids. That was probably the biggest thing I learned."

We surmised the Monday morning divorce was off!

Blessings rolled in like waves

Bobbie began, "There are so many blessings." She recounted with joy that because of the Valentine's program, their daughter, Bretta began to grow and change from a rebellious teen to a Godly woman.

At 17, their son, Chuck, had entered the military and when he came home, he saw the change in his family. They were treating each other differently, and his parents' behavior had changed. Truthfully, he didn't like it one bit! Chuck's complaint: 'Why didn't you change and do this while I was home. I missed it!'

"So, for a long time", Bobbie recalled, "he was in rebellion against us but openly nice to us". He was not living the Christian life. Even though several friends tried talking to Chuck, it wasn't until their close friend spent some time with him that he came back a changed man. "The greatest blessing is having our kids here and watching them grow in their faith."

Another blessing was the way Bobbie's Mom was right when she said Bill would make a good preacher…a good missionary. That's exactly what God did with his life when Bill said, 'Yes' to God. Bill remembered these words: 'Now, you don't have to do it but you're settling for OK when I've got the best for you.' Bill's response: 'Lord, I can't do this thing You're calling me to! I can't be a missionary and head off halfway around the world! I can't be a pastor! I can't be those things but if that's what you want me to do, then you are going to have to carry me through'! Bill ended with: "And it's been the most awesome trip I've ever been on!"

She never gave up on me!

They both vigorously shook their heads as Bill said, "She never did give up on me and it's amazing!"

Bobbie reached up with both of her petite hands around his larger span and kissed his hand.

"And she's still stuck with me. That's the power of the commitment that God calls us to in marriage. Ours was a typical set of marriage vows. I can't remember them, but I know the vow that I made. Even in 1982, when things were pretty bleak, I just knew somewhere back in the recess of my brain, there was this thing about hanging in there. The understanding of commitment to each other comes out of the understanding of the commitment that Christ made for us. That's a forever commitment."

Tears welled up in his eyes as he struggled to get the words out. "It makes me sick to think what it would have been like had I actually gone through with a divorce that Monday. What if my heart had been so hard over the weekend that I wouldn't have heard that message?"

As they tenderly held hands, Bill quietly added, "She loves me, in spite of me."

"And you have me, too," Bobbie said in an almost whisper.

Steadfast love

Without hesitation, Bill said, "I appreciate the steadfast love that she has for me." He searched for the right words. "She blesses me because I've heard her say this to other women: 'My first commitment is to my husband'." Tears continued to flow as he groped for a response. "I've got news for you. That's not just a statement on her part. She means every bit of that and she lives it every day, every moment of every day. I am overwhelmed by that." More tears fell as he softly hit his chest with his fist.

"I went to a Promise Keepers conference for men in 1991. One of the speakers was Wellington Boone. He stood up and talked about men serving in their home. At the end of his talk, he said, 'I want to challenge you to go home and out-serve your wife.' My pastor and I made the same commitment. We said, 'If Wellington Boone can do it, we can do it'.

A week later, my pastor asked me: 'So, how's it going with your commitment to out-serve your wife?' I said, 'Pastor, I am absolutely exhausted'!" His loud laugh said it all! "Then my Pastor said, 'Praise God, so am I!' I said, 'I can not do it! For every one thing I do for her, she does ten things for me! I've tried, and I can't do it'!"

Bill looked over at Bobbie and with tenderness said, "I know that she loves me but it's a heart that's driven by a love for God and a desire to serve Him. It shows in everything that she does, not just for me or for her children or grandchildren but for everybody. She's the most amazing woman and for me to stop and think there was a point I didn't want to be with her anymore."

She smiled humbly and patted his hand. "He thinks he's not a servant, but he is. What other husband would make his wife's breakfast every day even when he's not here eating with me. He does serve me. When I had cancer, he did everything for me and just loved me and was right there with me through it all. I also appreciate his love for other people and our family. His steadfastness never changes. I appreciate him so much more every day."

Wisdom to share

Wisdom from Bill began by telling us what he shared with a young couple in premarital counseling. They had already covered many of the common questions on finances, sex and what to expect from marriage. They were in about the third meeting when he laid everything down and said, 'All of this is important for you to get ahold of now instead of going through failure to discover what you're supposed to do, but none of it is as important as a relationship with the Lord Jesus Christ. It's not just salvation. That's just the beginning of the adventure. It's how much you let Christ be the center of your lives from this point on'."

"It was like a light bulb came on in that young man's eyes. I told him, 'You got to get your act together, Kid. You're getting ready to get married. You're going to be a husband. You're probably going to be a father. You need to get this relationship with the Lord where it needs to be, and you need to commit yourself to making Him first in your life'.

I said the same thing to her. 'Tell me on a scale of one to ten where you think you are in your relationship with the Lord? I mean a relationship that depends on Him, that seeks Him, that wants to know more of who He is'?"

She just looked at me and finally said, 'Maybe three.'

'Is that sufficient for you? Is that an OK place to be in a relationship?'

'No'.

"So, I got the joy of helping them both understand what He requires of them and what He wants them to do, not because it's a commandment, but because He loves them enough to want them to have the very best. The very best is a total consuming love for Him and a desire to want to follow Him. It was such a joy to see the change that happened at that moment.

I had not met her father until a few minutes before the ceremony when he came to me and said, 'I want to thank you for the time you spent with them. My daughter is so different from that little girl that I knew just a few weeks ago. There's this intensity of an understanding of what marriage is supposed to be that I don't think she understood until they spent time with you'."

Bobbie laughed, "I can't follow that!"

"Yes, you can, Darlin'."

She meekly but confidently began her advice with, "First and foremost, Jesus has to be the center of the home, then out of that follows everything else. So many women think it's being involved in something at church, but your first ministry is always to your husband. Women often say, 'I'm serving God by doing this and they'll forget about their own husband. So many Moms I know give their total attention to the kids, regardless of their husband. It's like, 'I got kids now so forget you.'. I would have to say the main thing is to make sure that you serve Jesus first and then your husband. Put Jesus first in everything. Simple."

Make it fun!

Bill added, "Golly…make it fun and don't think you don't have to do little special things. Don't ever get to that point." A while ago, he did something special for Bobbie and remembered how much it blessed his wife. "It's no further than a voice away from Him to say, 'Lord, show me how to love my wife.' There's this confidence that nothing is too small for my God, and He will give me the desires of my heart and give me the answers I need to show me how to love her the way I am supposed to love her."

Bobbie's voice cracked: "I would just add that marriage gets better all the time. You think you love so much and life's so good, but there's just this amazing way that

God makes it so much fun to grow old together."

He said, "We find there are new ways we support each other. To me, it just seems like there is a new freshness every day in our marriage. I wish I would have had that on day one of our marriage because there were moments that first year...Golllllly. We got along and all of those things, but I don't think either one of us had any concept of what love was."

A different kind of love

Bobbie struggled with these few words directed at Bill that say so much. "I have sometimes thought, 'When did I start to love you?' I can't say when." Tears began as they looked into each other's eyes. "I know I didn't love him when I married him."

Copyright © Tyler Ogburn Photography

"I loved her, but it was not the love that we've got today." This truth was evident each time they looked at each other and hesitated long enough to make more than eye contact. They were making heart contact.

"It's a different love. I cared about him but nothing when you try to compare it with what we have now."

Bill said, "You're exactly right. We are genuinely, overwhelming, shockingly in love with each other." Their laughter rang through the house as he continued, "Our kids, sometimes, raise their eyebrows at us when we make little remarks or we're playing dominoes and I'll just reach over and lay a big lip lock on her. Our son will say, 'Dad, get a room!' or 'Do you want us to leave'?"

Bobbie wiped tears and laughed at the same time. "Our physical relationship in our marriage is better than it's ever been. At 74 years old you kind of expect..."

He quickly shook his head with a 'NO'. "I'm sorry but maybe because we love each other more or just because we're relaxed and don't have frustrations of things we have to do."

"It's an intense love," she smiled. "It's Jesus...what else can you say. Jesus is the answer...and that's not a cliché. He is the answer!"

No mediocre marriage

Miracles still happen today. A marriage that nearly died was brought back to life. God revived them for not just a mediocre, run-of-the-mill kind of marriage. He revived and renewed a marriage built solidly on Him.

Bill and Bobbie? God wanted the best for them, and they weren't (and still aren't) about to settle for anything less than His best.

John & Debby – You're Not in This for Yourself

MARRIED 41 YEARS

"And this is the testimony: God has given us eternal life, and this life is in his Son." I John 5:11

Maybe you thought he used some smooth 'line' to get her attention, but he was actually waiting in the typical long line at college. Boring! The guy behind him asked, 'How long is this line going to take?'

'I don't know', John answered, 'but I'll ask this gal in front of me.'

He took one innocent look into her face and, "I was struck by how beautiful she was!"

Conversation came easily as they found they had a lot in common, including the fact they were both PKs (pastors' kids). When she asked if he was going to seminary to be a pastor, he answered, 'No, I'm going to be a Biology teacher'. (Remember his answer for later in their story!)

John recounted, "Debby said she was kind of lonely out there. I answered, 'Oh...really'?"

They were both breaking up as Debby said, "I DID NOT mean it in that way!"

"So," John smiled, "the wheels started to turn. Most good-looking girls have their noses up in the air. She was different." We're not sure if it was because of his 'good-looking girl' remark or 'she's different' but Debby was now bending over in uncontrollable laughter.

He patiently waited for her to regain composure and continued, "She's connect-ing with me. She's talking...actually treating me like a human being!"

As John moved further into his version of their story, she continued to have difficulty putting on her serious face. "Well...since I'm older I asked her, 'Are you a Junior or a Senior?' In a falsetto voice he gave Debby's answer, 'No...I'm a Fresh-man'."

She hadn't caught her breath from her last outburst of giggling, but somehow managed to hold it in as she glanced over at John. He closed his eyes as he shared his next thought that day: 'Oh...great! I've got a sister that young!' He did admit in those few minutes, his attitude towards dating changed. "Now I thought, I'd like get to know this person as a Christian sister. No pressure." As Debby finished up and left the line, he thought he'd never see her again. 'Great! I lost my opportunity! If she comes back, I am going to ask her out.'

"Surprise! She did come back!" When he asked her out, "There was a five second pause that seemed like an eternity. I was thinking 'no way'! Except she was saying, 'Yah...that would be fun'."

Their chance encounter took place in the line where students drop or add classes. John quipped, "I was dropping a course and adding a wife!" They were now both enjoying his humor.

"I was very impressed because he just seemed so non-threatening. I felt I could trust this guy and I didn't even know him. He's not going to try to put any moves on me!" she teased. "When he did ask me out, I was shocked. I said, 'Yes'. He could have been some horrible man." (At the time, she had no idea he was 28 to her18.)

Impressed

On their first date, she was impressed with his Datsun 280Z. 'Oh, my Dad has a Datsun!', she swooned. John quipped, "She was not impressed that it was a sports car but that it was a Datsun like her Dad's!"

As innocently as she said it that first date, "I didn't know what a sports car was."

John, nearly bent over in laughter, explained her Dad had a Datsun B210 (not even close to a sports car!). "Quite a bit of difference! So, I was impressed with Debby because she wasn't impressed because of the car I drove."

Not such a smooth move

He didn't even hold her hand on their first date. According to John, "It was going to be a one-time good deal. Nice evening out. Period. So, I brought her back to the dorm after a nice evening and I said the fateful words: 'Have a good semester!' I guess she could have killed me!"

She was thinking, 'Great! What did I do? I must have really bad breath!' Thoughts were spinning, "It's like he hates me, and I really think he's pretty neat'."

John admitted his hesitance was based on their age difference, but his 'less than smooth' dismissal was redeemed two weeks later when his cousin was looking for a double date for a football game. "I didn't have a black book with loads of names!" That's when Debby's name surfaced in his memory bank as a candidate for the double date.

"We went to a football game and then to a dance. Neither one of us can dance...but it's like we fell in love. The age difference went out the window. We spent nights in her dorm just talking. We couldn't get enough of each other. So, the love affair accelerated."

Debby called home to tell her parents she was bringing John home at Christmas to meet them. She was a little concerned how she would introduce John and his family. She told her Dad John's name and he responded, 'Oh, is he a pastor's son?' 'Yes'. Her dad's voice smiled, 'I think I know his Dad!' 'WHAT?' Debby and John were both grinning as she told us their Dads were seminary classmates!

"I couldn't have cooked this up," John said. "No way...that's a God thing. Absolutely!"

"My parents LOVED him! If I had said 'No', I think they might have forced me to marry him!"

"Her Dad and I were together alone that weekend and he said, 'If you and Debby were to get married...' John looked up with eyes bugging out as he realized the green light just went on!

Her dad continued a different line of questioning, 'Sure you want to be a Biology teacher, but what is God's highest will and purpose for your life?'

"He started planting seeds for me going to the seminary."

'As a Biology teacher you would be right up there. On a scale of 1 to 1000...you'd be 750. If you went to seminary, you'd be up at 950.' Debby and John both laughed loudly at her dad's 'subtle' hint.

"I bought into it. I started thinking and praying and I thought: 'Yah...maybe God will have us as a team. I wouldn't be going to seminary by myself. Debby seems really fit for being a pastor's wife and we would go together.' It just started clicking and making sense." That's when he changed his career course.

What made you fall in love?

Debby looked down a little embarrassed as John began, "From a guy's perspective, she's gorgeous! Physical attraction was there but she loved the Lord and it was genuine. I wasn't used to being around women that had such a mature faith at that stage in their life. So, that was attractive. Her faith was solid, and she was grounded and a woman of prayer. She was also just fun and giddy, too."

Debby used her falsetto voice and reached over to touch his arm as if she were swooning over him, "Ohhh...Johnnnn!"

He laughed and then continued his thoughts at that time in their relationship. 'I can't believe a Christian can be that gorgeous and be well grounded. What a combination!' He crossed his arms smiling. "Before going to Pacific Lutheran University (PLU), after being out of the military and being an older guy, I prayed for a spouse for the very first time the summer of 1976, before meeting Debby. I was reaching 28 and for me, the clock started ticking. 'Well, maybe I'm not going to find anybody'. But--that first week in school God proved me wrong."

Check list for a man

Debby had been in a serious relationship in high school but wasn't sure about his relationship with Christ. When he asked, 'What are you looking for in a man?' She said, 'I really want somebody who's a strong Christian...who loves the Lord, and of course, a Lutheran would be nice. Scandinavian would be nice, too.' She then realized she was telling this boyfriend all the things he was not. She was almost convinced there is no such person like that. Debby added, "...but I think God put those desires in my heart."

As she looked over at John, her voice cracked, and tears streamed down her cheeks. They intertwined their arms and she said, "When I met John, he was everything plus more." Now, the 'happy tears' made her eyes sparkle with fun.

"I had blue eyes, too!"

She giggled, "And blond hair."

"I used to!"

The 'special' proposal

Their proposal? "Real special!" he said.

Debby laughed, "This is good. You probably haven't heard one like this!"

"I had visions of going to the Grand Canyon...something very romantic." However, his 'Gray Ghost' hot 280Z was having transmission issues, so they didn't have a vehicle to go there.

She smiled, "That's because we weren't going to go up there alone. My parents wanted my sister to go with us."

"Kind of a chaperone", John said.

"Well, she's my best friend....so that was fine. I didn't know he had anything up his sleeve."

Since that romantic trip didn't work out all that well, he returned form the Grand Canyon without proposing to Debby. They later went on a little drive about five miles away. "It was just a bump in the road, and I was teaching Debby how to do straight stick in the 280Z. She was driving when I said, 'Pull in here.' It was a Circle K (gas stop convenience store) right by the propane gas tanks."

"Very romantic!", Debby said as she in mock tenderness rubbed his arm.

"I put my cold, clammy hands on her shoulder and she immediately thought she was doing something wrong. I said, 'Would you marry me?' In front of a Circle K in Huachuca City, Arizona."

In response to his proposal, Debby laughed uncontrollably because she thought he was joking. "When I discovered he was serious...it was like: 'Absolutely! I'm not going to turn YOU down'!"

"And that's our proposal," John grinned and rolled his eyes.

Feeling neglected

John and Debby were not different than any other married couple in the world. No matter how they tried, they were not able to avoid challenges. One of their earliest came with John's calling as a pastor and Debby's as a pastor's wife. After their first daughter was born, he was the solo pastor in a church. Debby had this beautiful baby daughter and yet, she was feeling neglected.

After less than a year at this church, Debby noted, "He was working extremely hard to be the pastor God wanted him to be and that he wanted to be, and the church would maybe expect him to be. He was working so hard at that...I felt, to the neglect of both our daughter, Kjersten, and me. I remember writing a kind of letter to him. I don't like to write but this actually made more of an impact than what I thought it would. He still has the letter."

"I've got the letter in my drawer to this day," John said with a little snicker, "with all the socks on top of it. Every now and then, I will see that letter and 'ahhhh...it's a reminder'."

They remembered the letter said something like, 'I didn't know marriage was going to be like this. You're leaving me in the dust. I guess I don't count.' After receiving the letter, John said, "I backed off. Modified. Adjusted. I don't know exactly how but we would have more outings. My day off would definitely be more of a day off than work. That caught my attention. Forever I'll keep that letter in my top drawer." With an eventual total of five children welcomed into their lives, it became even more important to have that reminder handy.

Not just two people in love

Marriage is not just about two people in love. It more often is complicated by lots of other people in the mix...such as children!

As a little guy, their special needs son, Karl, suffered many seizures caused by high fevers. John recounted, "We didn't quite know what was going on until we moved to Tucson where he had five grand mal seizures in 12 hours." At age five, he was diagnosed with epilepsy and had a shrinkage on the left side of his brain which would affect verbal memory. "I cried like a baby when I found that out." John admitted, he thought Karl's future was pretty much set in stone. He was going to be a disabled person.

Debby shared about an extremely difficult childhood for Karl, even earlier than five years old. "He was <u>very</u> angry and would have outbursts. He's also had ADHD with learning disabilities. I remember for a while, he had a knife fetish. If he was angry, he would grab a knife and start chasing whomever was in his way. That was tough on the whole family."

John added, "He would go into rages. We got a lock on his door…on the outside and he put holes in that door." It was easy to see they both struggled with the necessary actions they had to take to keep Karl and the rest of their family safe during one of those rages. They both have tried to second guess if that was the most helpful decision because when confined to his room it took so long for Karl to calm down.

They intertwined their arms more tightly as Debby said, "When we took him to doctors, they would look at us like…" she screwed up her face as she continued, "…like…'you're the bad parents. You don't know how to care for your child'. We were like: 'No duh! We need help'!"

Some relief came when they moved to California and located a neurologist who they felt actually listened and got him on the right medication. John said, "He mellowed out and was manageable, although we were on the edge of our seats a lot." Sometimes, they were waiting for the next seizure to happen or a new behavioral problem to surface.

"When you think of family dynamics, it affects the other kids, too." Debby added, "He was the center of attention for many years."

John agreed, "He got all the energy and attention to the neglect of the others."

Making the right decision

Their oldest daughter, Kjersten, was in her final year of high school when John got orders from the Air Force to relocate to California. They admitted this was the greatest challenge of their marriage and the most difficult decision they had to make…even while in total disagreement with each other.

She wanted to stay in Montana with her friends and continue with her singing group at her high school. She wanted to graduate with her class! Much the same situation happened to John his senior year of high school. Even though there was an offer for John to stay with his coach's family, his parents chose <u>not</u> to allow him to stay behind.

John remembered how painful and difficult it was for him his senior year. He didn't want that same thing for their daughter. He felt she should be able to stay while they moved to their new assignment.

Debby's face still displayed the sadness of that time as she said, "It really hurt!" A Christian family offered to let Kjersten live with them, <u>but</u> they had only met this family about two weeks before the move. "For me, it was just tear your heart out and stomp on it!" Her eyes opened wide, 'Aghhhhh…how can this be God's will? How can we leave our daughter? And how can she want to stay'? "I felt like John didn't understand me or maybe even try and yet, am I really trying to understand her situation? It was about me!" she struggled. "That's what hurt so bad. It's hard for a man to understand a mother's heart!"

With tender but pained eyes, they looked at each other, "I think Debby saw it as rejection of family. Kjersten didn't want to come to be with us and we should be together as a family." Debby shook her head in agreement as John said, "Whereas, I saw it as I wanted the best for Kjersten. That was #1. I didn't want her to go through what I went through. I was convinced I was right and maybe Debby deferred to the fact that I was the head of the household."

She shook her head in agreement. They had talked this dilemma through, and both had their voices heard, but John humbly continued, "The final decision would be mine."

Their oldest daughter stayed behind when they moved. She flourished that year and graduated with her class. Debby admitted it took a few years to get over that very difficult time and realize it <u>was</u> for the best. "Yes, it does work the best if you pray about something and your husband is saying, 'No...this is what I believe it has to be'... Defer to him, even if you don't agree...that is the best."

Even though, at the time, it caused compounding stress in their marriage, they both felt it also drew them closer together. John agreed, "A united front did help us."

Teamwork was work!

They took some parenting classes and found they had different parenting styles. John smiled as he admitted, "I'm more permissive."

Debby rolled her eyes, "I'm permissive already! That's the scary part." She put her fist to her forehead, "Somebody's <u>got</u> to be strong! Oh, my goodness...we're really in trouble!"

"One time, John was trying to get our first-grade son, Peder, to play the piano for the nursing home. So, John said, 'Peder, would you like to sing this Chipmunk Christmas song at Bethel?' Peder's like, 'NO!' So, John told him: 'I'll give you a Game Boy if you do it'."

'YOU SAID WHAT?????', was all Debby could get out of her mouth!

John demonstrated Peder's reaction by pumping his arms up in the air, "He jumped up and down and said, 'YES...I'LL DO IT!' For me, that's one way to get it done!"

She could smile about it now but remembers thinking, 'AGHHHHHH...we can't be using bribery to get our kids to do stuff! That's horrible!'

"Never saw him more enthusiastic," John smiled. "Yah...our styles are a little different." The corners of his mouth turned up into a 'mock innocent' grin as she gave him 'the look'.

However, the parenting course they took and eventually taught others, did help them to develop some improved skills in dealing with the challenges presented by their son, Karl, as he was growing up. "He's 25 years old now and he's turning into a fine young man. He loves the Lord. He's very concrete. Very structured." John continued with his loving tone, "He has a girlfriend who is autistic. We wonder where that's going to go but, God has brought us through some difficult times before and He'll do it again." Debby smiled in agreement as John continued, "I think Karl has a good future and he's working through a disabled young adult program at Sears. He loves being in the receiving room with his box cutter."

Debby didn't flinch with the truth, "When he started, we wondered if he was going to be a serial killer..."

"That thought," John smiled, "did cross our minds. That box cutter scared people at first but then they trusted him. He likes to work. I think he's got a future."

As they walked through parenting, they walked as partners, as a team...even when it wasn't always easy.

First time apart

John's military deployment to Guantanamo Bay was tough on the whole family. The 180-day assignment was John's first deployment and the first time they were apart for any length of time. To say the least, it was tough.

"Anything that could go wrong, did go wrong. The transmission went out in the van a week after I left. Debby had no knowledge of cars but was left with trying to figure out if it should be repaired or buy a new car. She no sooner got the vehicle issue solved when health issues cropped up, not only with Karl's seizures but with Kjersten contracting pneumonia. As if that wasn't enough, Debby then got pneumonia."

Asking for help wasn't exactly on her 'easy' list but God sent a friend from their military family to check on her. The friend literally dragged all the 'sick bodies' to the hospital while her son took care of the other four children at their home.

In the days of no internet, no Skype, no cell phones; only letter writing and voice recorded tapes were the main form of communication. Phone calls were frustrating because of the incessant echo. Even if Cuba was only 90 miles off the coast of Florida, it was as if they were on the other side of the world from each other. Deployment wasn't easy, however, they not only survived that separation but came out of it stronger as individuals and as a team.

Crisis of faith became stronger faith

John had served in military chapels and civilian congregations over his career. Just prior to retirement, he sensed a calling as a pastor to one more congregation. John said he felt like God was saying, 'Finish strong. Get re-energized'.

His last church, however, challenged every word of those statements.
With disunity in the congregation, there was not unanimous support of their pastor. "I had a crisis of faith. I did not want to preach." Debby saw him struggle through that and was a tremendous support.

"The amazing thing...I didn't go through any deep depression like a lot of pastors. I came out relatively unscathed. I was not wounded and beaten up even though it was the toughest call in my career in ministry..." John recalled journaling and praying more during those three years than any time in his career. "I definitely reached out to God for all the help I could get. So, I didn't finish strong from the human standpoint, but I know God called me there for a reason. If nothing else, there was a positive side of a difficult call."

Debby looked lovingly at John, "It's was just so tough to see him go through that." Her voice got stronger and louder, "And so undeserved. Yet, I wanted to love those people because God loves them.

John proudly told us how amazed he was by Debby and the strength she brought to their partnership in ministry. "If someone hurts me, she doesn't make things worse... She's wonderful in that environment."

Debby teased, "Sometimes I <u>want</u> to!" Then in a more serious tone she said, "God gets us on our knees one way or another."

Blessings times 5

There was no waiting to answer our question about blessings! They agreed their greatest blessing is their five children.

"It's amazing! Debby would have a dozen. I keep teasing her that in the Air Force, every assignment we would have another child." He made a cutting motion across his neck, "Debby, this has got to stop somewhere!"

They both laughed at her answer, 'But why???'

Many times, they have had people notice and give positive comments about their family. John said, "I think our family has blessed others. That does our hearts good to know we can be a blessing. Another great blessing is the fact all five of our children love the Lord and are walking with Him. It could be one or two out of the five that could care less, but they <u>all</u> love the Lord and there's nothing better."

Debby said, "With 33 years of having children at home, I was a little scared to be empty nesters but by the time the last one left the nest...it's very nice. It's fun now!"

"We now have some freedom to do things together," John smiled.

Advice for you

When asked about advice they would give, John said, "Typical answer, 'Marriage takes work'. A lot of forgiveness. It's easier said than done! We preach a good message about forgiveness but that's one of the hardest things."

Debby added, "We like to try and do something every year that's just for our marriage."

John said, "Spiritual renewal and those kinds of things enhance our marriage. I would recommend that for young couples to never give up renewing their marriage. That's probably our downfall... taking each other for granted."

He remembered the day before their wedding, he was bragging about how he and Debby had so much in common...Christians, Lutherans, Norwegians, pastor's kids. Her cousin said, 'Because you have so much in common, you are going to take each other for granted all the more.' John said, "That stuck with me."

"I take him for granted," Debby turned her eyes and heart toward John, "and I'm sorry."

She added this advice: "Remember it's a partnership. You're not in this for yourself. If God has led you together, He wants this marriage to be a blessing, not just to you but to each other and also to the world. People are watching to see if a Christian marriage really does make a difference. I know that I have prayed that our marriage would be an encouragement to others."

"Both of us are non-assertive," John said, "so for us, there are very few conflicts. But, when the water is smooth you have to be concerned what is underneath. Are there things going on underneath that you're not aware of? How you're feeling? Are there times you've disappointed your spouse?"

She reminded us, "No marriage is perfect. You've never arrived. There's always more to learn and grow."

Rare in this world...

"We're a nuclear family and that's more and more rare in this world," John said. Neither of their parents were divorced so they have had good healthy examples of marriage in their lives. That is something they believe is unusual and extremely valuable in today's world. They know they have been given a rare treasure.

No matter what was thrown at them, they knew they were not in it for themselves. That was their testimony to the world...and to you.

Eddie & Dianna – From the End to the Beginning

MARRIED 38 YEARS

"Rejoice always, pray continually, give thanks in all circumstances; for this is God's will for you in Christ Jesus." I Thessalonians 5:16-18

Most stories don't begin with the last chapter...

When Dianna went to Hawaii several years ago, every one of her late husband, Eddie's, family had given their lives to Jesus.

"Every one of them!", she exclaimed. "To see the end from the beginning…I know it was worth everything I had to go through for that!"

"God tells stories from the end to the beginning," her smile brightened. So, it is from the end to the beginning, we share Dianna and Eddie's story.

He always wanted to go back…

Eddie always wanted to back to Hawaii, the place of his childhood. He was coming full circle as Dianna tenderly carried his ashes back to a beach named Hau Bush. This was a place he surfed and spent time with family and friends. It was the very beach where Eddie and Dianna, along with all of their family, had spent their wedding night. It was the place they took their children when they were growing up. "Memories from that place are special, and so were the times when just Eddie and I would go alone and look out across the vast ocean. Together we made memories during the tender times on that beach. I remember standing beside him there when first his father passed away and again when his mother went home. He always said he'd like to return there, so I planned to make it his final resting place."

They knew they would need to be 100 yards offshore to spread the ashes, so a boat would be out of the question. Their son, Jason, offered to take his Dad out on a surfboard. An appropriate final journey for a guy who grew up in Hawaii and spent many hours riding the crest of the next big wave on his own surfboard.

With Eddie's ashes cradled in his hands and flower leis around his neck, Jason paddled out to deep waters. Farther and farther he went until he was past the last breaking wave. As he tossed the ashes, a breeze caught them and formed a rainbow in the sky. Eddie was back home.

The leis quickly followed into the water with some lazily floating back to shore. According to Hawaiian tradition, that meant they would someday be reunited.

A Cinderella beginning

"We met with a paper clip." Dianna had just finished basic training and checked in at her new base with suitcases in hand. As she was passing by Eddie she crossed into his line of sight. "He was shooting paper clips and he hit me. Right between the eyes. I dropped those suitcases and I said, 'I'm going to git you!' And lock stock and barrel, a year later I did!

I felt like Cinderella. I was in the Air Force in Colorado Springs and I met a man from Hawaii. Now who wouldn't want to go to Hawaii. Who wouldn't want to marry a man from Hawaii?"

Scary wedding!

Once he made up his mind, he wanted her, Eddie bluntly announced, 'We're going to get married this afternoon.' She said, 'I don't know about that'. He came right back at her, 'No! We're going to get married this afternoon!'

"He just told me what we were going to do and then he went and told his Dad. His Dad said, 'Wait just a minute. You need to talk to somebody'."

They found a pastor who quizzed Eddie and said, 'Yah, Eddie's ready.' "They had no clue that I wasn't ready because I wasn't interviewed. After that, he left me at a store to go buy a dress. I was numb...I was scared. I wondered if I was doing the right thing, but I didn't have the courage to say, 'No'."

They were married by a Justice of the Peace and then met his family at Hau Bush Beach for a party. "That's where it began! Right after we came out to the beach, I watched him say 'Hi' to his family and then get on his surfboard and paddle out. I knew then I was in trouble."

It seemed at first glance Eddie was married to the ocean more than he was to her! "My father-in-law told me later, 'I looked at your face and I saw one scared woman'."

"That's how I was. I was scared. I thought, 'What have I done?' So far away from home, marrying this guy and I really don't know him."

Culture clash

Though they lived in Hawaii, his family was Japanese to the core, even wearing the traditional Japanese kimono. Eddie's grandmother came from Hiroshima, Japan. Her future husband worked on the sugar cane plantation in Hawaii and needed a wife, so he ordered one from Japan. Along with him, she got the bonus of nine children to raise.

Dianna's family? She described them as total Kentuckian; 'down-home folks' who did lots of huggin'!

Those two cultures, like oil and water, weren't about to mix!

"When I went to meet his family, I walked right on in the house and hugged his Mom. Little did I know, I was supposed to take my shoes off and go in and bow to her. Then, I was supposed to go to their Buddhist altar and bow down. Then I could come back out and I would be received. Later in the day, Eddie's Mom told him, 'More better you marry Japanese'."

It must have been a challenge for that little Kentucky gal to eat strange things without rolling her eyes or possibly gagging! Rice without cinnamon and sugar? Fish with eyeballs? That might have been enough, but she was also expected to eat them with chopsticks! A few chopstick lessons from her father-in-law and plenty of years of practice and she was finally proficient in actually getting more food to her mouth than on her lap.

His culture said women were subservient and needed to do what they were told. No questions asked and do it now! "One day my father-in-law rolled an empty beer can towards my mother-in-law. She got up and got him a new one...honored him. His Mom was in the kitchen busy cooking one time I was there, and he rolled the beer can to me." Her eyes lit up the room as she broke into giggles, "I rolled it back!"

Social customs were even more of a challenge when she observed, "When Japanese have a party, if there's not a fight, it ain't a good party. I feel the Hawaiian culture is very broken. We lived in Hawaii four years and I would see women with broken bodies...broken hearts. I saw them as prideful people, too, because they boasted in their men all being strong, but inside they were hurting."

Faith clash

She was not only the first white woman added to the family; she was the first Christian. All of his family were practicing Shinto Buddhists. Dianna sadly told us, "I did not know one Christian Hawaiian that was treated with respect. They could not have a conversation that didn't hurt."

Eddie wanted to know about the Christian culture, so he went to talk to the chaplain on the base. The chaplain adamantly refused to tell him. He told Eddie, 'I don't condone this marriage. I won't have it.' With a puzzled look, Eddie said, 'I don't want you to tell me about Buddhism. I know all about that. I want you to tell me about this Jesus man.' Again, it was, 'No'!

Dianna's face saddened, "That broke my heart, because I thought, 'That's the Jesus I serve'. When I realized the chaplain wasn't going to share my Jesus with the man I was going to marry, maybe I didn't want Jesus either. Maybe I was on the wrong track because the chaplain told me if I married him, I would be breaking all of God's laws and I wouldn't be accepted by Him."

Later in their marriage, someone told her there was a Buddhist man who could help her understand his family's faith. "I thought, 'OK...I'll join the Buddhist religion. If the Christian church doesn't want me, I'll go that route, but first I got to check it out because this Jesus means a lot to me."

The Buddhist man she was sent to had become a Christian. "Pastor Cho showed me that Buddhism is not the way and Christianity is. That's how I got saved. In my excitement, I shared it with Eddie. I about choked him to death because he became totally unglued. He didn't want to hear it...not from me. He told me to be silent and if I had something like that, to do it on my own and never in front of him. That was very tough!"

Faith challenged

"My faith challenge came when I had to believe in a God who would protect me because my husband's culture said he could dominate any way he chose. Sometimes it was with his fists, other times it was with his tongue, other times with deadly silence or manipulation. I remember one time I had gone into the bedroom because I was so devastated by what was going on. There was dysfunction in our home. There was abuse. I went in my bedroom and I yelled at God. 'You know...I promised to love, to honor, to cherish. So, why aren't You in there helping me? Why aren't You there with me?' I said, 'So help me God! I brought You into this marriage, but I don't see You doing anything! You're not protecting me. You're not there for me!' I was crushed. I said what I'd been thinking...out loud."

Her head moved slowly back and forth, "You'd think letting go like that, it would get better...but it got worse...so it could get better." There was a time when she was hospitalized after Eddie had been drinking and pushed her out of a moving car. "When they asked me how it happened, I wouldn't tell them. You don't talk about your husband in any negative way and I was holding on to that fiber that said I was to honor and cherish him."

The military had a way to take care of people after domestic incidents like theirs. He was sent away to Korea. "I remember while he was gone, I told the Lord, 'I will trust You if You don't let him hit me again. I need to know You're real. I know I've cried out to You. I know You've sent him away and I've gotten some reprieve. What's going to happen now that he's back? Are we going to start this same chapter again? Are we going to finish it off? Do I leave'?"

She found somebody new

"While he was gone, I wrote Eddie a letter and said I found somebody new and it was Jesus." Evidently, he didn't understand what that meant because when he came home, he tried to take a swing at her. She told us his arm was stopped in midair as if she was protected by a huge angel. "The fear that came into him was horrific. He ran out of the house and went right to the priest I had been talking to."

If you stay...

"One of the questions I asked, 'God, can I leave him? I'm out on an island. There's nobody I trust. I've got two little kids. Can I leave him?' I waited, and I heard God say, 'Yes...Yes, you can leave him, but if you stay...if you stay...I will bless you. I will bless you'.

I knew He meant what He said because after that, when things got rough, I immediately ran to God. He was my source of comfort. I wasn't being hit anymore but the verbally abusive words caused bruises. I got closer and closer to God because I had to run to Him more than I ever had before...and He would soothe it."

I was so wounded. I didn't want to feel. I didn't want to be hugged. I saw a counselor two days, and on the third day, the counselor just wasn't there."

It seemed no one was there for her. She walked back out to her car and put her head on the steering wheel. 'God, I don't know what to do. I'm weak. I don't know what to do at this point.'

"There was nothing left. Eddie had crushed our marriage. It was burnt and charred beyond recognition. He had done things that had hardened him and made him feel he was all alone. Even though I kept loving him, I know he felt a lot of regret because he couldn't do it any differently. He didn't know how."

His island

She shared about a time when God revealed something through a vision that impacted her greatly. "God showed me an island that was so burned and so charred, it was worse than any volcano could ever be. Eddie was standing on the middle of that volcano looking up. I could see him, but I knew he couldn't see me. He was screaming at the top of his voice. 'What do you got that I ain't got'?"

She remembered the fear in his face; something she would never forget. "He was screaming out the most horrendous fear, 'What do you got that I ain't got?' So, I said, 'All you got to do is say His name. Just say His name!' He yelled it again and again and again: 'What do you got that I ain't got?' All of a sudden, he screamed, 'Jesus!' at the top of his lungs and he didn't mean it in a cursing voice like I had heard before. He meant it that he was desperate for Jesus."

With each new military assignment, it made her wonder if that location was the 'island' in her vision of Eddie screaming. Would this be where he would get the answer to his question, 'What do you got that I ain't got?'

With each move to a new military base, she would also grow in her faith. "He would give me Godly women; women He knew I needed. They would love me unconditionally. Love me when I was grumpy, frustrated or angry."

Not about to give up

"He taught me I was stronger than I thought. I was not about to give up! The blessing of not giving up was continuing to walk the walk of a Christian in front of people that had never seen it before...like his family members. Continuing to show them that I loved them but would not participate in some of their dysfunction, like the drinking. There were times when there were drugs available. My mother-in-law opened a book to read to my children and inside of it was a leaf of marijuana. She used it as a bookmark. My kids didn't know that the Japanese altar in the home was for the dead. In explaining to them what I believed, there were people listening. I might be sitting on the front porch on the stoop because I had just been chastised in the house, but as I was sitting there, people were listening and watching." As she lived out her faith, it was a visible example to those around her.

Promise without proof

Dianna had received assurance through prayer that her whole house...their whole family would be saved. Still, she agonized about those in Eddie's family who didn't know Jesus. That desolate island Eddie stood on seemed to cause a ripple throughout his entire family.

Every time it got hard, Dianna looked up and reminded Him, 'God You promised'! When she questioned God, 'Why don't I get to see it happen?', she knew the answer was, 'You don't have to see it! God promised it...Abraham didn't see it. God promised it...the prophets didn't see it. God promised it...Dianna doesn't have to see it.' She understood first-hand what it meant to walk by faith and not by sight!

What about Eddie?

There was so much Dianna appreciated about her husband. "Eddie knew how to be a team player; he just didn't know how to play it at home. The only time Eddie got applause from his dad is when he played well on the ball field. He stayed in that frame of mind: 'If you do good, you'll get praise. If you look good, you'll get praise'. He looked for affirmation, but he also gave it on the ball field...just not at home." Her face winced a little as she said, "When people talked about him at his workplace and on the ball field I was thinking 'That's a totally different man than I know'."

"One of the traits that I truly admired was that he said what he meant. If he said he was going to do something, he did it. When he was around people who frustrated him, he knew how to hold his tongue (just not at home). He wasn't sure about his abilities but if I encouraged him, he would see it through. He tried to compare himself to other people and I think his weakness was that he didn't think he had it in him. I saw more in him than he knew he had. He wasn't as strong as he acted. There was a lot of brokenness.

His brokenness started really, really early when he was a child. He lived with multiple members in his family and I think he got criticized by a lot of them. I grew up in the fields of Kentucky where we were told to run, roam, find, investigate and we were encouraged." Two totally different views of family and life.

Communicating when they couldn't talk

When their marriage was on the rocks, the military sent her to a psychiatrist who gave these instructions: 'I want you to write letters to each other. Set the timer and write for five minutes how you feel. Not what he did but how you feel.' That's exactly what she did.

"Eddie wrote me back. We had gotten to the point we couldn't talk to each other, but we could write to each other. That's how I found the power to forgive. He could tell me how he felt rather than yell at me about what he wanted me to do or wanted me to be for him. That worked. So, we used that technique until we could do it with our tongue and we could learn to forgive."

Open wound

"I look back now, and this is still an open wound in me because there are times in my marriage I want to forget completely. And then there are times when I think, 'I've been healed so well now that I can empty that tonight and be OK'. I have to take the shadow of what Eddie was away because it will hold me back. I also can say, 'I've been through it and I've survived, and I can help others not give up'."

Just as God often sent women who would teach and encourage her, He also sent women who needed someone to walk alongside them in their pain. Dianna was often that woman. She was only able to do that through the healing of her own brokenness.

Hiding the truth

"I was taught to honor a man. You don't let him be seen as anything less than the best. I did protect him. My children didn't know that I was that abused. They suspected it, but they didn't know it until after he died. We were in Alaska for our first Christmas without Eddie. I opened up about the abuse and my daughter, Jenny said, 'Now I remember.' Janelle said, 'I thought so.' My son, Jason, just stood there…. I hid it from them. They didn't need to see that. There would be times I would go places with them to take them away." She felt her children needed to be children and not have to be exposed to abuse.

"Eddie had a 'runaway spirit', too. I ran to get them away from the conflict. He did it to punish us. There were also threats of suicide. 'You ever leave me, I'll kill myself. It'll be your fault'."

"Covering up his mistakes was dysfunctional on my part. I could have helped him or at least tried but, I was dysfunctional and broken, too."

Shield of laughter

Like a rosy morning sunrise, her smile slowly began to appear. "Then God gave me the gift of laughter. Eddie would be so ugly, and I would laugh at him. I wasn't laughing at him to make him look humiliated. I was laughing at him to show him that was not the way he meant it. A man wouldn't say it that way.

I had to learn to answer, 'This is how I feel', and never accuse him with...'You made me!' I am responsible for my actions and reactions but you're responsible for yours.

You learn to laugh...you lighten the load! I can't take those things so seriously because each one of those things would be an arrow. If I want to blunt the arrow and let it fall to the floor, I need to do something about it. My shield was 'Let's make light of this' or 'Let's bring it into laughter.' You can do that if you got the Holy Spirit to do that. He's good at it!! He's got quick comebacks that are not hateful or ugly."

Throwing beer bottles...or not?

"If I was very, very frustrated, I got to the point I wanted to throw something. I remember one night, taking some of his beer bottles and I threw 'em. Crash! Threw an ashtray...60 million crystal pieces all over the driveway. I never threw them at Eddie, but I threw full bottles of beer in the trash. Caps on...exploding! Yup...you can be angry, and you don't have to keep all that pent up. You can throw an orange until it's smashed. You can find ways to vent. You don't have to keep that anger. I learned when I was frustrated, I could clean kitchen cupboards. I could clean 'em, and then I'd be too tired to fight.

Give him time to diffuse, too. Space is good. Redirect anger into something constructive. If you don't, you will find yourself in that rut."

Quit praying for me!

Dianna couldn't quote the Bible around Eddie! She was not allowed to say the word, 'Bible' around him, but she found ways to love him unconditionally and to be the best wife possible. It served as a testimony for him to see God's love.

Sometimes Eddie would point his finger right in her face and say, 'You quit praying for me cuz it hurts!'

"I didn't stop!!", she smiled.

He was different

She didn't see Eddie cry out to Jesus like she had experienced in her vision, but by the time he died, she had started to see he was different. "He wasn't abusive anymore. His words were still very sharp, even the night he died. That afternoon, he pretty much daggered me, but he was different."

That evening when he was home alone, he died very suddenly from a heart attack. There was no bedside confession for her to hear.

After Eddie died, Dianna said, "I came back home and went into the bedroom standing over that spot where he fell. I was thinking, 'I don't want to be in this bedroom anymore. I don't want to even go in there.' The Lord just kind of put His hands on my shoulders and said, 'Dianna, that's not a pit to hell, that's a portal to heaven. That's where he met me. Eddie cried out My Name that night'."

One by one

After Eddie's death, his family came to faith in Jesus – one by one. The first to come was Eddie's grandmother and then an Auntie and her sick husband. Dianna went to pray with them and would tell them, 'I don't know this Buddhist god. I only know Jesus.' As she prayed and shared, much of Eddie's family was again standing on the sidelines listening. They caught the 'over spray' when she talked about Jesus!

"The toughest one was Eddie's brother. He would stand with his arms crossed over his chest in front of me. I hadn't heard from him for about five years after Eddie's funeral."

She had written a book about Eddie titled, 'The Journey: Ask Me, I Was There', and in it had shared the path each one of us could take to salvation. Little did she know Eddie's brother got his hands on that book and had been sharing it at his church. "His book got lost so he called my son, Jason, and asked if he could get another copy. Jason let me know, so I bundled up some books and mailed them. I got a letter back saying, 'I had no words to say, but in my heart, there was so much I wanted to say. I want you to know next Sunday I'm going to be baptized.' The last time I went home to Hawaii, all of the grandchildren had been saved, too!"

Would I do it again?

"This morning, thinking about this interview, I wondered, 'If I had to do this again, would I marry him...knowing what I now know?' Because of how many people got saved, I had to say, 'Yah...I would. It was worth it'!"

From the end to the beginning

In the end, Eddie's ashes floated on warm Hawaiian waters. About her marriage, Dianna said, "God brought treasures out of ashes." God knew the end even before the beginning took place!

Jack & Dianna – A New Beginning

MARRIED 3 YEARS

"LORD, my God, I called to you for help, and you healed me." Psalms 30:2

A fter the death of her husband, Eddie, Dianna saw the end of one story and a new love story begin.

A rather sneaky friend arranged for her to be a prayer partner with Jack, a bachelor at the church they attended. After the prayer meeting, she thought to herself, 'He really knows how to pray!' Almost everyone was gone when Jack asked Dianna and another lady to pray specifically for him. He had his hand on Diana's shoulder and he knew God did something in his heart. God was preparing him for their future.

He was a patient man and one year later in that same prayer room – no one else showed up but Jack and Dianna. That is where she got her first kiss and she said, "I shook like a leaf!"

They dated seven years (a long wait for a guy who had never married).

"Jack coming into my life is totally different. He is a man of God who truly lives the walk. It took me a couple of years to even trust him. Years! That's how broken I was."

She knew without a doubt and said with bold confidence, "This was designed by Him. God uses the past to propel you into the present. Your past prepares you for what God has for you now." He did that for Dianna when He mended the hurt of the past and gave her a new beginning

Josh & Ashlee – Biggest Blessings from Hardest Times

MARRIED 12 YEARS

"How abundant are the good things that you have stored up for those who fear you that you; bestow in the sight of all, on those who take refuge in you." Psalms 31:19

Copyright © Kim Hoppert Photography

Boring! Boring! That's how Ashlee could describe her day. She was sitting in a model home her Dad had on the real estate market. With nothing else to do, she got on the computer and opened CatholicMatch.com.

Josh had just graduated from college and moved to Minnesota to start chiropractic school. Boring! might also have described his days killing time until chiropractic school began. One day he found himself on the internet looking at information for a conference when he stumbled on the link for CatholicMatch.com. "Wow...I had no experience what-so-ever with any of that, but the people seemed very genuine so, I put my profile up." In the Fall, when school started, he found himself a little less attentive to the dating site—<u>until</u> he got her email!

Love at first sight!

Ashlee broke into a smile. "I fell in love with his profile right away!" They talked online a couple of times and then met each other in person. "It was definitely love at first sight...love at first date."

"Absolutely!" Josh beamed. "I just felt very drawn to her and her personality. I could sense there were some values that were there and that's been kind of important to me all along."

She admitted her Dad was really nervous about her meeting a guy online. "I am the oldest of 13 kids, so Josh had to meet all of them before we went out on a date," she snickered. For 'safety insurance', her brother and his girlfriend came along as chaperones. "My parents would have it no other way!"

Expensive first date…

The four of them went out to dinner and then wanted to all go together in the same vehicle to downtown Minneapolis for ice skating. They were going to drop off the extra vehicle when her brother's girlfriend rear ended his car. Recounting their first date brought out unbridled laughter because they remembered for Ashlee's brother and his girlfriend, it became a very expensive first date…somewhere to the tune of $3000 in car repairs!

Ashlee said, "It was still an awesome first date! It was all 'up' from there!"

How old???

When asked how old they were when they met, there was a lot of giggling and smiling going on! Ashlee said, "I have to think how old I really was...because I'm pretty sure I didn't tell the truth on my profile. I think...I said I was 21...but I was actually 18 or 19. I was young. I didn't go to college. I went right into real estate."

They met in December and were engaged in July. In a rather unusual move, Josh staged his own surprise birthday party and one of the last presents was a ring for Ashlee. All along, Ashlee was working to plan what she thought was a surprise birthday party for Josh. "The joke was on me!"

They were married the following summer when she was 19 and Josh was 23. Their wedding was what Ashlee described as, "Absolutely gorgeous...a fairy tale come true. It was what I always dreamt about. It was the perfect guy and starting a life with him was wonderful. My Dad was such a God-filled man and when I met Josh, it mirrored my Dad in such a beautiful way. Josh had such a compassionate heart. He was so caring, and he was very giving of himself to other people. I think I am wired that way, too…so, I was just drawn into that so much. I was very excited to start our life together."

No fairy tale

After wedding cake was put in the freezer…the fairy tale turned into real life.

Ashlee said, "Most of the challenges we faced had to do with our children. In any marriage, I guess some financial challenges, but that seems to come and go. We seem to bounce back from those things a little more easily. When it comes to family, I think that really puts us into more of a crisis mode."

"Our first pregnancy actually ended up in miscarriage," she smiled sharing the memory. "That was really a challenging time because we had just gotten married in August and found out in January, we were pregnant with our first. You haven't really lived life yet at that point so, you just start telling everybody that you're pregnant. We had literally been picking out cribs at 12 weeks. Just beautiful...but then...to get the news that there is no heartbeat."

The baby's heartbeat ceased at eight weeks, but the pregnancy went to 12 weeks when the doctors had them deliver the baby at home. "That was a challenge because we had only been married a few months." She held her hands over her chest, "We...really had to come together and be there for each other at that time. It was really just a sad time. Through that, we even knew the dignity of that little baby. After I delivered, Josh put the baby in a little casket, and we had a service at church."

They buried their first little life in March and in June found out they were pregnant with Levi. "We were cautious," Ashlee said, "but excited again at that point. We went through the summer and then on September 26th, we went in for an ultrasound.

It took a long time for them to come out and actually talk to us. They said, 'You know we definitely see some challenges here. We're going to send you in for an MRI'. They told us the baby's brain had not fully developed. This meant he could touch a hot surface and not realize it was hot. He may never know how to tie his shoes." Holding her hands on her heart Ashlee said, "It hits you like a ton of bricks! Then they told us we actually had a diagnosis of holoprosencephaly (a malformation of the brain taking place in utero, many times accompanied by other disabilities). Then you go to the internet...which is always the worst thing to do but the only thing you know to do. It was just heartbreaking to know what you were potentially up against with anything from one eye to no nose or no stomach."

They tenderly looked at each other as Ashlee shared, "I just remember crying in your arms a lot. You try every...try to change this. You find yourself asking for a miracle. There was definitely a time during this pregnancy, we had to just hold each other and be together. It wasn't a long-extended scenario. I think both of us knew exactly what this child was meant for. We grieved for a little, but I think we both understood that there was nothing to grieve about because Levi was exactly the way he was going to be. I think we were selfishly grieving for what we wanted but that wasn't who Levi was."

We witnessed sadness in their voices but even more so, we witnessed their deep love for the child God had entrusted to them. "We picked up and had a really beautiful pregnancy with Levi, not knowing if or how long he was going to be with us. They told us to buy a casket instead of a crib because he probably wasn't going to make it."

"Early on," she continued, "we were given the option of aborting. I think we both just shut that out as soon as we heard about it." They both gave a little laugh as she said how they felt about the medical personnel who made that comment: 'We won't be seeing you again! We just don't even want this negativity!' She tossed her hand in the air gesturing for that thought to go away. 'This isn't in our world!', she held up her hand in a stop sign.

Her voice could only give a clue of the depth of emotion she felt. "I think in a world that is so against him...how could we be anything but for him." As they shared their determination to care for Levi, they kept their eyes on each other. "He just needed his Mom and Dad so much. It didn't matter what specialist came into our life. If they weren't 100% positive about Levi, they just didn't even enter the story."

Easy delivery – Complicated life

Levi was born in what they described as the easiest delivery of all their children. When he came into the world, he had a really strong heartbeat and lungs to match. He was whisked off to NICU where they confirmed many of his physical systems were compromised. Ashlee shared the list with us: "He had an underdeveloped eye that never opened. He couldn't eat and couldn't keep his food down, so he needed a gastric-tube. He had an imperforate anus, so a colostomy was performed. He eventually needed to have a sphincter tied around his esophagus to prevent acid reflux from burning his throat. He had hormone imbalances and as he got older, his physical condition got more complicated and more painful for him. He would receive narcotics to control the pain and that would slow down his bowel which caused him great pain."

His life was a constant series of hospitalizations and surgeries. It was not unusual for them to hear doctors tell them Levi was not going to make it.

Ashlee's voice cracked, and tears streamed down her face, "He taught us so much during that time about suffering. You really learn to embrace it because it's temporary and if you treat it the right way, it has the ability to change the world. It definitely changed us."

Almost in awe she said, "We knew that we had a 'saint' in our midst. It was beautiful because he would fight his battles and to him, it was worth it to live. He lived to love and he loved to live." Josh nodded his head in full agreement as she said, "It didn't matter to him what he was having to endure...so it made any of our challenges quick to get over after Levi touched our lives."

New life

When Levi was six months old, they found out they were pregnant with another baby. They were now faced with the fact they had about an 80% chance of having future pregnancies be born just like Levi. Ashlee said, "I was scared. We were both scared. The doctor said, 'You're going to lose this pregnancy if you don't take progesterone. Your body is rejecting this pregnancy right now'."

They were challenged to decide if they were going to prolong this new little life growing inside and bring it to term. The cold, hard facts were staring them in the face...again. Were they willing to gamble that it might be a recurring situation where they would be bringing another child into the world to suffer? They looked to their church and the church just said, 'Be open to life. You're a Mom from the beginning and you need to be open to life.' A priest said the words: 'Be guided in love and never in fear. So, if all you do is in love, then you have no fear. Then you would just love this baby from the beginning, and you would do whatever it took.'

They stepped out together in faith and Josh gave her the progesterone injections. When it was time for the ultrasound, they were told, 'It's a scan of a perfectly healthy baby girl.' A challenge in their marriage that could have divided them became a beautiful moment of trust. As they walked side by side, God had worked together in their hearts to make this decision.

Challenges came daily

Josh spoke about the challenges in their marriage of caring for a very sick child, "When you ask about challenges…frankly, we didn't fight an awful lot, if ever, about many things. If there was an issue that came up, we would try to first identify the issue and then take the necessary steps to overcome it. When you are faced with a situation like Levi's where there were a lot of health concerns, there are so many things that were unpredictable. Just as soon as we thought we were sliding into this nice routine of doing things, things would deviate, and the flow of life was completely disrupted. When that happened, I think it was important for us to stay grounded and understand…'You know what? He's going through far more than we are.' I think it was just important for us to keep that in mind."

Ashlee laughed, "There was no planning! It was survival!"

Finding balance

It was constant work to find balance. "We would go many, many, many days on end where she would be at the hospital with Levi." The arrival of baby #2 added more challenges to their relationship. Ashlee gave a deep sigh and shook her head in agreement as Josh continued, "We wouldn't have much of an opportunity to see one another because I had to be there for our little girl, Gianna, too."

"We would maybe cross each other at the hospital but I think a big piece of that was knowing when to give the other a break. Constantly through Levi's life, I felt like I had to remind Ashlee to take care of herself because if she let herself go, she wouldn't be able to be there fully for other people, including Levi. We needed to give one another a break…not necessarily only in time but also in our emotions. Sometimes we reached a tipping point and we had to recognize those points and then be able to give time to heal." For Josh, the outlet was often exercise. He would get to a point where he finally would say, 'Stop! I need to work out!'

"I would go until I just ran myself crazy." She admitted struggling with the guilt of wanting to be Mom to her new little one, and yet needing to be with Levi even more. In retrospect, she can now see how Gianna's compassionate heart was formed by watching her Mom care for Levi.

She was trying to treasure each moment she has today with Gianna. "It's all in God's timing…even when you doubt and wonder why this is happening. You just have to trust."

"I don't know how I could have made it through without Josh. It's been the right balance of giving and taking care of each other. Josh has never been spiteful. Never been jealous. He's never been the 'that's not fair' type. He's always been so giving."

Josh's view of Ashlee was a mirror image of her remarks, to which he added, "She is just such an amazing Mom to our kids. Patient."

At that point, Ashlee screwed up her face and laughed. He finished his thought, "I am not saying she hasn't been tested but just very giving of herself. I am just so appreciative of that...especially with the intense needs and care that Levi required."

We only do intense

Gianna celebrated her first birthday in May and Baby #3, Bennett, was born in July. "When we found out we were pregnant with Bennett..." Ashlee hesitated as she put the fingers of both hands over her mouth and then spread her hands out toward us. "I am open and honest!" She gave a slight laugh and continued, "I was trustful, but I was kind of like...'Have you forgotten about me, Lord?' I have Levi and then I had Gianna who was almost one. We had three kids under the age of three with Levi's difficulties on top of that. I was just really, 'Wow'! We don't fit in a double stroller anymore and I have oxygen and two feeds hanging out of it. This is going to be a challenge!"

"On top of that," Ashlee and Josh looked at each other as she said, "Bennett had implanted into scar tissue from the C-section with Gianna. So, there was a lot of medical complications for me during that time. That was another challenge---my health. I had placenta previa (the placenta is low in the uterus and sometimes positioned over the cervix), so at any time it was just a ticking time bomb. If I went into labor, I could bleed to death. That really hung over my head: 'OK...if I go into labor, I have this medically fragile child that needs his Mother and then I have a very feisty almost one year old that climbs'," she laughed, "and turns the microwave on by herself'."

At that point, she put her hands on her chest and gave out a long breath. "Whooo! If that was not enough, my placenta was growing out of the uterus and into other organs." They looked at each other and she spoke after a short pause, "It was a was a very challenging time for me just trying to keep my heart and soul in check."

She smiled, "We delivered Bennett five and a half weeks early because he was healthy, and they wanted to take care of things while everything was stable. He also was in NICU for lung development and that's how he entered the world!" Those perinatologists (maternal-fetal medicine physicians) know us by name!" She slapped her forehead and laughed heartily, "It's awful!"

Josh was smiling and calmly said, "It was very intense. I remember that day..."

According to Ashlee, "We only do intense!"

It took prayer

Josh said, "It took prayer. Prayer from others as well to keep us grounded through that. I felt not only were we living with the circumstances of our lives but where I could be potentially...losing my wife through that whole process. Until it was over, there was no certainty, so it brought a lot of anxiety to the table."

When they said she might need a hysterectomy, she explained, "I really think that was hard for me, sad for me because I came from a family of thirteen and I loved a big family. Josh came from a family of five. I think, both of us had envisioned something different than we had been given."

Her eyes lit up and her effervescent personality sparkled as she said, "We didn't end up having to have a hysterectomy and to this day, we are both open to life. If we were pregnant again, we would honestly be rejoicing because we just know how precious it is. Life is a beautiful, beautiful gift and if you have a couple years together or a whole lifetime...it's just how you spend those years."

Blessings in hardship

Ashlee said, "Definitely, our biggest blessings have come from our hardest times. I think kind of holding hands and going in there together and coming out of it. That in itself is a victory. It's a true blessing from God and it makes us stronger. So, when we come up to these hard times in our lives, we kind of just embrace them because you know from past circumstances, 'Hey...this really IS going to make us stronger if we do it right.' Then, you have the ability to touch other people by it."

She noted, "There are so many times where people don't have hope. They don't know what it is. Don't know how to get it. We've learned when you can just say 'yes' to God and be courageous about it and say, 'God...whatever...whatever you have for us...we're OK with that'."

When people are in awe of their lives, they both push back any hint of pride because they feel, 'No...we just said, yes to God. That's all!'

Letting go

"Josh had actually taken Gianna out to a family reunion in Iowa and I stayed home with the two boys. I don't know why. We just decided it might be too much for Levi with all the commotion."

She hooked Levi up to his feeding that night but as usual he never really slept much. When he didn't sleep, Ashlee didn't sleep either.

"It wasn't uncommon for me to be up at all hours reading books to Levi. That night, I was just like, 'Levi...' she pressed her hands on her sleep starved eyes. '...I have to sleep for just a little bit'. So, I put the oxygen cannula in his nose, and I laid him on his side. He always slept right next to us, so I could feel him breathe." She gave a little laugh, "His whole life he slept next to his Mom.

When I woke up the next morning at about eight, all of his alarms were going off. His food pump and his IV alarms were all going off and I was in this little bit of disbelief."

The words were coming harder for Ashlee as she softy said, "I looked at his face and he was blue. The oxygen cannula was on top of his nose. I just screamed like I knew." Fighting back tears, "I put him on the floor, and I tried to do CPR. I called 911. I knew he was gone. I ripped the cords out of the wall and just took him and laid him down in the middle of the entry way. This whole big rush of people came in and were trying to resuscitate him and they were trying and trying. I was just like: 'God...You can't...No!', she looked up with pain in her eyes. 'I need him...I need him. Don't take him from me. I need him'!

There was a time I was just holding him, and I was praying. I was holding what they gave me...like his foot or toe maybe." She looked up at a painting they have on their wall titled, 'Divine Mercy'. At the bottom of the picture it said, 'Jesus, I trust in you.' "At that moment, I just told them to stop and I said, 'He's in heaven and just let him be there'." She smiled through the tears, "And, that's how it happened."

Josh's perspective began with their mutual decision for Ashlee to stay home from the family reunion with Levi. He was requiring more oxygen during the night and it seemed, as always, his life was a precarious balancing act. They were all too familiar with Levi's oxygen levels which could drop to 84% one second and then bounce right back up to 94% the next. "So, you kind of get immune to that alarm going off. Especially in Ashlee's case, there were many, many, many nights she was up until three or four in the morning. That seemed to be Levi's pattern. He would stay awake until three and then sleep until ten, eleven or twelve the next day."

He left for the family reunion but was in regular communication with Ashlee. "Saturday morning, my phone was dead and so my sister came running into the room and said, 'Ashlee's trying to get ahold of you! Something must be going wrong'!"

When he was able to speak with Ashlee, the paramedics were already there, and she was breathless, 'Levi's not breathing, and the paramedics are here working on him!' Josh commented, "I guess there have been so many close calls, I didn't know what that meant at that point."

Ashlee shook her head in agreement as he continued, "Frankly, Levi had fought through so many things and you're like: 'Well...he's not breathing...he'll come around'." His face broke out in a wide smile as he said, "That was my attitude: 'Levi can overcome anything'!"

When he realized something was different about this, his smile faded into the words struggling to leave his mouth, "I grabbed my daughter and grabbed my bag and out the door we went."

He struggled in the hotel parking lot to load his bicycle on the car rack. When he couldn't get it loaded, "I just dropped to my knees and said, 'Why'?" He could barely get words to form and tears filled his eyes. "I just remember the day was rainy...just downpouring. I had never been to Okoboji before and I didn't really recall how I got to the hotel. I didn't know how to get out of town. I was on the phone with Ashlee the entire time and within about 15 minutes they pronounced him gone. It was a...long road home. That's a drive I'll never forget."

Free of pain

Struggling with words, Ashlee's tears continued to flow. "You don't know the day or the hour. It's easy to let him go because he's finally free of that body. That's what gets me through. To know that he doesn't have to carry that anymore," she wiped at her tears. "That is definitely the thing that brings me so much joy, but I miss him terribly."

She admitted, "I miss the fight of caring for him. I miss everything that was in our house because it meant that we were fighting for him. Now it's just kind of empty. We moved since he passed away and that was good. It was good to distance ourselves a little from that because I truly want to be happy. I want to be happy that he's happy."

One of the other Moms with a child with this same birth defect said, 'Levi's still around, so what are you going to do for him every day just like you do for your other kids? I think you need to be happy for him because he's happy. Would he want to see you being sad?' Ashlee answered her, 'Of course not'. "So, for a little while that was my mission just to be happy for Levi. Then it became more of a mission where I just felt an intense need to share him and his message and what he had been through and truly the joy that the suffering brought."

Why?

"I know for a period...that night has been a struggle for Ashlee. I know that she has on more than one occasion with her intuition, saved Levi's life. I think she wanted to beat herself up because how could she not identify there was something wrong. The reality is that Levi had challenges and it was his time. I asked myself, 'Why was I not there?' Was that situation presented because it took our daughter out of that environment which could have been very traumatic for her? I know Ashlee

Copyright © Kim Hoppert Photography

gave so much of herself. She did everything she possibly could to keep Levi comfortable and give him the best quality of life she could."

Ashlee closed her eyes, "I really feel like God put me into a deep sleep, so I would not fight it...", she gave a small laugh, "because He knew I would." She opened her eyes, "I just have to give that to God."

"Just to give you some perspective," Josh said, "I had only left our family three times Levi's entire life. That was it. I wouldn't even have gone, had I not thought things were stable. It just wasn't how we did things. For whatever reason, God said, 'Hey, take a day trip'..."

As she finished his sentence, '...I've got some work to do,' Ashlee laughed lightly with her beautiful smile.

Throughout Levi's life and through his death, anger at each other or at God was not a part of their relationship. "I know it's easy to get mad and spiteful," Ashlee said. "At that point, there's so much vulnerability because you are suffering. He's really putting something beautiful before you if you can just trust Him. There were definitely times I was tired, but I was never tired of God or of the journey or anything like that. It was hard, and it was a challenge, but I was never angry at God for it."

Together they embraced their situation. It doesn't mean it didn't cause pain or struggles, but they felt it often served as an eye opener to other people. Ashlee's face brightened, "I know we spent so much time in the hospital they didn't even need the last name. It was just, 'Levi's here!' How Levi ministered to those people! He never spoke a word and yet people knew the love that I had for him and I would do anything for him. Many were so touched by a little life who never walked, never talked. They saw something deeper. It was so beautiful to be his Mom."

Our inspiration

Josh said, "He was just such an inspiration to us. Levi never gave up so, why would we give up on each other. Maybe Levi was given to us to help protect our marriage. Maybe our marriage wouldn't be as strong as it is. Maybe it would have played out differently had he not been the thread that brought us closer together. Sometimes I feel like it's almost an advantage we had that existed over other marriages." Smiles emerged at that truth.

Redefining their purpose

For so many years, Levi <u>was</u> the purpose of their lives. What would they do now? What would bind them together? Josh said, "There's definitely beauty and love that exists within challenges. I think moving on and re-defining where your purpose should be. When Levi was here, it made it really kind of easy for us to identify what our purpose was because it was such a big thing." Now they would look a little deeper for that purpose. Some of that is found in the numerous ways they can share Levi's story with others.

Advice from the heart

Looking back on his life, Josh began, "I think it starts when you are really young. My Dad wasn't overly vocal, but I think I learned through his example of persistence and finding common ground in certain challenges throughout life. These things were kind of instilled in me, especially by my Mom. She would always say, 'That's part of character building and you're going to need this and you're go-ing to use this down the line'. In life, it became really apparent like, 'BAM'...'This is why she was talking about this'."

He thought a moment and continued, "I would say it's really important to iden-tify somebody you want to spend your entire life with but know there are going to be challenges. Ask, 'Is that the person you want next to you when you are going through those challenges?' Remember, things change. You go through different sea-sons. We're still learning. Things are going to continue to evolve and we have to be ready for that."

Ashlee's advice came through her Dad. "When I was growing up my Dad would always ask me when I was dating: 'Is that the best Father you can give your children?' As she looked down and laughed, "I would always be: 'No, it's not'. When you take your emotions out of it and it's a real thing: 'Ohh...that's for my children. It's not about me anymore. Is that really the man and the qualities I would want to give to my children'? When I met Josh, it was a resounding 'Yes'! That was really clear to me at that point."

She smiled as she said, "<u>You</u> have to be the person you want to marry, or <u>you</u> have to be the spouse that you want."

Josh added, "I feel if we ever hit a rough patch or an area we could be working on...I look internally. 'What can I do better'? It's a question I constantly, constantly have to be asking myself. I think that's really good advice for life in general. I am a business owner so if business isn't the direction I want it to be, rather than pointing fingers to some external factor...I've got to look within, fix all that and if there are still problems...then, I need to reevaluate again."

Ashlee related marriage to her own life as a child. "Growing up with thirteen kids, it's like a drill sergeant", she hit her right hand on her left palm like 'chop-chop'. "My Dad ran that ship like nobody's business. He would come in with the white glove and say 'This is dirty! Dust it five more times'," she laughed. "That was just how I grew up, so, that's how I knew to parent." It was easy to see she loved and respected her Dad and how he brought up his children.

"However, I learned, my children don't respond to that type of discipline: 'Get your chores done. Sit down. Eat dinner!' That wasn't it. It actually drove them further away. This isn't working. What needs to change?' It turned out that I can't preach to Gianna. I need to hold her, love her, cuddle her. I have her tell me what's wrong and we work through things like that together. I didn't know that." It was also true in marriage. What worked for another marriage could be great advice but might not be the best approach for them in their own marriage.

The most poignant piece of advice from Josh: "I don't think we ever tried to point fingers. We just give everything to each other. I think that's how it works. We don't hold anything back. All of our hope, all of our dreams...everything we are we do together. If there's ever a hiccup, we quickly get over it because we share the same vision."

Final word

Together, they fought for their little Levi to have the best and longest life possible. They fought to help their other children live as normal as they could in the least normal of circumstances. They fought for their marriage even in the greatest challenges. The only thing they didn't fight was each other! "Marriage can be a lot of work," Josh smiled, "but it's definitely worth the fight!"

They adamantly agreed. Their greatest blessings came through the hardest times!

Peter & Ellie – Marriage is Important

MARRIED 5 YEARS

**Copyright © Nitram Photography 2014,
Chris Martin**

"Therefore, as God's chosen people, holy and dearly loved, clothe yourselves with compassion, kindness, humility, gentleness and patience." Colossians 3:12

We pray these words from Ellies' Facebook post will bless you as much as they have blessed us.

Elie's Tribute

"Peter is the only family member I got to pick.
Three years into our marriage that still feels like a big deal to me.

The honeymoon was great. But you know what's been even better? Having a husband that can deal with unexpected family events.

Two months before our second year of marriage, my Dad had a massive stroke on the right side of his brain. The sadness I experienced felt endless.

My husband came with me to visit my Dad in the hospital almost every night for an entire summer while my Dad fought to survive. He gave me hugs and space and lovingly refilled my styrofoam cup with cold water and ice chips. That's love.

The hours of wiping away my hot tears, holding my hand and cradling my heart is love. Months. Not hours. Not days. Not weeks. He did this for months.

Then six months after Dad's stroke, my husband suited up in scrubs to hold my hand during my emergency c-section. I was in labor for 36 hours and the nurses discovered my son was positioned to be born with his head spun 180 degrees in the wrong direction with the umbilical cord around his neck.

When my son was born purple and struggling to breathe, my husband rushed with the hospital staff to the NICU. He made sure the first moments of my son's life weren't completely traumatic and spent alone.

He adored our son through wires and pumps. He agonized over the heart monitor hooked up to my son's doll sized chest and analyzed the numbers closer than any Cardinal's baseball game.

He made sure our son was safe. He slept on an uneven mattress in my hospital room as I recovered from my delivery and rallied for another day.

THIS is the love I know.

Marriage is important.

Look for someone who is kind and dedicated. Someone who is okay with sadness and change and can deal with life's insanity. Find someone who will go to the grocery store and buy you chocolate and cheap wine after a rough day. (Or be that person for someone else.)

Finding your person feels like all the fairy tales, but with a lot more inside jokes and belly laughs.

It starts as a feeling and builds into a shared lifetime."

Ted & Barbara – Grab Ahold of Jesus and Hang on Tight

MARRIED 62 YEARS

Copyright © Larry Marx

"The LORD makes firm the step of the one who delights in Him; though he may stumble, he will not fall, for the LORD upholds him with His hand."
Psalms 37:23-24

N early drowned waiting

He was back from college for the summer and coaching the swim team. She was a junior high swimmer trying out for that very same team.

"He was teaching a lifesaving class and immediately asked me if I would be the victim and go down to the bottom of the pool. So, I'm down at the bottom of the pool and he gets busy talking...and talking...and talking...and I finally had to come up for air and said, 'Are you coming to save me or what?' Barbara and Ted looked at each other and laughed like the teenagers they were at their memorable first meeting.

Immediate attraction

"He had good looking legs!" Barbara playfully teased when asked about her initial attraction to Ted.

From Ted's point of view, he remembered Barbara walking across the far end of the pool. "I saw this girl and my eyes just about popped out of my head! She had this beautiful dark tan with a very white bathing suit. I just thought, 'Wow!' Then this thought came to me: 'That's going to be your wife someday'."

Needless to say, he was so smitten, he 'unselfishly' offered to pick her up on his motorcycle at 0-dark-30 each day for swim team practice. "My Dad agreed," Barbara said, "that I could ride on it TO the pool and that was it. Nowhere else...just TO swimming practice!"

After about a month of early morning rides, he got up the nerve to ask her to a church youth group picnic at the beach. Her Dad was a little hesitant because of their age difference but finally relented. According to Ted, "We just became very, very good friends. We did some other dating, but it was a little awkward because I was 19 and she was 14."

Barbara laughed, "Which today would be illegal!"

Ted looked over at Barb, "It was then, too, but still her Dad didn't seem to mind. It was all kind of around church...dances with our youth group and that kind of thing. Then, we just really fell in love with each other...or I did."

"I knew I liked him, but we never had the stipulation that I couldn't date other people. So, while he was away at college, I dated other boys, but nobody ever really interested me."

He shrugged his shoulders, "I dated a few girls while I was in college. None of them interested me much either."

Surprise backfired

When Ted was home on holidays, they always went out together...except. Barbara sheepishly explained, "This one time he came home unexpectedly."

"I just thought I would surprise her." It was a surprise all right! Barbara had been invited to a party with a male friend. They were going as a couple and she wouldn't break the date. Obviously, that didn't go over very well with Ted!

"It really hurt my feelings, so I just kind of washed my hands of Barbara." In college, his summers were committed to ROTC, so he couldn't coach the swim team.

Instead he was a lifeguard on the beach. "She would come and sit under my lifeguard stand and try to talk to me and I would just sort of..."

"I would come out there all the time and sit there making him look at me and talk to me."

"But I was holding my own. I was holding my distance from her."

"I wasn't going to let him get away! I finally realized I really, really did like him!"

During that time, Ted had her picture in his wallet and regularly gazed at her beautiful face. "I just really was waiting for myself to get off my high horse." Barbara lightly giggled as he related how he continued to 'hold out'. When he came home from college after graduation, they didn't see each other at all. Off he went to pilot training until he had time off to attend his sister's wedding.

Wedding boo-boo

"Of course, Barbara was at the wedding. I saw her...and I thought, 'Ohhhh...', he twirled his head around, 'she's so beautiful! I've got to knock this off'!" He approached Barbara and told her he would come back to get her and take her somewhere after he took the maid of honor home. As he was walking out to the car, his Dad pulled him aside and said, 'It's the best man's job to take care of and date the maid of honor after the wedding, so you take care of Connie tonight.' "So, I took care of Connie and I never went back and told Barbara anything."

Surprised they didn't find Ted dead the next morning, we asked Barbara what happened that night. "I sat there, and I waited and I waited and I waited and I waited. His cousin asked me if I'd like to go out (and his cousin's a real looker!). I said, 'No, Ted's coming back for me.' Later, I thought, 'Shoot, I missed a date with Dan!' I sat there and sat there and sat there and he never came so I started walking home...in the pouring rain! I didn't know what happened to him or why he never came back. I was a little upset!"

Realizing he was oblivious to Barbara's plight, he said, "I tell you...I was terrible! I was terrible! I was the king of my universe, so I never gave it another thought. She was just so in love with me and wouldn't let me go."

Barbara couldn't figure out what happened to him, so she finally called his mother and asked for his address, so she could write. The letter wasn't angry. It was kind and concerned. She told us she held herself back because, "I didn't want to say, 'What the heck happened to you...you doo-doo'?"

The letter came

Without any further contact with Barbara, he drove to San Angelo for his next training. He was there two months, when he got that very kind and forgiving letter from Barbara. only asking him what happened to him the night of the wedding. "I looked at that letter and I went into my roommate and said", 'Dick, I'm going to get married in a few months!' Ted and Barbara had a good, hard, long laugh with each other over the audacity of his statement!

They wrote each other until he came home for Christmas vacation. The first thing he did was buy an engagement ring. He went to her dental office and the minute he saw her with her dark tan against that white uniform, he must have had visions of her in that white swimming suit when he first met her! "I almost melted right there on the floor. I said, 'Barbara, I've got something very important I want to share with you tonight. Would you go out with me?' She said, 'Sure'. So, we went out and watched the ocean", he laughed.

They leaned into each other as Barbara snickered, "We used to call it watching submarine races." Now she was the oblivious one! She thought maybe he was going to ask her to go steady again. Instead, he said, "'Would you marry me?" Shocking question, but her shocking answer was, 'Yes'!

Ted came with his best romantic speech which consisted of: 'Well, let me have your finger'. "I put the ring on it, and we were so happy we could hardly stand it!" Watching them giggle and laugh through their story, we felt as if we were right back in their car by the ocean, reliving that touching moment with them.

Long way from home

Immediately after the wedding, they headed to the desert of West Texas. Barbara had just turned 19 and had never been away from home. She was snatched from tropical Florida and planted to a dusty yard, devoid of grass and filled with tumbleweeds. "I thought if you couldn't see the end of the world from there...we were pretty close." She was alone in the house all day and didn't know anybody. "I had a lot of growing up to do really fast, especially learning not to be afraid by myself." Barbara grinned as she added, "Oh...and I couldn't cook either!"

Ted rented a house which he described to her as much like the house she lived in growing up. What he said and what she got were two entirely different things! Ted laughed so hard, he had to hold his chest, "I'll never forget the kitchen! Green kind of oil cloth wallpaper with roosters all over it! One bathroom had this wallpaper with huge big lilac blooms in pink and purple on black background." By now, Ted was laughing so hard he couldn't stop. When he finally caught his breath, he told us it didn't take Barbara long to see it was nothing like the beautiful home in Florida where she grew up.

"But she loved me enough. In fact, she really loved me. She hung in there. I had to get up at 4am for early morning flights. She would get up and fix breakfast for me. She was just a perfect wife," he started laughing again, "but when I came home about noon she was still in bed."

"I got to where I could get up and fix a whole breakfast of bacon, eggs, toast...the whole nine yards and never wake up. I would hit the bed and I would be out like a light."

Honeymoon faded

In the first few months of married life, her only challenges were learning to live in a barren desert and learning to cook for her new husband. Their lives were filled with fun in the water and in the air! Every weekend they would be out on their boat fishing and water skiing. They joined the Aero Club and Barbara even got checked out in an open cockpit plane. Ted's wild side surfaced, and he treated her to some loops! It could be the only challenge Barbara faced on that ride was staying alive!

That is, until their lives took an upside-down loop when she got pregnant about nine months after their wedding. Their baby was due the same summer the Air Force base was closing their pilot training program. They would be pulling up stakes to transfer to Florida. Barbara had six more weeks before her due date, so they planned to drive to Florida and have the baby there. At her next appointment, the doctor warned, 'If you leave, you won't get 10 miles down the road'. And they wouldn't have! That baby had another idea!

Two days later and five weeks early, Mark was born. He weighed in at nearly six pounds, but his premature lungs gave him a 50/50 chance of survival. They were not allowed to travel with him until he gained some of his birth weight back. All their household goods, including the baby clothes and Barbara's regular clothes, had been sent ahead to Florida. Ted had to buy her some clothes to get her out of the hospital and also find a fully furnished apartment to rent for a couple of weeks.

Barbara came from a whole family of girls, so she was thrilled to have a little boy. And little he was! Ted could hold him on his forearm to give him a bath in the sink. He was so tiny, that even after two weeks and gaining enough weight to travel, the doctor said they couldn't take him unless there was an air conditioner in the car. Ted started laughing, "That's when we traded our boat AND our old convertible to get a car with an air conditioner!"

Mark was so small he couldn't nurse so they had glass bottles that had to be sterilized on a hot plate as they traveled. The motion of the car kept him sleeping all day but at night he would be up every two hours eating. They drove all the way to Florida with their sterilizer, bottles and two extremely tired bodies.

Throw in a war...

Their marriage went on as normal until Viet Nam arrived on the scene and Ted would be deployed a long 14 months. "Barbara," Ted tenderly explained, "was all of sudden going to have to be mother and father to our children."

By now their children were nine and seven and as Barbara described it, "They were not young enough to have baby problems and not old enough to have teenage problems." They bought a home near both of their families, so that if something happened to Ted while he was deployed, it would be a good place for their family to live.

"I was so proud of her!"

Barbara's challenge was raising the children alone. Ted's challenge came when he returned from Viet Nam and had to make the adjustment back into the family. As many military families know, when Dad is gone, the kids have no one to go to but Mom. When Dad returns, that habit is still there, and they continue to go to Mom. Dad can be sort of an afterthought...the extra guy around the house. Many military families were not prepared for such a challenge, including this one.

Sometimes the effects of war don't surface immediately. That was true for Ted. "I didn't know it at the time but about two years ago, after talking to some people at the VA, I discovered I did come back from Viet Nam with slight PTSD (post-traumatic stress disorder). It wasn't really severe like some of the guys, but I saw enough action to come back with enough PTSD to throw me off."

As he looked back, he noticed before Viet Nam, he had a very high work ethic. He wanted to be the best he could be as a flight instructor and math instructor and even pursued his Masters' degree. "I don't think we had any troubles between us, but after I got back from Viet Nam things weren't the same." Even though he occasionally drank before heading to Viet Nam, when he returned the drinking started getting heavier. He had another tour as an instructor at the Air Force Academy but this time, he admitted, his work ethic wasn't at a very high level.

"We went out camping and had a lot of fun together with the kids, but I was just not the same guy. I didn't know what was wrong with me. I just really didn't understand why I was..." His voice trailed off as he hesitated and then added, "I'm just sick I was that way."

Drinking got heavier

Following Viet Nam, they finished their three-year tour at the Air Force Academy followed by language school to prepare for an assignment to Venezuela. "Once we got there", Barbara said, "the local people would just as soon we go home." That meant we were confined to a small group of American military friends who all stuck together. As much as they had fun, it was also when the drinking got even heavier. Barbara said, "That really upset me!"

"My buddy and I would go to lunch at the embassy and have three or four martinis and go back to work. That was nothing. Venezuelans did the same thing, so it was no big deal. Then, we would get together at one of the houses when we got home after work and go at it again.

I tried to stop drinking many times and couldn't!" he explained. "I was angry at myself for the way I was because I knew I was about to lose my best friend and my kids. I really didn't have any idea what to do, but I had a feeling it had something to do with God."

On January 1, 1975, while still in Venezuela, Ted was sitting in the living room by himself...frustrated and desperate. He slammed his arms down on his knees as he repeated his words from that night, 'God, I have got to find you this year!' "I made that statement to God and although it didn't sound like one, it must have been a prayer."

About three months later, he was attending a church service where the Gospel message was presented. He said the prayer to receive Christ along with everyone else in the service, but felt his heart wasn't really in it because nothing changed in his attitude. He sadly said, "I was the same."

Not Alabama...again!

Ted digressed to explain he had always been given every military assignment he wanted. One assignment he never wanted again was Montgomery, Alabama. "It was 1959, and we lived in a roach infested apartment in the south part of Montgomery. They treated blacks so badly I couldn't hardly stand it. I would go to work and travel 15 mph through the white school zone and 35 mph through the black school zone. We had a black officer in our little group, and we couldn't have them over to our house. You couldn't have blacks in your house except as domestic help and they had to come in the back door."

"It was against the law," Barbara added.

"I told Barbara, 'We are never going to live in Montgomery again'!" After the tour to Venezuela, he put in for San Antonio but this time, the Air Force decided to send them back to Montgomery...exactly where he didn't want to be! You will come to see, as they did, that the undesirable assignment came with a God-designed purpose.

After reluctantly moving back to Alabama, they reconnected with some friends they had known at a previous military assignment. They were invited to attend church and a prayer and praise group with them. Ted said, 'Barbara, we have done so many religious things our whole life. I don't want to do any more religious things'."

"Besides", Barbara laughed, "we didn't know what a prayer and praise group was!"

Their son said he'd been there one time and they were a 'wild bunch'. Now, that was helpful information! So, every week they would get invited and every week they declined. After about six weeks, Ted finally said they were going one time to get them off their backs!

He said, "We went to the prayer and praise group and there were about four or five couples that were just beaming, so happy and so joyful. I thought, 'I wish I was like that.' They started talking about Jesus and started singing about Jesus and they started praying to Jesus and they started reading the Bible about Jesus. It was Jesus and Jesus and Jesus, and I said, 'Hmmm...they are just soo joyful.' So, we kept going back and kept going back."

Ted said, "On New Years' Day, 1976, I was sitting in my den reading my Bible. I was reading John chapter 15 where it says, 'I am the Vine and you are the branches and if you abide in Me and I abide in You, you will produce much fruit but apart from Me you can do nothing.' That caught me. That caught my heart," his voice cracked, "and just ripped it out of me. I knew at that moment God was calling me to come to Him. I got down on my knees," again his voice broke and tears started to fall as he shared the words he said that day, 'Jesus, please forgive me and come into my heart and be my Lord and Savior.' "And He did! Right away. I was just so joyful I couldn't stand it."

He drove me crazy!

Barbara gave her best, mock-whiny voice, "He drove me crazy! He told me I had to do that (give my life to Jesus) too and because he told me I had to do it, it made me mad!"

Ted smiled from ear to ear, "She didn't know what to do with this new guy!"

"He would start leaving brochures and tracts all over the house," their shoulders met as they shared their laughter. "It was mainly just stubbornness on my part because the Holy Spirit had been working on me overtime and yet, I was just so upset with him because he was badgering me and badgering me."

He kept taking her to the prayer and praise group and visiting other churches. They were attending a crusade at an Assembly of God church when Barbara said,

"The minister gave a call at the end and I don't know how I got down front. It was like the Holy Spirit picked me up and threw me down there, because I don't remember getting up out of the pew. I gave my heart to the Lord and got up a new person."

What caused the change?

Ted's face brightened, "Jesus!"

At that point, his drinking was way down, but he still enjoyed a drink every night after work. They were out with friends for dinner and everyone ordered water or tea and Ted ordered alcohol. As they were all walking out to the car one evening, one of the guys put his arm around Ted and said, 'You know, you really need to stop that, Ted.' "So, I did. That was the end of that. It did have a big impact on our marriage."

One of their biggest tasks was trying to convince their own teenage kids they weren't crazy. They literally thought their Mom and Dad had turned into 'Jesus Freaks'!

Promotion...or not?

The morning the list for promotion to Colonel would be coming out, he read the first of his three daily devotions. It was Romans 8:28, 'And we know that all things work together for the good of those that love the Lord and are fitting into His plans'. Ted raised his hands in the air and gave a huge smile. "I thought, 'Aha...I'm going to be on the promotion list'!"

His boss called him into the office and said, 'You didn't make the list'. He hung his head as he told us he went back home for lunch and read his second devotion: Romans 8:28...'All things work together for good... Then he read his third devotion. You guessed it: Romans 8:28 - All things work together... "I said, 'OK, Lord...I believe it and I know you've got something better for me'."

No promotion and a dead-end job! How could that be something better? Then, through a series of inexplicable situations, Ted wasn't promoted to Colonel, all because of a letter he wrote for his Commander. He was appointed as Deputy Commander which was almost impossible to understand because there were three or four guys that outranked him for the job. That didn't matter to the Commander. He wanted Ted! God definitely had something better in mind!

He had just been in Washington DC, so he was less than excited to get news he was being sent back there again for a conference. To upset Ted even more, there was no room for him to stay on the base, so he had to go to a local hotel. The next morning three guys at the hotel were sitting together at breakfast. "This great big guy comes in and walks around. People around the room are saying, 'Come over here, Lew. Sit with us!' He walks around and comes over to us and says, 'May I join you?' First thing out of his mouth was 'Jesus'! He started talking about his job and Jesus, and his family and Jesus, his job and Jesus. I thought to myself, 'You can't do that in the Air Force', but Lew did!" That's when Ted knew God brought him back to Washington DC to meet Lew!

Ted held his hands out in front of himself with fingers entwined to demonstrate the relationship he and Lew had from that day on. They were assigned to different bases, so at the end of the conference, they would go home but their lives stayed connected. Ted gave a fit pump into the air, "That's where it all kind of began!"

Start what?

Time passed and Ted came home with a letter from Lew. He said, 'Honey...I've got some exciting news! We're going to start a ministry!' From that letter, Ted and Lew formed Son Shine Ministries International, a Christ-centered resource specializing in ministry to families.

Barbara laughed as she recounted her response, 'That's the dumbest thing I ever heard!' "That was my spiritual answer and you can put that in the book! Ted went on and on about preaching and teaching and I said. 'What makes you think you can preach anyway'?"

"She didn't want to be a part of a ministry. She wanted to travel!" Well, she got her wish, because during the course of their active leadership of Son Shine Ministries, they traveled to thirty countries!

Didn't have to look far

It didn't take them long or need them to look very far to both agree their greatest blessing in their marriage was sitting right next to them.

Ted said, "As we have grown in the Lord, in our relationship with Him, our relationship with each other has spiraled upward. We are over the physical part of marriage, but we just love each other more than we have ever loved each other. We're on the same page spiritually. We get up in the morning and sit here for maybe two to three hours just reading our Bibles, praying, having our quiet time side by side. When we both finish, we pray together. Our relationship has been so great!"

Barbara added, "I think it's growing closer as we have gotten older and the kids are on their own and doing their own thing. I have had a few challenges...thinking I would die from lymphoma and then having multiple sclerosis. My MS is starting to take a toll on me..."

"...plus her back surgeries and hysterectomy."

"I can't do a lot of things I used to be able to do, and he has to do a lot of them for me. That's a real big blessing in how he takes care of me. He's has quit teaching English as a Second Language because he doesn't want to leave me alone for three hours at night. He has made some sacrifices to make sure I am well taken care of."

Ted answered humbly, "It's so neat to have more time with her."

Just wanted to get a break

Barbara said the only time she ever thought about leaving him was when they lived in Venezuela, but she had nowhere to go but Columbia. As you can imagine, with that option, her thought of leaving him didn't last very long. "I just wanted to get a break. I've never thought about divorcing him...never!"

Ted went through a time in Venezuela, as well, when he was so disgusted with himself, he thought his family would be better off without him. He admitted as he was driving over the winding mountain roads, he once thought, 'If I just hold this steering wheel straight on a curve, I'll go right off, and no one will ever know the difference.' That was a fleeting, but very real thought in his mind.

They were adults now

There seemed to be a lull when their children were adults, and everyone seemed to be doing well. Until…their daughter, Wendy, who had been married about 14 years and had two children, went through a divorce. Barbara said, "It just seemed like her whole life unraveled from that point on. She just couldn't hold anything together. She couldn't hold a job. She couldn't function very well, so she started self-medicating."

There was a sadness in Barbara's voice as she continued with Wendy's story of marrying a former drug addict. She was soon taking methamphetamines, to the point where she heard voices. She traveled with her husband who was a trucker and there were times they would come home and stay in Ted and Barbara's home. On one of those nights, Wendy got a butcher knife and Ted had to wrestle it away from her. Another time, Barbara woke up with Wendy standing over her with a bat. Barbara said, "She scared me to death so, we would wedge a chair under our door at night."

It was frustrating because Wendy was an adult and they couldn't force her to do anything. They made phone call after phone call trying to get her help. She wasn't willing and nothing they could do helped. Barbara said, "We had never heard of this before, but she finally got addicted to BC powder (a powdered aspirin). She would take four at a time and a couple hours she would take four more. She would just eat those things. She had them hidden in her purse. She had them hidden in the truck. Her husband said every crack was stuffed with them until they finally killed her because she bled to death while on a cross country trucking trip with her husband."

As parents, it was very difficult for them to not be able to do anything to help their daughter. Ted said, "I tried to think back…'What did we do wrong?' That was a very, very tough time."

The most difficult thing Barbara faced was the memory of seeing Wendy for the last time in a cold storage drawer in the hospital. She cried as she continued, "It's always bothered me."

That wasn't the end of the story. When Wendy's husband, Charlie, was diagnosed with cancer, they put a bed in their living room. He stayed in their home for one and a half years until he died. They did everything they could to help him, too!

Pulled them together

Barbara smiled, "I think it was pulling us together."

Ted agreed, "Oh, I think very, very much so. We would cry together, discuss and talk about what we could do. It did really open up a lot of conversation between us."

There was never any resentment from either of them toward God. "No not at all," Ted said. "There was never a time when I was upset with the Lord. In fact, I think Wendy really loved the Lord, because she would sit over on the couch and read her Bible for hours when she was living with us."

"So," Ted said, "the Lord assured me she was with Him. Once we knew that, we knew she was OK. That settled us down and gave us peace."

In addition, being surrounded in prayer by Christian friends gave them strength to carry on. The support they received and continue to receive from their son, Mark, and his family, has been immeasurable in their lives.

Advice for you

Ted's tender voice began, "My advice is to grab ahold of Jesus and hang on tight. I don't care what background you are, you need to go to a church that teaches the Bible and get into the Bible and read it. Become a born-again Christian. God will do it if you search Him out. Jesus said, 'Anybody who seeks Me will find me'."

With confidence, Barbara said, "Remove divorce from your vocabulary. Scratch it out of your dictionary. Divorce is just a cop out...taking the easy way out."

Ted added, "You made a commitment in marriage. You keep that commitment. A covenant. You don't break it. I think that's what held us together even before we became Christians. Just a commitment."

Their advice included finding mentors. Shortly after giving their lives to Christ, they met their friends, Lew and Sandy and began partnering with them in ministry. They were more than partners...they were mentors." Ted said, "We were so new to our faith and had so much stuff the Lord had to clean out. We didn't quite see it at the time, but when we look back on it, we see how much they mentored us during those first ten years of the ministry."

Standing tall

Alcohol, war, numerous military assignments, PTSD, death of a daughter, lymphoma and MS. One might think their shoulders would be bowed down with the weight. Not true with Ted and Barbara! Their shoulders were straight, and smiles filled their entire faces with brightness. They knew they weren't walking their life journey alone. Even though they might stumble or fall, they had each other and they had Jesus holding them up.

Gary & Vicki – Commitment... Their Glue

MARRIED 50 YEARS

"The LORD is my rock, my fortress and my deliverer; my God is my rock, in whom I take refuge..." Psalms 18:2a

Any romantic love story could begin as theirs did: A young, beautiful college coed lingers on an open balcony. He glances up and then takes a second look. 'My, those are <u>good</u> looking legs'. Ok – OK...that remark maybe wouldn't make it into a romantic novel, but <u>really</u>...that's how it happened!

"I was dating another girl at the time, so I told my friend, 'You and I need to go on a double date'." This guy wanted nothing to do with a double date because he didn't know anybody to ask. "I said, 'I tell you what. If I can line you up with somebody, would you double date'?"

Now, who could argue with that! That's when Gary leapt into action and found out the name of this mysterious balcony girl with the good legs. "I asked her out for my friend. She accepted and that's the first time I met her. It wasn't <u>my</u> double date...it was <u>hers</u>."

Persistent!

Vicki knew who Gary was and more than that, she knew his car which came with a reputation for making a unique sound as it went down an alley appropriately titled 'Echo Alley'. She was also aware that he came with a reputation Vicki described as 'less than stellar'. Gary scrunched up his face at that comment. Add this to the mix was the fact Vicki was aware he had dated his current girlfriend all through high school and college. "It was pretty well accepted on campus that they would eventually get married." Those seemed to be enough caution signals to make any young woman hesitate.

"Later when Gary called me and asked me out for himself. I was going, 'WHOAAA! Wait a minute! NO, NO, NO, NO, NO!' She made movements with hands like umpire calling 'You're out!'. She put on the brakes and told Gary, 'You and Linda are a thing. I am not even walking into that hornet's nest'!"

'We broke up!'

'Yah...<u>sure</u> you did!' (She was not easily persuaded, so he actually called her at least three times before she ever gave in and agreed to go out with him.)

Gary innocently grinned, "I was persistent."

Not exactly Mr. Smooth

A couple of days before their actual date, they were walking out of the Student Union. He casually draped his arm around her shoulder and asked, 'What would you like to have to drink Saturday night?' Vicki gave him a puzzled look to which Gary responded, 'Oh, you're leaving it up to me, huh'?

'Oh, God, what am I doing with this guy?'

Later, his roommate brought a little clarity to the situation when he said, 'Gary, you just asked one of the most religious girls on campus what she wanted to drink!'

Clueless, he responded, 'Oh'...'

He gave it the 'old college try' to attempt a way to bring redemption for his glaring error. "On our first date, I took her to the most romantic place I knew...the cemetery."

Vicki was all smiles, "Needless to say, he had a hard time convincing me to go out with him the second night!" And, by now we were thinking Mr. Smooth was destined to be out of the romantic novel business!!

The legs? The car?

Legs caught his attention at first glance, but it was her laugh he noticed on their first date. " I just thought she was nice. A good girl. A fun date." He admitted at that point he had been dating lots of different girls trying to find one perfect, fun date.

Vicki smiled, "Gary was fun...and oh yes...his car was a 1965, cherry red, Belvedere II Plymouth that had a really hot engine in it. It always looked perfect and it was a fun car to be in." This was one girl who obviously knew her cars!

How long did it take?

In spite of his dating bloopers, Gary said, "We kept dating and about the third week, I decided she was the one...but...I still had to convince her! We had our breakups in that course of time. I couldn't understand why anybody wouldn't think I was the greatest thing on earth!" At that, Vicki laughed and shook her head in agreement.

It took a little longer for Vicki! In fact, she said, "I knew I was in love two days before I walked down the aisle," to which they both gave a hard, long laugh.

"To be really truthful with you, we were sitting outside the dorm when he looked at me, grinned and said, 'You know, my Mother is just going to love you!' I looked at him and said, 'What does your Mother have to do with anything'? She raised her voice in a testy tone, 'Besides, who said I am going home to meet your parents'!"

She was definitely the stubborn one in the relationship. "He asked me to marry him, I don't know...two or three times. He asked me to marry him the night of the Spring Formal and I said, 'No'. He took me back to the dorm and things were pretty chilly. When I got home from church Sunday morning, he had everything of mine packaged up and at the dorm. There was a note saying, 'I'm done! I won't ask you again. It's over.'

"OK, it was decision time. Even at that point I wasn't sure that I loved him. I just was sure I wasn't ready to let him go. That's when we got back together again."

I finally know I want him!

Vicki's family was taking a long vacation that summer and would be traveling near Gary's hometown. He drove to meet her, and it was on that trip, she finally knew she wanted to be with him.

When they returned from vacation, Gary came to Iowa and proposed. Her final answer was 'Yes'. "You get caught up in this whirlwind of wedding plans but, I can truthfully say," she looked at Gary, "I had reservations the night I walked down the aisle. Not so much reservations about you but just reservations about 'Am I really ready to get married?' 'What on earth am I getting into.' 'What am I doing'?"

Gary admitted he had those same reservations but teased, "When you marry the perfect person (meaning himself)...there are high expectations."

'Oh God, this is for real!' She made a funny face and continued her thoughts in a very soft voice. 'Ahhhhhhh...Can I turn around now?' Even with those questions and doubts, she continued the walk down the aisle where they began their journey together.

Distance brought unity

Their marriage began with their joint decision to serve on staff in a children's home in Maryland. It was a long way from both sets of parents, so basically, they had to do it on their own as young 20-year-olds. They were house parents in charge of court committed juveniles, ranging in age from eight to sixteen. Vicki could now see how that particular job caused them to work as a team to prevent their charges from conquering and dividing. She felt it gave them great experience they would use later in life with their own children.

After about nine months, Gary took a new position still located far from their families. "That first Christmas, Vicki was so home sick and to call home was a big thing. It cost money and we didn't have a lot of money. It was sad to see her like that but here was nothing I could do. We got through it. We had to do it on our own. There were no other choices."

Mixing business and family

A few years into their marriage, they made the choice to become part of the family business with her dad serving as CEO and as Vicki called him, 'Chief Enforcer'. Gary smiled, "That's a nice way of putting it," and then they both laughed. "I don't know how we made it through."

"It was very difficult, and Gary was only 23 at the time but was given a huge amount of responsibility. He handled it fine, but Dad was 600 miles away, trying to micromanage what he had given Gary to do. It was a really difficult situation.

I was far away from family and had a newborn baby and a husband that was working 18 to 20 hours a day." You could hear the residual pain in their voices as they spoke about this challenging time in their marriage and in Vicki's family.

Some years later, they took their business experience and decided to break away from the family business. Her Dad felt they were taking his 'trade secrets'. "Basically, he said we could either stop what we were doing, or he would slap an injunction on us. When we moved forward, he slapped an injunction on us. Gary and my Dad did not speak for nearly ten or twelve years. It was a long time!"

Effect on their marriage

She couldn't hold back tears as she said, "The effect on our marriage was not as much as you would maybe think." However, it was easy to see she was troubled over the lack of relationship between her husband and her Dad.

"I remember lying in bed thinking, 'What can I do? These are the two men I love the most in my life and what can I do to bring them together?' Ultimately you recognize there is nothing you can do. I can remember one night while I was in bed praying, I was muddling over all of this again and again and again and again. There was the image of packing your troubles and taking them to Jesus.

I laid there that night and I put all the emotions I had and all of this situation in a box. I remember seeing Jesus sitting there and I walked to His feet and bowed and put the box there and walked away. I said, 'Jesus...there's nothing I can do. I recognize this is ALL yours!' and I walked away. I had let go of it and at that point, I told Gary, 'You know, the kids (age four and seven) need to know their grandparents'." She smiled as said Gary never forced her to make a choice between him and her Dad.

"I finally said, 'I'm going to take the kids and I'm going home for a visit'. We spent time with Mom and Dad and it was an OK trip. Each summer after that, the kids and I went back to Iowa and visited. This went on for nearly eight years, when Gary and I were sitting at a restaurant having a cup of coffee. He looked at me and said, 'Maybe it's time to go home for Christmas'." She wiped tears streaming down her face.

Gone on long enough!

They made plans to make a surprise visit to Iowa for Christmas. Everyone knew but her parents. Their visit would be their Christmas present.

Vicki said, "Mom heard somebody coming up the steps. She turned around and saw us and just stood up and screamed. Dad looked around to see what the commotion was, and he looked at us and I think he screamed, too." She wiped tears as she continued with sadness in her voice, "We just stood there and cried. So, the barrier was broken but until the day my Dad died, he never said anything to me about, 'I was wrong. I shouldn't have done it'."

Gary continued her story, "That's when the farm economy bottomed out and her Dad and the business were struggling back there in Iowa. It was not a good time for them. They didn't have anything. They were at a low point. So, it's like, 'Give this up. This is stupid. This has gone on along enough'!"

They were eventually back working with her Dad's business. "That's when I had to go through the process of understanding that Dad, for whatever reason, did not understand how to form or maintain relationships and the joy that come from relationships. I finally said, 'You know this is my Dad and if he were any other person, I would probably have very little to do with him. Because he is my Dad, he deserves a place in my life'.

Vicki also came to learn that her Dad's main goal in his life was to make his parents proud of him. She felt he died never feeling total acceptance from them. With compassionate tears forming in her eyes, she said, "It affected everything he did."

With kindness, Gary shared this simple truth: "When you marry someone; you marry their family."

Not just family challenges

Vicki said, "Like everybody else, we faced financial ups and downs. The last 13 years we have also dealt with health issues." Gary was diagnosed with multiple myeloma and has undergone several bone marrow transplants and many chemo sessions as well as experimental drugs.

"We faced the health crisis and the prospect of his death and me being a single person. We got through that by understanding where we are in our relationship with Christ and understanding that's the basis of everything." Their faith was strengthened and has carried them each step of this journey.

Blessing in humor

They both laughed together as Vicki said one of her blessings was Gary's sense of humor. "Warped as it is!" We sensed that many days his sense of humor was the thing that lightened their heavy load.

When they were going through the biggest challenges, Vicki could remember saying, 'I am sooo blessed. We have two really good kids that for the most part caused us no grief growing up. They were good teenagers. They were fun to be around. They did well. Good marriages, even with its ups and downs. I have always had a roof over my head and a pretty good one'."

He patted her on the shoulder, "She's easy to live with!" It must have been an inside joke because they both laughed hysterically!

Vicki smiled, "See...sense of humor!" We were all laughing so hard it caused Gary to look over at us and pipe in with, 'Mike, don't fall off the chair please.' That made the room erupt in snorting laughter!

Guard your marriage

Gary admitted, "Leave? Oh, I'm sure there were times I thought it. If it was...it was a short term, passing...and then reality is like: 'Well, leaving...that doesn't sound like something I want to do'." When asked what kept them together, Gary said very seriously, "What are the options? Not too many and they aren't any good."

He quickly and confidently said, "I've always maintained you don't put yourself knowingly in a situation where you become tempted by another woman. Stay away from the obvious. There were opportunities while I was out there. I was with wheelers and dealers and some with not such good moral character, but I would never allow myself to be drawn knowingly into that situation." He would always ask himself, 'Why would I want to do something stupid?' He laughed, "My favorite saying right now is: 'You can't fix stupid!' And that is stupid!"

Vicki said, "Commitment kept us together like glue. We have talked about this and see many marriages today are the event, not the covenant. For me, the ceremony of marriage was a covenant and it was one that I didn't have a right to break." Gary shook his head in agreement. "So, whatever I thought was an issue and was wrong in our marriage, walking away was not an option. Life is choices. What kept me in the marriage over the years was the conviction of the covenant that I made with Gary," tears began to flow, "and that I made with the Lord on September 9, 1967."

Gary got that trademark grin of his and said, "Besides that...I'm perfect!" Together they caught the humor, even as Vicki chuckled through her tears.

He then put on his serious face to explain, "It's not short term. There's going to be a lot of rough spots. You can use it as a reason to quit or you can use it as steel sharpening steel. I guess over the years, we've used it as steel on steel. Besides loving each other, I think we like each other."

"I think Gary's last comment is one piece of sage advice. You have to like each other. You have to enjoy being in each other's company. Maintain a sense of humor. I don't care what you're going through, find a lighter side to it. When Gary was diagnosed with cancer, he also happened to have two broken arms at the time and a titanium rod in each arm. Instead of just kind of doing the old 'woe is me'...we began to chuckle and laugh about his arms saying, 'Well, someday they'll become wind chimes'!"

Gary joined in the exuberant laughter as she said, "It's finding some way to put some levity into the situation so you're not always holding your hands to the side of your head screaming, 'Ohhhh...the sky is falling...the sky is falling!' What's going to happen tomorrow? No one knows. Live in today. Leave yesterday back there or you'll keep trying to drag yesterday along.

Don't take yourself too seriously'. In the grand scheme of things...you're just a little speck. Have fun with it. There are times to be serious but don't be sooo serious."

Vicki said, "It's important to have mutual respect."

Her husband smiled, "And give some grace."

Gary shook his head in agreement as she continued, "I think to understand marriage you have to know it only works well if a marriage is Christ centered. There has to be something bigger than you."

Moving closer

When their interview began, Gary was sitting with his arm casually draped over the back of the couch. Vicki had her arms crossed in front of her...as if putting a little emotional distance between them. As they told their story, they leaned into each other as barriers came tumbling down. Sometimes hearing your story from your own lips is a reminder of why you fell in love in the first place. So, it could be with Gary and Vicki.

Milestone celebration

In 2017, they celebrated their 50th anniversary with family and friends in the mountains of Colorado. One of Vicki's favorite memories of Gary is him puckering up for an anniversary kiss.

Written by Vicki - August 20, 2018:

"What a sad joyous day this has been! After a long gallant battle with multiple health issues for the past 13 years, my dear husband and life mate of 51 years, earned his angel wings. We will miss him so. Everyone that has crossed his path has a Gary story. As you remember him, chuckle about your favorite memory and remember him warmly. His enjoyment of life will be missed.'"

Our view

As we gathered with family and friends to celebrate his life, there were indeed many Gary stories. One thing Gary left with us was how his faith got stronger as his health deteriorated. He inspired us. Let the story he and Vicki walked, inspire you.

Ward & Bretta – Love Story Still Being Written

MARRIED 34 YEARS

Copyright © Tyler Ogburn Photography

"Strengthen the feeble hands, steady the knees that give way; say to those with fearful hearts, 'Be strong, do not fear; your God will come'." Isaiah 35:3-4a

W hen asked their wedding date, Ward proudly proclaimed, "seventh day seventh month!" When asked what year, he said, "It was a good year!" That's when she burst out laughing and he gave his innocent smile!

Yes, our time with them was filled with lighthearted kidding and private snickers over inside jokes. It was, like a good cup of coffee, up to the brim with sweet moments of memories. Their eyes often were over the brim as tears splashed down on their cheeks. Won't you join us on their journey?

It all began...

They were so young. She was just 16 and he was 20. They met at a meeting held by Son Shine Ministries located in Texas. Ward was there with another girl, so he and Bretta didn't spend any time together, but she <u>definitely</u> noticed he was cute. Unbeknownst to them, God was putting the puzzle pieces together as both Bretta's family and Ward would be joining that same ministry the next year.

When they moved onto the grounds of the ministry center, Bretta and her parents lived right next door to Ward. At first, they got to know each other as neighbors but soon became friends...in fact, best buddies. Bretta was a senior in high school and Ward would walk her to the school bus many mornings. Even when they moved down the road, he would come and get her and pray with her before school.

"He encouraged me all the time in my walk with the Lord and we encouraged each other." At one point, Bretta remembered telling a friend, 'I wouldn't mind going out with Ward.'

He did a 'Crash and Burn'

Ward was eventually engaged to another woman and six weeks before their wedding, it was called off. He described it as a 'Crushing...Crash and Burn'!

Bretta remembered the excruciating pain she saw him experience. "It was really bad...really, really bad. So, I just kind of helped him through that. He was hurt so deeply and struggled to get over the breakup. He needed somebody. Then, somewhere at the end of that year...I could sense our relationship changing."

When Bretta went with her family to Georgia for Christmas, Ward made a cassette tape singing to her and talking to her the whole time. She said, "So, we sort of both knew and it kind of scared us because we had both been through other relationships. It was just this feeling...this hesitancy."

At one point later in time, they were standing across from each other as the ministry was having prayer for a mission team being sent out. "Ward looked across the circle and our eyes met. He told me at that moment the Lord spoke to him and said, 'She's yours! Rejoice!' It scared him half to death," her laugh resounded.

Ward met with Bretta's Dad to ask if he could marry his daughter. Her Dad said, 'Let me see the ring.' "I showed him this ring and he said, 'Nope...too small!' Then he said, 'I'm just kidding!' He said, 'Yes'." Her Dad, ever the kidder, definitely had this young man shaking in his boots for a minute or two!

The Engagement

They talked many evenings as they sat on a swing under a big oak tree. Ward said, "That particular night, I had the ring in my hand, and she kept trying to hold my hand." The memory of that night brought a grin to his face, "I had her ring in my hand so, I kept clenching my fist."

"I didn't even realize I was trying to hold his hand. I wasn't consciously thinking, 'Why won't he let me pry his hand open?' It didn't even occur to me there was a ring."

"That's when I asked her to marry me."

Bretta's eyes began to sparkle. "He asked me to pray about being his wife. I said, 'I already have! YES!' We got married seven weeks later!"

So, you have a young lady who just turned 19 and a 23-year-old guy planning to be married. Doing the right thing, he took her to meet his parents for the first time. "On the way down there I asked her, 'How old are you anyway'?" Ward broke up at the memory and Bretta had a funny look on her face as she shook her head back and forth in mock disbelief.

According to Ward, "That wasn't the only funny occasion on that trip. We were sitting there in my Mom's church on a Sunday morning and they did birthday blessings. I thought, 'Oh no...I forgot to get Bretta a birthday card.' I knew it was coming up, but I just completely forgot. So, I slipped out of church and got a birthday card...or something. Been a lot like that ever since!" Bretta's smile broke into 'couch-rocking' laughter and so did ours as we tried to imagine the scene.

Explaining the almost four years difference in their age, his face took on a more serious look. "I valued her maturity and her sincerity for wanting to serve God. That's one thing that really impressed me."

Challenges from the beginning

Ward had just completed his missionary training and would be moving to serve in California. An admiring look left his eyes and locked on to Bretta. "So that made a whole change for your life...not just getting married..."

She finished his sentence for him. "...and moving thousands of miles...half way across the country from my Mama."

Ward added, "We always say that was our hardest year of marriage."

She had a look that told us she remembered it as if it was today. They shared a house with their ministry partners whom they loved but she added, "We just really didn't get a chance to just be the two of us."

"Yah...", Ward sighed. "I wouldn't recommend it!"

God gave them a beautiful house that had been converted from a barn and Ward described it as, "Looking out the window of the living room, with this huge wall of windows, and you could see Sacramento when the lights came on at night. The American River over there in the morning with the sunrise. It looked like someone just poured out a ladle of silver or mercury or something...silver ribbon. It was very beautiful, but...we had to go through another couples' bedroom to go to the bathroom."

"Which," she giggled, "was fun for them, too. You know what I mean. We didn't even have walls in our first bedroom upstairs...just the studs and sheets."

"That was a GREAT idea!", teased Ward.

Added was the fact Bretta was missing her Mom and Dad. She managed a little laugh as she said, "And you know you are just learning how to love somebody else and not be selfish. That's against your natural inclination. All those things made it a tough year."

How did they make it through their first year? Ward said, "Obviously the Lord got us through it with a lot of prayer."

She smiled, "Probably the hopefulness of the future...like this wasn't forever."

"Because," added Ward, "God was obviously doing things in our lives at the same time."

One year into their marriage, it came! The BIG change! They received a missionary assignment to Australia and would be moving there with Bretta's parents. They were expecting their first child <u>and</u> for the first time they would be living <u>alone</u> in their own home! Their dream assignment: living in Australia, working with her parents AND the bonus of not having to walk through someone else's bedroom to get to the bathroom!

Bretta said, "I think they were some of the best years of our lives!"

Drew them closer...

They had a daughter and a son while living in Australia and another son was born to them after they returned to the United States. Bretta said, "Like all parents, there have been both great joys and great struggles in raising children and teenagers, joys and struggles in being parents of adults and married adults and joys and struggles in being grandparents." The tenderness for her children was evident as she looked down and tears filled her eyes.

Referring to the effect parenting struggles had on their marriage, Bretta said, "I think it's made us closer." Ward agreed as she continued to wipe tears from her eyes. "No matter what is going on in our lives, it is so vital as Christians, that we press into God and His presence."

Ward said, "God is not surprised by anything. When we make mistakes or watch our children make mistakes, we are prone to ask: 'Jesus...why don't You get in there and do something about this'?" His voice cracked as he spoke quietly and deliberately. "It's easy to quote Romans 8:28, ('And we know that in all things God works for the good of those who love Him, who have been called according to His purpose.') when things are going good." Tears streamed down their faces as Bretta smiled and looked at her husband. Ward told us it is still just as true when things aren't going exactly like they thought it would. "God is still God and sovereign over our lives and our children's lives."

Tough times

Even through tough times, they never felt like giving up on their marriage! Ward struggled with tears and words as he said, "The tough times, I think, have confirmed what I saw in Bretta, and what the Lord showed me about her in the beginning." He couldn't continue as he reached over to grab not a tissue, but a paper towel to wipe his tears. She gave a slight laugh and smiled at this tender man of hers.

After a pause, Ward began by saying: "Having each other. For me, just knowing Bretta will be there no matter what. Just the encouragement she is in my life. I don't know where I'd be without her." Tears didn't seem to stop as he spoke lovingly about his wife.

She replied with tenderness, "I think it's amazing we can fall more and more in love with each other. When you first get married, you think...'Oh...I just love this person with everything I have!' But, the blessing of growing old and growing deeper in love with each other has just been phenomenal. I could never have imagined."

"I can't relate to the guys who complain about their wives." He wiped his eyes again as he finally was able to speak, "A blessing to me are my in-laws." By now, Ward was crying again and Bretta smiled in agreement through her tears. "I can't...," he struggled for words, "...I can't relate to the in-law jokes."

"I can't either!"

Ward admitted he often wondered why his father in law, Bill, didn't just kill him! At that, Bretta attempted to hold back a full-out guffaw.

She said, "We made so many dumb mistakes! They were always so gracious and loving and supported us even when we made stupid decisions. Sometimes they would give us the advice we needed to hear, even if we didn't want to hear it. More often than not, they just would say, 'Alright...you just live your life and you have to make your own decisions'."

Trying to follow that example, now that their own children are grown, they have learned to ask the Lord to keep their mouths shut more than open. At the same time they are also asking Him for wisdom when they NEED and ought to speak.

From frequent transplant to roots dug deep

Ward spent most of his life moving to new places every four to five years. From Florida to Venezuela to Pittsburgh in the middle of the winter! From Pittsburgh to South Africa. Boarding school in Tennessee. Graduation and on to Texas.

His parents wanted to see the world...and they did. "I have been to almost every country in South America. We've been to a lot of places you've never heard of. It's neat to remember those things and all the places we traveled...but, I never...past the age of five got to see my grandparents more than at the most, a month a year. I didn't grow up with my cousins. I didn't realize how valuable family was and how close you could be as family."

As he wistfully spoke about Bretta's family, the salty flow wouldn't stop. "So, you know just seeing Mamaw and Papaw (Bretta's grandparents)..." He struggled to find the words to express his heart. "They never worried about going to a nursing home because they knew the family would take care of them. That really means a lot to me," he said through his tears.

His own family was spread all over the map, meaning they might have a family reunion once every 15 years. With Bretta's family, it's family reunion season every summer. "We have three family reunions a year. Seeing the value for family here is a neat experience for me. Getting to know Bobbie's parents was very meaningful to me and formative in a lot of ways." He saw so many things in Bretta's grandparents, especially PaPaw, that he wanted to emulate. He also watched his in-laws take loving care of their parents.

Bretta added, "The way they care for each other. It's such a testimony!"

"And that's not a slight to my parents. It's just very different. My Mom comes from a big family." Their family could be in the center of Rome and in the middle of a plate of pasta when Ward would ask: 'When are we going to get to Grand-mommy's?' His voice wavered, and tears returned. "I loved that place...at Grandmommys! My uncles are just a few years older than me, so they were kind of like big brothers and heroes to me." It was easy to hear the yearning in Ward's heart.

He craved and longed for the nearness of his family but didn't resent them as he said, "That's just the way it was. Everybody had dreams and had to pursue them."

Bretta could see her husband was much like his Granddaddy in that he was always helping others. "Because there were times when we'd be expecting him home, but he stopped to help somebody on the side of the road. He would just go and help...even though it has driven me crazy sometimes." She looked over and spoke to Ward, "I admire that in you...that willingness to just always be there and serve others. That's something I really appreciate in you. I think you got that from Granddaddy."

How they see each other

Without hesitation, Ward said, "I especially love Bretta's love for our family. Not just our kids but for all the family," he made a wide circle with his arms. "I love her enthusiastic devotion. I was going through a rough time. I was saying: 'What if no one stands with me in this issue?' She said, 'I will'!" His voice cracked, and his head went down in heartfelt humility, "And she has."

She spoke confidently to husband, "I have always loved your sense of humor. Our kids love your sense of humor even though they make fun of both of us," she snickered and covered her eyes. "That's what kids do...they make fun of their parents. The goofy things we do and say and laugh about...but your sense of humor was one of the first things that drew me to you besides your beautiful, dazzling, handsome eyes!"

"It wasn't my hair?" he said as he rubbed his shiny, bald head.

She bantered, "It's a good thing it wasn't!"

In a more serious tone, she said, "But the strength I've seen in you...even when you didn't feel like you were strong. Your devotion to me. You always make me feel like I'm the most important person in your life." Their smiles covered their faces. "I know it's a given but not in every marriage. Even things like when we joined the gym...you were like: 'No, let's do it together!' The fact you want to do things with me all the time and we want to spend time together. It's a blessing. The way you father our children, even though you feel like you've made a lot of mistakes. They love you and they know you love them."

Ward gave a teasing smile, "I don't know if you've noticed, but Bretta's pretty intent on having a good time no matter where she is or what she's doing. She enjoys being with the people she's with. That's a lot of fun watching her."

"Even though he has to rein me in sometimes. He would say things like, 'You need to settle down just a little. Did you have too much coffee today, Bretta'?"

"Watching Bretta and her Mom is a lot of fun because they are best friends. She tells me I'm her best friend..." he scrunches up his face and in a quiet, almost whisper says, "but really her Mom is."

"My best girlfriend", she wiped away laugh tears.

What you need to know

Bretta began, "Hold tight to Jesus...always. You're going to have times when you may wane in your affections. Or things are just rough or you're exhausted because you're a new Mom. Jesus never fails, so be holding tight to Him!"

Ward admitted he had no clue how exhausting being a Mom actually was until he saw his own daughter become a Mom. He knew he didn't do a good job in that department so his advice to other Dads was to, 'pay attention…'. "You're young and just married...and it's so easy to wanna. 'I wanna go play basketball with the guys or I wanna go there…' Realize the treasure you have in your wife and build on that relationship. Encourage each other in Christ. Make that a priority early on."

Godly mentors

Ward said, "Find a Godly mature couple that you can go to and talk with…that can point you to Christ...that can point you to the promises of God...to the Word of God...how to live it out, walk it out. Get involved in a good church." They both felt belonging to a church family and praying together helped them from feeling like they were living life on an island.

Bretta said, "We're still learning, working, processing everything He's been showing us about prayer lately. I think praying together on a regular consistent basis is so crucial. Praying when you're mad just doesn't work very well," she laughed.

Not over

Ward and Bretta are not hoping and praying for every difficult thing in their lives to disappear from their story. That's because they know and trust they will move closer to each other and to Jesus through those hard times.

Like lingering over a good cup of coffee, their life is filled up to the brim and flowing over with sweet moments they are living together as their love story continues to be written.

Copyright © Tyler Ogburn Photography

Wilton & Joyce – Rocky Start to Solid Ground

MARRIED 46 YEARS

"…He set my feet on a rock and gave me a firm place to stand." Psalms 40:2b

This 'not so loving' love story began in 1972 at the cab stand at the entrance to Chanute Air Force Base in Illinois. Wilton was a part time cabbie and would drive Joyce from the gate to her job inside the base almost every week-end. "He used to ask me when I was going to take him out for a beer." Her final answer? 'Oh…hang it up! Forget that'!

"The fare was supposed to be seventy-five cents but," Wilton laughed, "I let her off for fifty cents!" His generous discount, however, didn't impress her one bit!

Eventually, one of Joyce's friends started working at the base, so she and Joyce would take a cab out to the base together. When they got to the cab stand, the two of them and Wilton started talking together and eventually with her friend as a buffer, they could at least have a civil conversation.

Their first date had a little bit of a rough start. "When he asked me for a date, I said (and I wasn't lying), 'I'm having company coming this Sunday and I really need to check the house and get it all cleaned up before they come, so, I can't go with you'." He was not easily dissuaded so he called Joyce's friend, Wanda.

Joyce tattled on him. "He whined to her!"

"I did not! Wanda told me, 'If you're not man enough to call her again, I'm not dealing with you'!"

He mustered the courage and called her about a week later. Joyce said, "You know those deals when you want to say one thing and something else comes out of your mouth? Well, he asked me if I would go out on Saturday. I'm sitting there thinking, 'I don't want to go out', but I said, 'Yah...I'll go out'!" We laughed as she looked down like she was giving the phone a crazy 'how did that happen' look.

It had been a long time since Joyce went on a date, so she suggested he come over to talk about where to go on their date that weekend. That's when Wilton met Joyce's two-year-old son, Gene...over a cup of coffee. Yes - that's right! Over a cup of coffee. Wilton was drinking a cup of coffee and little Gene was sitting in his highchair staring at him. When Wilton asked what he wanted, Joyce said, "He would like a sip of your coffee... he likes coffee...black coffee.' He put the cup on the tray of the highchair. Gene picked it up and drank the whole thing. Even though Wilton was shocked, that was the beginning of a relationship that would continue with Wilton's eventual adoption of that coffee drinking little toddler.

They dated a few times and were just getting to know each other when Wilton was being sent on a five-week temporary duty assignment to Texas. Before he left, he asked if she would like to marry probably the poorest guy in the world. She said, 'Yes'.

While in Texas, he wrote her a letter and asked if they could get married in Las Vegas. She agreed with one condition and flew out to tie the knot. When the assignment was complete, he came back to Texas and fulfilled Joyce's one condition for marrying in Vegas - renewing their vows at the Base Chapel with their children and her parents as witnesses.

Instant Family

They started marriage with instant family. Wilton had three girls and Joyce had three boys. They were just getting settled in their new assignment in Texas, when he got orders for Germany. Lots of details had to be completed before that overseas move, including the adoption papers for little Gene and securing military housing in Germany. Within about two weeks, Joyce and four of their children were on their way to meet Wilton in Germany. After graduation, their oldest daughter, Sue, also joined them.

These newlyweds had a full house and their lives were filled with lots of noise and laughter. By now, they had added their son, Jimmy to the family. There was always some kind of excitement and if there wasn't any, the kids would create some. In the winter, they enjoyed sliding down the hill on cardboard into an abandoned coal pit. Gene got a bicycle for his birthday and decided to use his bicycle instead of cardboard and ran right into the side of a German owned Volkswagen. What could have turned into an international incident was nothing more than a smile and a nod from the owner of the vehicle who was more worried about the little boy than his car. Never a dull minute for this couple!

Military life...

Joyce loved to travel and enjoyed the new adventures and shopping their life offered. However, one of the most difficult years took place when Wilton went on an unaccompanied tour to Turkey and she and the children went to Florida to be near her parents. If you can imagine this: no internet, no calling cards or cell phones. Wilton was authorized one call a month on MARS (amateur radio operators) and occasionally, Joyce could talk to him if she was able to get a MARS call to Turkey by routing it through Germany. (That was definitely going 'around the block' in order to talk to each other...while the radio operator was listening in!)

As a typical military wife, Joyce did what she needed to do, which often meant she needed to be Mom and Dad to the children, as well as decision maker, discipline giver and budget juggler in his absence. When he came back home, they had to learn how to live together again as a husband and wife and as a family. Their common bond and focus of most of their activities centered around their family. Even though all of their children did not live with them full time, they made family a priority and worked to keep those connections with each of their children.

Dragging baggage...

Looking back over their lives, Wilton was brought up in church but at about 17 years old, quit attending. He graduated from high school and went into the military where he intentionally stayed away from church. God, with His sense of humor, had him assigned to a job at the base chapel.

"I always knew God was there for me if I needed Him", but it seemed Wilton never needed really Him. As a young man, his church shopping seemed less like a serious attempt to find a church and more often like a dating service where he spotted women who might be potential partners!

Everything in life went smoothly for a while and then he entered a marriage that lasted three and a half years. He followed it up with a second marriage lasting ten years. Joyce was wife number three, but he confessed he was still not at the point where he would admit he needed Jesus in his life.

Joyce's first marriage lasted nine years. She said, "By that time, I was still married but pregnant with another man's child. My first marriage ended in divorce and now I had a baby but never married the father of my child." Two years later, in 1973, she and Wilton got married.

There was no denying they were both dragging baggage along behind them. Nothing too heavy that God couldn't carry!

What changed?

God did the changing...and He changed Joyce first! "I loved the Lord. I took the kids to Sunday school and church. Wilton would stay at home or say he could go worship the Lord by fishing. My challenge in that situation was keeping my mouth shut. 'Want to go to church with me?' 'No!' 'Want to come with me?' 'No!' By the time we got to our new assignment to an Air Force base in Idaho, the Lord said to me, 'Quit nagging him. He's mine and I'll take care of him'. He did take care of Wilton and He blessed me when He did."

If there was any work to do at the chapel, Wilton was there. "If you had hot dogs or hamburgers to be cooked or work to be done...even carving a ham...those things I loved to do. Just sitting for that length of time to listen to somebody talk...I just couldn't do it."

Even though he occasionally came to Sunday services, Wilton admitted at that time, faith wasn't important in his life or in his marriage. That is until they were married about 19 years and he attended a men's retreat. When he got up Sunday morning of the retreat, everyone else was already in the chapel. He said to himself, 'I'm not going any place!' "My right foot hit the floor and it bounced right back into bed. I put it out there again and the same thing happened. I said, 'I'm NOT going anywhere! I still ain't going'!"

As much as he didn't want to go to services, "I got my body turned around and put both feet on the floor and finally got my pants and shirt on. It was about 150 yards up to the chapel. It was two steps forward and one step back, but I finally got up there!" He was having severe pain in his back and some of the men met him at the door of the building and anointed him with oil. All that battle to keep him from going to services couldn't keep him from Jesus. That was the day he decided to turn his life over to Christ.

Since that time, Wilton said, "I'll be honest, I think Joyce and I got to know each other a lot better because we were now doing the same things together. We went to church together, prayed together, read Scripture together."

Want to call it quits?

Wilton was shaking his head 'No'!

Next to him, Joyce was adamantly shaking her head, 'Yes'!

"We were married in 1973 and in 1979 we moved to Florida. It was just one of those things. I had been to a women's conference and when I got home, Wilton asked me to do something I really didn't want to do. I thought 'Why did I ever get into this marriage. Why did I do this? I don't want anyone telling me what to do!' I had no way to leave. No money. No car. It then came back to me from the women's conference I attended: 'You're not to leave your husband. You're not to leave your husband.' I said, 'Father, if I'm going to stay here, you're going to have to keep me here'! That's exactly what He did. It's as if He took my mind and completely turned it over and changed it completely. I never had that thought of leaving again. Never!"

What made this marriage different?

When Wilton was asked about marriage he said, "I'll be honest with you. I hated living alone. I hated frozen dinners. I hated little or no companionship. I dated a few other women before and didn't feel comfortable around them."

Joyce looked over at him and asked, "Why did you stay in this one?"

"Compatibility." They agreed they have different viewpoints on some issues but rather than argue about them, they have agreed to disagree. He added, "We, like a lot of marriages, have our little ups and downs and spats once in a while, but we're always able to reconcile our differences."

What did divorce teach you about marriage?

"I learned to look deeper," Joyce said. Looking at the surface things in her first marriage caused her to focus only on those things that were wrong her husband.

With sadness in his voice, he said, "Trust!" His first marriage lasted a little over 3 years when he was faced with a divorce he didn't want. About marriage number 2, he said, "I knew from the start that was a mistake... I thought there were better things in life, but I didn't know how to get there. At times, I felt like I was lost." He wanted to trust but found he didn't know how.

Joyce admitted she didn't feel like forgiving her ex-husband. "Sometimes it was like I had to speak it out (forgiveness), speak it out and finally it was there."

Wilton said, "It was hard, especially with my first marriage. It was awful hard. When the divorce papers came through, I sat down and cried. I was heartbroken." Even after all these years, it was obvious they were still painful memories.

If you are struggling

Wilton's advice if you are struggling: "Pray! Pray! Lots of prayer!"

Joyce said, "Seek God. Seek His advice. Christian counseling. Jesus is the only way to bring you back together. If it's going to happen, that is what is going to do it. Pray. Communicate. If you don't talk to each other, you will never know what the other person is thinking or what they truly desire."

This marriage is different

They could have stayed in the pit of the past, but as Wilton said, "Expectations are different in this marriage. We no longer talk about the past. We look forward into the future. In the years we've been married, we have learned a lot of things, not only about ourselves, but about marriage and how to trust one another."

"My Mom was a yeller," Joyce said. "She would yell out the back window for us kids. So, did I. I went to a Christian conference and a couple months later, I realized I was no longer hollering. My sister-in-law said to me, 'You're different'. You used to just do what you wanted to do.' I said, 'I respect my husband and I ask him if it is all right or if he minds if I go and do that. Generally speaking, he will say, 'No problem' but I still choose to ask him."

They have learned from past mistakes, but they don't dwell on them. They are working to build this marriage into a stronger partnership that will last a lifetime.

Joyce ended with these words: "I love and trust Wilton in absolutely everything! He covers me. He loves me. He honors me. He blesses me."

From rocky start to solid ground

The loving look between them (and yes…the teasing and joking) demonstrated that their lives and this marriage have been different! From a rocky start, they are now standing their marriage on the solid ground of Jesus!

Anonymous – We Felt Like Failures

"And we know that in all things God works for the good of those who love him, who have been called according to His purpose." Romans 8:28

Marriage is not lived in a vacuum

When they walked down the aisle it was just the two of them…giddy with love! It was as if no one else was in the room. Fast forward and soon there were diapers, long, sleepless nights of crying babies and then in the blink of an eye, their little ones had grown into young adults.

There's no doubt about it! This Mom and Dad <u>love</u> their kids! It also seemed, as with many parents, a good amount of their lives together centered around struggles in raising them. As she spoke of the many blessings and challenges, the tenderness and love for her children were evident as she looked down and tears filled her eyes.

They eventually observed their young adult children learning how to walk on their own. As with many other parents, sometimes they also watched them turned away from what had been taught and modeled for them. They chose their own way in life. Sometimes they turned away from the faith of their parents. She looked up with tears still glistening in her eyes, "That's hard."

Tempted to isolate

They acknowledged there were times they wanted to isolate themselves from other people because of their sense of failure as parents. He said, "That's foolish…but a very real temptation."

She couldn't speak for a minute before she continued, "But, we trust, and we know…we just believe God's promises… And we're still learning every day how to be parents to our adult kids."

She was driving recently when God put their youngest child on her heart. She felt it was like God was saying, 'You thank me for where your child is right now'. And that was what she did! We could almost sense that she felt some of the pressure lift that day as she made the choice to be thankful instead of turning to worry.

As parents, they knew they weren't the only ones going through this. However, he admitted, "I did catch myself regretting some of the thoughts I had about other people going through the same thing with their kids. Just a self-righteousness... It was easy to judge others, because we knew it <u>all</u>…<u>before</u> becoming parents!"

Sometimes the dreams and goals of parents for their children take a U-turn or head down a different road. During their most challenging periods as parents, they intentionally moved toward God and cried out for help. While going through those times, he said, "You feel a sense of 'What did I do wrong? What should I have done differently?' A lot of soul searching goes on." They admitted they were not perfect parents and have come to realize most parents, including themselves, do everything they know to do…the best way they know how to do it.

Greatest lesson learned

We believe the greatest lesson they have learned together about being parents is that they don't identify their kids by the choices they have made. She spoke for both of them as she said, "We think of the wonderful, warm, joyful, caring, kind people they are and the joy and fun we have being with them. They are great adults!"

Praise when you're hurting

They may have questioned their parenting, but they never blamed each other! She fought tears and pushed past the breaking of her voice. "One of the things that stood out for me was the Lord saying, 'Just keep praising me…even when your heart's broken. You just have to praise Me and trust Me.' You do feel that hopelessness. Praise is so hard when you're hurting." A mother's love for her children overflowed as her stream of tears didn't slow.

God is bigger

They agreed if they had a 'parent do-over; there would be a lot of things they would change. However, since they only have one shot at it, they have come to understand and trust that God is bigger than the things they regret or the mistakes they have made. They believe that is one thing extremely important for all parents to remember!

Raising their children could have divided them. Instead, it drew them closer to each other. Even through their perceived failures, God was and still is bigger than any mistake they ever even thought of making!

Glenn & Margie – He Has Loved Me Ugly!

MARRIED 38 YEARS

"A cheerful heart is good medicine, but a crushed spirit dries up the bones."
Proverbs 17:22

Copyright © Princess Cruise Line

First time – same wife! (Glenn's quick-witted answer to how long they have been married.)

Consummate joker, he got Margie laughing even harder when he said, "I know how long we've married, but I just can't do the math!" (Don't let him fool you! This is coming from a former Air Force and commercial pilot and now college professor!)

Reminiscing

They linked arms and snuggled up closer to each other as they reminisced about growing up only 22 miles from each other but never meeting until they were in college. Margie was walking across campus with a friend and walked by Glenn's dorm. Her friend introduced them to each other and when this sweet, little Southern gal found out he was from King's Mountain, North Carolina, she said, "I fell in love immediately! I was so happy to find someone from home!"

Margie couldn't hold back her laughter, "He was home! That was my attraction. He was comfort."

"She was petite and cute and that's nice to start with but, I would also agree with that familiarity. When we were introduced, I was like: 'I already know some of your family'." That initial attraction got them interested enough to take a second look.

'Come back later...I'm off to fight a war!'

After dating a couple of years, they split up and went their separate ways for the next three years. Glenn's version of the split went something like this: "I was in Air Force ROTC in college and my dream and my goal was to be commissioned and fly airplanes. Margie didn't exactly look like any of the planes I had seen in the Air Force inventory. She was nice, and she was fun...but just couldn't go as fast as an F111." The bottom line – she wasn't quite as interesting as those dreams and aspirations of his!

"I was in no way mature enough to be a husband and accept the responsibility of a husband...nor, was that my interest. I would have been a terrible husband as a college student or 20-something year-old. I was focused on my career—and that's why when I graduated, I said, 'Hey...I'm off to fight the war and fly airplanes'!"

Margie always remained friends with his parents and like a good match-making Mama, she made sure Margie's contact info got to Glenn. After he sent her a birthday card, they agreed they would meet when he came back home on a break. No big plans. Nothing spectacular, but after they were sitting and talking with her stepmother that night, Margie beamed, "He doesn't believe this, but I KNEW within two hours I was going to marry him."

She broke into giggles as that familiar gleam in Glenn's eyes teased, "I call it entrapment..."

The long-distance friendship continued but didn't satisfy either for long. They needed to be together. She traveled to see him for a week and that's when she knew it was meant to be. "Before I left, I told my stepmother, 'I'm going to Montgomery and I'm going to talk that man into marrying me!' That might be what he referred to as entrapment!"

When she got back home, her stepmother quizzed, 'Well, did you talk him into it?' Margie's answer? 'I'm close...I'm close.' Joy filled her face as she told us how much her stepmother 'adored' Glenn. "Every time I would go home...if there was ever anything in the local paper that had his name on it, she would have it plastered on my mirror."

Glenn chimed in, "Saint Glenn, of course!"

"So, when we got married, she was very happy until she realized he was taking her little girl across the 'pond' (to England)!"

Write me a note

Glenn, grinned, "When I left to go down to Montgomery, I said, 'Write me a note' and she did…every day." He called that time, BCP (before cell phones)! When they were together, their conversations were much like topics covered in most pre-marital counseling. "It was the fact we were interested enough in each other now that we wanted to find out these things, so we started asking questions." It seems back then, pastors didn't do premarital counseling, so they did their own.

They dated a year and a half…enough time to get to know each other's family and each other well. After a three-month engagement, they were ready. They had matured and had experienced a little bit of life, Glenn smiled, "…and now our soul was looking for that partner."

Healing from wounds

Margie said, "I had come out of a very possessive relationship, so I knew what I didn't want. While I was dating this other guy, I knew he was not my life partner. I prayed for three solid years for someone like Glenn. Someone who would be more interested in dinner parties than pot parties. I prayed for a Christian who could love me for who I am today, who would forgive my past transgressions, that would be a good Christian partner. Three years I prayed…never knowing it would be someone in my past."

Everything new

The wedding was followed very shortly by lots of 'new' in their lives. "When we went to England. I was a new bride…new to marriage, new to a new country, new to military life. It was very hard. Yes, it was very exciting…but it was very, very hard. When I got over there, I spent a lot of weepy moments Glenn did not know about. He's got a brand-new bride and she's crying all the time."

Glenn smiled tenderly as he kept his eyes on his wife. She struggled with finding anything in common with the other military wives. At that time, she described herself as 'a quiet, shy little girl who didn't know how to carry on a conversation'. After a New Year's Eve party, she cried, (actually Glenn said she was 'bawling'.) 'I don't know what I'm doing. I am completely out of my element!' "I was scared."

How does a young wife make it through all the 'new' in her life? "Loving Glenn. I was just loving Glenn so deeply and so purely."

"The other thing that helped me through was the Officers' Wives' Club. They asked me to be the Assistant Treasurer. I had a job. I had a purpose. I got to know the people. I got involved."

A unique kind of help came from her innovative husband who made flash cards for her. "I didn't know the military acronyms. I didn't know what TDY (temporary duty) meant. I didn't know what Squadron Coffee was. I didn't know the aircraft. He made little index cards and he would come home and quiz me on all of this stuff. He helped me through that time."

He added, "The challenge of being newlyweds…as you now have a new partner. Although you may have dated, and you think you know each other…now when you are thrust into being in the same household 24/7 you realize, 'Oh…I guess we haven't discussed <u>everything</u>.' There are still things you are learning and getting accustomed to."

They chose for Margie to be at home rather than working, so when bills came in, Glenn remembered thinking, "Huh?..I have to pay all the rent? You're not contributing? Wait a minute…the grocery bill is twice as high as it used to be. Oh yeh…that's right, but then, I do have somebody there to eat with at the dinner table. So that was a benefit." As he looked over at his wife, a teasing smile soon crept across his face…and brought her to giggles.

Not just one of the guys

Glenn remembered a time he learned just a little bit more about taking his wife's needs into account. "I walked into the kitchen and said, "Hey…I'm going over to the pub for a while."

They laughed out loud as she tattled, "He never invited me to go with him!"

"Then, she said something about, 'Am I invited'?" At this point, Glenn hit himself on the forehead with the palm of his hand. Evidently, when he lived with a bunch of guys, if he made that statement about heading over to the pub, they would just say, 'Well, I'm coming, too.' That's when it hit him that he now had a partner and he had to take her needs into account, too. She wasn't just one of the guys who would invite themselves along!

Benefit of separation

Glenn saw another benefit in their lives. "We got married and three days later, we were back overseas where I had been stationed, so we got started the first two and a half years of our marriage overseas. We were away from our families and away from anybody that could muck into our marriage and mess it up. Everything that we did was our own responsibility, whether it turned out well or whether it turned out to be a flop. It was kind of up to us to sort it out, make the friends, use our resources…but you didn't have all these somebodies stirring the pot and trying to influence it because that's the way they thought we ought to be acting."

There also wasn't instant access to Mom and Dad to solve their problems. "So, we did a lot of growing. We learned to talk. We learned to communicate. We took walks. We integrated ourselves into the community. I always feel that living overseas for our first few years of marriage is what really solidified our relationship."

Margie interjected, "…and we didn't have TV either."

NO TV?? What did they do at night? Glenn said, "You came home from work and ate dinner…and we sat around and made placemats. We made Christmas ornaments together. I recorded music on our stereo. We sat by the fireplace and we talked, and we communicated. We could actually do that because we didn't have so many of the distractions and the interruptions that we sometimes allow into our lives today."

Even today, Margie said, "We make a habit after dinner to sit at the table for 45 minutes and have a conversation. Because we didn't start out with TV, we just don't watch it. We spend our time together."

Road not so smooth

She shared about a period, when things in their marriage were not very smooth. "Glenn was not in the happiest of work situations. I had started to work full time, which I had not done before. We had agreed in the beginning of our marriage that I would not work for the first two to three years...to give ourselves that adjustment time. After that, I always worked part time. When I went to work full time, we both had the same expectations...that I would do the cooking, the cleaning, buying the groceries, paying the bills and working full time. It was hard to keep up with all of that."

They discussed her work situation and prayed about a solution. Her schedule was reduced to three days a week, however, on weekends, Glenn was still out flying and building time as a flight instructor, so he was still doing less at home. She admitted thinking, 'You're out there having fun and I am cleaning house and doing da-da-da-da', she counted on her fingers. Solution: communication. "We came up with a better division of labor so that he pitched in and helped out." At the time they were going through it, there was a strain, but they both agreed the challenges they faced were few and minor compared to many other marriages.

No book big enough!

When asked about the blessings in their marriage, Glenn's exuberant answer was, "You don't have time enough to listen! You can't write a big enough book for that!"

Her eyes glistened, "We live in such peace and contentment and love and happiness and total support of one another. It's just unreal and the things God has allowed us to do and see together. I really believe the reason we've been able to travel as much as we have is that God knows how much we enjoy seeing His world and how much we appreciate its magnificence and beauty. We don't enjoy museums. We enjoy God's nature.

He's my best friend. I'd rather do anything with him than any of my girlfriends." She interjected with a big smile, "He's not high maintenance...girlfriends are!"

Once when out traveling, a couple asked them, 'So you've been married this many years. What's the key?' Glenn said, "I had to think for a moment. Then I said, 'There are three things that are a common thread in our relationship. I call it the three Cs. It's Christ, it's communication and it's companionship. It's a good tripod to build upon because you have got to have your focus right."

He explained further, "#1 – Christ is the center. We try to live from a Biblical perspective, saying that Christ is the center of our marriage and of our lives. That also means that you are focused on one thing. If you are both focused on the same thing, you are moving in the same direction and you're usually not fighting against each other in competition because you are moving towards that one particular goal.

#2 – Communication has always existed. Sometimes people say, 'You can almost complete each other's sentences'. That's how you know...because you communicate. That's how I know what's going on in her life and the same with me. Don't try calling us during dinner because we won't answer. That's our time together.

#3 – Companionship. She is my dance partner through life. We do share ballroom dancing as one of the things we love. When we get in frame (the shape formed by the shoulders, arms and hands in dancing), we can become so attuned to each other that when we dance, she knows exactly what the next move is because I telegraph that to her so subtly.

She's my best friend and everything we do...it's just fun to do it together. A prime example is this past summer when we went to the Italian Culinary School." He smiled literally from ear to ear as he said, "Wow...what fun! How many guys do you think would have that much fun with their wife in the kitchen cooking?"

Her reaction: "Best vacation ever!"

A fourth C

As she thought a moment, "I could add a fourth to the three Cs. Compromise." They were going to place some curbing around their landscaping. She wanted a nice bright white and he wanted something that blended in with the mulch. He looked at me and said, 'Margie, I really let you have your way in just about everything. I'd like to have my way in this one'."

She said, "I looked at him and it only took me a fraction of a second to respond. I said, 'You are absolutely right...but can I be present?'" Laughter rang out!

"I wanted a lemon tree. He very calmly said to me, 'Margie, I'm the one that mows the grass. I'm the one who's going to have to pick up the dead lemons and all the garbage around it'."

Glenn teased, "We don't have a lemon tree!"

She laughed as she uttered one word: "Compromise."

Pick our battles

They try to remember to choose their battles. They have both learned to ask, 'Is this important enough for us to get into an argument? Is it important enough for us to be unhappy?' Most of the time they feel the answer is 'No...it's not that important'. They agreed some things were not worth fussing or fighting about.

"I don't like fighting with Glenn. Sometimes, he might hurt my feelings, but then he also knows to just leave me alone. I have to pout for a couple of hours."

Glenn whispered, "Oh yah!"

"Once I've pouted a couple of hours, I come back to him and then we will talk it out." To that, Glenn shook his head up and down while she snickered. "We never, ever go to bed angry and we don't let it go past a couple of hours. I can't stand it. Why spend days and days being angry when you can talk it out and move on being happy and loving one another and loving life?"

It seems their biggest argument of their marriage might be how high to hang pictures on the wall! "I finally got him trained. It took about ten years!" She now laughed until in unrecoverable hysteria.

He responded with a fake stony-faced look. When she regained her composure she continued, "I said, 'Glenn, pictures are supposed to be eye level. He looked at me dead serious, 'But, Margie...they ARE eye level. They're MY eye level!"

Glenn lobbed back a little bit of sarcastic humor, "So what I really started doing instead of compromise, I just started buying short houses!" Actually, he thought hanging the pictures so low made him feel as if they were in a house built for Munchkins. And with that, he did his best Munchkin impersonation which was greeted by Margie's enthusiastic laugh!

Lasting appreciation

Margie's tender comment came quickly. "I can trust Glenn. I can depend on him. He is a Godly man. I know that in his decision making he prays about it. I can just trust him in every aspect of our relationship in our lives."

It was a painful time to be so far away when her father was in a nursing home in North Carolina. "That just killed me. That was tough, but Glenn was very supportive during that time. No matter what I am going through, I always have my faith and I have the Lord Jesus. Then I have a husband who is going to stand behind me. Even through sickness and illness and pain, those are the things that bring me peace. My heart breaks for the people who don't have that."

Support might be the key word for Glenn's appreciation. "She takes such care of me in backing me up in everything that we do. She supports me in the things that I do, so that it makes it possible for me to go to work, to teach these college students...and I can do that so enthusiastically because she is my background support."

"She has so much wisdom. She has so much wonderful counsel that she gives to young women...young college students and these young men. People seek her out. It just makes my heart explode with joy when I see her and listen to her talking to some of these people and giving them counsel or direction or guidance. That's a jewel that is priceless."

Her smile didn't exactly expand past her sweet face, but it came very close as she listened to Glenn's comments. "To have that in a partner, in a woman that has that kind of solid foundation, Scriptural foundation, a Godly foundation and now is passing that on because people will listen to her. They love her, they care for her, they listen to her. It's going to make a difference in someone's life. How wonderful to think that she's mine!" Margie grinned in humble response.

A family?

After working with young couples, Glenn shared his insight into when he felt they might consider starting a family. "I think that it's critical that you grow together as a couple. As newlyweds...there's still a lot of growing together and learning (about) each other. When you introduce the responsibility of a family soon after you become married...I think you are robbing yourself of that opportunity to grow and bond together...as a couple." They don't claim to be experts but offered what they saw in that discussion held early in their own marriage. Glenn said, "We think it's important to wait at least three years before we start a family and that gives us the opportunity to grow and bond together. As time went on, of course, we mutually chose to kick that can down the road a little further and a little further. Then, mutually chose, maybe children were not part of our plan. That has worked out very, very well but only because we discussed it and agreed upon it."

Margie was excited to tell us how they have been blessed to work with children. "I worked with Girl Scouts in Idaho. We worked with church youth in Idaho and Colorado. And now, we have these wonderful college kids we work with who totally have our hearts." (They have recently moved into working with a group of young married couples in their church.) "So, we don't feel like we missed anything. We feel like we have an overabundance of blessings through these kids." In a recent visit with them, they talked about an upcoming trip to New York City where they would visit three of their adult 'children'! They could hardly contain their excitement!

If they wrote a book for you...

In chapter one titled, 'Promises'...Glenn would say, "I've only made two promises. #1 – My oath of office when I joined the military and #2 – my marriage vows standing before God and another human being who would be my partner and witness. It is a promise I had to keep until the end. You don't break those kinds of promises!"

Margie's chapter would start with: "Do not expect your husband to read your mind. They can't read your mind, so if you think it...you'd better speak it. I found that even after all these years of marriage, Glenn knows me so well, but he still can't read my mind. If I ask him...he is more than happy to accommodate that need."

Glenn said, "My responsibility is head of the household. It says that in the Bible. It specifies what my role is and that I am to take charge of the household. You've got to do that in a Godly fashion. So that's what I always seek." In making decisions, they first do their research and explore all options together. That is when they sit down and talk with each other. "Then she'll say, 'The final decision is up to you'. I will make the final decision...but the important thing is that I will weigh in what her thoughts, ideas, desires are."

Confidently he added, "Someone has to be in charge. It's true in the military structure. It's true on an airline flight deck. You have to have a captain or a commander but like a good commander, you take all the information that you can get to make the best possible choice."

Happiest time in my life

Margie claimed, "I'm the happiest I have ever been in my entire life. I love being home and supporting Glenn and supporting him with whatever he's doing with the college kids and what we're doing together. I have never felt that I had to have a career to be fulfilled." She spoke from her heart as she said, "I think it's the peace and contentment that comes from the Lord being #1 and the peace and contentment in our lives as a married couple. I really do believe I only have peace through my faith."

As she spoke, that 'Glenn' grin had not left his face. "I LOVE coming home to her. We have moved all over the world many times over the last 38 years…but where ever we are, where ever we are living…that's home. It's the peace we have that is the blessing that's so fun to come home to."

He has loved me 'ugly'!

Their quick wit surfaced when she told us Glenn has loved her 'ugly'! She pointed to her eyes and said, "These are laugh wrinkles." Pointed to her mouth and said, "These are kiss wrinkles."

Glenn's response was, "And you're going to get a whole lot uglier!"

Their laughter bounced around the walls of their home! And…that, ladies and gentlemen, is Glenn and Margie!

John & Nancy – He Couldn't so She Did She Can't so He Does

MARRIED 41 YEARS

"Consider it pure joy, my brothers and sisters, whenever you face trials of many kinds, because you know that the testing of your faith produces perseverance. Let perseverance finish its work so that you may be mature and complete, not lacking anything." James 1:2-4

When they stood beside each other and repeated their wedding vows, they had no idea what the next 40 plus years would bring. Would they have tied the knot if they had known there would be an empty bank account, cancer, panic attacks and depression, lawsuits, criminal charges, house arrest and probation?

Absolutely…because, it was love at first sight! Wellll…at least for 50% of this couple!

I'm going to marry him!

It all began at a going away party...for her! She was moving out of town and that's when her girlfriends decided she needed a party. So, a going away party it was. You know how that goes! Lots of single guys came because there were lots of single girls coming!

"I was sitting clear across the room and when John walked in, my heart just stopped." And at that, John had a huge smile but turned his head away in embarrassment. "So, I went to my friend and said, 'Introduce me to that guy'."

'Ok'.

'No, NOW!'

'What's the hurry?'

'Cuz I'm going to marry him!' (Now you know who the 50% of the couple was that felt 'love at first sight'!)

John's funny side surfaced when he responded with: "I went to the wrong party!" That got them both laughing as they looked at each other.

John's version

There was no guessing from John's facial expression that his response to the party invitation from his friend Tom was less than excited. Not dissuaded by John's lack of enthusiasm, Tom threw out some bait - 'It's going to be a lot of single girls and nurses and stuff!'

He admitted it wasn't the enticement of having single girls at the party, but he went because he had nothing else to do. In a room full of people, he only knew Tom. That's when he met Nancy. No fireworks or flashing lights. Just a couple of dances together.

"You actually had eyes on somebody else, didn't you, John?"

"About three others." They both burst out in laughter as John continued, "I was just wandering around talking to people and these girls would give me phone numbers (which I had to eventually throw away). Then, Nancy came up and that was it. I didn't think much about it at the time."

This might be the stereotypical picture of the oblivious man!

He liked the poodles...so he stayed!

After they started dating, they were driving together one day, and Nan thought, 'I wish he'd ask me to marry him.' "And since he didn't", she chuckled, "I think I said, 'When are you going to marry me'?"

Ever the tease, John jabbed, "We were driving on the freeway and the doors were locked and I couldn't get out!"

John and his first wife had been separated for some time, but he kept putting off filing the divorce paperwork. He would soon add that to the top of his 'to do' list because, in the middle of the freeway, they decided to get married when his divorce was final.

"He moved in with me and two poodles. He liked the poodles, so he stayed. I was in love with him long before he was in love with me."

The wedding

He called his Mom with the news they were going to Las Vegas to get married. "Even though she sounded excited, she actually thought we were going to go to Vegas to gamble. She didn't hear the married part. She just heard Vegas! Nobody in my family knew about our wedding and so no one showed up.

When we got back, that's when my family asked, 'How was Vegas?' 'What do you mean how was Vegas? I told you we went there to get married.' Everyone looked at my Mom like…what?" That's when John put on the 'they thought Mom was crazy' look on his face. The newlyweds probably didn't think it was quite that funny on their wedding day, but now they both roared hysterically over the 'Mom mix-up'.

Baby? Sooner than later!

'If you want kids, you'd better get pregnant. I give you a year'. That was the comment made by Nancy's doctor when he told her she had cervical cancer. She had surgery to remove that area of the cervix, but along with surgery came the warning that the hormones produced in pregnancy could make the cancer worse. Not only did she make it past the year deadline, but they had their first son, JR, 18 months after her surgery. Three years later they were blessed with their second child, Christopher, and the cancer never returned!

Lean times

Pregnant with their first child, John lost his job and they didn't have money for rent. "I remember the first time I walked into a welfare office asking for assistance. I was crying and the lady helping me started crying." John had to give up his pride, as welfare helped with the hospital bill and food for one month. They could feed their new baby with formula given by their pediatrician. During those lean times, many of the essentials, including clothes, a crib and diapers were donated by people from their new church.

The arrival of their second child, Christopher, found John in a new job with the Forest Service. New job – new challenges! They often needed to juggle their work schedules and find childcare for the times John was working up in the mountains and Nancy was working night shift as a nurse in the local hospital. An older friend, Mary, 'adopted' their two little boys as if they were her own and would stay with them at night.

God's provision

Tears welled up in her eyes as Nancy said, "We were very blessed!" Looking back, they recounted many times God provided for them. "It was the middle of the summer…100 degrees and our refrigerator died. Then the garage door split right down the middle. 'Where are we going to get the money for this!' That's when John came home with a check for his work uniforms." (That check always came in November—not in the middle of the summer!) "It was exactly what we needed plus ten dollars! Thank you, God!"

When they couldn't afford to build a home, God sent a builder who said he would accept whatever the California Veterans' loan would pay, if they did some of the work. They put in many hours of sweat equity, but when the roof was being put on their home, Nancy's Dad died. While they were back home for the funeral, the builder and his father finished the roof for them. "You don't think about the blessings until later," Nan said, as she and John continued to clasp hands and gaze at each other, seeming to soak in the memories of shared miracles.

I was her challenge...

While we were talking about challenges, John looked down slightly, "I guess I never really grew up. I was still thinking and acting like I was single. When I was working for the forest service, we always had these drinking/pizza parties. I would go, and she would stay home with the kids. I was her challenge for many, many years..."

Nancy snickered, and she looked over at John, "Should I tell them about the hole in the dining room wall?" Without pausing for his answer, she went on, "We were trying to move our waterbed out of the apartment, and it wasn't moving like we wanted it to. We were stuck in a little bedroom with this great big waterbed. We couldn't get out <u>and</u> couldn't get the bed out, so he just took the screwdriver and threw it at the wall. So, there was this hole with a screwdriver sticking out of it."

"I've always had a problem with my temper and..."

"But you never took it out on me!"

"No, I never took it out on her. Occasionally I would yell, but usually I tried to bottle it up. My way of dealing with it was to leave and go somewhere. 'I don't want to talk about it anymore. I'm sorry...I just want to go over here and let myself cool off and then everything will be fine.' Her idea was, 'Let's talk about it...NOW'! Now she knows to just let me go out to the garage and when I come back it's like nothing ever happened."

I lost him

It wasn't just finances or communication that challenged them. At one point later in their marriage when the boys were both gone from home, John became very ill. The psychiatrist thought John had just bottled up everything over his lifetime and never let it go.

Nancy said, "I lost him for about two years because he wouldn't leave the house. I had to give him Valium to take him to the doctor. I cried to God, 'Give him back! I want my husband back'!"

She walked alongside her husband on the road of depression and panic attacks over several years, but by that time, as with many who suffer long term mental conditions, most of their friends had disappeared. It was 'just the two of them' but the eventual result was an even tighter bond between them. Nancy barely got the next words out of her mouth as tears streamed down her face. "God got us through."

One big mistake

Nancy quietly began, "I made a big mistake. I went into real estate and I would say," she paused and looked over at John for verification, "I was obsessed with the money. It was so easy and so fun. They looked at each other laughing, "I guess the nicest way to say this is that I worked with someone who turned out to not be very honest. Let's just say, because of that, we went through some real tough times. Lost our house. Lost pretty much everything." She cried so hard she struggled to get out the words. She looked over at John through tears, "...You tell it, John..."

He stepped in to finish her thought, "We had big problems because....because it got us into a lot of legal problems that we are still dealing with."

They were both former California State prison guards, always on the enforcing side of the law. Now they were on the other side of the law. They were shaken as they experienced the legal system operating in a way they never expected. They struggled with fact they were considered guilty until they could prove their innocence. "As a plea bargain, we finally ended up accepting felony charges, so they would drop any potential charges against our son who also worked with the same company."

By then they were living in Nevada and traveled back to California, in order to separately serve their six months of house arrest. It was a long year of separation.

It seems like a story with no hope, but John smiled, "...it brought us back into line. In real estate, the money was easy, and we weren't thinking about God. It was just 'there's the money...let's go get it. Let's sell houses...let's do this...let's do that!' We got a little blind to it and then we got in over our heads."

John admitted that was the point at which their faith got stronger and to them, God was visibly present in their lives and in their circumstances. "It's like God was saying, 'You need Me!' He used many things to get our attention and He got our attention! Personally, I don't think I ever looked at it as God working till much later."

Seven-year battle

Through the seven-year court battle, they were often discouraged and worn down emotionally and financially. There were many times their future seemed uncertain.

However, Nancy said, "All the way through we have just been praising God and praising God and praising God. Yah...we got stuck with the charges.... We got what we got and did what we did. Now all we have to do is pay off..." Nancy laughed as she looked over at John, "a bunch of money we didn't take and don't have. But, it's OK... We believe it is not being taken from us. It is being taken from God. We've never starved. We've never slept under a bridge. God has always provided."

At times, like any of us would, Nancy and John went through feelings of hopelessness. They felt despair and abandonment. However, despite everything they faced, there is a thread of strength that can be seen in them as marriage partners and as individuals.

They never wasted time blaming each other. No moaning about the injustice or trying to justify their actions. This protracted legal battle has not divided them, only brought them closer.

Give up on your marriage?

"Give up? Not really...", John said as he looked down at their clasped hands, "I don't think I ever did. I don't think that thought ever crossed my mind. That would have been too easy an out..."

An emotional and emphatic "No..." came from Nancy as she dabbed at her eyes. "I think sometimes, because we were both married before...we were more willing to put a greater effort into this marriage and staying together. We didn't want to go through that again."

"Christopher was about five years old when John and I were going out for the evening. We were spatting about something. It wasn't a big thing. Christopher came in and said, 'You two are fighting.' I said, 'No - we're just discussing, Honey.' He said, 'Does that mean that you're going to get a divorce?' I looked at Christopher and said, 'Oh no, Honey...we can't afford a divorce'." She laughed almost hysterically as she shared Christopher's parting 'OK', "as he walked out of the room."

"That was all he needed to hear," John added.

She smiled, "If we wanted to get a divorce we would have still had to live together because we couldn't afford..."

John finished her sentence as they chuckled, "...we couldn't afford to live apart."

Lessons learned

When speaking about his first marriage, John began, "...it was 'me'... I don't think it worked out mainly because of me. I think I got married too soon and wasn't ready. I think I have learned to work harder at it instead of trying to take the easy way out. Maybe to listen and quit being such a jerk. In my first marriage...we weren't in church. We just did it on our own..." He knew they needed to put Christ at the head of their family. He said, "That was the hardest part because it was hard for me to let go and not be in charge of everything."

It was obvious Nancy's lessons from her first marriage came with much pain. She looked up, "...It was difficult for me to trust again. One thing I had to learn was to trust John." Even though there were tears, we could sense God had healed her heart because she felt no driving need to elaborate on her ex-husband's offenses against her.

Tears were welling up in her eyes and quiet sobs lifted her shoulders. "I was a little defensive at first with John because if you're burned once... Tears flowed freely as she paused. "I realized in a very, very short time that John would not hurt me. Never, never, never!" Their hands were clasped tightly together and stayed that way throughout their entire story.

They both believe honesty is extremely important in marriage. Nancy was totally honest with John from the very beginning when she told him she had a son she had given up for adoption. It was a blessing to both of them years later when that son, Jeff, searched for his birth mother and found her...and his new family. Because they had been honest with each other, there were no surprises. Nancy and John were able to rejoice together in having Jeff back in their lives.

Not all pain...and so much gain!

It would be so easy to concentrate on all they suffered through their forty plus years of marriage. Instead, they chose to see the blessings and all they gained, beyond the challenges.

"John was such a good Daddy! He learned to change diapers and rock Christopher when he had colic." Crying made it difficult for her to speak. "God gave me...someone...who takes care of me every day." She looked over at John as he kidded her with a goofy look, "He cooks, cleans and does laundry. He does it all'!"

"Nancy has a lot of health issues. The warranty wore out and I'm stuck with the car!" he teased. In a more serious tone, he said, "That doesn't bother me. I take her to all of her doctor appointments because I need to know what's wrong with her, so I know how to deal with it. If she isn't feeling well, I take food to her in bed. She's got so many medical problems, but we take them in stride. It's just another bump in the road. I started seeing her health declining and I was like, 'I guess I'll have to step up a little more myself to take up the slack where her health was hurting'." I know sometimes she wants to throw in the towel, but I tell her, 'It's going to be fine'. That's part of being 'hitched'. You take the good with the bad. Till death do us part," he got that teasing smile, "either that or until she kills me—one of the two!"

Bonus blessing

Another blessing came in the pint-sized package of their first grandchild, Tobin. For much of his life, their sweet little grandson lived close enough to spend many fun

days at Grandma and Grandpa's house. They didn't just sit on the couch and watch him play. They blessed him by getting down on the floor to play and let him spend plenty of time on their laps reading stories. The bond forged with their grandson, also bonded Nancy and John together with a united purpose.

Picture a wheelchair

They live this simple explanation of partnership: 'When he couldn't do it, she did. If she can't do it, he does.' John said, "That's the way it works!"

If she were sharing advice with a young couple contemplating marriage, Nancy would say, "Look at that person when they are seventy or eighty or even next week, if they should get into an accident. You need to look at them and envision them in a wheelchair and you pushing that wheelchair. If you can envision that and be willing to take care of all of their needs...then marry that person." That advice has come from a very real part of their own story.

Parting story

They both snickered as John shared this parting story. After their second son, Christopher, was born, John's Grandma started giving them all kinds of gifts. She showered them with boxes of crystal and all kinds precious family heirlooms she had never given them before. She said, 'I wanted to make sure you guys were going to stay married and I figured with two kids you would!'

They didn't disappoint Grandma! They not only stayed married, but they grew in their love for each other and in faith in God! Even through the most challenging times, when one couldn't do it...the other one did!

Norman & Nancy – Loss Created a Strong Bond

MARRIED 34 YEARS

"Praise be to the God and Father of our Lord Jesus Christ, the Father of compassion and the God of all comfort, who comforts us in all our troubles, so that we can comfort those in any trouble with the comfort we ourselves receive from God."
2 Corinthians 1:3-4

Broke all the relationship rules…

Out of Norman's mouth came, "We did everything wrong. We broke all the rules."

They definitely broke the TIME rule! Together they spent five weeks in San Antonio, two dates about a month later, and six months of correspondence. Nancy then flew overseas to visit him for eight days before deciding to get married! Whew!

"We didn't have quantity time," Nancy admitted, "but we did have quality time that included long walks and even longer talks."

Cautious beginnings

He was in the Army Medical Department and she was a graduate nurse attending training to become an officer. Of course, when the nurses came to town, all the guys in the Medical Service Corp wanted to meet them. Nancy had been hanging out with Pete, and as they headed to a dance, Norman just 'happened' to be in Pete's car. She described, "Just group dancing. That was it. I had already been burnt a couple of other evenings with Army guys, so I was going to go out and just have fun. The next day, Norman came knocking on my door, and asked if I wanted to go out."

Trying to keep a safe distance, Nancy told him rather nonchalantly, 'It's Pete's birthday, so we were already planning on going out, but you could join us if you want to.' The cautious arm's length invitation evidently didn't deter him. He joined them and they spent most of that evening talking together. By the end of the night, Norman and Nancy were a couple.

What made him come back the next day? "I think her energy and smile. I think there was a spirit with her that was just attractive."

Distance didn't stop them

At the end of the five weeks, Nancy was off to her new assignment in Virginia, and Norman was soon heading to his assignment in Germany. Maybe you're wondering how this love story was going to continue with so much distance between them…

"Of course, I (with a huge emphasis on that word 'I') was ready, but Norman wasn't ready for any kind of commitment. Obviously, without a ring on…I was going to be in Virginia, and he was going to Germany. We agreed to be friends and were going to write to each other. We also agreed to see other people. After dating an Army lawyer, I realized, 'I think Norman's the one for me'."

Norman smiled innocently, "I was clueless!"

She had more words to use than he did, so she wrote him an eight-page letter, baring her whole heart. She went to visit him in Germany, and at the end of that short visit, it was as if they were never separated. They both chuckled as Nancy said, "But…Norman was still scared!"

"I just wasn't sure that out of 100 million women in the world that this was THE one. So, I thought about it, and prayed about it all week. I knew Nancy wanted to get married, and yet, I wasn't sure. I finally decided that if I didn't ask Nancy to marry me at that time, we would probably go on with our separate lives. I knew eventually, I would have found another girl, and maybe fallen in love, but it would be different because Nancy was different than anyone else. Everybody had their special attributes, and I said, 'I want what is different about this girl!' So, I decided to jump in out of blind faith". The corner of their eyes wrinkled as they laughed at his comment.

Norman struggled with finding the perfect time to ask her – so he didn't! That is until Nancy was packing to go to the airport. That's when he blurted out, 'Stop packing! Stop packing! I need to talk to you! Nancy, I know that I said I'm not sure if I'm ready to get married, and now I know I'll never be ready to get married'." They both laughed hysterically as Norman said, "She panicked!"

"I thought he was breaking up with me!"

Their laughter roared as Norman said, "She wouldn't let me talk! I kept saying, 'Wait!!!! Wait!!!! Wait!!! I know I will never be READY, so I just have to decide without being ready. Will you marry me'?"

"I was in shock! Of course, I said, 'Yes'! 'But, you're asking me now--ONE hour before I'm going across the Atlantic??? We had to decide..."

Norman laughed because this time the tables were turned. "Now SHE had to decide!"

"In the Army, I couldn't bring Nancy to join me in Germany unless we were married. If we were going to be 3000 miles apart, there wasn't any point in having a lengthy engagement because we wouldn't be together to develop that relationship. So, it was either thumbs up or thumbs down...no in between. I said, 'Let's get married as soon as you can plan it'."

Nancy recalled, "My life was in upheaval. I hadn't passed my nursing boards, so I was getting out of the military. I was thinking about going into the Peace Corps. I really didn't know what I was going to do." Then came the proposal! When it came down to it, even in the chaos, they both knew they wanted to start their lives together. So, they sat down to plan a wedding date.

So much for normal, unsure, hesitant Norman! She said, 'yes' on Memorial Day and they got married in October!

When did you know?

"I don't know that there was any one minute I knew I loved her. It was really sort of a conscious decision to move forward or not. I had to decide that I loved her or decide that she was a nice person I enjoyed spending time with but would move on to someone else. There was emotion, but it really wasn't an emotional decision. It was 'yes' or 'no'." He playfully put his finger to the side of his head like a gun. By now, he was laughing hysterically as he told us he 'pulled the trigger' and stepped into marriage!

When Nancy described how she knew, she said, "My heart would go pitter patter when I got to talk to him." They both smiled at each other, "I was in love...still am today."

We all laughed as her husband innocently smiled, "I guess I thought I would figure it out later."

Needed 'Husband 101' course

They were living in Germany, far away from family and their support. There was no one to help guide them. "I was this new husband, and I was like, 'OK...good bye. I'm going off to work. I'll see you when I come back.' It never even occurred to me that I should be concerned what happened to Nancy during the day if she wasn't working and was stuck in a foreign country. She couldn't even speak the language." They both smiled as he said, "I had no idea what I was doing as a husband!"

When life changed

They cruised through more years of military service but life as they knew it changed when Norman left the military and went to grad school. Nancy had been a stay at home Mom to three children for the past five years, and all of a sudden, had to go back to work full time. That change challenged both of them. After grad school, it took two years for Norman to find a permanent position. In the meantime, Nancy had received her nursing license and was working as a registered nurse for a home health company. When new management came in, she lost her job. Now there were two unemployed people in their home. They remembered how they had to work together to survive that drastic change in their lives.

He told us he didn't know if he ever felt like their marriage was at risk but there were definitely his own challenges dealing with finances, being unemployed and not feeling useful. During that time, they held onto each other, and believed times like those made their relationship stronger.

Feel like giving up?

Nancy quickly answered, "Oh yah!"

"She was hoping I would figure this marriage thing out. I still didn't."

Yes, the dreaded and often expected 'seven-year itch' made an appearance. Norman said, "We were having some issues. I think it was the first time we actually tried to go to a marriage seminar or get some books to read. When we first read, Gary Smalley's book. 'The Five Love Languages', we found out both our love languages were 'Quality Time' - spending time together."

"With him working long hours, I didn't get to spend time with him, so I didn't feel loved. Norman's love language was also quality time, so we had to make time to spend together. At that point in our marriage, we really tried to work on our relationship."

And then there were kids!

No surprise to them! Working on their relationship before kids was much easier. With kids, it was definitely a 'conscious, hard fought, carve out the time' decision to spend time together. Nancy reminded us, "If you don't hold onto your marriage during that time, it can really fall apart."

In the midst of kids, jobs and normal life, they went through what Norman described as a 'dry' time. "We weren't communicating well. We weren't emotionally close. We were just going through the motions rather than feeling and acting on the love we had for each other. We didn't know how to get over the hump. We did some marriage counseling and it showed we were willing to work at it to get through it."

Nancy couldn't deny there were times she used the 'D' word (divorce). However, she felt they were empty words because in the very beginning of their marriage, they made a commitment to never get divorced. "It's a commitment to each other. Even when you have problems, you have to work through those problems. God wants a commitment to each other - forever."

Loss glued them together

Her voice saddened and her voice grew quieter, "Nine years ago, we lost our 18-year-old son, Ryan. I heard after the loss of a child, a lot of times, people wind up divorced. We just looked at each other and said early on: 'We're not going to be a statistic. No matter how hard this loss is, we are not going to get divorced. We are going to work through this grief together."

They described Ryan as a very healthy teen. He had just graduated from high school and was accepted to the University of North Dakota in aviation. He wanted to be a pilot since he was six years old. Their daughter, Cara had just graduated from the University of Washington in Seattle and got a residency at Duke in North Carolina. Middle son, Mark graduated from high school and was working full time. It was the perfect time for their whole family to travel out East for a family reunion. Nancy and Cara drove cross country to the gathering in North Carolina and on the morning of July 2nd, Norman and the boys had an early flight to meet them.

Norman clearly remembered that morning as if it just happened. "I woke up our oldest son, Mark, and then went to wake up Ryan. As soon as I opened the door, I

knew something was wrong. He wasn't the right color. He wasn't breathing and hadn't been breathing a long time." He struggled as he searched for words, "It happened in the middle of the night sometime. The night before, he had heart palpitations, but he had been lifeguarding and doing swim lessons. I thought he was just tired. I sent him to bed and he never woke up. I had to call Nancy and tell her over the phone. That was tough."

Nancy told us, "It took four months for the cause of death to be determined. Ryan had his wisdom teeth out exactly two months to the day he passed away. The coroner believed bacteria from his teeth traveled down to his heart causing a very rare cardiac sarcoidosis."

He explained that sarcoidosis is an autoimmune event where the body attacks its own tissue. Doctors thought the bacteria

went to his heart where his body fought off the bacteria and then kept fighting and killed the heart. "It was sudden. There was nothing we could have done."

Nancy's voice saddened, "We weren't able to say goodbye to our son, so that has been a hard part of our journey."

Impact on their marriage

They paused and looked at each other before explaining the impact Ryan's death had on their marriage. Norman began, "I would like to say that going through that has made our relationship stronger, because we have that experience in common and pulled through it together...but it wasn't immediately like that."

He paused, "...When Ryan passed away, God said to me, 'Do you trust Me?' I was like, 'Yah Lord, I trust You...<u>but</u>'. And He said, 'No...do you trust Me?' I said, Yah, Lord...I trust You <u>but</u>...'. He said, No, do you trust Me?' I said, 'OK, Lord...I guess I'll trust You.' I gained a peace through that, but Nancy didn't have that peace right away..."

Nancy struggled, "That was one month after Ryan's death...and so, I couldn't comprehend that..."

"She couldn't comprehend how I could have peace after Ryan had passed away. I knew it immediately, and then the only question is: 'What do you do about it?' Because if God had given me a peace in my heart, how do I give that to Nancy? She wasn't ready to accept it. I think there was even a degree where she felt like it was a betrayal. 'Either you don't love him, or you don't love him the same way I did.' That was difficult, but I knew it was just part of how Nancy had to grieve, and how she had to deal with it.

It wasn't anything in me," continued Norman. "It was the grace of God that got me through."

"So, unfortunately for me, I felt like I was grieving alone. Our daughter, Cara, was in North Carolina. I knew our son, Mark, was hurting but not talking about it and Norman said, he was 'over it'..."

"Not over it...," Norman said quietly. "I had a peace that Nancy just couldn't understand for quite a while. We did have the experience in common, and we did rely on each other, but at the same time, we were dealing with it very differently."

Several months before Ryan died, Nancy recounted, "I had a dream in the middle of the night that he was found cold, dead in his bed. I woke up and I was like: 'Where was that from?' To me, it was a nightmare. I never told anyone, not even Norman. I had forgotten about it. The minute Norman told me that Ryan passed away, I felt like the Lord was whispering, 'Nancy, I was trying to warn you I was calling Ryan home.' That gave me a lot of peace in 'the Lord gives, and the Lord takes away'. Our children are a gift from God and they're God's children."

It wasn't over

At that point, she started to question God, 'OK, Lord...I understand You called Ryan home but why did You have to take my son?' She said the same statement for about four months until one day, her pastor preached, 'God is God and doesn't have to tell you why.' Nancy said, "I had to accept that.

I did...I did accept it, but it took about two years to find the joy. The first time we went to church after Ryan passed away...the tears just streamed down my face— but I couldn't worship. I just kept trying to find the joy again and finally...," she struggled for words "...like the lightbulb went on. I heard, 'Joy is in My presence' and that has stuck with me. I was like: 'Yes!' The joy is in Your presence, Lord! So, after that, I started to feel a little bit better, but it's still a journey. We've got good days and bad days."

They had Ryan's remains cremated, but it wasn't final until about four years after his death. Nancy said, "We were able to bury him, and have him rest in peace which also gave me peace. Everyone's grief journey is unique, and you can't shorten it. Norman's was way different than mine, but you just have to go through the grief."

They learned men and women grieve differently, and everyone grieves at a different pace. Nancy attended a support group for Moms who had lost children from age 18 to 23 years of age. They also went together to a Grief Share program at their church to help them in the processing of their grief.

According to Norman, "The grief is never completely gone. I miss him every day, especially when we go up into the mountains. Ryan loved the mountains, so he is a part of me every time I go to the mountains."

With painful honesty, Nancy shared, "It never goes away...it gets easier but when people say, 'Oh, get over it'...you don't get over the loss of your child."

Blessings in their marriage...

They have had more than their share of grief, but when asked about the blessings, Norman began with this statement: "The greatest blessing in marriage is not some great event, some big thing but the biggest blessing of marriage is just sharing our lives...just being together, and having Nancy be a part of me. I'm not complete without her."

She added, "Also our children. Cara is 28, Mark is 26 and we had Ryan until 18 years. They are our lives. We like to go on adventures and vacations, spend time with each other...building relationships. We were so blessed that we had so many memories with Ryan. He did more in his short 18 years than most people did in a lifetime. So, we cherish the memories we have. I tell people...'Make memories, because memories don't just happen. You have to make them happen'."

Norman nodded, "Building memories is important. That's something I would counsel younger couples who are considering splitting up. You may be able to put your life back together, and find someone else, but you won't have that history. You won't have those memories that you had if you stayed together. You've got that accumulation of years of memories and that's not replaceable."

You might as well make it good!

They looked at each other, and both snickered as Norman shared this wisdom: "If you're stuck together...you might as well make it good!" (As they were leaning into the laughter, we could imagine those words on a best-selling wall plaque!)

"Communication. Communication," Nancy said, "is the most important. You share your highs...You share your lows...You share when you're hurting. You just have to communicate....in good times, and in bad times. I'm a talker, and Norman is more inward. There are times when I want to verbalize why I'm angry, and he'll just be quiet and not say anything. That bugs the heck out of me!

Always say you love each other every day. Don't take each other for granted, because too many people don't show that love and affection. If you don't, it will die."

Norm shared wisdom learned in their own marriage, "You can't put yourself first. That is a challenge, but also a blessing, because it takes you out of yourself. You need to be willing to say, 'I'm willing to sacrifice what I want, because I love Nancy enough to put her first, and allow her to have what she wants or what she needs.' It's not just about me!"

"It's not all about self or what the other person does for you in return. I have to do for Norman just as much as he has to do for me," they looked deeply at each other, "because we love each other."

They are such different personalities, so it means working on how they communicate and resolve conflict. Norman is more of a thinker when he processes things. Nancy is a talker, and needs to verbalize, in order to process. Through the advice of a marriage counselor, they learned to write down what was bothering them, and then go out for coffee and talk it through together.

As an internal processor, Norman said, "You know, a lot of times, talking about it is worse than the problem itself...or it felt like it to me!" They looked at each other and laughed as he added his normal question during conflict, 'Is that a big enough problem that I actually have to talk?' "It makes me get out of my comfort zone. It's a challenge but it's also a blessing, because I need to learn how to communicate."

Nancy added, "You can't take everything seriously. Life is too short. My motto is work hard, and play hard, because you have to enjoy each other...enjoy life."

To all you guys out there...Norman teased, "Marriage...I'll figure it out next year!", to which they both gave out a long round of laughter.

God first

When talking about the place their faith had in their marriage, Norman said, "In our own hearts we are actually selfish. If we don't have a foundation of faith in God, and if we don't have His Spirit supporting us...our natural inclination is to put ourselves first. That foundation of faith in God allows us to build a strong relationship, because we're dependent on God first, and then we can love each other unselfishly."

"One of the things that did attract me to Norman was the fact he was the first person I dated that did have faith. When I went in his room there was a Bible. We went to church together. God grew us together and united us. He made us one in our faith through all those years."

Norman said, "It was also essential...a make it or break it proposition...that the woman I married HAD to have faith in Jesus. Even though, at the time, neither of us were walking that closely with Him, but we did at least have that first step."

Faithfulness

Nancy ended their love story with this: "God is faithful, and if we seek to follow Him, He will make us faithful."

No marriage comes with the guarantee it will be devoid of bumps, bruises or catastrophic crashes. Through joy and sorrow, they forged a strong bond because their strength came from the One who is faithful to carry them.

Terry & Madelyn – They're On the Same Team

MARRIED 44 YEARS

"Two are better than one, because they have a good return for their labor: If either of them falls down one can help the other up. But pity anyone who falls and has no one to help them up." Eccl 4:9-10

W hat was a small-town girl doing moving all over the country…and the world? Wasn't she supposed to settle down like all the other girls and marry a local guy?

Oh, Madelyn was a small-town girl all right, but, according to her, "The 'pickins were slim' in the guy department. I didn't want to be stuck…I wanted to get out!"

At one point, she was dating Terry's roommate but after spending time around Terry, she discovered she had more in common with him than his roommate. That's when she 'sort of' got rid of the roommate and let Terry know she was available.

When they went out for the first time, "I just remember opening the door thinking, 'Oh my gosh...he's here for me? He's here for me! How could I get someone this good looking'!"

Terry's first impression of Madelyn: 'It's a girl and she isn't short!' At which they both laughed out loud!

Their love story timeline: Met in August, engaged in October and married in February!

Terry acknowledged, "I can tell you I never had a plan...I just..."

Madelyn blurted out, "He just did it!"

Her family thought it was too fast. His family was in England, so his Mom got a letter saying, 'I met a girl.' The next letter said, 'We're getting married'. So, his Mom wrote him this letter...20 pages long!

About that letter...

As the result of that letter, Madelyn got a call from Terry saying, 'I'm not coming over.'

'What??' She had a shocked look on her face as she related that phone call.

'Well, I got a letter from my Mom.'

'What??' "It didn't make any sense!" Finally, two nights later, after he had worked through a few issues, he came to visit. She asked if she could read the now 'famous' letter from his Mom.

She teased him with a sigh as she remembered finding the pages tossed all over his car. "Yah...page one was over here... page two was back here, page three was over there, page four..." She reached her arm out as if she was gathering pages from the far reaches of the car. "Evidently, he was tossing a page as he finished reading it.

So, I read the letter and with relief, I said, 'Terry, all she's doing is saying, 'Are you sure? Make sure this is the one you want.' His Mom had been through a divorce and didn't want him to go through the same thing. She was being a mom and looking out for him and being careful."

Whew! After maneuvering through all the panic, they narrowly escaped the demise of their relationship and went on to plan the wedding.

Starting out alone

They walked the aisle at age 19 for Madelyn and 21 for Terry. To the chagrin of their friends, eight months after their wedding, they packed up and headed overseas to England with no family or friends anywhere near. In fact, military life forced them to move ten times in 24 years. (If you don't want to do the math, that's an average of about two years at each duty station.) Many military marriages dissolve under the constant stress of relocating their families and adjusting to an entirely new life. When asked how this challenge affected their marriage, Terry remarked, "It didn't push us away, so it had to draw us closer together."

"I had to because he was all I had. I had no friends to call. We didn't have text messaging or cell phones then. I think, that can be a problem today. Technology makes it so easy to call home. Even back then, phones were long distance and it cost so you didn't just pick up your phone and call home. When you don't have close family, you have to rely on your spouse."

Made it positive

As far as the kids and frequent relocations were concerned, Madelyn admitted, "There were stressful times, but at the same time, they were good. We were positive with the kids. We always told them...'you GET to move...you GET to make new friends...you GET to live in a new place...you GET to see new things'."

Terry said, "That worked until our last move...the hardest move because the kids were leaving tenth grade. It's really hard to come into a new school at that age and make friends because the cliques are already formed. That was the only time we saw that the kids affected. They verbalized it more than ever before." During that time, open communication with them was extremely important, as well as standing united as a family facing new challenges together.

Time alone was rare

Another challenge military life presented was pointed out by Madelyn. "We needed time for ourselves, but we didn't always have someone to drop the kids off with or someone to come over and take care of the kids. So, we were with our kids all the time. We made it through one day at a time," they both smiled in agreement. "I think talking a lot after the kids went to bed...trying to figure out the issue and what we needed to do to fix it."

Give up?

Their corner of their eyes crinkled with laughter as Terry said, "Give up? Not me anyway!"

They were still enjoying the hilarity when Madelyn made an attempt to evade giving her answer. "Could we go to the next question?"

Finally, ready to answer the 'give up' question, she said, "Through our families, I knew how much damage divorce could do. The word 'divorce' was not allowed ever...ever, ever. Neither one of us ever spoke it. It wasn't allowed and when you take that out of your conversations, the only thing left is to make it work."

She continued, "Give up?...bottom line... It wasn't what I wanted but it just played in my brain for a little bit...a day or two. I was thinking, 'What would I do? Where would I go?' We were a military family. Going home for me wasn't going to be an option. I couldn't go home to my parents. I didn't want to go home to my parents. I really can't answer how I got to that point. I just remember that for one moment...for maybe 48 to 72 hours..."

"The reason?" Madelyn paused, "...my prayer life was probably down. I was probably not reading the Bible and that was my fault. If I'm doing what I'm supposed to be doing, then God's going to take care of that for us. I just think you have to stay close to God because it is not humanly possible for us to get along with each other. We just can't. It has to be a God thing."

Terry candidly commented, "I come from a family where my parents divorced, as well as several of my siblings, so it was like," he let out a big breath of air. "...it was something I wasn't really interested in!"

"We both believe strongly that this was our marriage," added Madelyn. "I was supposed to stay in our marriage and in order to do that, it wasn't an option to leave the marriage."

Plenty of blessings

Terry shared, "Part of the blessing was moving and being together the whole 24 years of military life. A lot of people go TDY (temporary duty) for a year or remote assignments (overseas to locations where families are not permitted). We've been together the whole time."

Madelyn gave the one exception when Terry had a TDY to Saudi for 45 days. "It was a long 45 days! A normal TDY would be a few weeks and he was back so, for him to go to Saudi...it was so far away. At a certain time of the day, he knew he could call the base and the base would patch it through to me. Calls didn't always help because whatever was going on at home, he couldn't fix anyway. Our son, Scott, was a teenager and I was going through a hard time with him and Dad wasn't here."

"With no cell phone and no internet, we used a lot of prayer because I didn't know the answer. I couldn't see what was going on, but I knew something was and that was frustrating. Terry was not there to help me. We did make it through with...perseverance...lots and lots of prayers...because it was one day at a time."

Releasing responsibility back to him

When Terry came back, they both had readjustments to make. Madelyn said, "When they leave, you quickly do everything. It's all yours and it's just really easy to step into that. So, coming back, I think as a wife, it is harder to release some of that responsibility." She had to remind herself, "I don't have to do it all anymore. He's home. It's not my responsibility. So, 'back off'!"

When asked if he ever had to tell her to back off, Terry laughed and sarcastically said, "No...we get along sooo well!"

"He never says anything!" she laughed. "He just waits for me to work through it. He's just sits and waits. Quietly." She admitted it can be frustrating at times. "Yah...because communication isn't sometimes there. He is just waiting for me to get through. I may be ranting and raving and he's just like, 'OK...when you get through'...."

They both laughed as Terry said, "Of course, when she's ranting and raving, she can't see me and I'm probably making faces."

Different personalities

Terry and Madelyn have very different personalities, so they handle problems differently. Terry said, "Wait and see. There are things in life a whole lot worse than whatever it is that is bothering me at the time."

Madelyn wasn't out husband shopping, so she said, "I was blindsided with him. I didn't expect him in my life. When I think God picks that person, then He complements me and helps me through those challenges. When I know he's silent, I know I've got to work through an issue. When he's waiting, I know I've got to work through it. Anybody else might have been combative with me and that would have been a big problem. You can't have two people together that are going to be at each other all the time. So, for one of us to be calm and waiting, is a good thing. He does have moments when he'll speak back to me and I'll have to go, (gulp) 'OK...grrrhrrr.' I just marvel that God put us together and that Terry puts up with me."

We knew NOTHING!

The biggest smile emerged on Terry's face as he explained what he loved and appreciated about his wife. "The fact that she puts up with me...still. She is all around nice!"

"I like that he's stable. We have been talking about retirement. I had a goal originally to teach 15 years. Recently, I got it down to 12 and now I am probably down to 11. His whole outlook is, 'Look...you don't have to keep doing this. You just don't. If you need to retire...you need to retire'. I like that about him because he looks at the big scheme of things. He is able to calm me down and he just takes that pressure off.

I think we were so naive when we got married. When you're young, you think you know everything. We knew NOTHING!

We grew up so much by being in the military and doing all that traveling. That caused us to grow up and see things outside our own little world. I'm not saying we know it all now, but we know better. I don't have to prove anything to him, and he doesn't have to prove anything to me. We are comfortable with each other in all instances. We kind of know how the other one is feeling. We can sense when things are not good, or we are in a situation when things are tense and maybe the other one needs rescuing. I just think it's better."

"Initially, when you're in love, it's L-U-S-T. But," Terry said with a smile, "as you get older, it becomes love--H-E-A-R-T."

Madelyn responded with a resounding, "Wow....that IS good!" Her comment brought Terry one of those ear to ear grins.

Lessons learned

Terry liked something he saw his adoptive Dad do. "Mom would get mad and he would say, 'I'm not going to argue with you'." Snickering, he continued, "So that is probably something I carried over."

"Yep," Madelyn smiled, "there is nothing the wife can do if the husband will not argue. The wife is stuck not arguing. She is left having to think about...'Why are you arguing? Why are you frustrated?' and 'What do you need to do about it'?" In her own marriage, that time of reflection prepared her to then be able to go back to Terry so they could resolve the conflict together

Advice to young couples

Terry said, "It's a journey." He snapped his fingers, "It's not: 'OK, we're married and now I know everything. I'm going to be the best person there ever was.' No. You have to learn to take the bumps and learn from it."

"Marriage is a lot of work," interjected Madelyn, "but at the same time, the blessings far outweigh any of the trials. Someone once told me....'Don't ever go to bed mad. Always tell them that you love them and have the foundation of faith.' Being a Christian doesn't mean it's perfect. You are still going to have trials but it's the only way to ensure that you are going to get through the trials."

Terry's last piece of advice was said with a teasing smile, "Don't get old!"

Madelyn had a little bit of a faraway look as she said, "I just shake my head and think...'How did we get here because it seems like yesterday, we were in our 20s and 30s. I think at this age, we are very comfortable with each other and at the same time, we are about to begin a new journey. Soon, both of us will be retired. We've not walked that way before, so we don't know what to expect."

Terry said, "There are a lot of people who turn 60 or 70 and start acting like people who belong in a nursing home. Always remember, inside you there's a 20-year-old!"

Madelyn agreed, "It is all perspective. Can you get out and do things? Well, maybe you can't go as fast as you could before or as far as you could before but do what you can. Don't just sit there and say, 'I can't do it anymore'."

Same team

So much of their story centered around being a team when no one else was around to help. When other couples might be running to Mom or Dad for advice, they were living thousands of miles away where they only had each other. That meant they spent their marriage wearing the same team jersey.

What could have seemed like a handicap became one of their strongest reasons to bond together. Wearing the same team jersey isn't just for their favorite Yankees. It is a life lesson they have lived and learned in their marriage

Orville & Sheila – A Steady Diet of Miracles

MARRIED 32 YEARS

"He performs wonders that cannot be fathomed, miracles that cannot be counted."
Job 9:10

If our plans go as we are talking about," Sheila smiled, "we will celebrate our anniversary by taking a motorhome trip to Canada and Alaska. Hopefully it will work out."

Orville piped up, "What...the marriage or the trip?"

"Both!"

If that was any indication of how their story (and their lives) would go, we needed to prepare for a few laughs…and more than a few miracles on the horizon!

Hands held tightly

Throughout the entire interview, they held hands as if this was their last few minutes together. When you hear their entire story, you will come to understand why.

How it all began

Sheila was a young widow, working full time. When she came home from work, her seven-year old daughter always wanted to go to the swimming pool. "I sure as heck didn't feel like doing that after working all day. So, I saw this ad in the paper for an inground, vinyl liner swimming pool. It was pretty cheap in comparison to what I thought a pool might cost, so I called to get somebody to come give an estimate. So, this gal set up the appointment but," she looked over at Orv, "instead, <u>he</u> shows up."

It wasn't all that normal for Orv to be coming to give an estimate on a pool. And, here's why— "I had been running a very successful business. In a nutshell, I got a big head about myself. I had real estate investments and we were doing a wind farm and money was rolling in. I started taking pride in what I was accomplishing and took my eyes off the Lord.

In 1982, we were just getting ready to open a big retail showroom and the Lord allowed me to remember the last thing to come out of my mouth as I was locking the store up for the grand opening the next day. 'You finally made it, Orv. You made it to the top.' I got in my truck and headed to my new home when a pair of headlights came across the double yellow line and I got nailed by a drunk driver. I woke up one and a half years later and had amnesia for a total of two and a half years. During that time, I lost everything. I was homeless and penniless."

He continued his rather surreal experience, "When I woke up, I finally figured out I didn't have a house, or anything left. A fellow I knew was a contractor, so I got a job with him. He asked me if I could wire houses. I said, 'Sure' and then I went and got a book on how to wire houses. I wired a subdivision of houses for him and before that I had never wired a house in my entire life. I started saving up my money and needed to decide, 'What do I want to do with my life?' I said, 'I think I would like to build swimming pools. I've never built swimming pools before. I'd never even seen a swimming pool built before." He passed the test for a California contractor's license. "Now, I am a swimming pool contractor who's never built a swimming pool before."

Sheila kept her eyes on her husband and smiled as he continued, "I found a kit pool we could build, so now I had to sell a pool AND learn how to build it. So, I put an ad in the paper, and we got a call from...Sheila."

His post concussive syndrome caused memory loss which meant he was normally not the one who would go out to make a presentation. His business partner's daughter had a doctor's appointment that day, so Orv went in her place. He nervously made the presentation and, "This nice lady (Sheila) bought the pool. Then I had to figure out how to build it! That's how we met!"

We laughed in disbelief as Sheila said, "I had no idea he had never built a pool before and never asked to see his references."

Orv laughed, "Thank goodness because if you ever asked to see the work I had done, I would be in trouble. I'm sure some houses I wired are..." Laughter came even harder, so he couldn't finish the sentence!

The attraction?

Orv got that teasing look in his eyes and said, "Sheila was dating a doctor and an Air Force C5 pilot and she ended up falling in love with a homeless man who used to be a pilot and wanted to be a doctor."

"He was just a very nice man."

Orv snickered, "A terrorist...a nice terrorist."

Sheila was also snickering, "He looked like he was a terrorist. He had this bushy black beard that was out to here and big glasses. But--he was a nice man." They would talk when he came over to work on the pool. One day he saw the old 911 Porsche in the garage and Sheila asked if he wanted to buy it. Orv just laughed at the thought of this homeless guy buying an expensive Porsche.

"I didn't know he was homeless. Orv asked why I was selling it. I said, 'Well, it was my husbands and I don't really want it.' Innocently, Orv asked, why her husband didn't take it with him. Sheila said, 'Wellllll....little hard to do that. He died'!" She thinks that was when Orv got interested in pursuing a relationship with her.

Relationship problem

According to Orv, there was just one slight problem. As a result of the accident he had only a five-minute memory span. Everything that happened ten minutes ago, he didn't remember. He would promise his associates he would do something and five minutes later it was as if it never happened. "I ended up alienating every person I knew because they thought I was lying to them. Then, of course, they thought I flipped out. Nobody put it together that this was part of a memory loss from the accident. They thought I was just a jerk, so I really didn't have any friends left at that point. Sheila was a friendly lady and actually liked me just for who I was. So, we kind of developed a friendship." It seems that at that time, anything more than a friendship was a scary proposition for both of them.

Cheap living

He had no money and would survive on a dollar a day back then. "After working all day, I would go to Holiday Inn. At their bar, for dollar you could buy a beer and with the beer you could have all the hors d'oeuvre you could eat." He usually ate his one meal a day there. "I hate macaroni and cheese, but Sheila was always fixing the neighbor kids and her daughter, Nikki, macaroni and cheese. So, if I hung around a little bit after work, she would feed me macaroni and cheese."

Their eyes crinkled in laughter as Sheila said, "Well, if he doesn't leave, you invite him to eat."

Orv put them both into hysterics as he finished with, "...like a puppy waiting for a bone."

Pool is done...Now what?

When the pool was done, he needed an excuse to keep coming back to see her. He said, 'My son has never been able to swim in any of the pools I've built. (Well, that was true because this was the first one he ever built.) Sheila said, 'Bring him over. The kids will have fun.' So, he did!

That's when the neighbors seemed to get a little protective of Sheila. They asked her, 'What kind of guy is this? He's never taken you out! He just comes over and hangs out but never takes you out?' That's when Orv decided he needed to take her out.

Problem #1...When his business collapsed, he still owed the federal government and the state of California $265,000. Every agency, including IRS, Workman's Comp and Social Security seized all the funds from the business and garnished the accounts. Orv said, "Every penny that came in went to the government until the $265,000 was paid. I really didn't have any money." Obviously, Sheila didn't know that side of Orv.

"So, I went to this place called Dave's' Giant Hamburgers and found out how much it was going to be to take Sheila, myself and Nikki to get a hamburger and a drink. They didn't have fries, so I didn't have to worry about that. They gave me the exact amount with tax. So, I saved and scrimped and finally came up with enough money to take them out to Dave's Giant Hamburgers. As I was getting ready to pay for the three things we ordered, Nikki grabbed a bag of potato chips off the counter. I didn't have the money to pay for it. It sounds crazy now, but that's the way it was. I was so embarrassed, but I said, 'Nikki, you don't want those. They are full of cholesterol and salt and they're not good for you'!" That's when Sheila lost it!

As if reenacting the event, she threw her arms into the air, "She's seven!"

Orv said Sheila looked at her daughter and said, 'Put them back, Nikki. I've got a whole bag of chips at home. You can eat the whole bag if you want.' They were laughing so hard they could hardly look at each other!

When they got back to the house, Sheila blurted out, 'Somebody better do some talking!' That's when Orv explained the accident and the fact he didn't have the money and why he was so embarrassed. That's when she started putting things together. He saw by her response that she was a compassionate woman, a good listener and not judgmental. That revelation didn't put an end to the relationship, but only made it grow as they spent the next year getting to know each other.

When did you know?

If you could put it in a capsule...Orv said he knew he loved her when he got dysentery. No, really!! Dysentery!

He sold enough swimming pool kits that he qualified for a free trip to Puerto Vallarta. So, he went to Puerto Vallarta...by himself. While he was there, he got dysentery and thought he was going to die. "As I was dying in that room...I realized how much I cared for her. We've always told each other that we liked each other." They were a little cautious so, Orv said, "We were actually in 'like'...we weren't in love. I decided when I get back, I told the Lord if I lived, I would tell her how I really felt. When I got back, I told her I was in love with her. She said, 'Well, I like you, too'." At that point, he knew he needed to pull out all the stops. He took her on a drive to a very nice little restaurant close to the coast.

"On the drive out, I asked her if she would marry me. She said she would have to think about it. Well, that didn't go exactly as I planned." Even her lukewarm answer didn't deter him. He said, "I found a keeper."

She was concerned. "There were issues with Nikki…especially after the potato chip thing!" They both laughed when Orv said, "Nikki holds a grudge!" They both remembered a time when he came to visit, and Nikki answered the door. Sheila came out after her shower and asked who was at the door. Nikki said, 'Nobody!' She had slammed the door in his face and went back to watching TV.

Your final answer?

A short while after the proposal, Orv recalled Sheila saying, 'I have been thinking about your proposal and before I give you my answer, there are three things you have to consider. #1-If you marry me, you take my daughter, too.' Orv thought, 'Eeewww…can't we just sell her?' That was a tough one. Then Sheila said, #2 - 'You have to understand, I can be a real serious b____ '!"

Sheila reached over and hit him on the chest, "Of course, you had to say that one!"

Then he explained her reason #3. 'If I say 'yes' and I marry you, understand this is a life-long commitment. You are committing to me and I'm committing to you and there will be no running around. If I find out you're unfaithful, you have to understand, I'm a nurse trained in the use of surgical instruments and you have to sleep sometime!'

She giggled and then Orv slid in, 'Hmmm...I can handle that but I'm not sure about Nikki!'

As if Sheila's heart melted, "I had been praying that if I got married again, God would bring me a man that was like my Dad...loved his family and a Godly man. That's what I really wanted and that is what I found in Orv."

"It's interesting how God works. She fell in love with me when I had no investments, no money to my name. I was just trying to pay off that debt and keep a business together. People would say, 'He's just after you for your money.' Hey…she had a job, a house, a car!" Even with his kidding, it is evident in the way he looked into her eyes that money was never what attracted him to Sheila.

Miracles commence

They would soon get used to miracles and Orv told us the first one was about to arrive shortly after they got married. "We hadn't bought our rings and didn't have the money to do it. A friend of mine said, 'I'm selling this piece of property and you need to move your bulldozer'. I thought it was gone with everything else, but I had no loan on it, so it didn't get repossessed." Orv went to look, and it was still there. "I fired it up and it still ran so I put an ad in the paper and sold it."

The money bought their wedding rings, paid off their credit cards and paid for the honeymoon. "The Lord provided so I was able to provide something for our marriage." That wasn't the only miracle! He also found out he owned two homes. but no taxes had been paid on them because of his amnesia. He quickly paid the taxes and they were now free and clear.

"By the time we got married, we owned two houses, had all of our debts paid off and had our rings. So, God, at the very last minute, gave back some of what I lost. She fell in love with me when I had nothing and yet by the time we got married, we were comfortable financially."

Need a kid-sized miracle

Ahhhh...the kids! They had 'potato chip' denied Nikki and Orv's son, Aaron, who lived with them part time. Even though they had the same rules for both kids when they were at their house, Aaron escaped those rules when he called his Grand-mother to come get him if he didn't get his way. That made for frequent clashes between Nikki and Aaron. Sheila threw up her hands in mock defeat when she told us they also defended each other when you least expected it. "Once a kid was beating up on Aaron and Nikki went in and just nailed him. Go figure!"

Discipline was often a hard thing. Sheila said, "They were both spoiled for one thing. Nikki was angry with God...angry with the world when her Daddy died. She was so stubborn and so 'in your face' that Orv left discipline up to me, since he was the stepdad."

Orv said, "She told me if I touched her, she would call Family Protective Ser-vices."

Sheila said, "The kids would play us against each other. 'Mom said I could...' Of course, I didn't know the other part. Same thing with him." They felt many of the challenges in their marriage were in dealing with their children. This miracle didn't come instantly but came as they stood together to make their newly blended family work.

What? Another miracle?

Sheila told us, "I got a viral infection while we were on our honeymoon and they thought it was bronchitis. Six months later it hit full tilt. I had a viral infection that settled in my heart and caused lots of heart damage...viral induced cardiomyo-pathy." About a year after they got married, she was medically retired from the Air Force. It couldn't be cured so she was being treated, hoping to keep the heart from deteriorating.

"She just kept going downhill. In early 1994, she woke up in the early morning trying to get out of bed but instead just flopped around and mumbled." Orv got out of bed and turned on the light. Immediately he could see she had suffered a massive stroke. "Her whole left side was drooping. She had no use of her arm or leg on one side. I scooped her up and ran her into the hospital. She had a blood clot in her heart that was about the size of my thumb. With each heartbeat you could see it move. It was held on by a thin little piece of thread. We were told, 'If that threads breaks, she'll die'. They did a scan of her brain and a large portion of her brain had no blood flow to it. It was dead. They couldn't give her blood thinners because it would thin the bloodstream and allow the clot to come loose and it would kill her."

At the end of day #2, the neurologist said, 'The chance of recovery is very slim. She'll have to stay bed ridden for at least six months. We're hoping the heart will encapsulate the clot.' Orv went home that night realizing she would maybe never be able to walk or talk again. "I was pretty depressed. It wasn't exactly how I expected our marriage to go. I just felt the Lord remind me of a Scripture: 'In all things give thanks'. So, I got in the shower and started singing praises to Him. As I was singing praises to Him, I felt this overwhelming...it wasn't a voice I heard...just an overwhelming knowledge of what I was supposed to do. I was to take Sheila. Leave California. Sell everything and go. That made no sense at all. She couldn't be moved. It was impossible, but I just felt it so strong. I said, 'Lord, if that's what you want me to do, then I'll do it but you're going to have to make a way'."

When he got to the hospital the next morning, she was sitting up on the side of the bed. "She stood up and raised both hands over her head and said, 'Praise God, He healed me overnight!' God had healed her. She could stand. She could talk."

"I woke up and everything was normal."

Orv gave a wide smile, "Of course, it blew the doctors away. When the nurse saw her, she said, 'Get back in bed! That blood clot!' (Remember, if it broke loose, she would be dead!) They took her back in to check on the progress of the clot. They did the echo again and there was nothing there. No clot! They looked and looked again. They reviewed the original tape from the original echo. They said, 'We don't understand. There's some anomaly.' One doctor just kind of hung back after the others left and said, 'It's no anomaly...that's a miracle'!"

Sheila's smile spread across her face, "And that's truly what we believe it was. We are sure!"

That 'shower' feeling

However, Orv couldn't get that feeling from the shower out of his mind. He told Sheila, 'God told me we are supposed to sell everything and leave.' She said, 'Well, that's stupid! God's not going to tell you that!' They had two kids who were a junior and senior in high school. Not exactly the best timing. They shared it with their small group from church. They told them they were out of their minds and Orv's business partners weren't all that crazy about the idea either!

For him, the questions and arguments just wouldn't stop coming. 'Where are you supposed to go?' 'I don't know.' 'What are you supposed to do?' 'I don't know. 'This is just what I feel God told me.' 'How do you know it was God?' 'I don't know...I just feel it was God.' 'Well, there you go. You felt it.' "So, I realized, it really was stupid and didn't make any sense." That feeling was put on the back burner, but not entirely gone.

The effects of the stroke on Sheila totally disappeared. Amazingly, the brain scan showed she had this large part of her brain that was dead. In spite of that, she miraculously functioned as if she had never had a stroke. They both felt their lives went back to normal.

The end?

"A year and half later, I woke up at one o'clock in the morning and Sheila was laying there in bed. Her eyes were open and glazed over and she was cold. Sometime during the night, she had a cardiac arrest and died. I was doing CPR on her but couldn't get any oxygen into her. I knew it was fruitless. She can't go that long without oxygen."

The ambulance was on another call, so it took them a half an hour to get to their home. Orv and their daughter, Nikki, were doing CPR all that time. When the emergency personnel finally arrived, they asked how long she had been without oxygen. Orv said when he told them, "They kind of rolled their eyes and drove her to the hospital--shocking her (heart) all the way."

They got every prayer chain they knew praying for Sheila. "Shortly after she was in ER, the doctor came out and said, 'I am sorry, there was nothing we could do for her. She went way too long without oxygen. None of her organs are even viable for transplant. There was an erratic, periodic heartbeat and every once in a while, there is a gasp of air, which is not uncommon...but she was brain dead." The doctor told them the time of death had already been declared, but if they would like, they could be in a room with a heart monitor on Sheila. When they saw the flatline they would know it was over.

They sat quietly by her bed. "Hour after hour it would be this flat line and all of a sudden there would be this little blip and then flat line, flat line, flat line and then little blip. Every once in a while, there would be a little gasp and then she would go thirty to forty seconds and then a little gasp. It was hard because I knew she was already dead. I just sat there and held her hand. Her eyes were glazed over and there was no blinking and her kidneys weren't functioning."

If I could only turn the clock back

He held her hand for about 10 hours. "I finally just said, 'Why God? Why?' Immediately, that same voice I didn't hear but felt in the shower when He told me to leave California, just spoke into my spirit. 'Why didn't you leave when I told you to?' It just hit me like a ton of bricks. I promised God I would do something, and I didn't do it. I said, 'Lord, forgive me'. If I could only turn the clock back and go back to when You first told me. I would let nothing stop me from doing it.

After I was done praying, I put some saline drops in her eyes. When I did, her eyelids fluttered. I called the nurse and said, 'Her eyelids just fluttered'."

'No, Honey...they didn't flutter.'

'Watch', as I dripped some more into her eyes."

With a puzzled look, she said, 'That's unusual.'

"I looked down and there was a stream of urine starting in the catheter tube. The nurse said, 'Her kidneys are coming online!' Pretty soon, everything was buzzing. Within a few minutes Sheila sat up on the gurney, grabbed her chest and said, 'Oh my God! Oh my God! What happened to me?' (We had broken all her ribs doing CPR.) The Lord brought her back!

They flew her down to Stanford University Hospital. The Chief Cardiologist said, 'Before you see her, I have to talk to you.' I thought, 'Ooohhh, something's wrong.' He said, 'I just need to show you all this.' They had all the strips from the paramedics and the hospital and the lab work and everything. She said, 'This is the first time, I have ever seen a documented person that is dead and has come back. This is a miracle!' It's unbelievable.' Sheila's in there chatting and talking to everybody like nothing had ever happened!"

We're leaving!

With Sheila's condition miraculously reversed, Orv couldn't let go of what he felt in that shower! He told everybody, 'We are leaving California!'

'Where are you going to go?'

'I have no idea.'

'What are you going to do?'

'I have no clue!'

When the house sold, and details of their business were settled, they bought a motor home and headed East and then eventually to Texas. When they got to each of those locations, they knew it wasn't where they were supposed to be. That's when Sheila remembered receiving a flyer advertising 'living with your airplane'. They previously owned an airplane, so they thought they had nothing to lose by heading to the Ozarks to check out this piece of 'airplane living' property in West Plains, Missouri.

When they arrived in the Ozarks, Orv's response was more than negative! 'I tell you one thing...this is ONE place I would NEVER live'! As he repeated the statement he made that day, all Sheila could do was smile and look up at heaven as she shook her head back and forth.

He continued by sharing his introductory statement to the realtor. 'We're not interested in buying anything. We're just curious about this flyer you sent out about 'living with your airplane'. "So, he took us out to this little old farm. There was an old rickety barn that leaked and inside the barn was an airplane where a guy also had a bed, a refrigerator and a stove...and maybe his chair. Literally - he lived with his airplane. That's a taste of the Ozarks!"

Sheila laughed, "Not MY taste!"

They agreed to go on a little tour of the area. While out touring, the realtor's wife called with news of a house that just came on the market. They agreed to take a look, but once again told the realtor they weren't going to buy anything.

Orv said, "We walked into the house, which was nothing like it is now. It was just a little boxy old ladies' house. All we saw was the kitchen and the kitchen was nothing to look at. That's when the Lord spoke to BOTH of us that time and said, 'You are buying this house'!" He said, "One little drawback, we didn't want to buy this house!"

She remembered saying, 'Orv...we need to go outside and talk! This is weird!'

Orv felt God gave them a price to offer but it was quite a bit less than they were asking. It just came on the market, so they were sure it wouldn't be accepted! Aha...that would be their 'out'! As crazy as it might sound, the offer was accepted.

Orv said, "So, now we bought a house and we hadn't even seen the property. We saw the kitchen and we didn't know what the rest of the house looked like."

The next day when they went back, Orv spoke to the lady selling the home. 'We noticed yesterday you were crying downstairs.'

She said, 'As soon as you shook my hand, God told me you were buying the house and I had to accept the offer. That was it!'

After they signed the purchase agreement, Sheila got into their motor home and slugged Orv in the shoulder and said, 'What did we just do?' She threw up her hands like she was giving up, 'Why would we want to be here. We don't know anybody here and it's in the middle of nowhere'!

He finally felt as if he was right in the middle of God's will. "We are doing exactly what we're supposed to be doing. Sheila was still sick but I'm good and vibrant. So, I'm going to start a business. Got to make a living.

I went out and cut some firewood to sell and got bit by a tick. I got this weird rash and neither of us knew what it was. I got really sick and found out I had Lyme disease. I was in full blown stages of the disease. I suffered from that for about three years and now I was just as weak as Sheila was."

They would go to Wal Mart and stop the car right next to a shopping cart, so they could both hang on to it like a walker. Just getting groceries would wear them out for the day and they would come home and go straight to bed. Orv smiled, "Here we were right in the middle of God's will and both of us near death. I kept thinking that when you're obedient, everything turns out just perfect, but life is also full of tests and trials."

She proclaimed, "We knew all that God had done already in both of our lives. He brought us together in the first place. Healed me of a stroke. Brought me back from a cardiac arrest. I was living a pretty normal life even though my heart was not healed. It was going to be alright, even though all this stuff kept bombarding us."

Never 'why us?'

He said in a serious tone, "We never really thought, 'Why us'?"

"We didn't really ever doubt that God was there", Sheila said, "taking care of us."

"We learned we could depend on Him and trust Him. I didn't have an income, but we were able to survive on Sheila's medical retirement and a little savings." Once he had recovered from Lyme disease, She urged Orv to do something he had always wanted to do...get his commercial rating and flight instructor rating. "All of a sudden, people were calling me from all over the country to teach them how to fly helicopters. God's Word says He will give us the desires of our heart if we put Him first. It took the Lyme disease to get me refocused and to stop me long enough for Him to organize our life the way He wanted it to be."

By the way, God...we need miracle #3!

Meanwhile, Sheila's heart condition progressively got worse until doctors said she needed a heart transplant. On Friday, June 6th at 8am she was officially placed on the transplant list. At 8:30am her heart started failing. She was immediately transported to the hospital. The next morning when two physicians came in, they told Orv, 'We have a heart, but we don't know if she's strong enough. She is a perfect match for this heart, but her kidneys are so weak we don't know if she'll survive the surgery.'

He said, "We prayed together and said, 'Run another test.' They ran another test and," He gave us a thumbs up, " because she met the criteria. So, they whisked her in and sent a crew off to harvest the heart. It was a young man who had been shot. Before we knew it, she was having a heart transplant!" There is no denying the appearance of another miracle in their lives.

We all laughed as Orv said, "It took 20 years, but now we're honeymooning! We're the healthiest we've ever been!"

Had to depend on each other

When asked if they ever thought about giving up, they both shook their heads

from side to side as Sheila began, "I think, were closer through everything. I know that from the time we met and got married, until now, we've grown together a lot in our Christian walk."

"We had to depend on each other. When Sheila's heart was failing, neither of us wanted to say goodbye. We didn't want to be separated. That was probably the main reason Sheila didn't want to get on a helicopter and not see me again."

It was evident throughout the entire interview, they were not ready to let go of each other's hands. They were not fearful, but they held on tightly as if they wanted to appreciate today as if it was the last day they might be together.

Wisdom to pass along

Orv said, "If we didn't have Jesus, our faith in Christ, as our foundation, the stresses would have torn us apart. If Christ is not your Lord, if you don't put Him first...you will put yourself first. When you put yourself first there are going to be problems!"

Sheila said couples needed to be friends before they get married. "We were friends first and I think that was the really important thing to build our relationship on. Today, too many young people 'hook up'." She laughed, "I guess that's what they call it now."

As they worked with other couples struggling in their marriages, one frequent thing Orv saw was husbands insensitive to their wife's needs. He observed, "If she expressed her needs, he'd act as if, 'Well, that's stupid!' It could be something as simple as putting the toilet seat back down when done. Yet, if the husband is to be to his wife as Christ is to the church, willing to give his life, I usually ask the man, 'Would you give your life for your wife'?"

'Well, absolutely! Absolutely, without a thought!'

'But you're not willing to put the toilet seat down?'

"That usually causes him to ponder. If we say we're willing to die for our spouse," He said with a slight smirk, "we should be willing to do other things that aren't quite as drastic as dying."

Not all look the same

Their lives have been filled with illness, miracle after miracle after miracle and a giant dose of humor. Their marriage (and their miracles) might not look like yours, nor should it! But, consider this: God doesn't run out of miracles. He has enough left for your marriage, too. Restoring hearts, renewing joy or reigniting love aren't impossible for Him. It's Who He is…a miracle working God

Jim & Carol – Normal Got Snatched...More Than Once

MARRIED 8 YEARS

"God is our refuge and strength, an ever-present help in trouble. Therefore, we will not fear, though the earth give way and the mountains fall into the heart of the sea..." Psalms 46:1-2

Marriage blew up!

When an interview began as this one did, we knew it was going to be off the cuff, honest and hard hitting! As soon as the camera went on, Jim opened with: "Why would you want to talk to us about marriage. Both of us had marriages that blew up!"

As we listened, we found neither wanted a divorce!

Two weeks before he arrived home from his first deployment as a reserve chaplain in Iraq, Jim got a letter saying divorce papers had been filed. No counseling. No specific reason. It was just over.

"All the time I was married...there were other women who were attractive to me and there were sometimes I would think, 'I sure like being around her.' I never had the idea, 'How can I trade my wife in for her.' For better or worse...richer or poorer...I am going to stay married. I never had the feeling that I made a mistake and now I'm stuck'."

He went on to tell us how he and his first wife weathered the death of parents, agonized in losing a child and rejoiced in adopting a son. "We were a team. For our 25th anniversary we celebrated down in San Antonio. So, it was stunning. You could have knocked me over with a feather when I opened up that letter!"

Carol said very little about her first marriage but commented, "I won't say I am completely healed of everything. I was talking about love to my second-grade class and one of the students said, 'Well, if you're supposed to love everybody, why don't you love your ex-husband'?" Struggling to explain, she told her student, 'I can love him because Jesus says to love everyone. I can love him that way, but I don't like him at all. And Jesus never said we have to like everyone, did He'?

We both had hope that our first marriages would last. I know that I prayed and prayed and prayed."

As they told their stories, there was still a hint of pain in their voices...and in their eyes.

Internet dating 101

Jim, a reserve Army chaplain, was sent to Afghanistan where he was injured. He went to Ft Benning, Georgia, for evaluation and recovery. After nine months, he would be released. He didn't have a home, a car, a wife or anything. He said, "I was bummed out because they made me come home. I was doing chaplaincy work over there and I didn't want to come home."

To pass the time, he bought a computer and got on the internet where he found a free Valentine's special on e-Harmony. He was single and thought he might be ready to get into the dating scene. He admitted to being very inexperienced, but he felt this could help him learn how to be sociable. He connected with a number of women from all over the country and Carol was one of them.

Carol had only joined e-Harmony for three months. "I figured...If I don't meet anybody in three months...I wasn't going to meet anybody." Admittedly, a couple of connections she made on e-Harmony were failures. "I'm meeting all these losers. I am sick of this. I am taking a break." Just when she was ready to quit, she got a message from Jim. Even though she was determined to not date someone named Jim (because her ex-husband was a Jim) nor was she ever going to date someone in the military (because her ex-husband was military). "Don't ask me why but I finally said, 'I guess it won't hurt'."

At first, they communicated through e-Harmony, then e-mail and very quickly decided they wanted to see each other. That's when they began using video on Skype. They would often talk for hours as they got to know each other. Carol said, "Skyping was a big step. He sent me some pictures, and some looked like he was in a prisoner of war camp." No wonder! The background for his photo was his barracks...a cement block building.

"It was like every night he would be there. Usually I would come home from school and put on pajamas and just relax. Here I am, doing my hair, putting on a nice shirt. It was like a video date. He was very unique. It was just really easy to talk to him. It would be every single night. I had to get up at 5am and I was coming to school tired. Almost by April, I knew there was something different about him."

Carol is very gifted in making greeting cards, so she began sending cards to Jim. Usually they were more like...'thinking of you' or 'hope you're having a good day' type cards. Jim said, "I covered the wall in my room with them." Even though they were just friends, he felt encouraged by the cards, but he told her he didn't want to hear anything about love! NO hearts!

Her mouth drew up into a smile. "Every once in a while, there would be a heart in the stamp and then I would get a lecture...'Remember, I told you...no hearts...NO hearts'!" What started out as friendship gradually grew to love but he told me he still didn't want to hear anything about love. Even though he was divorced, Jim was still hoping his first wife would change her mind. He felt if he could just give her time to settle down and heal, she would come back."

During that time, Jim was still an inpatient in rehab and not able to leave the hospital. From the time they began communicating in February until July when they met in person, about all they could do was talk and talk they did. Without the physical distraction of being together, they learned about each other and found they had an overwhelming number of things in common:

- They each had a son living with challenges
- They were both professionals...he was a pastor and she was a teacher.
- They both had the same church background.
- Jim is ADD, so he knew what Carol was talking about when they would discuss challenges in her classroom with ADD students.

He was finally released from the hospital and was able to travel. On the way to see his family, he stopped in St Louis to see Carol. She said, "All it took was one look. It was like..." She motioned with her hands like fireworks going off.

Jim said, "She opened the door. I looked in her eyes. I saw those little freckles and I just fell in!" They both broke up as he dramatically dropped his head on her shoulder.

Even while he was driving to see Carol, he admitted if his ex-wife had called and said, 'Let's make an effort', that would have been the end of his relationship with Carol. He knew he couldn't go back but he kept hoping against hope. However, when he saw

Carol it was, 'OK...the past is done'. They both would have married immediately if they could have. The only thing holding them back was the fact that he still had to travel to Colorado, and she had signed a teaching contract for the next school year.

When she announced she and Jim were getting married, the staff at her school reacted with: 'Oh my goodness...you're marrying somebody you met on the internet!!! This is horrible! This is horrible!' Carol said, "It wasn't just one person...it was everybody!"

'You're doing what? You're doing what?!!!'

"Then I said, 'I'm going to have to quit my job'."

'You're what?!!

Before the proposal, her daughter, Amanda, who is in the Air Force said, 'What are you doing talking to that Army dude? You know Army people have problems!'

Jim leaned over and whispered with a teasing tone..."Yah, but Amanda's in the Chair Force (his nickname for Air Force)!"

They decided they would get married as soon as he was released from the military. She put in her last day of work on October 15th and drove to Ft Benning where he was still u treatment.

Sweet tea and brownies

They got married on October 20th in a rather funny series of events. They were going to get married at the courthouse, but when Jim called his pastor, he said even though it was Bible study night and people would be there, he could marry them right then and there.

Jim called Carol with, "We can get married tonight." The only one who knew they were getting married was Carol's daughter, Amanda. They knew their other children couldn't attend because they lived all over the place. Amanda just happened to call from Germany, so Carol told her the news.

'What!!!' Amanda shouted over the phone. 'Have you got your nails done? Are you going to get your hair done? What are you going to wear? Is he going to get flowers?'

'I don't know! He's not going to see my feet anyway and he doesn't care!'

Amanda was off the charts! 'What are you going to do?'

'I can fix my own hair.'

'No, you can't!'

Well, yes, she did! Jim came with flowers and Carol picked out something to wear.

He smiled, "We wore our Sunday clothes."

Carol said, "We went over to the church and those in the Bible study were our witnesses." The Bible study group added a special touch by hosting a little reception with sweet tea and brownies.

I cried through the whole thing." "I didn't cry for my first wedding. I 'shoulda' cried and run out the door! At my first wedding, I was standing at the back of the church and the thought was going through my mind, 'You don't have to do this. You don't have to do this. You can leave. You can turn around and run out. You can leave.' I didn't listen. This time, I didn't hear, 'Turn around and leave'," she laughed. "I think I was so overwhelmed that this man loved me."

The next night they were out for dinner when his Mother called. 'Did you get married yet?'

'Yah, we're married,' and she hung up.

Carol said, "When she hung up, she got on the phone and told everybody before we had a chance. His kids were angry we didn't tell them."

He added, "We were supposed to at least give them a heads up it was coming. I never even told anybody except my Mom that I had proposed to Carol."

She l smiled as she continued the story, "Earlier, when he went out to Colorado, he was happy and smiling and people asked: 'What's wrong with you?' He finally told them he had my ring." Evidently, he didn't give them a clue about when that ring would go on Carol's finger! Within seconds of hanging up the phone with Jim's Mother, there was a barrage of phone calls. Carol put it on Facebook and got all these hits immediately. That's when she got more 'You should have told us' comments!

Carol laughed as she said, "They were acting like we're were the kids and just did it at the spur of the moment. And...the whole business of being an internet romance!" We can definitely say, this time around Carol and Jim were anything but traditional!

Now she could send hearts...

Remember Jim's aversion to receiving any hearts in the cards he received from Carol? After he proposed, and went back to the Army post, Carol sent him a card filled with a whole bunch of punched out hearts.

"I opened up the envelope and all these hearts come falling out. 'Ok...she's making up for lost time'!" Together they grinned at the memory.

Who said challenges?

"When he asked me to marry him, I realized he still loved his ex-wife."

Jim interjected, "And I still...I don't dislike her. I felt sorry for her because I figured her whole reason for leaving me was because of my going away. She's the one that actually urged me to go on the first military mission. I said, 'I'm going to be gone for eighteen months. Now that's a lonnnng time'." He got his family together and met with the people of his church and they were all supportive. "So, I did...I volunteered for it. That's why it was a surprise to me."

"I knew he still had love for his first wife. 'OK, can I live with that? Will I always feel like I'm second best?' I realized that Jim loved me but when we first got married, he talked a lot about his ex-wife."

"Like she had died....," Jim said. "that's more how it was to me."

Carol looked over at Jim, "One night we were in bed and you started talking about her. I honestly felt like she was laying between us in the bed and I said, 'I don't care if you talk about her at breakfast. I don't care if you talk about her on the couch. But I don't want to hear about her when we're lying in bed because I feel like she is right there between us.' You looked at me a little surprised and went, 'Oh...that's reasonable'." She laughed, "And that was the last time that ever happened." In the eight years of their marriage, Carol said he talks about her less and less.

About her first marriage, Carol said, "I don't feel like I was bitter but there was still a lot of hurt. There have been tears...because if I talk about it, I will cry." She broke down in tears for several minutes before continuing, "Jim showed me the love of Christ." She wiped tears from her eyes, and said, "It's different being married to Jim. We talk about everything."

Jim teased, "Sometimes when people ask us how long we've been married. I'll say, 'over 30 years...just not to each other'."

Carol would look at other couples and remembers thinking, 'I wish I had a husband who would stand by me in church. They're so good together! Why can't I have that?' "And now...God has given me the desire of my heart."

Pain and grief piled on

Another challenge they both faced was the results of Jim suffering from PTSD (post-traumatic stress disorder). Jim accepted his diagnosis of PTSD but didn't like that term because he felt it wasn't adequate. "Police, firemen and emergency personnel can experience some horrible things," he continued, "but there is something different (in the military) about people wanting to kill you and knowing that's your job to go face people who want to kill you. Every day, there was someone outside the wire that wanted to kill me. We just lived under that awareness and that has a different kind of a strain."

As a chaplain, he was professionally trained to help soldiers ward off PTSD. In civilian life, he was part of a team that went to fire and ambulance departments to assist with PTSD. "Soldiers have a different kind of a depression and grief than what you see in the civilian world. I look back at some of the pictures she had of me and I think, 'Wow...I did look like I came out of a prisoner of war camp."

Jim served for two tours in Iraq of twelve months each and a nineteen-month tour in Afghanistan. "PTSD already began on my first deployment. It was emotionally very, very strenuous. I had civilian training to deal with PTSD and when that was discovered, they actually put me in charge whenever there was a line of duty death or catastrophic injury. Humvee blown up or something like that. They would bring that crew in to me and I would talk with them and do the debriefing. I was not prepared to deal with that...about 130 soldiers over that years' time. I soaked up a tremendous amount of anger and grief..."

After his first tour, Jim said, "When I was ready to come home. It was to the aftermath of Hurricane Katrina and I ended up having an extended tour to New Orleans. The living conditions there were worse than anything I had seen overseas. There were 25,000 soldiers in a convention bay. Fights...all kinds of stuff."

On his military deployment, he survived several rocket attacks and an ambush but no matter where he was stationed, as a chaplain, he could only fight the enemy by watching and listening to soldiers. One thing after another was piling onto to his sagging emotional shoulders. "Then, of course, with my wife filing for divorce...I came home and didn't have a home. I lived at a homeless shelter until I found a one room boarding house where I had to pay cash on the barrel to stay there each week.

I was a reservist in the National Guard, but I couldn't find a job. No church was going to call me to be a pastor as long as I had this divorce pending. I got this idea that if I would slow the divorce down, maybe she would reconsider....so, I volunteered for another tour." His voice took on a more serious tone, "When I came home from my second deployment, I had already been taking medicine for depression from the first deployment. I started having trouble with language. I spent three months at Ft Knox getting my head put together."

After a slight pause he said, "The divorce was finalized, and I still didn't have a job. Still didn't have a place that was home. My brother let me stay with him for a while.

So, I called up Washington, DC and volunteered to go back. They sent me to Afghanistan. Then, I was actually physically injured. I was in a vehicle roll over and got my head hit and got a TBI (traumatic brain injury). I came home, and they put me in the hospital in this Warrior Transition Unit. I spent nine months in that recovery unit. I had to have language therapy, physical therapy, cognitive therapy. All kinds of stuff they put me through before they would let me go home. When I came home, there was still the PTSD I was dealing with. It was just something I learned to live with...that constant feeling of grief, sadness, sorrow."

Looking at her husband, Carol said, "I knew he had PTSD, but I didn't know what it was. Since we've been married, he had a couple of PTSD episodes which were big challenges and stressful." She got a call from the ER one day saying, 'I think we have your husband over here and he's having an episode.' She remarked, "That's only happened a couple of times at home. That's definitely for better or for worse and it wasn't any reason I was going to leave him. The possibility of those things happening are always there. Going to counseling has helped to deal with it."

She has never known me how I was before

Jim said, "The biggest challenge I faced was because of my mental condition. I didn't want to go anywhere, I didn't like to go out of the house, I didn't want to do anything. She helped me with that. She would say, 'Do you want to go shopping?' My first thought would be, 'NO' and then I would think...'I need to get out'. She helped me and still helps me to want to go out, otherwise I would just as soon stay in. She was actually a big part of helping me recover because I also had someone I could talk to and it didn't have to be about combat."

Carol looked over at him, "I met him how he was then and fell in love with how he was then."

"She has never known me how I was before."

Did everything together

Jim started, "The greatest blessing is that I have a friend and I don't feel like she has unreasonable expectations. We're not just single people living in a house to-gether. We have a close relationship. It doesn't require a sexual nature because one of the problems I have...that goes with my condition. Between the medicine I take and the mental condition...it's not a thing. That was never a part of our relationship in the first place. We're very intimate with each other...cuddly, hugging and kissing. I have someone who admires me, likes me and fusses over me."

"He said he wasn't used to getting 'smooched on' all the time." She reached over and planted a big kiss on his cheek as they both broke down in laughter. "It's a blessing that we enjoy each other's company. We are not only lovers; we're friends."

When they moved to Indiana, there was no family near. and they never really made friends who invited them to do things together. Carol said, "We did everything together because..."

"...there was nobody else to do it with!" Jim said as they both broke into full faced grins.

Carol said, "We didn't have traditional dating, so we made a good foundation."

He added to her comment, "Because there wasn't this hot and heavy time...it was like we continued a gentle, easy going relationship."

"Our relationship," Carol said, "comes first. Our relationship with the Lord comes first but I mean, our relationship is above a relationship with kids, or friends. We're first for each other."

What do you appreciate?

Jim said very seriously, "I appreciate her hair." They both burst out laughing as those trademark teasing dimples appeared on his face.

"The first thing I appreciate about him is his relationship with the Lord. That's really important. I wish you could hear him preach because other people knowing about Jesus is important to him. I've learned so much. He has a wonderful sense of humor that he can make me laugh. Sometimes, too much," she giggled and looked over at Jim smiling.

"I appreciate that she appreciates me. It's a guy thing. I like being useful. I like having purpose and she says, 'You are valuable.' She affirms me. I don't need it to exist. I've learned to be my own man and don't have my identity wrapped up in what other people think about me but the fact that she is very supportive and very affectionate and fusses over me. Little things like trimming the hair in my ears." Carol teasingly hit his arm. "There's nothing I NEED from her but there are all these things she does...just are extras I appreciate and enjoy. I also am comfortable knowing my issues are not unsolvable problems for her and she is able to cope with me."

I could lose him!

"It was very hard when he went through open heart surgery because it suddenly occurred to me that I could lose him. When you get married and you're young, you think you have your whole lifetime together. When you get married in your 50's, as Ian, my oldest son, put it: 'Well Mom, you two might as well get married, you only have a few years left anyway.' We've had eight good years. Last year, it suddenly hit me, I could lose him.

I have this thing. I have to get all my scrapbooks done before I die. When the possibility of death was actually at our house, I didn't see him scurrying around trying to get things gone. He was not even worried about any 'let's get all the scrapbooks done' kind of things. I think he was ready to go. He was more like, 'If I die, I'm going to be with Jesus. I'm not worried about it'. That was eye opening for me. At first, I was distraught inside but actually before he had the surgery, I had peace about it. I didn't want him to die but if he did, I knew where he was going and somehow it would be all right."

The two became...

We could see how two totally different personalities, with heart wounds, head wounds and spirit wounds, had taken the broken and weak parts and combined them together to become a 'stronger body of one'! Neither of them expected the other to be everything or do everything. They are willing to be and do whatever is needed at the time to love and encourage each other.

'Normal' got snatched...again! (Two years after initial interview)

Life is fragile. They know this more than many. The day we began to put words from their video interview onto paper, w got a message saying Jim was involved in a motorcycle accident and had suffered severe spinal cord injuries. His spine was almost completely severed at T4 which means he is able to move his arms and hands but will never walk again. Carol's comment on Facebook following the accident was: "Our lives will be changing dramatically."

Jim finished months of intensive therapy and rehabilitation and was released to return home. Some changes have been made to their home, including a ramp, a lift and an electric wheelchair. Carol was right. Their lives will never be the same. There is much Jim is no longer able to do for himself, so Carol has become his main care giver.

Never leave!

It takes us back to these words spoken by Carol during their initial interview: "I'm with him. He knows I am with him no matter what. There isn't <u>anything</u> he could do that would cause me to leave. And I know he's not going to leave me."

Carol's words of commitment to Jim those many months earlier were not just words. They were a pledge and a promise to God and to Jim. Words she would soon live out in every day of their lives.

Yes, their normal got snatched more than once! PTSD. Traumatic brain injury. Divorce. Motorcycle accident. They have had more than their share of tough stuff marauding like a herd of wild horses into their lives!

Jim made us laugh in their original interview when he said, "Both of our marriages blew up!" We think this marriage blew up, too! Only it blew up with more love and a greater commitment...no matter how many times they have had to adjust to a 'new normal'!

Floyd & Marcia – Didn't Know If We'd Make It!

MARRIED 44 YEARS

"He is the Rock, His works are perfect, and all His ways are just. A faithful God who does no wrong, upright and just is He." Deuteronomy 32:4

F ell in love with their own love story

At the conclusion of their interview, we thanked Floyd and Marcia for sharing their story because someone needed to hear it.

Floyd said, "We needed to hear it ourselves! It confirmed...it gave an exclamation point to our story."

We thought maybe...maybe...as they relived it, they fell in love with their own story all over again.

God's design

Marcia looked over at Floyd, "We know it's God's story and He's the One who ordained all of this to happen, so it's not our design but God's."

Floyd agreed, "I can say it was a work of the mighty hand of God."

It might be difficult for some to understand how both of them, being divorced, could be part of God's design but Floyd went on to explain, "I do not advocate divorce for anyone because marriage is supposed to be for life." However, they both understood how God used their previous marriages as an extremely important part of their life experience. Through that difficult part of their lives, God would help them make the changes and adjustments they would need for <u>this</u> marriage. He used their pasts to shape them for their future together.

A terrible beginning

Floyd rushed in with how their lives together began. "That's a terrible story. We met in a bar!" Marcia laughed as he went on to say, "I was quite inebriated." Since he was single, it seems a friend wanted to introduce this lonely bachelor to someone. So, there he stood in front of what Floyd described as 'this wonderfully attractive, young woman'.

"In spite of my condition, we hit it off and I asked her for her phone number. She reluctantly gave it to me. I called her the next day, when I was sober, and she actually agreed to go out on a date."

Marcia shook her head as if in crazy disagreement. Then, she went on to tell us how it <u>really</u> happened: "We did meet in a bar. My friend introduced us. I could tell he was not sober. I was probably polite but not overly so. So that was it. He went to the bathroom and I went home. A few nights later, my friend and I came back to the bar and Floyd was there. I think he was intentionally sober that night, so, he came over and introduced himself again. We had an amiable conversation and I reluctantly gave him my phone number because I didn't really want anybody to know it. A couple of nights later we had our first date."

Two versions of the story ended with the same result...a first date.

Family date

Their first official date was bowling, which by the way, included Marcia's three children and Floyd's daughter. They both broke into snickering as Floyd looked over at Marcia, "You embarrassed me with your score."

She smiled, "I got a 200...by accident!"

Romance built

They continued to date and as they got to know each other better, the romance began to build. "He told me on the second date he wanted to ask me to marry him."

Referring to his more than speedy declaration of intent, Floyd teased with that innocent smile of his, "Well, I'm ashamed of myself!"

"After we spent many long hours really getting acquainted, talking over early breakfast and late into the night. It was a feeling, knowledge...whatever you want to call it...that we were supposed to be together."

Floyd said, "We emptied out our 'closets' to each other. We went out into long, deep conversations about our past experiences, past marriages and what we wanted for the future."

They both shyly smiled as Marcia said, "From the time we met until we got married was six weeks!"

Our shocked reaction: "Six weeks!!!"

She was the target!

She knew without a doubt what attracted her to Floyd. "I can tell you! He was an older guy and I was a single Mom with three children. He was stable. He was an Army officer and he had a career. He was not a kid and basically, I had previously been involved with immature guys. I saw in him stability and, honestly, my feelings were: 'This man could be a good Dad for my three children.' That's what made me feel I could marry him. I wasn't in love and that didn't come until about a year or so into our marriage when I really understood what love was all about."

On Floyd's third consecutive military tour to Southeast Asia his previous marriage ended. Of course, that opened the door when Marcia came into his life.

She teased, "I was the target!"

They laughed even though Floyd quickly retorted, "I wasn't going to say target."

Marcia also felt he was just the kind of guy who couldn't stay unmarried. He needed to be with someone. And she was that someone!

Not the first time around the block

Coming from previous marriages, when they made the decision to get married, they both knew what they did and didn't want in a mate.

Floyd had a hint of sadness in his voice as he related that his first wife had emotional and mental problems causing her to be admitted to a psychiatric hospital for six weeks. That experience caused him to become more cautious of any women he met.

His smile brightened, "Marcia was a young attractive woman to whom I had been properly introduced. It was very natural. I didn't see anything I didn't like. It just seemed to be what it ought to be. It still is after all these years."

Count the blessings

"The biggest blessing in our marriage," Marcia said, "was that the Lord called us to Himself about four and a half years after we were married. I think another blessing is that we were best friends. A lot of couples do not seek friendship or are in lust instead of in love. We built a friendship and I think that is what has maintained us through all these years."

When Floyd mentally tried to count the blessings, he said, "How much time do we have?" He continued, "We didn't know what God was doing at the time but after we became Christians, we could look back and see God's hand in every step. The first blessing is compatibility and mutuality. We were one, easily. We believed the same things. Our ideas about children's discipline were the same. We talked, communicated about everything...that was the key. Beyond that there was real love."

Not an easy road

It took a split second after we said the word 'challenge' for Floyd to say, "Kids!"

Early in their marriage, Floyd's 12-year-old daughter came to live with them. Marcia also had a 12-year-old daughter. She said, "Those two were..."

Floyd finished her sentence, "...conspiring!"

"They were constantly jealous of each other of or the other ones' parent," Marcia observed. "There was constant strife and competition!"

They now had a combined total of four children. (You might call that 'parents outnumbered'!) It seems if one of the kids didn't think of something, the other did.

In their experience, Marcia said, "Sometimes, blending families can be difficult beyond belief! We weren't the Brady Bunch and there were times I was just about at my wits end!" They had no option but to turn to each other for support. "Even so, there were limited things Floyd could do as a stepfather."

"As step-Dad, I was sort of an outsider - an add-on to the family. I didn't have a lot of authority, so that was a challenge of 'great proportions'!"

When they were assigned to Germany with the military, Marcia's two daughters decided to stay behind with their Dad. "When we left for overseas, just a few months into our marriage...", Marcia's smile faded, "we had to leave the country without my two oldest children. My dear husband was so kind and compassionate, always ready to do whatever would help me through that difficult separation. That was the hardest thing I had ever done, but they both soon were back in my life."

Sinking for the last time

There was so much jealousy and competition in their home, but, Marcia said, "The main thing is that God was not in our lives. We had no anchor. I think it was at that turning point of my life, when I was really sinking for the last time when God pulled me up."

It was then Marcia surrendered and gave her life to Christ. Floyd was kind and went to church with her. He even encouraged her in her faith but claimed he didn't need it. Marcia grinned, "But the point was, the Lord needed him." Six months later, Floyd gave his life, too.

Anything change?

"Big changes," Marcia said. "I'm sure the children all observed different parents. I don't know that they were completely happy about it, but they all went to church with us. I don't think it was a life changing situation for any of them, but our home life changed. We were no longer relying on our own understanding. We were leaning on God."

Eventually, this blended family became a blessing as Marcia shared that Floyd adopted her youngest (Floyd thinks <u>she</u> adopted him.) "All three call him Dad."

Life spared

"Eight days after Floyd became a Christian (within the first five years of their marriage), his colon ruptured, and he almost died. And...God keeps sparing Floyd's life!"

He's the Energizer Bunny™. He's fallen from a ladder and broken his ankle in five places. He has fallen from the second story of a home under construction, to the basement through the stairwell and survived with nothing but bruises and a minor fracture in his spine. BUT because of CT scans, it revealed he had an abdominal aortic aneurysm. Floyd reminded us a rupture of that aneurysm would have been fatal, so it was immediately repaired. It was the fall that saved him...again!

However, that wasn't the end! He has had an unplanned pacemaker followed by a quintuple heart bypass. He teased, "For an old coot in my 80s, I tell people, 'I'm vertical and mobile'....and in love! I'm blessed!"

The medical challenges Floyd faced were not faced alone. Marcia walked right beside him and said, "It has been total reliance upon God."

They want to tell you...

"Trust in the Lord in all your ways and He will guide your paths," Floyd paraphrased Proverbs 3:5.

Marcia would tell you, "If you are a believer, do not marry someone who is not a believer. That's almost doomed to failure. Do not marry someone who isn't your best friend. Above all, be best friends first. Too many people can get into a marriage and find they really don't like their spouse. They might love them...but you have to like your spouse, too."

Floyd added, "I don't think we realized we had become best friends until it already happened when we were well into our marriage."

Marcia stressed premarital counseling for every couple. "I think every couple and family, should be completely devoted to reading the Scriptures and praying together. I think that's really key in raising a Godly family."

Floyd didn't want to leave out one key he felt essential in marriage, "Be really aware of the other person's feelings, emotions and expressions. They might say something or do something out of the ordinary, so it is like waving a white flag." He gave his arm a wide swoop over his head to demonstrate someone crying...'I need help! Pay attention to me!' "You've got be able to attend to those signals. Be aware."

They ended their advice with Floyd speaking candidly about compromise. "You're glad to do it. It isn't like you're giving up something that really hurts. Because of love, I would yield to her and she would yield to me. The vow to love, honor, obey...you've got to be ready to really do it."

Relationship barometer

When asked about the state of their marriage, Floyd didn't hesitate to indicate their relationship barometer pointed out they were always growing.

Marcia tenderly added, "It deepens, especially as you start seeing old age approaching. This is your life's partner. This is someone you want to live with the rest of your days. You care about them...it doesn't stop when you get sick. It doesn't stop when your money is short or whatever the circumstances. You are in it for the long haul. God doesn't take your vows lightly."

Living their vows

At one point in their marriage, Marcia remembered thinking, "I didn't know if we'd make it! I didn't know how much we could take!" They didn't have to be sure they could make it, because Jesus was sure enough for both of them. He never quit on them and they never said 'quit' either. That was a vow they made over 40+ years ago and they continue to live that vow today!

Anonymous – I Stepped Over the Line!

"But the Lord God says, 'See, I am placing a Foundation Stone in Zion—a firm, tested, precious Cornerstone that is safe to build on. He who believes need never run away again'."
Isaiah 28:16 (TLB)

It takes courage for anyone to open wide the door or even allow others to gaze through the windows into their homes and hearts. There are times when professional reputation or personal preference call for some interviews to be done anonymously. This is one of them.

You don't have to...

As the interview began, he struggled with his emotions and his words. His wife looked over at him with compassion, "You don't have to if you don't want to."

"I'm trying to figure out how to say it..." He looked up as he began, "I put something in front of my wife that would challenge any person to ask, 'Do I want to stay married to him.' I allowed myself to be curious enough about a relationship with another individual who was a divorcee." He explained how they often worked together on projects and eventually he felt she gave signals she wanted to be even closer to him.

He took a slow breath in, "One night after a meeting, she came into my office and we talked a little bit. Too much silent time happened and there we were. I allowed myself to cross a boundary, a physical boundary of kissing her. I have no idea why. I didn't love her like 'this is the love of my life'. Not at all, because I wanted to be married my whole life to my wife. I didn't want that to be different, but temptation was there... and...I crossed that boundary."

That can never happen again!

He took a deeper breath as he continued, "I remember going home that night and feeling like, 'Well, that's something that can't ever happen again.' It was something I wasn't planning on saying anything about to my wife. When I got home...I don't know if it was the way I was acting, or your intuition..."

He looked over to speak to his wife, "And you said something like, 'What's going on'?" He seemed to push himself to continue, "Right away, I was put in a place where I wasn't ready to keep on lying. I felt like it was put before me and I needed to say something...and I did."

She began slowly, "I just noticed a change in him. There was something about him. It wasn't just when he came home that night. It was what I noticed recently, so I ended up asking him. That night, he told me some of the most hurtful things. He said he really cared for her." At that point, all she could think in response was, 'And, what does that mean for us'?

Crushed

"I was crushed. In my marriage, I would never in my wildest dreams think that something like this would ever happen! I didn't have a lot of boyfriends before my husband, but I prayed for a man who would love the Lord and love me. When this happened, I was devastated!"

Her painful account continued, "Once the kids were in bed, I spent a lot of my time in the walk-in closet, on the floor in the dark...crying because I just didn't know where to go. I kept thinking, 'I'm not good enough! I've never been good enough'!"

"I did that for weeks. That's why the house wasn't cleaned." They laughed together over the memory of their messy home during that excruciating period of time.

With tears filling her eyes, she spoke quietly, "I just didn't know what to do. I had nowhere to go. I couldn't call my Mom because I didn't want her to think bad of him. I was also very protective of him. I didn't want him to lose his job, so I knew I couldn't tell anyone."

When asked how she dealt with the secrecy, she said, "I talked to myself a lot about my life. I kept busy with the kids. You just go on...even when you can't talk about it! I know I was carried (by God)."

Broken trust

With sadness creeping across her face, she said, "I didn't know if I could believe that it was just a kiss." Her voice trailed off, "I wanted to believe it but for a long time...but...I didn't know..."

Once composed, she added, "Before this happened, we were so in touch with each other. We could answer each other's sentences. I knew what he was thinking. This changed everything! I didn't know any more what I thought I knew about him."

Their world was turned upside down! It seemed as if the truth she once knew could no longer be trusted to be the truth. As a result, she became very adept at 'faking it'. She developed the ability to leave everyone around her with the pretense of her sincere happiness, even when doubt crowded into every thought in her mind and in her heart. Despite the smiles on the outside, her mind was tormented with the question: 'Can I trust him?'

Decision time

They came to a crossroads where a decision had to be made. "I didn't know if I should leave. I didn't know if I should stay. I didn't know if I should just take a vacation and leave him with the kids and let him see what it's like," she laughed lightly. "I didn't know. Then I decided maybe I wasn't being intimate enough, so I would be more intimate so maybe he would love me more. That was really hard because I don't know that my heart was in it, but I didn't want to lose my marriage. I wanted him to love me."

Her choices became, "Do we become a statistic, or do we choose our marriage?" She had experienced so much divorce in her own family, she knew she didn't want that for her life. Her ultimate choice was to stay and work on their relationship.

He came to realize the relationship with the other woman wasn't going anywhere and yet, he wasn't readily willing to tell the other woman to move out of his life. There was a professional relationship with her and on a personal level he didn't want her to feel like he was using her. He knew this relationship was wrong but admitted he was reluctant to put a close to it. He said, "It lingered just long enough to inflict some damage." It was easy to tell his admission was painful for his wife to hear.

Speaking to his wife he said, "I probably didn't want to hurt her (the other woman) and I think it was really hard for you because it made me seem wishy washy. It let you think that maybe I was entertaining the idea of going off in another relationship. Obviously if the shoe was on the other foot, it would kill me...and yet, I did this to you. I am blessed that the boundaries beyond just that kiss were maintained, but in some ways, that didn't seem to matter. It was still a boundary that was broken. A person can forgive, but I can't expect somebody to forget that."

Even though roughly 25 years have passed, it obvious how this wound between them was still tender to the touch. He looked down slightly as he explained, "Every once in a while, it comes up as a hurt and I think there is forgiveness. We talk through it and everything, but that sense of 'how could that happen' is still there."

Happy face – Sad heart

Her eyes saddened, "I think I've learned to hide a lot of things. I think I've been good at that a lot of my life...to give a good impression. I don't think anybody who knew us thought that anything was off." She became proficient at putting on a happy face so no one would see inside to her sad and broken heart.

What changed?

She came to realize she couldn't take her marriage for granted. She needed to put time and effort into it. She looked over at her husband and said, "Being crushed taught me that he's human." In a tender moment, he put his arm around her as she said, "And it took you off this pedestal I had you on, which was probably a good thing."

What didn't change?

With a strained look on her face, she told us the thing that didn't change: "The other woman didn't go away. Arrangements were made so they didn't work together any longer, but she was definitely still in the picture." She eventually arranged to meet with the other woman, who also happened to be a friend. She confronted her but even though the woman said she knew it was wrong, she admitted she cared for him. This was a pain that kept on giving and giving.

She smiled at the most important thing that didn't change, "Christ is the cornerstone of our marriage!" She knew He was the firm foundation upon which their marriage was built and that would never change.

God held us!

At first, she went to counseling alone and then they went together. "That's a time when God held us through it. It's knowing Christ died for me and has forgiven me for all my sins. He also gives me the opportunity to share that forgiveness as well (with my husband)."

"For me," he began, "I think the same commitment to marriage was there. People talk about soul mates. I don't necessarily buy into the soul mate kind of stuff. To me, you learn your commitment with that person you are married to…whoever that person is. When you make the commitment, you make the commitment. Commitment to marriage is something that holds."

Path toward healing

"I realized my husband was not perfect (and neither was I) but he was forgiven. When I was hurting, I learned to concentrate less on me and tried to understand what he was lacking. I asked, 'What can I do' more than I asked, 'What do I want him to do?'"

What would you say?

When asked what she would tell a young wife who came to her with this same story, her answer was: "You are at a crossroads. What do you want to do? It always takes two. Does your husband want to make your marriage work?"

He gave a one-word answer: "Forgive."

"I made mistakes, too…", she admitted. "Just different mistakes. Accept each other's differences and know God will bless your marriage."

Healing from a broken trust or a broken heart isn't over quickly. She would remind that young wife, "It takes time to learn to live in your new normal. It takes time for healing. It's all been forgiven, but it took me years and years not to bring it up."

"I'm grateful for what we journey through." He turned his head and as he spoke directly to her, "and that you are here and committed. Many things aren't perfect and maybe not always good but there are a lot of blessings we share. We share a lot of good life."

She smiled, "Any hope I have has to start with the hope God gives to me."

How could this be good?

She believes the Scripture from Romans 8:28 to be true. It says, 'And we know that in all things God works for the good of those who love Him, who have been called according to His purpose.' Believe that to be true? Yes, she does! However, it wasn't an instant fix.   She spent many years along the way wondering how something that felt this painful could ever be good.

About a year after giving this interview, we spoke again and there was a sense her heart had lightened. She spoke about how she now understood that sharing this broken part of her life could possibly bring good by encouraging other women who might be living through her same journey.

When the foundation shakes...

The earth trembled beneath their feet and the cause...this event...could not be undone. However, when the foundation of their marriage began to crumble, it was commitment to Jesus and to each other that held them together! Through the shaking and rumbling, God was indeed the Cornerstone of their marriage and will continue to be no matter what storm threatens!

Phil & Vickie – Their Deeper Love Came With a Cost

MARRIED 58 YEARS

"I have told you these things, so that in me you may have peace. In this world you will have trouble. But take heart! I have overcome the world." John 16:33

W hen we remarked on their 58 years of marriage, Vicki's laughter rolled out into the room, "Yes, that's a big Wow! It's only God's grace!"

Phil paused before he spoke. "For better or worse. I had no clue what that meant. In those 58 years, there have been a lot of 'betters' and there have been a lot of 'worses'. Vicki was 19 and I was 24. I don't think we had any idea what the next 58 years were going to be like or what they might bring."

Mom picked him

Vickie rolled her eyes, "I had no idea about life...period. I was a very young and immature at 19. I don't know if I could have survived on my own at that time."

Phil remembered when he came to the door of her parents' home, Vickie's mother claimed when he rang the bell, she felt like an angel tapped her on the shoulder and said: 'This is the one'!

Well, Mom might have known he was the one, but Vickie wasn't so sure. 'He's the one!', was a mighty huge claim for a blind date! (And Vickie didn't even do blind dates!)

No huge fireworks for him either, but he proudly announced, "There were probably a couple more dates because three weeks later...we got engaged!" That's when their hysterical outburst encompassed us!

Vickie contained her composure long enough to tell us her brother was getting married and she thought she probably got caught up in all the excitement. Not only did they have an abbreviated friendship, they had a six-month engagement...something she would not recommend!

Communicating...or not

Their greatest challenge, according to Phil, was communicating.

"He didn't communicate..."

"But I was cool...", quipped Phil.

"If I talked emotions, he would push that away," she demonstrated by pushing both hands away from her chest. "That actually set us up for many lonely years. I think we were married ten years before we really could talk to each other about something that was meaningful." Phil nodded his head in silent agreement as she continued. "We talked about kids. We could talk about life but nothing that involved emotion. It was very lonely." During that time, Vickie admitted to suffering from emotional separation and isolation.

Something changed

Phil was taking a class at work that trained staff how to communicate with their peers, employees or supervisors. He thought it was just part of his job, but Vickie's view differed, "I feel like that was God...pure and simple."

She remembered him coming home from work one night and pulling their stools up in front of the dishwasher. He talked non-stop...just like the floodgates opened. "I'm looking at him and thinking, 'What is this? Who is this?' It was nothing I had done or tried to make happen. It was something that was provided at work, and it gave him tools to be able to talk. It was just amazing. I think that was probably one of the biggest miracles..."

Phil completed her sentence, "...that was a serious breakthrough in our relationship!"

He didn't want to hear anything about it!

Vickie said, "When I heard you could have Jesus in your heart, it settled it all for me. I was so thrilled. I understood. I became a Christian and then it became even lonelier, because he didn't want to know anything about Christ or being a Christian."

"You tried to tell me..."

"Yes, I did, and you said, 'Don't shove that down my throat!' I don't want to hear this!' If I had taken up golf, he would have wanted to hear all about it, but this was a spiritual thing and he didn't want to hear anything about it. I kept on going to church and praying and people were praying for him." It went on for 14 years and things began to change little by little. That's when Mark, a young pastor who lived down the street asked Phil to play basketball.

Phil loved basketball so that began their relationship. "One day Mark asked me, 'So, what do you think about the Lord?' I said, 'Well, Vickie does that.' I got out of his truck so, that was the end of that...at least for then." Even when Phil thought that was the end of that...Mark's friendship and God's spirit continued working in Phil's heart.

A rock marks the day

They have a rock located outside their house by their walkway. If you look closely, you will see written, April 10, 1983. That was the day they were sitting in church and the guy giving the message said, 'If you died today, do you know that you would go to heaven?' That question broke through the independent spirit surrounding Phil. He had always been able to do everything on his own, but right then he realized he couldn't. He stood in response to the invitation, however, Vickie had her head down, so she didn't see him respond. It seems everyone else did.

Vickie said, "Everyone came running. I got knocked out of the way! They had been praying and praying for Phil. Before that, I always felt like I had been alone. I felt like I was pretty isolated...even though people knew me, and I knew them."

She smiled, "Then, things changed. It was a real miracle!"

Phil broke into laughter as he said, "I was convinced that if I can be saved, there is nobody on earth that can't be saved!" They believe that one day had the greatest impact on his life and their marriage!

Regrets

Phil worked in the city, so he left for work about six and didn't get back home until seven or later most days...something Phil regretted. That left Vickie at home alone with three young boys.

Their middle son, Michael had been gone from home for about 20 years when he told his Dad he noticed how he was a different Dad to him than he was to John, his brother 13 years younger. Phil looked over at Vickie and said, "I always thought I was a pretty good Dad, but Michael noted the extreme change and said, 'It's not fair, Dad! Why weren't you like that when we were little'?"

Vickie looked over at Phil and encouraged him with the reminder of some good times with their older sons. "The older boys would go play basketball with Phil and his buddies. This one guy said, 'Yah...he comes in and runs rings around us with these two kids.' That was fun. It was good for them."

The older boys, Stephen and Michael, were a year and a half apart. Phil said, "The older boys ...I was gone a lot. The older guys had to deal with me the way I was. With John it was a lot different." There may be regrets, but it is apparent all three have a great relationship with their Dad today. "I love them dearly and I believe they love me equally."

Sparks fly

Phil admitted their marriage wasn't perfect. "We still have the communication challenges..."

"Oh yes, we do...."

"Sometimes I hear something a different way than she intends it and vice versa..."

"And sparks fly!"

When speaking about arguments, he said, "I say something and then she comes back and then I have to come back." He made motions with hands as if climbing a ladder. "So, there's that escalation phenomenon." He told us he learned somewhere along the line, if he can just stay there without climbing up that next step, the argument can be diffused.

Neither walked out

She matter-of-factly reported how many times she wanted to give up when she said, "MANY!"

Shaking his head back and forth, he described it as, "Often...Often...Often. Yes...often!"

When asked why she stayed, Vickie said, "I felt like I never had any place to go. My parents didn't want me back," she giggled.

Phil's response was a little more practical. "Where am I going to go and be able to afford to live on my own and still pay for them?" He looked over at his wife, "So, for me, those thoughts didn't last. We would get into a fuss and I don't know if I said it out loud as often, but I thought: 'This is it! I've done all I can do! I'm out of here'!" Phil said he always talked himself back out of it.

In a calm voice, Vickie said, "I can remember days like that when he said, 'I'm leaving you'."

His adamant response, "I never said that! I said: 'Do you want me to leave'?"

They laughed together as Vickie teased, "No one ever left...but he traveled a lot!"

Phil shook his head back and forth, "We said we got married for better - for worse. There was a lot of those kinds of 'worse', but in spite of those, we did have that commitment to each other."

Vicki added, "And to our children, too."

He whole heartedly agreed, "And to our children. That kept me from walking out the door...or her from walking out the door."

Through worse

They had plenty of 'betters' but some of their 'worse' came in waves of pain.

They got a call saying their oldest son, Stephen, was experiencing a horrendous headache. It was so painful he was banging his head on the wall. After several visits to physicians, his wife, Jessica (then his girlfriend), got through to the emergency room where they found he had a tumor. It had grown so much it had eroded the orbital bone around the eye.

Phil winced, "That was horrible. They did this craniotomy, so they could do the biopsy." He was in intensive care about five days. His condition deteriorated to the point that he was drooling and would fall asleep mid-chew when eating. It was finally decided he would need to have the tumor removed. Phil explained, "They did a double craniotomy," and demonstrated with his hands over his skull how they popped off both sides of his skull. The laser surgeon was going to cut that thing out but told us afterwards that he looked at it and it was about the size of a grape. He went in there with his thumbs and just coached it out. "He said, 'I'm pretty sure I got 100% of it'."

Vickie exclaimed, "What surgeon says that? Ever...ever...?" After surgery when Vickie looked at his forehead she remarked, 'Steve, you got a facelift for free!' That even got a chuckle out of him.

There were so many miracles surrounding them. Stephen had no medical insurance but the county where he resided had a program that would pay medical bills of uninsured individuals. They took care of it all.

Phil said there were guys in San Quentin Prison, some nuns in Russia and people they never met who were praying for their son. Vickie said, "Just amazing...just amazing! That united prayer. That's what got us through."

Stephen still experiences some double vision but has learned to live with it. Phil said, "He probably doesn't even think about it anymore."

Can it get any worse?

About three years later, their youngest son, John, went out to ride a motorcycle he had rebuilt with a friend. Phil and Vickie didn't like motorcycles and had talked to him about it.

'I'll be careful, Dad.'

He and a friend were heading to watch a motorcycle race, and as they were getting off the onramp to the freeway, the friend saw John's bike come sliding past him without John.

When he realized what happened, he quickly moved his bike around and blocked freeway traffic. John was laying out in the middle of the road and even though he looked fine, he wasn't talking or moving.

Phil relayed the miracle of people provided in this emergency. There was an EMT who 'happened' to just be going by...

"...who stopped," Vickie added. "There were so many calls to emergency that they jammed the lines and all kinds of help was right there."

John had torn an artery in his arm. There were physicians who 'just happened' to be in the trauma center practicing for their trauma certification when they brought him in. Word got out quickly and soon John's friends were lining the walls of the hospital three or four deep in order to donate blood.

Phil and Vickie received word of their son's accident and rushed to the hospital. When the surgeon came out to talk to them, he said, 'We're trying to save him.' Vickie asked, 'Are you trying to save the boy or are you trying to save his arm?' He was trying to save John.

Microsurgery to reattach the arm was not a possibility, so surgeons decided they would have to amputate his arm. He was in the hospital for months as his arm, following amputation, would require debridement of tissue that could only be done in stages.

There is much pride when they spoke about John. Phil said, "He's such a great guy! He was right handed...and now he does everything left handed."

Vickie said, "Pretty amazing things he can do!"

Their smiles quickly marched across their faces as Phil said, "He can cut his own toenails. He figured out how to do these things. He cuts his fingernails with his feet. I never heard him say...'Oh me...poor me.' That's what I think is more amazing. He didn't want to stay in bed... A lot of times...people won't even come out of their house. He was up and ready to go a lot sooner."

Phil said, "I have heard many people tell stories about how this kind of a trauma destroyed a marriage. I believe it brought us closer together. I KNOW it did..."

Vickie agreed, "Because we had another focus...our focus was John...not us."

Like a soap opera

Vickie said, "That was John, which was very traumatic. My baby..."

Then we come to Michael...their middle son.

She felt it was much like living a soap opera during those years. "Phil's Mom was dying, and we were down in San Jose at the hospital. Michael, who was living in Texas with his family, flew up to see her. He was looking kind of 'peeked' and he said, 'Mom, what do you think about this?' He showed me his arm," as she pointed to the inside of forearm near elbow. "It had a red spot...dark red..." She knew when a line started going up the arm it needed to be seen immediately.

Michael's wife thought he possibly had the flu or some other bug and just needed antibiotics, so they could fly home the next day and see his own doctor. The physician in the emergency room said, 'No...he's not going anywhere! This is not your decision. This is my decision!' Michael was admitted to Critical Care Unit with infection that had spread throughout his entire body. He was there about seven weeks, with five of those in an induced coma to promote healing of his body.

The orthopedic physician was afraid the infection was going travel up his arm and reach his heart. Phil said, "They were going to amputate his left arm..."

Vickie broke in, "To save his life..."

Phil, with agony in his voice, said, "This was two or three years after John lost his right arm." 'I can't do this', he said in the softest voice as if he was only saying it to himself. Finally, he agreed, 'OK...if that's what you have to do...that's what you have to do to save his life'."

When they wheeled him out of surgery, the physician explained they made an incision from inside the armpit to the inside of his elbow. 'The flesh is healthy. There's nothing wrong so I can't amputate.'

Phil related a story in Scripture where a young boy died, and a prophet came to pray over him, 'God, give this boy back his life.' The boy lived. The people in their church were praying that Scripture over Michael at the same time as the surgeon said he wasn't going to amputate. God gave Michael his arm back! But…that wasn't the end of the story.

He was still in ICU and eventually had to have a tracheotomy, an incision in the trachea (windpipe) made to open the airway. Phil told us, "They had cranked the ventilator up to 11…which was as high as it could go…"

Vickie added, "…and he had been on it as long as he could be."

They were told, 'There's not much more we can do.'

Every day, when they asked the lung specialist how Michael was doing, He would answer, 'Slightly worse.'

They would ask the kidney specialist, 'How's he doing today?' 'Slightly worse.'

Every night they would go home and pray for God to heal him.

"Prior to the infection, Michael rode eight miles a day on his bike. He worked out all the time. He was a black belt in Tai Kwando. Now he couldn't move. He was so fragile they couldn't move his bed at all. When they started therapy with him, they had an attendant on each side and a walker. He could barely take two steps and then back in bed."

Finally, the last week he was in there, their favorite doctor was in the room. When they asked, 'How's he doing today?', the doctor replied, 'Slightly better.' That turned the corner and he started to recover…rather quickly! Phil said, "I don't know if it was a week later, 'BAM' they were on the airplane and they were gone!"

Mad at God?

It was so much. How could any one family experience all of that trauma? When asked if they were ever mad at God, they both adamantly replied, "NO! No, No, No….gosh No."

Phil added, "We were so blessed!"

"We saw God's hands." Vickie smiled, "We were carried."

They felt carried by the many fervent prayers, by ministry received from the pastor of their church and the many meals and care provided by friends. They were even carried by unexpected, unusual people like a young hospital employee from East Africa, who decided he was Michael's best friend. He was not even supposed to be in Michael's room, but he would be in and out of there every day.

Phil said, "Michael recovered and the last time we saw this guy, he told us his last name. His last name is Charub, which means ''angel'. So, he's Michael Angel and he's praying for our Michael!"

Phil ended "There's the blessing…we still have our three sons with us."

Not over yet

Vickie laughed, "Then the last one was Phil who had this exciting heart attack." About five years ago, they were putting on their shoes to go for a walk. "He is in the family room putting his shoes on." She made a croaky, raspy voice to imitate Phil's call for help, 'Vickie…Vickie…' "Impatient, I thought…WHAT does he want now?"

'WHAT', she asked sharply.

He made a croaking sound, 'Vickie…can you come here?'

'WHAT DO YOU WANT? I'M PUTTING MY SHOES ON!' She interjected, "I get in there and he is literally rolling on the couch...writhing."

'I think you need to take me to the hospital.'

'Well, can you get up and get in the car by yourself?' (We are sure you can guess his answer to that one!)

So, here came the ambulance. According to them, that was only the first install-ment of this 'comedy' trip to the hospital. When the EMTs got Phil onto the gurney, they couldn't make the turn to get it out of the front door. All of a sudden, one of the EMTs said, 'OK...hang on,' as they tipped the gurney from horizontal to immediate vertical in order to fit out the door.

Phil could hardly contain himself as he said, "Then they put me in the back of the ambulance. 'Here...chew these four aspirin'."

'Can I have some water?'

'NO!! Chew 'em!'

So, we're driving down the highway when one EMT said to the other...'Well, what do you think we should do now?'

'I don't know.'

'What do you want to do?'

'Well, whatever you want to.'

Phil continued the story moving his head back and forth as if he was watching a tennis match. 'So, you guys know I can hear you?' At this point in recounting the story, Phil and Vickie gasped for breath as they leaned into each other with laughter.

Three Stooges activity aside, they transported him to the hospital all in one piece. The next day the cardiologist said, 'If I didn't know this was a picture of you...I think I would be looking at a picture of a perfectly healthy person because there was no damage done to your heart.'

Phil pointed to mid chest and said, "I have three stents here...none of which work anymore because my body made my own bypass. I've got to believe there is a God and He's in His heaven and He's alive today and He watches over us!"

Keep Him there!

Phil's basketball playing friend, Mark had a favorite saying: "Get Jesus in your life. Keep Him there! If you have to go through this in life, why would you go through it without Jesus?"

He's the One they would need to keep in their lives to make it through crisis after crisis after crisis. Their faith might have felt as small as a grain of sand on an enormous beach, but it was just enough to hold them up...to carry them through. He was enough to bond Phil and Vickie together through times when the whole world might have thought they would be torn apart.

They give all credit to Jesus for sustaining them through more than their share of calamity. Their deeper love came with a cost, but He not only sustained them, He has kept them growing deeper in love with each other.

Matt & Amber – God's Wonderful Plan

MARRIED 13 YEARS

"But the plans of the LORD stand firm forever, the purposes of his heart through all generations." Psalms 33:11

What happens when your plans come crashing down and your entire life changes? They weren't elaborate plans...just normal plans for a couple of young college students. They would graduate from school and then about three years later, start a family and buy a house. In a matter of seconds, that all ended.

Back to the beginning

Their relationship began at a fun-filled local carnival where a bunch of people from two small communities ran into each other. This little group, which included Matt and Amber, just clicked, and soon they started to hang out every weekend. Although Matt and Amber lived about thirty minutes from each other, they remained just friends who never dated until she went to college a couple of hours away.

"She was mysterious to me. I would be talking to somebody but felt like someone else was staring at me."

Looking over at Matt, Amber was all smiles as she silently mouthed: "It was probably me!"

"Every time I looked at her, she was staring at me, but then she would look away when I looked at her." Amber chuckled with a teasing sparkle in her eye! She thought he was cute, but she also thought he was a 'player' so, she wasn't really interested. However, when she got to know him, it was his sense of humor, dependability and loyalty that actually caused her to give him a second look.

The big proposal

They dated about five years before he popped the marriage question to the somewhat 'crabby, cramming for finals' love of his life. He remembers popping down on one knee and telling her: 'We've been together six years and I love you and might as well spend the rest of my life with you!' She actually remembered a little more romantic wording…but, by the way, even in the middle of exhausting finals, she managed a 'yes'.

Our lives were changed

Like any marriage, theirs came with challenges faced by every young couple learning how to live together. However, Matt recounted the unexpected, devastating challenge which took place early in their marriage.

"It was a swimming accident. Someone jumped off a high dive at the swimming pool and landed on top of me and broke my neck. (Matt's injury was classified as quadriplegia.) I was laid up in the hospital doing recovery and therapy. We then moved out to Denver for three and a half months for more rehab. We were on our own. No family there. We had only been married for a year and had this sort of thrown on top of us." He hesitated slightly, "We were trying to figure out what life was going to be like…trying to pay for everything…trying to find a small place to live."

Amber recalled, "I was down to a month of classes at school and two internships and I would be graduating. Until then, we were just focusing on getting through school. We were at the point where you are starting to think, 'OK, within the next three years we'll start having kids and we'll have a house'. Then all of a sudden, your dreams are just kind of…gone! You look to the future and you're like…'I don't know'." They were both shaking their heads back and forth indicating the hopelessness they felt. "I remember thinking, 'I don't even see a future'."

Matt described it as more like living hour by hour. He didn't want to look ahead and plan anything, because they didn't have a clue what the future would look like. Neither of them felt very positive, and Matt admitted to a period of depression. "Therapy wasn't physically as bad but emotionally it was horrible. That year, after getting out of the hospital and coming home was probably the worst time of our lives. When we were in Denver, we were always in the same room together. We were close to each other, but it seems like once we got home, we isolated ourselves from each other.

We would kind of each do our own separate thing because we really didn't know how to...to..."

"...to cope," Amber finished his sentence.

"You don't want to overstep that person's boundaries. This was something entirely new to me and entirely new to her."

"Our roles were different," Amber candidly remarked. "It's not just husband and wife anymore. I kind of took on a nursing role that became all consuming. It felt like my wife role was gone, so that changed the dynamics of our marriage a lot."

BA – Before accident

Before the accident, Matt would come home from work and make supper. She'd come home and study. Matt said, "We would eat, and then we'd have the rest of the night to do something together. Get hurt and your roles are flipped. It was almost like I was powerless to make supper or do anything like that. I had to shift the burden to her the whole time."

They were trying to figure out their new roles and discover how to find a little bit of balance. At the same time, they were trying to overcome barriers and find ways to make things adaptable, so Matt could help Amber with daily household tasks.

Marriages weren't surviving

Amber painfully remembered people in therapy with Matt who were getting divorced. In fact, they discovered the divorce rate was extremely high among couples where one partner was injured. "When the Social Worker was trying to help us find a handicap accessible apartment, she suggested, 'Let's just hold off on looking for a house until you decide if you're going to stay together'." At first, Amber firmly but gently pushed back, 'Well, we can look for a house. I think we're staying together.'

Still the Social Worker insisted, 'Let's just wait. Let's give it a little bit of time.' Matt remembers how she kept pushing the issue: 'Well, maybe if you're not happy you should just leave him now. It would just be easier.'

Amber said, "She didn't know us!" Finally, she adamantly told the Social Worker, 'No, we're staying together. We can look for a house!' However, she just wouldn't let it go, 'It's going to get worse, so you need to wait.' That response from the Social Worker may have discouraged other couples, but Matt and Amber seemed even more determined to prove her wrong.

Day by day they had to adjust through all of the physical and emotional needs that Matt's quadriplegia required. "When I got hurt, we were 23. I was thinking, 'We're in our prime. We're going to have some fun for a while.' Then it's like you get hit with this..."Amber finished the thought, "...and you grow up fast!"

Two became one...

When asked the question about giving up, immediately out of Matt's mouth came, "Oh Yah!" and they both shook their heads in agreement. "Not like even just give up on us, but there were times when I thought about calling it quits and 'offing' myself. I figured if I was gone, she could move on and have a better life with someone else...doing something with someone normal functioning."

His voice got stronger, "We knew each other so well. It wasn't like we'd been together only three months and got married. We were best friends!"

Amber said, "We were together six years before we got married so it was a pretty tight bond. Actually, now it's even tighter so it almost had the reverse affect. A lot of times, couples get up in the morning and they do their own thing and go to work. They come home and maybe get together for supper then kind of do their own thing again, but we are so tightly bound because I get him up in the morning. Our whole routine is just..."

Her husband finished her sentence, "...one!" They had to do everything together because Matt couldn't do it by himself. To us, they were a visual example right out of the Bible where it speaks about the two becoming one!

What about faith?

During college, Amber remembered doing their own thing which didn't include church. The last year before the accident, they started going to church more. Amber said, "I was starting to read my Bible every day which was something I don't think I ever had really done. So, then when the accident happened, I was actually mad because I felt like I was getting closer and..."

Matt interjected, "...then a slap in the face!"

About that time, Amber's cousin was doing a Beth Moore Bible study together with her husband. They sent the tapes for the 'Breaking Free' series and they started doing it together while in rehab. They believed it helped them in a very rough time.

She said, "We also became really good friends with the chaplain. We felt maybe the only time we really felt at peace was when we were in the chapel."

Amber was raised in the church, but Matt said it was a little different for him. He grew up where you were expected to go to church - even if you didn't want to. Some of the thinking about death he grew up with was more like, 'Once you're gone...you're gone. That's it!

"While we were dating, we would talk, but I just didn't understand him."

"Yah," he responded, "you'd get mad at me!"

She continued, "I grew up Lutheran and we were pretty involved in church. I was in youth group and my parents were elders and Sunday School teachers, but we were kind of a Sunday morning family...a private family. My parents believe and have strong faith but it's a quiet faith. We prayed at meals but other than that, we didn't talk a lot about God. He wasn't part of the day to day conversation. That's something we needed to change."

Matt felt their faith was gradually getting stronger. "When we were in Denver at the rehab hospital, I was at the low of the low. I was so mad at God. 'Why'? Why on earth did You do this to me? Do this to her? I am the one who is supposed to be protecting her! You're a lot higher than me. How am I supposed to do this'?

Now, over the years, I have come to accept it. Obviously, this happened for a reason. I can help other people who are in my situation. I would say, I am a work in progress."

Amber told us her faith has become deeper and stronger through this. "But, there was a point about a year after he was injured that I was like...'Done! Done with

God!' But then, the night we had a Bible study at church…I was like…'You've got one more chance, God'!" By now, she was laughing out loud as she remembered telling God, 'I'll give you one more shot with this Bible study and then I'm done'! A smile broke out on her face, "Then…I don't know. He brought me back!"

Matt looked over at Amber, "And He's been giving us good stuff ever since!"

The good stuff

Good stuff didn't mean it was always easy stuff. Amber shared, "Last year was really hard! It was a rough year. Matt was sick all the time and, in the hospital constantly (complications related to his paralysis). Then, my job was really stressful. I couldn't sleep. We'd been praying for health and a different job and it just seems like everything…," her voice trailed off.

Matt added, "We were trying to do the baby thing and it wasn't working. We got pretty low and we kept saying…2015…yup, this is the year! Then, 'Nope'!" They both laughed as they said they optimistically repeated, "2016…this is the year!"

"We had been looking for years for a house that would accommodate Matt's needs and couldn't find anything. We'd look at a house and by the time we began calculating some of the renovations…it was just crazy! Then, we'd think about building, and we'd see the prices were crazy, so we'd wait again. One day we came home and there was a 'for sale' sign on the twin home we were renting."

Their hand was forced. They had to do something. They thought building was their only option but now, they didn't have time to build. They had to be out! That's when their real estate agent called about a house for sale.

When talking about their home, Amber remembered, "At the time, we weren't 100% sure but we didn't have a choice. Now we know this is where we were meant to be. It feels like our house. That was definitely a God thing."

Matt smiled, "It feels like home!"

Hidden blessings

She said, "I think our closeness is probably the biggest blessing. Sometimes I wonder where we would be if it would have gone the way we wanted." She smiled sweetly, "By now, we'd have three kids running around, but I don't think we'd be as close as we are."

Matt shook his head in agreement and grinned as he said, "I've thought about that, too. I think we would have gotten on each other's nerves."

"And maybe had more separate lives," she added. "And, I don't know that our faith would have been…"

Matt said, "I don't think we'd be where we are now with it. We'd probably be going through the motions, not doing anything about it or doing anything to strengthen it."

A big blessing for Amber was trust. "Learning to trust when everything is out of our control. You think things are bad and then they get worse and they get worse again and worse again. You kind of have no option but to trust that things will get better. When Matt got injured, we had no other choice, so we decided to trust God.

When he was sick, the first instinct was to try to fix things on our own. I am hoping every time I will get a little bit faster with trust.

This last year, what kept going through my head was words from God: 'Just trust…just trust'. Trust in God. He is faithful. Trust in God. I did a Bible study for a while and at the end of every week, they'd say: 'And what did you learn?' I'd say…Trust." Amber was laughing as she said, "They probably didn't want to ask me anymore because I always had the same answer. Trust. You don't realize how bad it is until you don't have any other options. Then you just have to trust that God has a plan and there's some kind of silver lining even though you can't see it."

Becoming an advocate

She also learned she had to become an advocate for Matt. You tend to think everything is handicap accessible, but they soon discovered it was far from that. They found the costs associated with a spinal cord injury were astronomical. "In addition, if we go to a Canaries baseball game, there is handicapped seating, but it is priced toward the upper end, so you don't have options. Every time we go it costs quite a bit of money…so it's not ethical to charge handicap individuals more money. You want to go to the game, but that cost can be a barrier." To help others who are handicapped, Matt serves on the ADA Review Board for the city.

He became a member of the Christopher Reeve Mentor Program, with trained volunteers who go to hospitals to talk with newly injured people. At first, they were, as Amber called it, 'freaked out' when someone came to talk with them but eventually, they became friends with a couple who had kids and he had a job. Amber said, "It was good to see that kind of ending. If you want to work, there are still options. You're not completely dependent."

He said, "Eventually I had to make a career adjustment. I had a bachelors in Criminal Justice and was a cop. I went back to school and I am now working in electrical drafting. I can't even see myself working anywhere else. It's a great environment. They are so accommodating, and they get it. It's a real family-based business."

Amber laughed when she told how Matt was at a company satellite location where he normally didn't work. "There was no place to park so when one of the bosses found out, he printed off a handicap sign and put it on a parking spot for Matt. He was like, 'That's not acceptable!' Matt couldn't park, and he was just not going to let that happen!"

A steady companion

Matt has had his service dog, Teddy, for about seven years. "He's helped me a lot, not only physically but attitude-wise. After I got hurt and we came home, I was a bear. I was probably tough to be around."

We know Teddy personally and it is pretty tough to stay mad when he is snuggling up against your lap with those big eyes and warm nose. Matt gazed at his companion dog, "Teddy isn't like a piece of equipment but more like part of the family. He goes with me everywhere. It's weird if he's not around."

Amber said, "I always pet him and say, 'You're a blessing.' He's brought so much joy and we smile and laugh a lot more because he's just quirky. He's so funny and he can be a challenge. He's naughty!"

Matt admitted, "Every now and then he'll go rogue. He'll do things he's not supposed to do."

"If we leave and don't lock him in his kennel…he steals!" Amber tattled. "We came home one time and I counted 40 different things he had on the ground. I know he ate some things because I couldn't find them. He's very vengeful. He doesn't appreciate being left behind."

Matt laughed out loud, "We don't bring him to church anymore because he tried to eat a communion wafer out of the hand of the lady next to us!"

She said, "Teddy was right next to me, and when I saw him, I was like sucking air! 'Nooooo – you can't! You can't do that'!" They both laughed so hard they could barely stop. "That was the last day he went to church!"

Baby maybe?

"We've always wanted kids. I don't think Matt wanted quite as many as I did, but I always wanted a bigger family. So, that felt like it was a really big thing that got taken away. I think that almost bugged me more than a lot of the other stuff. We tried lots of different things to have kids on our own. We went through testing with in vitro. The doctor basically said, 'You can try this, but it probably won't work'. 'You can try that but that probably won't work.' 'You can try in vitro with genetic testing (which is a crazy amount of money) but that won't work either…but let's give it a shot.' He was basically saying. 'Let's pay $40,000 and you're probably aren't going to have a baby.' On their website their statistics are like 17% - which doesn't sound very good. So, I asked, 'Do we even have a 17% chance?' The doctor said: 'No'!"

They both felt as if doors were closing, until they spoke with some friends who have twins. They worked with a doctor in Denver and were willing to connect them with him. After a telephone meeting they were extremely encouraged. Amber said, "It was just a whole different attitude. He was like, 'You know what. You have a spinal cord injury. That's life. Life happens. We can figure it out. You have a 70-75% chance. You're a healthy girl. Let's do this'!"

He exclaimed, "They were phenomenal! When we walked in the door of the facility, we felt like 'This is where we're supposed to be'!"

"Matt and I debated a long time because going there meant more cost. We'd be gone for two weeks. I would have to use up all my vacation. He wouldn't get paid those two weeks, but it turned out to be phenomenal! We felt like asking everyone there at the clinic, 'Can we kiss you? You are being so nice'!

We had been trying two to three years with no results. This time we just had amazing…amazing results! They were able to use Matt's sperm and normally there are 14-15 eggs, but I had 28! Everything just worked beautifully. There's a lot of anxiety with in vitro because there are so many points where it can fail. God was definitely with us because the first try worked.

She beamed, "We couldn't have planned it better!"

Matt with (Elizabeth (Lizzy) born in 2016

They were all smiles when he told us they had nine more eggs left. When asked how many more children? They both laughed as they told us when their van is full…it's full!

Advice from their hearts

Amber's advice: "Trust God in your plan…in His plan. You can plan your life out all you want and it's not going to go that way so, you just have to trust that God has a plan for you. Even when it doesn't feel like a good plan. If you feel like there isn't any hope in your marriage, just wait and a year later, it can be completely different. So, it's normal to have those really rough patches. It's not something that is bad or means your marriage is over. It's something that helps you grow."

Matt's advice: "There are definitely going to be peaks and valleys and your valleys might be more than your peaks, but if you stay on the path, you'll eventually get back to the top."

What happens?

What happens when your plans come crashing down and your entire life changes? Ask Matt and Amber about God's wonderful plans!

His plan continues

Our hearts smiled as we shared their joy at the arrival of Joseph (Joey) on June 10, 2019. Along with Matt and Amber, we couldn't help but think: 'Our best plans are not nearly as wonderful as God's perfect plans!'

Rod & Wanda – Accept Each Other Without Conditions

MARRIED 47 YEARS

"My command is this: 'Love each other as I have loved you'." John 15:12

Solo interview

Wanda recounted their life story solo. Rod, her husband of 47 years, died two days before his 70th birthday. She said, "He was with Jesus 15 years in January".

Copyright © Sears Portrait Studio CPI Co

L ittle girl meets man

She smiled from ear to ear as she told us she was just a little sophomore in high school, and he was old enough to be in the Army. So, how in the world did they ever get together?

It began with a bunch of guys hanging over the fence whistling at the girls as they walked by on the way to school. "They were whistling not only at me but at anything that passed by!"

Rod locked eyes on her and told the First Sergeant, 'I'm going to marry that girl!' The First Sergeant said, 'No, you're not. Her father is a Lieutenant Colonel and you're not going to get anywhere near her!'

You would think that alone would slim down their chances of ever meeting, but a simple phone call changed everything. Her family didn't have a telephone, so she went over to the First Sergeant's house to use the phone. Rod was there...with a woman. They exchanged a 'Hi' and that was the end of that. Until...a couple of weeks later when Rod was back at the First Sergeant's house and declared he wanted to meet Wanda.

Group dating to a new level

"I thought he was good looking, but I had never dated. I was a little backwards. My girlfriends were all going out with guys in cars and 'necking' and all that stuff. I just didn't like that!"

She often went skating with friends, so when she met Rod, she invited him along to their regular Saturday night activity. Her mother made her a skating outfit but when Rod came to her house and saw the outfit hanging up, he took one look at it and said, 'You're not wearing that if you are going out with me!' Back in that day, skirts were midcalf, so she traded in her cute, short skating outfit for a midcalf skirt so she could go skating with him.

She was a little nervous about going out with Rod, so she set up a scheme with a friend. She and her boyfriend were to stop by Wanda's house about 15 minutes before they would be leaving for the skating rink. That way, she would 'have to' invite them along. Her planned protection for the night was security in numbers. When her plot played out just as she had planned, Rod responded, 'Oh, that's no problem!'

Wanda laughed, "He looked at my mother and said, 'Mom, you want to go, too?' She said, 'Sure!' so we all went skating!" (That night, they took group dating to a whole new level!)

Almost ended right there!

"We were all getting ready to leave and they had a couple's skate with the lights all low. I am looking for him and I can't find him anywhere." She told all her friends she would be there with this guy, so they all showed up with their boyfriends. Now, she couldn't even find him to show him off. That's when she saw him skating with some other girl. At the end of the skate, Wanda huffed, 'Hey, listen...we're in my mother's car. You don't need to go home with us. You can just stay with her!'

He convinced her he wanted to go with her. As they were driving home, he leaned close to her and said, 'Do you love me?' Wanda reacted boldly, 'What...love you? I don't even know you...how am I going to love you!' "Later, he told me I was the first girl that ever told him, 'No'. All the other girls told him they loved <u>him</u>. He was bound and determined I was going to love him, or he was going to know why! There you have it!"

She was 17 and he was 22! They met! Started dating February 28th! Married six months later on August 28th!

Too late now!

On their wedding day, she was waiting upstairs in the balcony and planned to come down when everyone was there. As she waited, Father Lafferty came upstairs and said, 'You can always change your mind'. She smiled as she remembered thinking, 'Too late now! Too late now!'

No fairy tale

When she first met Rod, it was perfect. He was very affectionate. She finally felt there was someone who cared for her. "After we married, the displays of affection virtually ceased. He didn't know how to respond to me. He was giving all he knew, but I didn't know how to pick up on what he was giving." Their whirlwind romance soon began to fade, and they struggled in their relationship. This was quickly becoming a 'less than fairy tale' marriage.

Culture clash

"We were from two different cultures. I don't believe skin color makes any difference at all but if you are from different cultures it means you are raised differently...with different priorities, different expectations, different values. With him coming from the Spanish culture and me coming from American culture, there was often a clash. To that equation, add a language barrier. When I went to visit his family, they all spoke Spanish. Of course, I was left out. I couldn't speak or understand, Spanish so things like that caused friction."

We all carry baggage

In a matter of fact tone, Wanda said, "Our young lives are shaped by people and circumstances." She felt there were many times in her life she didn't understand why she reacted like she did. She wasn't always sure of what triggered her negative feelings. She said, "Sometimes, we just react to them and in the process, we may unintentionally cause others to be hurt. Sad to say, when we marry, we carry all of this baggage into our relationship. This was the case with Rod and me."

"Through my life I felt unloved and insecure. These were the feelings of an only child who spent most of her time alone. I was never physically abused. My parents were good people, but they just did not have time for me. They were busy with their own lives which I did not fit into. We did not have family time, so whenever I was with them, I felt like an imposing third wheel." Wanda's parents divorced when she was 12 and that's when the shuffling back and forth began. She felt as if no one wanted her.

"When someone was kind to me, I was unable to accept it as love. I felt they were being kind out of a sense of duty or that they felt sorry for me. I didn't feel like I belonged or that they were glad to have me. I did not have a sense of how love was expressed, so I mistakenly thought it was by displays of affection. Hugs, kisses, holding hands told me, and the world, I was loved

Rod was raised in a family that didn't show much love either. If he brought home good grades, he was praised. Other than that, he was ignored." She struggled to find the right words. "I was looking for...I guess...love to me was affection. If affection was absent...there was no love.

Coming from two different families and two different ways of doing things...it was difficult. And...I was still a child. I went from my Mother's care to his care."

Being his wife was enough

Wanda said that according to Rod, "Asking me to be his wife said, 'he loved me'. He was giving his all by being a kind, loving husband and father, a great provider, and responsible person. I was proud to be his wife but somehow those feelings crept back in when I was not being reassured of his love by those displays of affection."

"I reacted by nagging him and trying to force him to change and to be what I needed. I think that Satan used my insecurity and blinded me to the way that Rod was showing his love for me. There was an underlying thread of discontent in me that continued throughout our marriage and blew up frequently with me demanding change. I did not realize that if something is <u>forced</u> it is not real."

This continued year after year until Wanda admitted, "It became an obsession in me. It was like a recording in my head replaying all of the times I felt unloved." Her mind kept repeating, "...without the displays of affection I was not loved, and I felt everyone else could see it...which made it worse."

With regret in her voice and in her expression, Wanda said, "For some reason, I was unable to see all he was giving. If only I could have recognized it back then."

Emotional distance

"Rod was quiet. He didn't talk much. He didn't talk about his family. Trying to get information from him about his family life was like pulling teeth. He was very closed mouthed about it. I don't think he wanted to remember...to think about it. He loved his family but there was a lot of heartbreak in his upbringing. He never wanted to condemn anyone; never wanted to say someone was bad or someone was doing this. He wouldn't talk about it. So, in that respect, I felt let down."

God, change HIM!

"Even though as years went by and I was still unable to see how he was really loving me, we still managed to enjoy lots of good times. We raised two loving sons who became Christians individually but still Christ was not the head of our home...nor was He leading us in our actions towards each other.

Now I was praying for God to change HIM." When she sought outside help, she was told, 'You cannot change a person...only God can do that'. "I DID NOT want to hear that! I was also told that Jesus was my husband and His love would fulfill me. I COULD NOT relate to that at all! I was having enough trouble being able to accept that God loved me. I knew nothing of His grace, so when things did not change, I felt separated from Him. I thought God had put this need to be loved in me and Rod was the one that I was supposed to get the loving from. If not him...then who?? To me...this justified my nagging and demanding."

After each blow up, she resolved to change. She would start doing all the things for him that she wanted him to do for her. He accepted what she had to give and never once pulled way. "BUT," she said, "...it did not make him change! Why would it? Instead of just loving him, I was trying to manipulate him."

The breakthrough

Throughout her marriage, Wanda always knew things were not right. She even read books looking for answers. "I wanted to say, 'If you loved me you would do this. If you loved me, you would do that'." Eventually, she realized, 'Well, if I loved him, I would have done this or that, too'.

A friend lent her a book and as she read it, she could see things that applied to her life but 'letting go and letting God' made Wanda balk. She then forced herself to read the book twice. "I knew I was not perfect but on the other hand, I was not so bad either." She finally realized she had been rationalizing by telling herself she was not as bad as other people.

"The Lord does not compare. I had not thought that doing things my way was not God's best for me. Plus," she laughed, "...my way was not working anyway!"

She was finally able to see it was not wrong to expect affection from her husband, but she was wrong in the way she was going about it. "It took the Lord a long time...to finally get through to me. But He did! He did!"

She read in Isaiah 48, 'I am the Lord your God who leads you in the way you should go, and I will provide a way of escape.' She realized, 'He will provide! I can't do it myself, but He can! IF I am willing'. "I wanted to be willing, but something was holding me back. I had to take time to think about what was being asked of me. I had to count the cost: 'What if the Lord didn't see it MY WAY and didn't change Rod to suit me'?"

Over several days she laid her friend's book down and picked it back up again. She learned it is OK to want and need love because that is the way God made her. "That is why He tells me in His Word over and over again, He loves me, because He knows I need to know."

She picked it up again and read about changing habits, repentance, forgiveness and openness. The next day she read about how Satan attacks marriages. "I could see I had been had! It made me mad that I had allowed myself to be deceived all of this time."

The next day, she was laying across her bed when her eyes fell on a book of devotions written by a chaplain. It opened to a prayer 'For the Enemy'. "Although my husband was not my enemy, I had felt hurt by him."

My prayer

As a result, this was the prayer she remembered praying:

'Lord Jesus, you have shown me some things that are very hard to understand and asked some things of me that are very hard to do. I know that in myself I am not strong enough, nor do I have enough faith or love to love Rod or pray for him as You would. When I see the years wasted with striving for what is rightfully mine, the hurt I caused those around me and the pain I have endured, all because I was unable to give it to you...it makes me sad. But, all of this time you forgave me and kept drawing me to the cross. You never gave up on me and sent me someone who cared enough to lead me to the truth of your Word. Lord Jesus, I know that You meant every word You said, and You practiced what You preached. So, Lord help me to see Rod through Your eyes and let my thoughts of 'rejection and hurt' give way to 'love and prayers'. Let me love him with Your heart and forgive him because You forgave and loved me. Show me how, Lord Jesus, to be like You. Give me the power to do it, too. Amen'.

I give up! God change ME!

"One day I finally just said, 'Lord, I can't do this anymore. If You want me to change...You want him to change...You want this situation to change...You're going to have to do it. This is it! I'm done! I can't handle this anymore'!

The next morning, I woke up and my heart was completely changed! I went in to make him breakfast and I was just filled with love for him. I just wanted to go and just hug him. If he never gave me another kiss, it didn't matter. If he never gave me another hug, it didn't matter. There no longer was a knot in my stomach or a hurt in my heart.

How this came about I don't quite understand but I know that it came from Jesus. Previously, I was not able to feel love for my husband, to reach out and touch him without expecting something in return. I did not tell him what happened to me because I didn't want him to feel pressured. I was committed to accepting him as he was and to love him whether he changed or not.

Although the love I felt for him was so strong, my change DID NOT come easy and it did not happen overnight. Satan still played the old recording in my mind. Each time I had to stand my ground and say, 'I have chosen to forgive', and I WILL NOT listen to this anymore! Then I consciously changed my thinking to praise and prayer.

It took about six weeks before the recording finally stopped. He was becoming more affectionate. I wasn't badgering him about it. You don't realize that if you keep saying to someone 'You have to hug me! You have to hug me! You have to hug me!'...and they finally hug me...what have I won? I haven't won anything because I forced them to hug me. The hugs have to come freely.

It was amazing how Rod picked up on my change and soon he was being more affectionate. It was like icing on the cake!"

He had it all together!

Describing how she dealt with Rod before God changed her heart, she said, "It's so funny. I kept telling him about God and how God wanted this, and God wanted that." As if she were thumping her Bible pointing it out to Rod, she said, " 'See, it says here in the Bible!

He already had it all together with God. I was the one who didn't have it together. Finally, finally...the Lord showed me.

After the Lord healed my heart...I was able to just accept Rod as he was and not expect him to change for me. That's the whole ball game right there. That was a lesson that was so hard for me to learn. I kept wanting...pushing and of course, the more I pushed, the worse it became."

She continued softly, "So when you pray, don't pray for God to change that person. If you are doing something I don't like, I don't ask God to change you...I ask God to change me and let me be able to love you like you are because that's how He loves you. He loves me just like I am. It doesn't mean He doesn't want me to change or doesn't want me to be better, but He will show me how to change and to be better, but...I can't change you."

Never leave

"No matter how hard some of these things were...divorce was NEVER an option for either of us! I think through all the years, because leaving was never an option, he put up with me. He was able to love me like I was."

Not all bad times

"We had a lot of good times with each other. He was easy going. I don't think he ever started an argument." Her voice lightened, "It was always me saying, 'We have to talk'! He put up with entirely too much from me. I look back now, and I wonder how he did it.

I was more of a disciplinarian than he was. He was more laid back and gentle. I was more, 'Do this! Do this! Do this!' I was more conscious of society. I wanted my kids to be well behaved. I wanted other people to like them."

Even through the pressure to be what their Mom wanted them to be, the boys grew into godly young men. "It blesses my heart to see them today. They get together and sing and play the guitar and praise the Lord. I don't think a mother can be any more blessed than to have her children serve the Lord."

Miss him every day!

Her eyes saddened a little as she told us this total transformation in her and in her marriage happened about two years before Rod died.

"Every day I miss him, and I think about him. I wish I could get a 'do over'," she laughed. "He was a good husband. He was a good Father. He loved his boys. He was very responsible person. A lot of times women say, 'I have to tell him to mow the yard!' I had to tell him to fix this! I never had to tell him anything. If there was something that needed doing, I would tell him, and he just did it. He took care of it." (She thought that made him a far better 'fix-it' husband than she was a 'cook-it/clean-it homemaker!)

Tried to be there

She spoke tenderly, "When Rod was sick, I just tried to be there for him. Touching, hugging and telling him that I loved him. By the time he was going through this, the Lord had already healed my heart, so I was able to see things I hadn't been able to see before."

When we marry...

"When we marry, we do not get any training, so we just give it our best shot. I have found that most problems in relationships are because of feelings. Many times, our reactions to our perceived hurts unintentionally hurts others.

As adults our lives are governed by the choices we make and the consequences of them. We can choose to be loving and kind and look for the goodness in people or we can choose to be disagreeable and only think of how this person is affecting us.

Forgiveness is a choice. It is not easy, but it benefits us first by setting us free of the stress that reliving the hurts causes. Second, it releases the other person into God's hands." She paused, "They say, 'sticks and stones will break my bones, but words will never hurt me'. This is not true. Words spoken by those we love can crush us...sometimes, even when said in jest. The sad thing is that once it is said, it cannot be taken back! Saying 'I'm sorry', does not erase what has been said or done. It can only beg forgiveness.

We have to learn to accept each other how we are. I just wished I had learned it earlier. All those years of tugging. All those years of feeling unworthy and un-loved. I look back now and see how he must have loved me very much to put up with all that stuff. Of course, he wasn't perfect. There were things he did and some things he said that hurt but balancing them out, my side is so much more."

Her eyes sparkled with her hard-fought advice to you: "Just learn to accept each other for what that person is able to give."

Tom & Joan – Always Stood Together

MARRIED 35 YEARS

"And we know that in all things God works for the good of those who love him, who have been called according to his purpose." Romans 8:28

Test of time

Can childhood sweethearts survive the test of time? How about 25 years? It seems Tom and Joan might be the poster children for long term friendship!

A junior high kind of love

They met in the 8ᵗʰ grade where Tom was the new kid on the block. "He was very quiet, very shy. He hung around with my girlfriend and me. I didn't know who he liked better, but I thought he was so cute because he was so quiet and didn't say too much. I invited him and other kids over to my house for parties. Of course, my parents were right there and caught us playing spin the bottle," she snickered.

Tom couldn't help but laugh as he explained their junior high gym class. "They brought in a dance instructor. The boys lined up on one side and the girls on the other. She would show us the steps, and would say, 'OK, now get together as couples'. Half the guys would turn around and run into the locker room." Tom and Joan both laughed uncontrollably as he said, "The teacher would be chasing after them!"

She said, "It was a junior high kind of love, but I really had my eye on him, whether he realized it or not."

They drifted away from each other in high school and both headed off to college. In fact, the same college, but on two different campuses in two different towns in Illinois. No way they were going to just 'run into each other'.

After college, even though separated by distance, Tom said he thought of Joan many times. They both eventually married...someone else. Their paths never crossed again...until their 25th high school class reunion.

Dance the last dance with me

Joan married a local man and stayed in the area to work as a dental hygienist. She was now divorced and never really had a burning desire to attend the reunion. A classmate said, 'Joan, you have to go. This is the 25th reunion!' She let out a deep breath as she remembered, "I had gone to the 10th reunion where people were talking about how rich they were and the big house they owned." However, she finally caved and decided to attend. At the Friday night social, she saw Tom and they talked. "I thought, 'Aw...he's so sweet'. I told him, 'For old time sake, dance the last dance with me'."

He was married, so she was positive he wouldn't take her up on her offer. However, at the end of the evening, he came for that last dance. "I didn't see Tom after that or hear anything until..."

He must be looking for a dentist

Later that year, Tom was served divorce papers for reasons he could never understand. "It was traumatic! 'What am I going to do now?' We tried counseling, but when I knew it was inevitable, I needed to move somewhere...do something. I couldn't live the life of a bachelor!" He was driving around looking for apartments and drove by an area where he thought Joan's office was located. He found it and dropped in to ask if she still worked there.

"The other hygienist came into my operatory and had a business card. 'Joan, someone wants to see you.' I thought it was a salesman. 'Have him check with Becky at the front desk.' 'Oh No, No, No. He wants to see you! He's not a salesman'." When handed the card, she discovered it was Tom.

Joan snickered as she remembered, 'What is he doing here? He must be looking for a dentist!' She was laughing so hard she could hardly speak. Tom told her he was looking for an apartment, and she innocently wondered why he was looking for an apartment at a dental office. "I have to laugh every time I think about it. When Tom said, 'No... I'm looking for an apartment. I thought that meant he and his wife were going to buy an apartment to invest in. I remember saying, 'Oh Gee...that's nice'." Her mistaken assumption caused her to laugh until tears streamed down her face.

Embarrassment aside, she also felt compassion. "When he said, 'No, I'm getting a divorce.' I distinctly remember saying, 'Ohhhh, I'm so sorry' and went over to touch his hand. 'Come back in about fifteen minutes and we can go for lunch.' We had a two-hour lunch where he told me about the shock of his impending divorce. I sat there listening as he poured his out his heart."

He surprised Joan by keeping the door open and said, 'Maybe we can get together again.'

She gave her truthful response: 'I don't date anyone who doesn't have their divorce papers first!'

Here comes Tom!

"After I got my divorce, I asked her out on a date. She told me, 'I'll go, but you have to bring your divorce papers, so I can see them'!" The room rang with laughter as they recalled that conversation. Tom grinned at the memory, "I think our first date I came with the divorce papers in one hand and a bunch of roses in the other."

After that first date, every night they talked on the phone for hours until one of them would fall asleep. They were engaged in February, without a ring...because he didn't have a ring. "You gave me that little ring. I don't know where you found it," Joan laughed. "In some bubble gum machine or something. He handed it to me, 'Here, until I sell some stock...here's a little ring.' Her answer? 'This is wonderful'!"

They started dating in January when the divorce was final and by the following September, they were married.

The attraction

"She was attractive. Beautiful personality. She was just a good, clean living, nice girl. We had an understanding in our Christian faith. Church was important to us."

Her attraction to him, "Ohhh...his steadfastness. His nature of sensitivity to the Lord was a big attraction to me. He's got so much common sense, and a lot of intelligence, too. He's very smart!" As Tom looked over at her she exclaimed, "Well, you do!" Then smiling back at us, she said, "And...He's just adorable!"

"What can I say?". Tom, looking a little bit embarrassed.

Faith and suds on the floor

Even though they were from different denominations, they had the same foundation of church. Family was important, as were good moral standards. Joan said, "God had His hand on us. We had our faith in Christ together."

Tom agreed, "Our faith has been so much stronger from the time we were married. It blossomed every year." One life changing event for each of them was attending a Cursillo retreat weekend. After Tom's four-day retreat, he came home 'higher than a cloud'!

Joan, however, wasn't exactly up in the clouds that weekend! She described it as 'a non-typical weekend'! Her mother's health was failing, so she was staying with them. Their kids were in and out of the house and Joan was just trying to keep up with laundry and dishes! She rushed to load the dishwasher and hurried to put the soap in. She came back in the kitchen about five minutes later to find suds all over the floor. She admitted to putting the wrong soap in the dishwasher. Unsuspecting, Tom walked into the house from his retreat weekend shortly after that bubbly fiasco.

"Where were you anyway? I thought you were going to be home early!" It wasn't exactly the greeting that he had hoped for after the spiritual high of the weekend.

He innocently replied, 'Oh, we stopped at the tavern on the way home.'

An explosion was in the offing. "I thought...'what kind of religious thing did he go to'?" They both laughed as Tom covered his eyes with his hand as he remembered telling her it wasn't strictly a bar but was also a restaurant.

When the 'suds' of that weekend finally dissipated, Joan agreed to attend her own Cursillo retreat weekend. That's when their lives and marriage were changed forever. They not only worshiped together but Christ was becoming the center of their marriage.

You marry the whole family

Someone once said, 'You don't marry one person. You marry the whole family.' Joan understood that quote as soon as she entered into marriage with Tom. Her main challenges were packaged into five teenage bodies. She had daughters, ages 13 and 18. Tom's daughters were 14, 18 and 19. That was a hormone explosion just waiting to happen!

He described his major challenge as trying to work with his ex-wife to remain connected with his girls. With no hint of bitterness in her voice, Joan said, "With the help of God we were able to get over that hurdle."

A man moved into their lives

After they married, Tom moved into Joan's condo with her two daughters. "It was five and a half years since I had been married, and their father was not around much so they only had me. Now, they had to adjust to Tom coming into their lives."

Tom agreed, "We had some hard moments...some very hard moments but we survived them, in faith. It is by the grace of God we persisted and grew stronger." They became true partners through the difficult parenting process.

Joan said, "We took the stance that we have to show our love to each other as man and wife. They were not used to that. My girls didn't see that. They saw their Dad as a raging guy, who otherwise was laughing, joking and never serious about things with them as children."

This was a new life for all of them.

When tensions boil over

There was a stressful time in their family that included Joan's mother moving into their small condo with a big hospital bed...the stress from a houseful of teenage girls...being newly married...and one daughter home after college. All of that stress boiled until eventually there was an explosion. Joan remembered emotions raging during one particular, but not isolated, incident.

Introspective, Joan said, "As in any family, there were complications with relationships, resentments and eruptions of frustration, and anger. Stress was high from time to time but thank God for His help. In His time and way, even hormones were no problem. We all grew into our 'new' family."

United they stood

No matter what happened, they were united. They always stood together. Those rocky times with the girls didn't pull Tom and Joan away from each other. In fact, they believe it cemented them even tighter in their marriage. Today, they continue to display strength by standing together.

As the girls have become adults, their relationship with Tom and Joan is a blessing. They believe that is because God healed and redeemed whatever had been lost between them! Tom said, "God is good! He has blessed us with eleven grandchildren, and one greatgrandchild. and they all love us as Grandma and Grandpa. It's wonderful!"

Lessons learned from marriage #1

Joan said, "In my first marriage, I kept thinking that it must be my fault. 'I'm not praying right for my husband. I'm not doing something right. God's not helping me. No one's helping. He doesn't even want to be helped.' That's when I learned I had to depend on God. It came to the point where he threatened my mother's life and pushed me down the stairs and across the floor and verbally abused me. I saw him start to turn on the girls. That's when I said, 'Lord, I don't think You want that to happen'."

"I wanted to have some sort of sign...an answer. The pastor at the church knew something was going on...something was wrong. So, the pastor just came out and said, 'What's going on? Joan, I think you should put a restraining order on him'." The pastor was willing to come talk to her husband, but he refused. When nothing changed, she finally had to take her pastor's advice and left her husband.

Joan smiled, "It was during that time...where God really used some very difficult times, and a very difficult man to draw me ever closer to Jesus. Jesus was my strength. He was my guide. He was my teacher. He was my helper. He was everything to me. As the marriage grew worse, my relationship with Jesus grew even stronger."

Tom added, "We were both divorced, and didn't want to go that path again. We didn't want that the first time we were married either. In our own hearts, we said, 'Divorce is not going to happen'...but it did."

Would they throw in the towel? At the same time, they both answered 'No'. They agreed they experienced frustration, adjustments and unfulfilled dreams in their marriage. "But", Joan added, "I think, if we didn't have our faith, our marriage wouldn't have lasted". Today, they are both firmly committed to never let the idea of divorce enter their minds or hearts.

Second marriage difference

Tom said, "We do more sharing. Maybe part of it was us doing marriage counseling. In my previous marriage, I relied on my ex-wife a lot. 'You take care of the girls and I'll do this.' He looked over at Joan as he shared his comment made those many years ago." Tom was introspective, "Maybe, I didn't take enough personal responsibility...didn't impose on myself."

Joan's tender smile appeared as she described how this marriage was different from her first. "I know Tom respects me, and I think he knows I respect him. We look to each other. Hopefully, the other person is fulfilled, and we see what we can do to enjoy one another."

Tom interjected, "Respect and trust."

They admitted their marriage was also made stronger as they served together. They were on the pre-marriage team at their church. They often talked about the topic: 'from singleness to marriage' and 'adjusting to married life' and moving from 'self to one'. Joan said, "Serving together was like renewing our vows every year. Each time we served, we would say, 'We never thought we would be doing something like this'. Serving together blessed our marriage in many ways."

Love and appreciation

Tom appreciated, "Her strong faith." Joan laughed lightly as he said, "She is a little angel. She is not only to me, but I see how she interacts with other people. People look up to her. She once said to me, 'I don't know why these people always talk to me and tell me their problems.' I said, 'I know why. You have a big heart and a big shoulder, and you've got 'I love you' written on your heart. They need that. That's why I love her. She's compassionate, loving, full of mercy."

"People come up and ask Tom for advice a lot. They look to him as a good leader and respect his opinion. He is gentle with people, but at the same time he can be firm. If you know Tom, you know that he means what he says. I admire that about him, because he shows integrity."

As she reached over and pinched his cheeks, they both laughed as she said, "And...he's adorable!"

Before getting married...

Tom's said, "Before you get into a marriage, know each other. By knowing each other, I'm not saying by living together. That's not knowing each other...that's distrust and lack of respect. Know each other where you are and understand what lies ahead. Marriage is not all love or only money either. You have to go into it sharing equally." Joan shook her head in agreement as he continued, "Too often people go into a marriage and say: 'What's mine is mine and what's yours is yours'. No - when we get married...it's ours. There is no mine and yours. You have to learn to have it all shared equally so the burden is equally cast thru hardships and good times."

Joan advised, "Definitely, marriage is part of your journey in life. Think of it this way, 'As you go through life, the highway's not going to be perfect. You're going to have bumps, ridges and detours. For that journey you need strength. The strength you will need would be your faith in Jesus as your Lord. If you have Him and the strength He gives, He is going to carry you through and over the ridges, bumps and detours. He'll be there for you. You'll learn to appreciate the life He gives you as a couple.' I think that's where I feel we've come from'."

Marriage is the best in life

Tom closed with this: "I think marriage is a sacrament...a sacred thing. It's holy in God's eyes. It's meant to be a strong relationship between a man and a woman. It's intended to be that way because we bring differences into our marriage. We come from different perspectives in life. A woman is the compassionate, loving...the mother. The man is the protector and provider in the marriage. That's the proper balance."

Joan looked over at him with tenderness, "I think marriage is the best in life. Life is just fuller."

Yes, their lives are full for these reunited childhood sweethearts. Sometimes, life was full of trials and tests, but as they stood together, their commitment has stood the test of time!

MARRIED 20 YEARS

"Jesus looked at them and said, 'With man this is impossible, but not with God; all things are possible with God'." Mark 10:27

Candidates for the impossible

Introduce two people who never wanted to get married again and it seems obvious they were candidates for the impossible. Dixie had been through a divorce four years earlier and was sold on remaining single…forever! Gary was also going through a divorce he said he would never want to repeat. <u>Except</u>, God loves the impossible! So we begin their impossible story.

A God meeting

They both lived in Florida, where Gary was pastoring a church and Dixie was a youth leader at another church. The youth leaders from both churches decided to hold an all-night youth event. Prior to the event, the teams got together for a planning meeting and that's where Dixie met Gary for the first time.

When Dixie walked in the door, Gary was still pretty fresh from his wife leaving. He thought, 'That sure is a pretty girl...but that's that'. "That was all there was...for the moment."

A few weeks later, Gary's daughter attended that youth event. "At the end of it my daughter said, 'Well, when the divorce goes through, Dad, I think you should date Dixie.'

I said, 'I-I-I-I-I-I don't think so. I'm not dating anybody...I'm done!' I was 44 at the time and I was done! My daughter just kept going and kept saying I should call Dixie. I just wouldn't do it. I wouldn't date anybody." Until one day...he finally gave in."

Dixie said, "I got a phone call from him at work one day saying he wanted to get together and have lunch with me. I thought, 'OK, maybe we're going to plan another youth event or something, so I agreed'." While they enjoyed lunch together, she eventually caught on that the reason for the lunch was a date. After that, he didn't take long to call and ask her for another date.

Guarded by the landlady

"Dixie lived with this elderly woman who was in her nineties who was very protective of her. I would go to the door and knock on the door. 'I was wondering if I could see Dixie'?"

"She would say, 'Nope...can't see her. She's busy tonight. You can't see her'!"
He rebutted, 'I kind of arranged it with her.'

She would come back with, 'Sorry...she's too busy'. According to Gary, this little lady was pretty gruff as well as unyielding.

"She was <u>very</u> gruff!" giggled Dixie. "Oh my goodness. She did not want me dating anybody. She wanted me to be her little friend that was living with her. I lived upstairs, and she lived downstairs and she liked that the two of us were little companions."

At this point in the relationship, they were determined to just be friends, but this little lady made sure getting together was an extreme challenge! Gary had to do things like get a little pebble and toss it up to second floor window to get Dixie's attention. This was before cell phones, so Gary actually resorted to writing on a helium balloon, 'Can I see you?' Then he would raise the balloon up to the window. (No! Really!!! We didn't make this up!)

"We had to get around my landlady. She really was a stinker," commented Dixie as she looked over at Gary with a huge smile.

Little by little

"Dating, little by little, I just began to fall in love with the girl. She was really amazing, and it turned out to be the truth...really amazing."

"I clearly remember," Dixie said, "we were at Wet and Wild Water Park at one of the youth activities for his church. He was across the way from me when the Lord said, 'That's going to be your next husband.' It was shocking! 'No, this can't be happening to me.' I resisted it for a long time and slowly but surely, I began to fall in love with him. I said, 'OK Lord, if it's your will'. I really felt it was the Lord who brought us together...and so here we are."

Attracted by...

"At first, the attraction was just companionship." She joined Gary's church and as she began to spend more time with him, she also began to learn more about him. "He was someone I could tell who really loved the Lord and was a good leader and very strong, very kind. He did sweet, little things for me. He would leave balloons on my car at work. I drove back and forth from Florida to Texas to see my kids every other weekend and he would leave me little cards telling me I was a great Mom. He was a good encourager."

Gary went back to memories of that youth event where they first met. He didn't spend the night there because that's what the youth leaders did...not pastors. He came back about 11pm just to see how things were going (or we think he possibly wanted to catch a glimpse of that beautiful woman).

"This girl here," he said as he lovingly looked over at Dixie, "was with her kids, doing stuff with them the whole time rather than saying, 'Ok, kids here's the activity...have at it. I'm going to talk to these other people.' She really cared about what was happening with her youth." That caring action made him feel there was something different about Dixie. "I think that's what really attracted me to her."

What did you learn about yourself?

After being divorced, they both eventually came to a place in their healing where they were happy being by themselves with God. Dixie said, "I got to a point where I was a complete whole person...just me and God...and didn't need anybody else."

Gary said, "Actually, at first, I didn't spend time alone when my wife left. My daughter was a teenager, so she was gone a lot. I'm such a social person, so I would go to people's houses, just visit with all the different friends in the church. I would get home at 11p at and I could just go right to sleep."

He thoughtfully said, "God had me begin little by little thinking...'Why are you doing this? Why are you doing nothing?' 'Well, I'm visiting my people'. No...I was doing it because I didn't want to be alone with myself. I didn't think very highly of myself, so I didn't want to be alone with myself and think about my short comings and...my failures."

"It sounds crazy," he continued, "but staying home wasn't easy for me but I started. Not that I had to read the Bible all the time, but it was just being quiet and letting God be there. It was amazing...little by little...little revelations began coming to me about my short comings and why I felt this way about myself."

He told God, 'Well, I failed in this area years ago and I was really a mess. I was terrible.' God said, 'Ask Me how I feel about it'. God's answer was: 'You did the best you could do with everything you knew. I'm proud of you.'

"That's when I realized God really liked me. Everybody knows He has to love you...that's kind of a given. He's gotta love you. The fact that He likes me and wants to be with me. So, I'm a likable person? I'm being successful in His sight? Wow...that's a really big deal. So maybe I'm not so bad'.

So, I began to see myself more as God sees me and it gave me self-esteem and confidence. I really began to believe I could do anything God called me to do."

How did you prepare for marriage?

After dating about six months, they knew they wanted to get married. They met with a mentor couple and during that meeting, they asked questions that made her think and pray about why she thought this marriage would be different. "They asked me why I thought this marriage would make it. They told me I needed to pray about it. I needed to know if I was going to marry Gary, it had to be a real commitment and not just a 'I feel like I love him right now' kind of thing."

They also went through premarital counseling where the counselor told them, 'You know each other's weaknesses and strengths. If you think you can't live with that, now is the time, before you get married, to say, 'I don't think I can do this'. "So, we had every opportunity to not get married if we felt like we shouldn't be together."

They originally planned to get married in a year, but Dixie said, "We both really felt this is what God wanted for us." Instead of dragging this out for a year, they shortened the length of their engagement and got married sooner than later.

Someone between them

Dixie took a deep breath as she walked into a painful time in their marriage. "This is when you've got to get real and share the terrible stuff in the past." She felt some women he knew had developed some attraction to him. She continued, "Maybe some hoped to be the next Mrs. and I was raining on their parade. I felt even some of the married ones...were wanting some kind of attention from him. If I was there, I would be in the way. Everyone kept telling me all those things weren't real and I was just jealous...but..."

We were aware this was still a very sensitive subject for Dixie as she continued, "In our marriage, it took five years to work through that. I felt there was an unhealthy attraction between Gary and another woman. They both were good friends and both kind of needed to be there for each other. I really felt like they had a history. They had known each other for years and he had only known me for six months."

There was a pained look in her eyes. She related that even after they moved away from Florida, there would still be long phone calls between the two of them. Dixie felt it was not healthy for their marriage. "Talk to her and get off the phone!

191

You don't have to be on the phone with her an hour. I told you not to do that'!"

Gary said he was sorry but was unsure how to accomplish that and get off the phone without hurting her feelings.

Dixie's advice was: 'Draw a healthy line that says...friendship.' "It was a big deal to me. In fact, it was the one time I thought I was going to leave him. I called my friend and mentor and said, 'That's it! I'm leaving him. I'm done! I've tried to work through this the best I can, and this has happened again and again and again and again. It's obvious. I'm done. I'm leaving'!"

Her mentor said, 'You've got to step up to <u>one</u> commitment in your life. Just once in your life be committed. Pray about it!' So, I got off the phone and prayed. God didn't say, 'Leave him' but He did give me a book called, 'The Power of a Praying Wife'. It was a 30 day thing. When Gary got home, I told him...'I'm going to go through this book. He got 'The Power of a Praying Husband' book. I said, 'At the end of the 30-day period we're going to get back together and see what we're going to do with this marriage.' At the end of the 30 days, we decided to stay together."

Tears welled up in her eyes as she continued, "It was like Satan was trying to break us up from day one! We had to put our foot down and break off that friendship. That's what it took for me to realize it was over, that it wasn't going to be a problem anymore."

Make or break incident

Gary said, "I remember an incident that really could have been a 'make us or break us' time. After a divorce, there are scars. I had in my mind if there was ever an argument or anything like that, we needed to stay right there. We needed to work through it and talk through it, settle it and it would be done. Then, we wouldn't have to worry about it building up into a bigger problem. Well, we had something come up and I said, 'Let's talk about this'."

She was pretty upset and said, 'No, I don't want to talk about it.'

'No, come on, we need to talk about it!' They both laughed as he said, "And she's walking away as fast as she could. She really didn't want to talk about it." Their faces took on a more serious look. I reached out and grabbed her arm and said, 'No, come on. Let's talk.' She pulled away. I grabbed her hard enough that the next day it left a bruise on her arm. I realized then...this can never, never happen again!"

What are you afraid of?

Gary went to a counselor and told him the whole story. The counselor said, 'So what were you afraid of?' Gary thought, 'What are you talking about? I'm a big boy, you know.' He repeated, 'What are you afraid of if you didn't talk right that minute. Why was that such a big deal?' "Then it dawned on me...'I already had one wife leave, I'm not going to have another leave'!" The realization finally hit him that his wife might not want to talk right that minute, but he pushed to talk it out so it wouldn't end like his first marriage.

He still marveled, "It was amazing God gave the counselor those words right then. It just showed me I was afraid...afraid it would happen again. That changed my life. Changed my demeanor. It made a really huge difference in our relationship.

I think if I had kept on and on through these little incidences, it could have potentially broken us up."

I don't give up on anything!

"Give up? No!" Gary said, "I don't give up on anything - EVER. So, 'No'— but I did think...'You know, this really stinks! The period we're in right now is really terrible and I don't like the way she talked to me just then.' I can really get mad but I'm not really one to say, 'Forget it...I'm leaving'. I just don't think that."

She smiled, "I have learned there are going to be difficulties in EVERY marriage. You kind of trade one bad thing for the next and at some point, you just have to come down to commitment. This is what I promised before the Lord to do...stay married to this man. Through the difficult times, I'm going to stay with him. Live life with him because even the next person I could find might be better in one way but worse in another way!" she laughed. "I really believe that's true".

Her adamant declaration: "I'm going to make this work with Gary, and this is going to be my last marriage!"

Nothing can stop us!

"I'm really not sure about our greatest blessing. Not that we don't have any," he laughed. "It's just which one is the greatest!" After a short pause he said, "At first we had a rocky road. Her experience with marriage was extremely difficult and so was mine. When you bring two people like that together...it's a lot of difficulty! The very first years were up and down, up and down. Then, little by little, I began to notice she would help me and encourage me. That's my love language...that's my deal, right there. Even if I'm fixing a door and she doesn't know anything about fixing a door, if she comes over to bring me a glass of water."

As he lifted his arm up high over his head, he said, "Boy...that makes me about ten feet tall". The smiles wouldn't stop as he continued, "That just rings my bell! She likes me! She helped me! She brought me a glass of water! Hmphhh...I'm going to beat this door!"

Laughing as they looked at each other, he continued, "It seems silly, but that's the way I feel on the inside! If she comes and puts her hand on my shoulder and just pats me, she doesn't even have to say anything. I know she loves me...but she likes me, too. You can love somebody and stick with them forever and ever and ever, but you don't really have to like them all that much. She does things that show me she likes me, too. If I ask if she has some time off work to do something silly like go to the movies in the middle of the day...she'll say, 'Yeh...let's do that!' Oooh my!" Gary's laughed, "I'm ready to go!"

His smile continued, "One of the greatest blessings for me is I feel like we're a team. I know for sure God brought us together and if we work together as one...nothing can stop us! That's what excites me! I feel like we can do anything God calls us to do...together. Whatever God has in the future for us to do, we will be good together as we help each other. He's a blessing to me because he's a real companion. We have fun hanging out together...out to dinner, to the movies or just hanging out watching TV at home. Whatever we're doing, we're good company...good friends.

When I first started my business, not all my days were filled up with clients, so some days I would go work with him. I think we got along better when we were working together," they both laughed, "than we ever did! He taught me how to do a lot of neat stuff and gave me confidence in using different power tools that I would never have done on my own. We really had some good experiences working together."

Lessons learned

According to Gary, "The greatest lesson I learned was not just to listen but to hear. Listening is hearing the words, but hearing is really understanding what effect it is having on the person who is speaking. My ex-wife always wanted me to spend more time at home.' I had to work. I was a missionary and then a pastor. I had all that work, so I didn't have a lot of time." He admitted he has now learned he could have arranged his schedule to match his priorities. "Even if I have to work ten hours, if Dixie says, 'I feel a little lonely or I wish you could be with me more'...BINGO...I gotta do that! I've learned to listen to Dixie and hear her...understand what she's saying."

Your kids – My kids

Dixie's' Mom heart' spoke, "It's important to really think about the kids before you get divorced. No one's going to love that child like their real father or their real mother. Don't take divorce lightly and think, 'Oh, I'm going to find someone else who is going to fill this person's shoes and make me happier'. When the kids get to be teenagers and get difficult, that's when the real parent will do things for that child that a stepparent won't. They just don't have that same empathy. They can know the kids since they were little bitty and help raise them, but still you can't replace the real parent when it comes down to it."

When they met, Dixie's children were about four, five and nine. Gary's son was already out of the house and his daughter was in high school. They recognize there were a different set of challenges for the younger children in divorce. "I think sometimes Gary felt like I put the kids in front of him." Tears begin to flow, "It's like you're trying so hard to protect your kid from anything."

"I had never been a step-Dad," Gary said, "and I wanted to treat them as if they were my own children. I wanted them to think and feel as if I treated them as a real Dad. That wasn't possible." Gary discovered and accepted that fact because they had a Dad already. "No other man could replace him in that position.

Then there's the discipline of the children when they do something wrong. I would discipline differently than Dixie would. With her divorce, there were guidelines on how you discipline. I couldn't comprehend that, so that part was very difficult for me. I honestly had to really...and it took some years...to really learn to just back off. I could be very kind and nice to the kids and do as much as I could with them and for them, but I had to really back off."

Admittedly, adding children from both families into the marriage, brought some additional stress and challenges. Instead of putting out the claws to protect their own children, they had to learn how to work together to develop solutions that were best for their whole family.

She laughs at my jokes

"He's a good provider. I had a few surgeries along the way and there was no way I could have afforded them on my own. Gary was always there to take care of me. I don't have to worry about that kind of stuff. God is really our source, but He always provides Gary with the work or whatever we need to get through."

Gary jumped in, "I think she's fun! She laughs at my jokes--that I know are really not all that funny!" They both laughed as he continued, "Sometimes, I even had good jokes. Sometimes she just laughs because she knows I need a laugh in my day. After I grew my beard she said, 'I'll give you a kiss, 'Mr. Prickly'!" His laugh resounded in the room, "I'd rub against her cheek and she'd laugh and laugh and laugh. She laughs a lot and she makes things fun."

Advice about marriage

"You have to give a lot of grace," Dixie said, "just like God gives us grace. I've had to come to the realization I am the biggest of sinners as anybody else and God doesn't have big sins and little sins. Sin is sin and it separates you from God. You've got to stay close to the Lord in order to stay close to your spouse. We have to forgive even if we think what the other person has done is way worse than anything we have ever done." She ended with, "Work on that marriage...it takes a lot of work. Be purposeful about it."

He said, "In order to come into a marriage, you need to be a complete person...by having a relationship, a really strong relationship, with God. He loves us and gives us grace. So many guys come into a marriage wanting that wife to complete him. That's a big burden. Let God do that before you come into a relationship. If two people are healthy and strong coming into a relationship...WOW! Then once you get into the relationship," Gary added with a snicker, "It's still crazy...because none of us are perfect."

Dixie's summarized, "Let God be the source of your own happiness and your own joy and your own strength. Don't rely on the other person to fill all those needs."

Important battle to fight

Their story may have started as impossible, but Gary and Dixie ended with this thought: "Marriage is an important battle to fight." The story of their hearts is filled with battles, many not of their choosing, but battles they were and are willing to fight. Instead of fighting face to face, they are approaching the battles that try to destroy their marriage by fighting side by side!!

Hollis & Carol Jean – A Three Sided Love Affair

MARRIED 49 YEARS

"Though one may be overpowered, two can defend themselves. A cord of three strands is not quickly broken." Eccl 4:12

Their love story began...

At least <u>his</u> love story began, since he fell in love with her first.

"She sat down the row from me and there was just something about this little red head that kept attracting me. It was during that time in my life, where I had dated but I had never been in love. The issue of love kept rising up inside me...'there's something different here'...'there's something different here'."

He looked over into her eyes and said, "God opened the door through a friend of mine who said to me one day, 'Hey, have you considered dating this red head named Carol Jean?' I thought, 'I'd <u>love</u> to do that'!"

"We were freshmen at college, and he was literally three seats to my right in Botany class, but I didn't notice him because #1 – he was very shy and #2 - I came to college to date older men. He was a freshman. Check that off your list! So, my freshman year, I dated anything that would move--that was older. That's the truth!" Hollis looked over at her and shook his head back and forth in disbelief!

"I know!" she took up where she left off. "God was dealing with my heart and in the Spring of my freshman year, I remember sitting in my dorm room with my back up against this wall and just giving up saying, 'God, I...I'm done...I'm through...I've messed up. Whatever you want to do...You do'! God took me to a Scripture and He just began to love on me as the Savior does and forgive me and refresh me. I was committed in the Spring just not to chase another guy...but all of a sudden, my eye notices him," she pointed to Hollis.

On this little college campus, everyone ate together in one dining hall. "For us girls, if you are interested in somebody, your peripheral vision is working fulltime. You kind of know where that guy is all the time. I'm sitting with my girlfriends and he had not asked me out yet but again, I was using manipulation...undoubtedly far more advanced than Manipulation 101!" She laughed and Hollis just had this wide grin on his face.

"I knew Hollis is about to walk down right behind me and I know he's very shy...so I need to help him, don't I?", she laughed. "He's about right here," she motioned with her arm. "He's walking, walking...peripheral is working and I shoved my chair out from the table and just looked up at him and batted my eyes."

By then, she was laughing so hard she let a little bit of the country come out of her and she started slapping her knee. Back to the eye batting encounter. 'Guess where I'm working this summer'?

Hollis pretended to yawn and now they were both laughing hilariously! She got a summer job at a hospital that 'just happened' to be a 15-minute drive from the farm where Hollis was raised. "I honestly didn't know what his reaction would be, but I knew if I didn't do it now...I'd never do it. I had to be that spontaneous. I think he was very polite because he's just a polite person. He said, 'Oh...that's nice.' 'OK'...and I scooted back up to the table with my girlfriends again."

This shy guy just didn't take the hint, so she mentioned it to her roommate who worked behind the scenes to get word back to Hollis. She smiled at her husband, "That gave this shy man the courage to ask me out."

Tennis un-date

He looked at her and displayed that little boyish kind of grin of his as she continued, "He asked me to go play tennis on a Sunday afternoon. I said, 'Sure! Sure?' I didn't know how to play tennis but, I was sure I could figure that out."

They both laughed out loud and she kept laughing when she said, "So, enter Manipulation 201!" So, on their first date, they were heading out of the dorm when Carol Jean piped up, 'You know...my roommate's boyfriend is pitching today. Want to go see his game?' And being the kind, considerate man that he was, Hollis agreed. They went to the game and 'Ta-da'...she never had to play tennis. In addition, she never let Hollis know she didn't even know how to play tennis!

Loved her before she knew it!

For all her planning and in her words, 'manipulating' going on, "I believe him when he said he knew he loved me before I knew it." She choked on her words and tears formed in her eyes as she said, "...and I'm grateful!"

"One of the things that just undid me about Hollis was I had never met a man so kind. I had dated a lot of men and in all my shallowness, I would go with the outward appearance. This guy", she looked over at Hollis, "was incredibly handsome and IS incredibly handsome." She made a 'Whooosh' movement with her hand and pointed at him as tears formed in the corner of her eyes. "That drew me to him, but I tell you, the staying power was the character of the man and how kind he was.

In the messiness and the pride and the arrogance and the manipulation and the self-centeredness and all that stuff what just whirls around an 18 year-old, God so mercifully gave us to each other. That's the simple truth."

He popped the question and she...

By the end of the summer, he was ready to pop the question. He arranged for them to go to a beautiful beach on Padre Island near Corpus Christi. Carol Jean reminisced, "There was a full moon coming up in the horizon. We were outside the car and I was leaned up against the car and the moon was shining on my face. He looked into my face and very tenderly asked me to marry him. I looked at him and I went, 'Nope'!" She guffawed at her terse answer.

All Hollis could do was shake his head as he recalled saying the only word he could get out of his mouth, 'What??'

In case he missed it, she repeated, 'No...I don't think so.

The bottom line...I said 'No'...#1 because it scared me because that's forever. I was raised by a Mom and Dad, that for better or worse lived together. I knew the depth and breadth of saying 'yes' and it scared me. Honestly, #2 - there was a selfish part of me that was kind of looking over his shoulder thinking, 'Well, maybe there's somebody better!!' Laughing and slapping her knee, she said, "I kid you not! I didn't say all that but that's what was going on the inside."

Hollis interjected, "Somewhere in this...she made the statement: 'You know...I've got places to go, people to see and things to do'."

Unbelievably, she mouthed those same words while he said them!

Not taking 'No' for an answer

Hollis continued, "Oh'...but in my spirit I was thinking, 'God, you still have some work to do in this young lady because she doesn't understand.' I don't mean that to be arrogant. That was just the reassurance I had that He had brought this woman to me...and...she just didn't realize it."

"No...No, I didn't'."

"It didn't deter me. I took her home that night. Said goodnight to her. Then I said, 'OK...God. If I'm wrong in this, then I need to know'." Open to God's leading, Hollis had to admit, "My heart's beating 99,000 mph, I am in love and I know this to be so different from everything else I've experienced." So, he went back to Carol Jean the next night!

"I held out for 24 hours," she laughed. "Aren't I a strong woman?"

Her heart caught up with his

Sitting out in the yard one night, she knew he was the one! He gave her what she calls, 'a lot of grace'. He didn't throw it back in her face but displayed a grateful, thankful heart until her heart finally caught up with his.

A wedding had to be delayed because Hollis was attending college on a track scholarship and if married, would lose those funds. That's when she headed to Corpus Christi to pursue a career and Hollis went back to college.

After one semester, she said, "God just cemented in that semester, this was not where He wanted me to be. He wanted me back at Howard Payne College. So, we did a lot of talking over the phone and a lot of things really grew because we weren't together physically. The friendship began to grow, and the trust began to grow. The character issues began to grow. So, we finally married in May of 1970 and then finished out our Senior year."

Advice from Dad

Hollis trusted his Dad's wisdom. "When he came down to pick me up from work after the night shift, we are sitting on the side of his pick-up. I said, 'Dad, I think Carol Jean is the one. Do you have any counsel for me?' He said, 'Hmmm...you just need to know '#1 – She's not going to live with us' and '#2 – She's your wife. She's not ours'."

Carol Jean, with a very straight face, gave her interpretation, "<u>You</u> gotta live with her!"

Hollis laughed, "I thought...that's pretty simple. I can do that...and that took away the stress. My Dad wasn't saying the word, but he was saying 'It's a covenant relationship and you don't break your covenant'."

Carol Jean smiled, "...wise man!"

Their journey...

Hollis said, "It's a journey of realizing even though we think we're giving 100% to the relationship and we're giving 100% to God's leadership...we're not!" They admitted God was training and growing them, and still is today.

About two to three years into their marriage, they moved to West Texas Boys Ranch, where they would be a part of managing 72 boys and 20 plus Staff.

At the same time, they were growing in their relationship with each other and were by now, raising a child and had one on the way. Hollis explained their choice, "All of those components drew us into either dependence on ourselves or dependence on Him in ways we didn't even realize."

During that time, they began attending a church where they were comprehending the role of the Holy Spirit in their lives and in their marriage. Hollis said, "Now we have the gathering of the Holy Spirit into our relationship and 'Wow'...this is changing things! This is changing how I look at my wife. This is changing how I care for our daughter. This is changing how we deal with the staff and kids. This is changing everything." God didn't only change their lives, He also began to prepare them as He changed their future.

She wanted NO part of it!

They loved their roles at the Ranch, his as Program Director and hers as part time Counselor. They were content and saw God use them to guide the boys they grew to love. That's when God shook up the norm and began to speak to Hollis about leaving the Ranch and go back to the family farm. Only...Carol Jean wanted no part of it!

"The challenge was not only for him to trust that God was saying to leave this place and to go farm, but for me as his wife, his friend, and as a mother of two children, it was challenging to believe this was God speaking. Pure and simple. I failed the challenge. I finally said, 'OK...I'll go' but, on the inside, I was dragging my feet all the way from San Angelo to Corpus Christi."

She laughed, "Being challenged is a good thing...rebellion is not! But...God knows what to do with rebellion. He knew what to do with a hard heart. At the age of 26, when we went to the farm, God got ahold of me in a way that I'd never been touched before."

Walking through this time, she had to ask herself some questions. "Was He faithful to me as a child when I asked Him into my heart? Yes! Was He faithful as He poured into me as a teenager? Yes! Was He faithful in college? Yes! Was He faithful now at Boys Ranch? Yes! But, when He put me on that farm, I knew, that I knew, that I knew I needed every drop of blood shed on the cross for me. God killed that root of arrogance...haughtiness. He killed it through a series of events because He loved me."

Hollis admitted he didn't know how to communicate God's direction to his wife. "Like all of us," he said, "it's one breath at a time and it's one heartbeat at a time. God was having to teach me how to walk in humility and teach me how to trust Him beyond what I hear my wife say....to hear her fears, her anxiety or her response."

He would sit in his office at night and plead with God for direction and for strength. 'Am I hearing You right? Is this what you're saying?' Through the process, God began to say to him, 'I want you to be able to release your wife from this (farm) vision...release her from it. Give her grace to come when she's ready'. I thought, 'That sounds crazy, but I'll say it anyway.' I sat down with Carol Jean and said, 'I'm not trying to make you be something you're not. As much as I understand, God is saying this is where He wants us to go. He is saying to me, '...just trust Me'. If you need another month to stay here and counsel with the boys, it's yours. I'm not afraid of that.'

"By God's grace, she said, 'I'll go'."

They both laughed in unison when Carol Jean said, "That's exactly what I said...'I'll go'...but with my arms folded across my chest."

And so, they began their totally different life on the family farm.

Marriage and faith entwined

When they moved back to the farm, he worked closely with his Dad. "I knew I was trying to perform for my Dad just like I was trying to perform for my wife. None of it was working and there was no peace in my reality."

So, God arranged for him to sit down with his Dad on the grass next to the barn. As they leaned up against the barn, Hollis confessed to his Dad about his struggle with allowing God to be the Lord of his life. 'You know, Dad. I have never really understood the Lordship so one of the things that He's done is He's exposed areas where I've...I've allowed, you Dad, to be Lord in a way that was disrespectful to you and I want to ask you forgiveness. Jesus is my Lord and He's teaching me how to walk in submission to Him and if I let you be my Lord, rather than Him...I'm dishonoring Him. I want to get this into balance so, Dad, would you forgive me for having it out of bounds'?

"My Dad couldn't say anything...just made the OK sign, implying 'I gotcha'! God's ownership (of our lives) has become the delight of our life rather than the resistance that we so easily were walking in. God was cleaning house!"

It was obvious their faith and marriage were inextricably entwined as Carol Jean began, "Jesus Christ is everything for both of us. There is such a maturation of knowing the best gift I can give to him is to be desperately in love with my Savior...his Savior, too. That didn't come overnight."

During this time in their marriage, it seemed to be typical for Carol Jean to think about Hollis, 'You've got to be my answer!' "He loved to love me in all those ways...as counselor and pastor but that misguided affection had to come to an end. There were sometimes repeat lessons where I woke up and knew my Savior was not to the left of me in bed. My Savior is Jesus Christ who shed His blood for me. I do love Hollis with my whole heart." She looked deeply at her husband, "But, he's second. It's true!"

We didn't have a clue!

As they have observed other marriages over the past 49 years, they were noting many of the couples they knew who were no longer married. "Sadly, many of them are not married now because there wasn't an understanding of a covenant relationship. It was more like, 'I'm in charge...you don't like it.' He pointed his thumb like an umpire, 'So, zip - you're outta here!"

They both agreed when he said, "We've had those moments where it's like, 'I've had enough of this. I want out.' Yet, that stability of the Spirit is what we chose to stand on, even though from our perspective it seemed pretty fragile. God's never fragile."

Carol Jean began pensively, "I believe the Bible period. I don't understand it all, but I believe it is God's love language to us. It's His love letter to us. It's Him saying, 'This is Who I am, and I want you to know Me'.

As a woman, He talks about submission. I believe in submission, but the challenge is always, 'How do I walk alongside this partner...this man that I am one with...in a submitted position and not lose what God is calling me to do'?" She folded her hands as if praying to demonstrate how those two things line up and intertwine.

She shared how the Holy Spirit had to be in the middle of her life explaining how He wanted her to walk in submission. 'This is what I want you to be about and I want you to bring it to your husband. Watch how I will use him to complement you or bring you into that unity of heart and mind.' If I don't trust Holy Spirit for that, I will either stuff it and walk in resentment or else I'll be domineering and say, 'If you don't see it...then you've got issues'!

When asked how to affirm each other and not lose her own God-given direction, she said, "If He is the Author and Finisher of our faith, then those things are going to work together. It's one of those mysteries that takes Holy Spirit to teach us on a daily basis."

Hollis said, "God has formed a structure within the family that He honors. We were both trying to do the best we understood. Head of the house...wife...husband...Mom and Dad...but we didn't have a clue! We were so invested in our ideas of what the husband should do and the wife should do. We had taken the cultural perspectives and we were trying very hard to make sure the Holy Spirit agreed with us." He laughed as he recounted his idea: " 'Jesus...this has gotta be right'!"

Screamin' and hollerin' in the barn!

Hollis said, "God brought us to this one refining point. It was an afternoon. It was hot. I was working in the shop about 50 feet from the house. Carol Jean came out of the house. She's upset! I'm upset! I don't even remember the circumstance, but it had to do with the reality found in Ephesians 5:22: 'Wives submit to your husbands as to the Lord, for the husband is the head of the wife, even as Christ is the head of the church, His body, and Himself its Savior'. We had no clue what that meant. It was distorted from my perspective of, 'Do what I tell yah.' and her going, 'Like hell I will'!"

He looked over at Carol Jean and added, "It was just stupid that afternoon with all the screamin' and hollerin' that took place in the barn. Both of us were shocked by God. Literally, it was that prod stick that the rancher uses with the cattle. He shocked us." His voice cracked as he struggled to talk. "It was His love so deeply that said, 'I can't let you go on like this. Hollis, I've called you to be head of the house.' I said loudly, 'I don't want to do it!!! I don't like it. It's not my plan. She does a better job of running things'."

There God was right in the middle of all their crying and shouting. Then He spoke to their hearts, 'But, I'm never going to leave you in this. I am so committed to you. I just want you both to agree with Me that My plan works.'

Hollis struggled with tears and words as he told us, "...and so in our brokenness, we agreed with God, but we were both skeptics. A couple of days later, as we loaded up the kids in the car, Carol Jean, said, 'OK...I want you to know I will no longer challenge your leadership in this family'."

She laughed as she said, "I think I used the word 'fight' your leadership."

He smiled as he relayed God's statement to him, 'Now, you've heard it. I've convinced her. Now are you going to let me lead through you?'

Finally, he came to the realization it was just he and God leading a family and he didn't know how to get there. In those moments, he gave God permission to be God. "Then, having no clue how to submit...we submitted...knowing there's nothing else that works so why not try this. We didn't understand that at the time, but we knew we were not going to go back to the old process that was such a failure."

Rejoice and be glad

Carol Jean began by reciting a verse of a song based on Psalm 188:24, 'This is the day the Lord has made. We will rejoice and be glad in it.' "Hollis and I love each other...respect each other. We would rather be around each other than anybody else. That's just a sign of God's transforming work in our lives because there have been multiple times where it was be around anybody BUT each other!!! We have been in rough places, but our marriage is forever being refined by the Lord."

She knew she was a people pleaser and would do just about anything to avoid a conflict, an action very toxic to their marriage. "Our people pleasing desire makes us," as Carol Jean put it, " 'dread the mess more than we fear God'. We all have a sense of self-preservation where our desire is to just 'go along to get along'." She began to recognize that the enemy liked to be right in the middle of their messes, trying to stop them from walking where God would have them walk.

"That," Hollis said, "is exactly what God is doing still today." He wiped his eyes as he said, "We can run our lives without Him and produce garbage or we can let Him run with us in His purpose and He gets to produce His beauty in us. That, to me, was the most significant thing He did from the beginning to start this process. He confronted us with lies we believed. He let us know the blood of Jesus Christ was great enough to forgive those sins based on the lies we believed, and the blood of Jesus Christ was perfect enough to empower us to start living in His righteousness we couldn't live in without Him. The rest of the journey and by His grace, we are riding on His wheels rather than on our wheels."

Value in each other

"What I appreciate and value in Carol Jean is that she has made a commitment of covenant, as I have. As much as the old voices and the old lies wanted her to stop and not be a part of this covenant...she's not stopped. That's an awesome, awesome thing. God continues to show me who she is from His perspective. When God speaks about Carol Jean to me, He would always call her His precious perfume." He looked over at Carol Jean and said, "I knew He was telling the truth when He first said it, but I shared it with her one time, and she didn't believe it. Now, I see her believing it. I see her living it. I know the joy that it brings to me because that's one of His promises He said He would do in her.

In my misunderstanding, I tried to help Him with it. It became pretty obvious, that it was stupid." Carol Jean cried as Hollis said, "There needed to be a shift in our marriage and God brought us through that shift. It was a wonderful, humbling process."

Walking around praying

In retrospect, Carol Jean said, "I heard stories that when Hollis was 18 years old..." She struggled for words and fought back tears, "...he would walk around the lake close to our college. His desperate cry was: 'God, if you're real...talk to me!' And the story goes that he would be out there yelling...yelling...crying out with his whole heart. This hunger to know God and to be known has just always been there in him."

In their sixth through thirteenth years of marriage, she realized when he went out into the fields or on the tractor, it was much like he had been walking around the lake again. "He came back a much better guy. It was a big shift. There was a countenance...there was a clarity. He was more manly...he was more husband...he was more friend. When Christ says, 'You might have life and life more abundantly'...I was seeing it manifested in my mate."

"In the last couple of years, I told him, 'Honey...the older you get the more ravenous you seem to be in the things of God...of what God wants to show you and what He wants to teach you. You are always going over that next hill'." She admitted, there were times when she was just plain tired...but NOT Hollis! "It's that fervor... I just so admire that because I am his. In covenant, what is his is mine and what God is doing in me is his. It's amazing. Everything God pours into me spills over to him. It infuses in him. It's amazing to watch that principle. I want more of God working that out in me."

As he smiled shyly, she told us if he has to walk into an intimidating situation, "God just brings him a love and a humility that levels the playing field." Her voice cracked, and she fought back tears. "I've seen it almost every day of my life. He's just not afraid because he's got both eyes on his Savior who answered the question of an 18-year old walking around a lake screaming...'God is'...present tense...'GOD IS!'

As Hollis likes to say, and I agree, 'It is so much fun to be a son of the living God'." According to Carol Jean, Hollis doesn't live a compartmentalized life. "He is the same with you as he is when all the lights are off and he's up to here with whatever spiritual battle. He is the same."

What should you do?

Carol Jean said, "First, have a relationship with Jesus Christ...invite Him into your life. Ask Him not only to save you from your sins but let Him be the Lord of your life...be your boss. Pray with your spouse. Don't worry about how to pray. Just pray together whether that's on your knees or in the car or laying side by side in the bed. Pray. Go to God together and say: 'Jesus, we love you. We need you. We want you. Teach us.' Did I say every day? Everyday!"

Reaching out to young couples through their ministry, Hollis said he was learning how to be very confrontational and yet compassionate. To simply say to them: 'We acknowledge you have an understanding of the kind of lifestyle you want to live, but we want to give you an opportunity to encounter the Giver of value and His Name is Jesus. You can look at us...a bunch of white hairs. You can make assumptions, but the bottom line is, we started out just like you and we thought we had a great handle on what life was meant to be. We lived it the way we thought was correct and God in His grace and His mercy said, 'Now time's up.' If not for His grace and His mercy, with that act of love, we would still be screwed up. We don't want you to be screwed up'.

A three-sided love affair

When their relationship began, they had what appeared to be a one-sided love affair. Hollis in love and Carol Jean resisting. They bonded to each other through Christ and it was soon a three-sided love affair.

"Though one may be overpowered, two can defend themselves. A cord of three strands is not quickly broken." Ecclesiastes 4:12

Randy & Gail – Lord, I Can't Do This Anymore!

MARRIED 45 YEARS

"But we have this treasure in jars of clay to show that this all-surpassing power is from God and not from us. We are hard pressed on every side, but not crushed; perplexed, but not in despair; persecuted, but not abandoned; struck down, but not destroyed." 2 Corinthians 4:7-9

Some women grow up thinking about marrying Prince Charming and living together in the little cottage with a white picket fence. According to Gail, that might have well described her childhood dream. Her Prince Charming dream came true when she met Randy in high school. One thing she could never guess was how the 'ever after' would turn out.

Prince Charming and the Farm Girl

Although they knew each other casually in high school, it wasn't until after graduation they began to see each other. Prince Charming lost his license and needed a ride to a party. "I couldn't believe Randy was asking me for a ride because I felt he was totally out of my league! He was a wrestling jock and so short, dark and handsome! By the end of the evening, he had asked me on a date."

"We went to the drive-in and he actually wanted to watch the movie...the ENTIRE time," she laughed. Gail looked adoringly at him and said, "He was a perfect gentleman. When I got home, I told my Mom, 'I just went out with the man I want to marry.' Three and a half years later, we were."

Randy rolled his eyes and rebutted, "I didn't feel like a jock." He put a lot of pressure on himself as a wrestler and when he didn't win the state tournament three years in a row, he felt like a failure. "Every time I did anything, I felt like a failure. I was liked in school, though I kind of felt alone," his voice trailed off.

"I knew that he was a jock and very popular. I mean, he was on the prom court but when I went out with him, he was just this very humble guy. That's what attracted me so much." She looked over at Randy, "In everybody else's' eyes you were a hero, but you didn't see that in yourself."

Randy firmly declared, "I would never go out with a girl, no matter how pretty she was if she thought she was better than somebody else. Gail was nothing like that. She was just a..."

Gail completed, "...a farm girl..."

Smiling as if they were actually back in those early days of their relationship, Randy finished her thought, "...a farm girl that was friendly and didn't think she was better than anybody. I liked that a lot."

Their inside joke

Gail broke into uncontrollable giggles and covered her eyes as if she was embarrassed. By now, they could hardly finish their sentences. Gail finally told us the inside joke. "The first night we were going out, he tried to get out of it. I didn't know it at time but there were a couple of other girls in the mix. He made a date with one of them for that same night so, he was trying to get out of our date."

His excuse to me, 'Well...I don't have wheels.'

'Well, I do.'

Excuse #2...'Well, I have a baseball game.'

'We'll go after the game.'

"I wasn't going to let him out of it, so I told him I would be at the park to pick him up after the game. I had on a pair of red hot-pants with suspenders. He was up to bat and struck out. He said it was because he saw me in my hot-pants, and he got distracted." Gail admitted she had to fight to win him over and eventually knocked all the other girls out of the running. In about a month, they were dating exclusively.

They talked about getting married one day and the most innocent marriage remark came out of Randy's mouth when he said, "Gee, that wouldn't be all bad." He felt most guys, including him, think about the sex but he said, "It went way deeper than that because of the kind of person she was."

"I remember that was when I realized he was more than a boyfriend. He was my confidante. He was somebody I truly trusted and he was my friend."

Speed bump

Every smooth road has a few bumps and when Gail got pregnant, Randy worried she might step on the brakes and not want to marry him. He said this was the first time he got a little scared.

As they went down the list of options, abortion was an absolute 'NO' from both of them! Gail said, "It about broke our hearts at even the thought of it. We felt, 'This is a real child! He was not a mistake!' Today, he is an awesome young man and we couldn't love him more. However, the pregnancy did make things kind of speed up in our relationship."

Would she accept?

They were driving out in the country when Randy pulled over and proposed. He lowered his eyes, "It wasn't very romantic..."

"No, but it was sweet. He put thought into it and it was the best he knew how to do," she tenderly patted his arm. "It was endearing and very unique. He handed me a diamond, but it was so dark I couldn't see it."

Randy laughed until his shoulders were shaking. "I don't think I said anything because you I thought you knew what it meant."

Gail joined his laughter, "He borrowed my car to get the ring and brought his brother to help pick it out." With joy in her heart bubbling to her eyes, she said, "I think then it was nice for the man to pick out the ring and present it to the woman. I have the same ring and hardly ever have taken it off."

Married but alone

Standing at the altar, they were both very young. Gail was 19 and Randy was almost 21. It seems Randy still had some young guy partying to get out of his system.

"I knew he had a little bit of a wild side, but I figured I'd be able to train that...calm him down. We always think we can fix people, don't we? It doesn't work that way."

Randy still enjoyed partying with his friends. He grew up in church but walked away from his faith as he started drinking and going along with the crowd. Today he is ashamed of that time in his life, but back then he didn't feel guilt over anything because he was running from God.

Gail said, "I didn't understand. My heart was so into our relationship and all I wanted to do was spend every waking hour with my husband. It was hard for me to understand why he would still want to go out with his buddies. It caused a lot of insecurities in me. I wouldn't say he was an alcoholic but more of a social alcoholic. When he went out, he went with the intention of getting drunk. So, I didn't know if I was going to get a call in the night from the police or the hospital."

She often felt married but alone.

The thing we hated saved us...

Five years into their marriage, Randy was 25 years old and serving in the military. They were expecting their second son, Nathan. Everything seemed normal until he came home from work one night.

"I asked him if he would take out the garbage. He said, 'No, I can't'. I thought, 'Well, you've done it hundreds of times before...why can't you?' He said, 'I just can't'. I stopped what I was doing and went out to see him face to face. He had a real pained look on his face, and he said, 'I just can't'. He turned around and was walking up the stairs...practically crawling up the stairs and I couldn't understand what was going on."

She was supposed to go bowling that night but before she left, she went upstairs to see how he was doing. What she found was her husband who said, 'I feel like I've got the whole world on my shoulders and it hurts so bad! It feels like someone punched me in the stomach and didn't remove their fist.'

She wanted to stay home but Randy insisted she go bowling because he thought he just needed some sleep. She very reluctantly left their son with a friend. "I got half-way there and realized I didn't have my bowling ball. (This was such a God-incident.) I turned around and went back home. When I walked into the house, I could hear this crying...but it sounded like a wounded animal. It took me awhile to find him, but he was on the floor in the corner in a fetal position...rolling back and forth...holding his stomach...crying like a baby. It was heart wrenching. I said, 'This is going to take more than chicken noodle soup. This is something very different than I've ever seen before'."

Randy was diagnosed with manic-depression - which is better known today as bipolar. Gail said, "Neither one of us were familiar with that illness. I thought it was something you would take a pill for and it would go away, but it turns out it's a life-long sickness that can come and go throughout life."

Before this depression set in, he remembered he didn't sleep and was running around at high speed all day every day. Then he got hit! He didn't know what it was, so he tried to mask it. It went on for three months and he soon realized it was getting worse. That's when he got a suicide plan together. "I was hurting her. I felt my family would all be better off without me. Somebody who commits suicide doesn't do it to hurt someone else. They think they are helping them." Gail didn't take her eyes off her husband as he struggled for words.

In his depressed state, he began to question if there was a hell. "I certainly didn't want to go there!" All of a sudden, the Scriptures he memorized in Confirmation started coming back to him. "That's when I knew God was real. The more I knew it the worse I felt. Then, I said: 'Jesus, you died on that cross!' I started bawling and I asked for forgiveness and repented. I said, 'Just take me!' I knew I didn't deserve heaven, but I knew I didn't want to go to hell. I cried out, 'I can't take it! I can't take it! God! You know I can't take it'!"

The next morning, five minutes before he was going to commit suicide, Gail came home and took him to the doctor. God did something in his heart during that time of agony. He no longer had to question if he had received salvation that day on his bed. He immediately, started getting into the Word of God, trying to figure out why he was so against the Bible. They both laughed at the absolutely radical change in Randy's life!

"When he cried out to God that night, He took Randy's hand and said, 'Come with me. I will be in your corner during this.' So, Randy's bipolar...literally the thing that we have hated most in our lives...is what saved us!"

Changed her, too...

Gail admitted she didn't know what happened to her husband. Yes, he was diagnosed as bipolar and put on Lithium to control the disease, but it was the life changes in her husband that had her puzzled. "I saw such change in him. He never went out to party after that. It was incredible."

When they moved to Colorado Springs, Randy was involved in helping kids and going to youth camps. It upset Gail to see him spending so much time on 'those' things. She met with a pastor but when he questioned her salvation, she was so traumatized that she ran out of the room crying, or as Randy said, 'more like bawling'!

God didn't give up on her. One evening they were invited to the home of some friends. Their kids were all outside playing together when the pastor and another guy from church stopped by to visit their friends, Mike and Linda. The kids pointed to Randy and Gail's house and said, 'That's where Mom and Dad are.'

They stayed for about an hour and invited both couples to church. The first Sunday they attended, they were sitting out in the parking lot when Gail commented, 'Everybody is carrying Bibles. Don't you find that a bit odd.' " 'I am not kidding", she laughed. "As soon as we got into the Bible and started getting into God's Word, it just opened up a whole new life for us. We had both received Bibles at Confirmation, but we never opened them. It just collected dust." They now know that evening at the neighbors was a God designed meeting. Gail shared a huge smile, "He allows circumstances in our lives to lead us to Him. It's just phenomenal when you think about it!"

For the first time in their lives, they realized it was more than having 'head knowledge'. It was having a heart relationship with God. "The drinking and going out," Randy said "...was pretty much gone."

She confessed, "I was a three hour a day soap opera addict. That desire went totally away. I guess the Lord decided I had other better things for me to do during my life."

He never wanted to be one of those 'Jesus Freaks'...those guys that ran around with tracts or something. He did, however, really want to make sure his friends knew about Jesus. "So, I went down to the bars and tried to tell my drinking friends." He laughed, "It wasn't too long before they said...'Get the heck outta here'!"

Problems gone?

They both agreed that their problems didn't disappear. Randy said, "I think the Lord gave us nine years with hardly anything related to bipolar. I think He did that, so I would grow for what was coming." For about 15 years, he was on Lithium to treat the bipolar. They found out from others with bipolar that it was extremely unusual to go as long as he had without an episode.

What's normal?

Their normal changed when he began to experience manic episodes. Gail said, "It is like having your battery charged up ten times over. You get this in your mind that you can do anything. That even includes driving and reading a book at the same time. He met a telephone pole doing that! He slept very little. He even talked faster. He would read a book like this", as she demonstrated flipping pages about every few seconds. "It's just incredible how the mind works." (Normally, manic episodes can last anywhere from two weeks to two months before a depressive episode might appear.)

"I just knew one day he would wake up and it would be the opposite and he would be in a depressed state. Lots of times, that depression required hospitalization. They told me that if he couldn't get out of bed or eat for several days at a time to bring him in. It's very difficult to bring your husband to the hospital and check him into the psychiatric ward. When they are so lethargic and just want to stay in bed the whole time...you have no other choice."

Randy eventually received shock treatments three times a week for three weeks. "They would always do the trick and he would come out of his depression." Her eyes grew sad as she continued, "Somebody asked me once, 'What is it like to watch your husband in this manic stage, knowing one day he was going to crash?' I gave that a lot of thought and got this vision of him being out to sea. Every time a wave would come, he would go further and further out. He kept getting swept further out and I was on the beach yelling, 'Don't go! Don't go!' but there was nothing I could do to stop it." Tears formed in her eyes, "I just had to wait for it to happen."

That began many years of what is termed rapid cycling; moving from manic to depressive state and back. It got worse after he got back from serving overseas in Desert Storm. In the struggle, Randy said, "I couldn't have made it without God. I wanted to kill myself. I asked God every day to take me if he wasn't going to make me better."

God wanted to use them

Randy was still in the military but was now feeling called to the mission field. Gail said her thought was: 'You've got to be kidding me! You're going to put me on an island somewhere with headhunters at 'Uki-aki' island!' "Then," she smiled, "we were introduced to SonShine Ministries (an international Christian ministry). Randy took early retirement and we went into the mission field."

He related his thankfulness for the 'God-thing' done through Son Shine Ministries. "You tell any other missionary organization in the country that you're bipolar and you're done. You aren't going to get hired. You're not going anywhere. The directors said, 'Take your medicine and come on'." Several years later, when Randy and Gail felt called to American Missionary Fellowship, again the leadership said, 'Come on...take your medicine.' God wanted to use Randy. Even with bipolar.

Greater than ever imagined

They served in many ways on the mission field but eventually God gave them a Christian TV show called *Spirit of America Hour,* filmed in Branson, Missouri. They were actually able to set up their props at the famous Baldknobbers Theater, with a five-camera shoot. "We would interview people that were sick of cancer, dying of cancer, being cured of cancer. We interviewed politicians, farmers...whoever wanted to tell their story...and of course, it had to have the Lord in it."

Randy laughed as he recalled how each interview would start out light and funny, almost like the Tonight Show. But...the last fifteen minutes was focused on how the faith of each interviewee worked into their life, followed by Randy offering that same gift of salvation to all the listeners.

She said, "People would say...'the reason we like your show is because it is unpolished, and it is speaking from the heart'." The message of Christ was in every show. They were accepted on an ABC affiliate show with the potential of five million viewers. "We were on top of the world. It got to the point, we didn't have to go out and look for people to interview. We were having people come to us saying, 'We want to be on your show'." They were still dealing with Randy's bipolar rapid cycling, but that didn't stop God.

Into the depths

Gail's face dropped a little as she said, "Then, one morning, Randy wasn't getting out of bed and I went in to check on him. I knew as soon as I saw him that something was wrong. He looked to me as if he had a stroke. Honestly, his hair grayed overnight. He was just very lethargic. I stirred him and got him up. As soon as I saw his eyes, I thought, 'Oh No....he's gone again. He's left me again'.

We drove to Fayetteville, which is about ninety miles away. When I went to check him in, they thought he was my Dad. He was scuffling his feet and he was looking down. He had all the signs of the worst depression I think he ever had. I thought, 'OK...we are going to have to do the shock treatment regimen again and it will be OK.' I went home without him and went back to my job. He didn't call me all week, which I thought was a bit odd. I went back the next weekend to bring him home. I was so excited and looking forward to it. He was not much different than when I brought him in. I had him home that weekend. He didn't do much more than sleep. I took him back on Sunday night and the next weekend it was the same thing. After the third week of shock treatments, they said, 'I don't know why, Gail, but it's not working this time. You're just going to have to take him home.' So, I did, and the weeks went into months. The months went into years." Randy's condition didn't change this time.

"We were in a dilemma. What were we going to do with our ministry?" They ran reruns as long as they could before they had to send a note to all of the financial supporters telling them they were going on a three-month sabbatical. They prayed something would change in the meantime but...it didn't. She felt one of the most difficult things she faced was shutting the doors of their 10-year-old ministry...knowing how much Randy loved it.

Surviving four years

Gail tried to explain, "You have to understand...Randy was diagnosed..." she struggled with tears, "...but...I felt..." As she cried, Randy reached over to hold her hand. Her sentences are halted by quiet sobbing, so he continued for her.

"She went through hell. In 98% of any bipolar relationships...the mate divorces them. It doesn't matter if they are Christian or not. They can't take what they've got to go through. They can't take it. For Gail to everyday have someone not even there. She didn't have anyone to look to or talk to. It was very difficult on her."

When she regained her composure, she said, "When that commercial says, 'When depression hits it affects everybody'...it certainly does. I got angry. I started reading my Bible less. I started praying less. I quit going to church because the few people I confronted with Randy's illness made comments that were more hurtful than encouraging. So, I internalized it. That's the last thing you want to do when you are going through something like that is to push the Lord away, but I did. It really cost me big time. I couldn't eat. I lost three dress sizes. It was like living with death."

Her method of coping was burying herself in her work with handicapped clients. "I just hated the thought of going home after work because I was always going home to a dark house. He would either be in bed or he would be in a chair looking down at the floor in the dark. There was no talk. There was no eye contact. There was no touch. There was nothing. It's hard to stay above that and on top of that and have to deal with life."

When one hurts...

She shared in his illness, "The hardest thing was seeing the pain in him. That's what marriage is. When one is hurt...the second hurts, too. We were one in this. I could...," her voice cracked as tears rolled down her cheeks. "I could feel his pain and I missed him. It must be a lot like when somebody gets Alzheimer's. I remember Mrs. Reagan talking about Ronald when he got to that point where there was no more talk. I could so relate to that because that's what we were going through."

"There was one time I remember sitting there reading a book and I looked up. Randy was sitting across from me," she smiled as if remembering that exact moment, "and he was looking at me. I looked at him and I said, 'Ooohh...I miss you.' He said, 'I miss you, too.' He looked at me for about twenty seconds and then his eyes went back to the floor and he was gone. How do you live with that? It's like seeing him die every day," she cried. "Facing death. They were to the point where they were ready to do brain surgery. They didn't know what else to do. We were ready, too."

He's back!

After two years, they were advised to move back to Wisconsin because that VA Hospital was the best one in the country to treat mental illness. Randy's psychiatrist said, 'I've got a good friend over at the U of Minnesota that is top in this field. I'm going to send you over there. I need to get a second opinion on you.' This doctor put Randy on an old school of medications. They said, 'It will be about six weeks and you will come out of it real slow if you come out. So, hang in there. Don't shoot yourself now.' Randy laughed at the thought. "Yah...whatever. I didn't believe them because it's been four years, and nothing worked." There are only about a dozen people in the whole United States that are on that drug regimen.

Gail smiled at Randy as he said, "They just thought it might work."

Gail laughed, "And it did! HE'S BACK!"

"Like a light switch," Randy beamed.

Randy's doctor said, 'I've never had anybody go that long in the depression phase. I was so worried.' Randy said, "He looked right at me and said, 'Your faith healed you. Not me. Not what I did.' I almost started crying." Randy and Gail both agreed they give credit to the meds, but the Lord did it!

"We know it's all the Lord! Praise God...that has been ten years. We have had the rapid cycling but it's more like this," she motioned with her hand like a gentle wave. They both see Randy a little tired but nothing like the depression of years earlier. Gail said, "He is a little more tired and certainly has some memory lapses, but he told me, 'I would rather die of anything than to die of depression'."

They stayed in Wisconsin for ten years and moved back to Branson about two years ago. Gail said, "We're looking forward to what He has for us in the future. We believe the Lord wants to get our story out, so people know with mental illness that there is hope. We have a whole list of people that have bipolar that have accomplished great things in life. We look back on our life and we've got three wonderful kids...three wonderful young men who are all married. We have eight grandchildren. Randy was in the military as a mechanic for C130s. It was considered a highly technical job and he did it very well. Then, we go into the mission field and we have the opportunity to have a show that airs to five million people. It just blows us away when we look back on our lives."

Randy said, "What He's allowed is incomprehensible. People need to understand that you give what you have, and He will use you whatever way you will let Him."

Wisdom about suffering...

"If you're in the Bible and you study suffering," Randy said, "you see that it's mostly a positive thing. All kinds of people suffer. Jesus suffered." He struggled to find the right words to express what their suffering did in their lives. He felt it could give you strength and help you to understand God better. As they have walked through suffering, he has come to acknowledge that pain is not a bad thing you should hate but something to recognize and accept, knowing you come out differently on the other side of that pain.

"After God told me that WE were going to get through this," Gail quietly added, "...that is when my heart turned, and I let Him back into my life again. Proverbs 3:5 just says it all. 'Trust in the Lord with all your heart and lean not on your own understanding'."

After a short pause she continued, "...there's suffering in the world. Look at what Jesus endured on the cross. There's nothing in the Bible that says we're going to live a wonderful, carefree life. We're all going to suffer something in life. I felt a change when I started asking 'What do you want me to learn from this experience.' He wanted me to die of all my 'yuk' and totally depend on Him for what He wanted to teach me through it. I think He has taught me to be more compassionate for people who suffer mental illness. He has definitely taught me perseverance and patience. Love one another. Everybody has baggage, but you can work through that, too. I believe we have gotten through the bipolar challenges because we did have each other. I can't imagine having to deal with that sickness alone."

He gave that great smile of his and added, "You have so much stuff to deal with. I don't know how I could have made it without an anchor. The anchor is Jesus Christ."

Gail looked over at him and said, "Humor is a good thing. I looked in the mirror one day and I thought, 'I don't recognize myself anymore. I look so down and out. I look so depressed myself.' About that time, a friend of mine, gave me a book from Barbara Johnson, *Stick a Geranium in Your Hat and Be Happy*. Barbara had been through a lot in her own life, and yet she was using humor to encourage others. I remember laughing out loud at that book. Sometimes, I go down to Hallmark and read some of those crazy cards. They're so funny. Sitting in a parking lot watching people and some of the funny things they do has really, really been therapeutic. It releases endorphins," she laughed. "If you are a care giver to somebody, take care of yourself. Whether that means going out for a brisk walk, sitting down to a good book, getting a manicure, pedicure...whatever. Do it because it's very, very important."

Stop a runaway train

Randy's goal through these challenges is to try to help people see no matter what is wrong in their lives, they can give it to God, and He can use it anyway He wants. "I am perfect example!" He also has come to understand how God has used his illness to stop him from becoming a runaway train and forced him to rest and take time to listen to Him.

Struggle to feel loved

Through the suffering, Gail struggled with feeling loved...by her husband and by God. "It was so hard to remember Randy actually loved me through this." The first routine question at the hospital would be: 'Are you suicidal?' Randy's routine answer would be 'No'. The second question, 'Do you have a death wish?' was more difficult for him to answer. After all, what Christian wouldn't want to go to heaven?

When Randy hesitated, or answered 'Yes', Gail felt as if she wasn't important to him and he would rather be somewhere else than with her. "I know he didn't really mean it, but it took me down a peg every single time."

Two different perspectives...

Randy helped us to see from the suicidal person's perspective. 'Look what I'm doing to my wife and my kids - my parents'. Randy looked over at Gail with sadness in his eyes, "Better for me but better for you, too. Look what I was doing to you."

He knew from his own personal struggle, "I'm telling you, those thinking about suicide are not thinking straight. The devil will just ride that to heck. When somebody commits suicide, I don't get mad at them. I just think...they got past that point..."

"He thought he would do me a favor by putting himself out..."

"And do everybody a favor...," Randy said, "but you mainly because you had it worse."

Gail's eyes dropped as her voice trailed, "It's horrible..."

Isolation

He may have felt isolated in his own body, but as Gail told us, he was not coherent or alert, so it was difficult to know what he was feeling. She knew isolation up close and personal and even isolated herself from God.

For a period of time, their youngest son, Danny came home to help them. Tears filled her eyes as she shared the memory. "I came home from work one day and he was on the other side of the door with his arms outstretched. I went into them and he closed his arms around me and said, 'Oh Mom, I had no idea what you have been going through'." Danny prayed for his Dad and played praise music to help lift his spirits. Randy remembered the praise music his son played but also remembered how he felt like a total failure.

They were both eventually isolated from people. Gail related that if Randy had cancer, they would have had people at their door all the time but not so with depression. People didn't know how to deal with Randy's depression, so most stayed away. This was a very difficult time for Gail as she even heard remarks like, 'What did you do wrong?' 'Have you been tithing?' 'He was sexually abused as a child.' Some thought he had demons, and most had a stereotypical view of depression. The truth is, with Randy's diagnosis of bipolar, it is purely a chemical imbalance. All the counseling in the world and even a change in his environment would not make the depression caused by bipolar go away.

Her challenge was making others understand, "It's no different than a diabetic that's low on insulin. With the lithium, the levels can go off." Even though it was obvious the pain of losing friends was long reaching, she admitted she wasn't very good at putting it out there, so people would know what she needed. "You know, it's not just something you go around and announce." She eventually felt so isolated that she pulled back even more so she wouldn't have to deal with people.

Feel blessed

There is no doubt they have had challenges in their lives, but three of the greatest blessings are their sons. Randy said, "They're doing a pretty good job in a world that's pretty bad today."

Gail added, "We never had to deal with drugs...never had to deal with alcohol...and having mental illness in the family, besides. That is another grace from God!"

According to Gail there are plenty of other blessings in their marriage. "The fact that we are together, as far as our Christian walk. We know we can grab each other's hands at any time of the day and pray. We agree on how to spend money. We've got a lot of friends now. I just feel blessed."

He confessed any money problems were his own doing. "Bipolar is not really noted for having big savings," they both laughed.

She said, "Compulsive spending. Another side effect of bipolar."

"For some reason," Randy said, "there's something in your brain that makes you think you can buy and make money back or something." We see them describe this challenge as a blessing because they recognize it is part of the disease and not willful irresponsibility. They feel they are blessed to be a team, working together toward the same goals.

"We don't have all the answers," she smiled. "We are still learning little by little every day. Little by little in every way...Jesus is changing us. We're never done growing and it certainly doesn't mean we have all the answers...because we don't. We're just taking one day at a time and trusting God in them."

I want to keep the one I have

Quietly she spoke, "Don't take any days for granted. Enjoy each one. You've got good days and you've got bad days. Just take each one that you can. When I was in such a bad state, I remember going home and falling to my knees and just literally beating the floor saying, 'Lord, I can't do this anymore! I can't do this!' He said, 'No you can't but WE can'!"

She would tell other couples, "Hang in there. Don't give up. It just seems like we live in a world--not devoting or giving any loyalty to your spouse. I praise God that we had conviction to be true to our marriage vows through all the mistakes and obstacles and challenges in life. I want to just keep the one I have. I don't want to have to break in anybody else." She smiled, "There is no problem in the world God can't work through, but you have to let Him do it. Let Him in."

Randy said, "Learn to forgive. None of us are perfect. I know it's hard to do but if you just want to have things your way all the time...it's going to be hard."

See it to the end...

"The fact that our marriage has survived 45 years of this," Gail said, "...I give God all the credit because only 2% of marriages survive mental illness. I know that for a fact."

"Friends even suggested I leave Randy during those four years because it was taking such a toll on me. I thought, 'What a selfish thing to do.' The thought of leaving Randy hurt so much worse than staying with him. I wondered how that could be right, not to mention who would take care of him. We are a team and we married for better and for worse...for richer, for poorer...in sickness and in health. We are going to see it to the end. Till death do us part," she lovingly looked at Randy.

He said with honesty, "I was at a point I hoped she would leave...it's terrible. If she could go somewhere and not have to come back to this...I wouldn't care... I wouldn't blame her. BUT she wasn't going to leave."

Paint a picture...

If we were to paint a picture of Randy and Gail, there might be plenty of dark colors and erratic patterns in the background but when we got to their faces, it would be a light bright enough to illuminate the entire room. They have had many seemingly hopeless situations, but they are not hopeless! The light in their lives? Gail said it best, "We're believing that better things are ahead. We give God all the credit."

Where are they now?

We had the blessing of meeting with Gail and Randy when they were back in Minnesota for another round of treatments for depression. They spent almost three months living with friends as Randy received experimental treatments with magnetic waves. They can't place their hope in the treatment because there have been no promises it will work. Their hope isn't in the present or in the future...but their hope is in Jesus, Who never changes even when they feel as if they can't do it anymore!

Jeremy & Lauren – Not a Typical Marriage

MARRIED 12 YEARS

"How, then, can they call on the one they have not believed in? And how can they believe in the one of whom they have not heard? And how can they hear without someone preaching to them? And how can anyone preach unless they are sent? As it is written: "How beautiful are the feet of those who bring good news!"
Romans 10:14-15

A dirty mud hut in Afghanistan with a bucket for a toilet. A 100-hour train ride to Western China...with a sick child...and virtually no Chinese language skills. Summers spent traveling 60 hours in the air and 40 hours of car time! No formal construction training, but three years leading the construction of a complex of buildings in Thailand.

Normal love stories usually don't include adventures (and challenges) of that magnitude! You will soon see, Jeremy and Lauren have their own unique love story!

Around the world to meet

With a heart for foreign missions, Jeremy had been in Africa doing a mission studies program and was then on his way to Afghanistan. First a stop in Perth, Australia, to complete additional training with Youth with a Mission (YWAM).

Lauren had a deep and long-standing desire to be a part of long-term missions and also headed to the same base in Australia for three months of training.

God took them around the world to meet!

Even though they were in different mission schools, they would see each other often, and their casual conversations turned into a friendship. That friendship deepened even more when they discovered Jeremy had a heart for Afghanistan and Lauren had been praying about two mission opportunities – Israel and Afghanistan. Their hearts connected!

Got to tell her!

Jeremy felt the connection with Lauren and told a friend, 'I've got to tell her I like her! I got to tell her!!' They both laughed as Jeremy repeated his friend's response: 'You can't! You can't! You can't! YWAM has a policy for that. There is no dating. You can't tell her! You can't tell her!'

'I got to! I got to! I might not see her again!' Jeremy was pulled by that desire, but he decided to trust if was the Lord's will it would work out. "So, I didn't tell her. Never said a word. Nothing at all."

Off they went to different parts of the world. He to Afghanistan and she, at the same time, heading to Cairo, Egypt, for outreach. In the Singapore airport they said their goodbyes. Jeremy's face drooped with a sadness evident as he said, "It was really, really hard."

So, missionaries in the field did not become too attached to 'back home', there was a policy that allowed them to email each other only once a week.

She was a little bit of a reluctant participant in this relationship, and for that she was often teased by her friends. "I was twenty-seven and had never dated. I was very determined that no guy was going to deter me from my call in the Lord!" She laughed as she said, "I was focused. I was going to the mission field and then God said to go to Israel next...so that's what I was doing!" However, when she got to Egypt, "I missed him a lot more than I thought."

Jeremy remembered pacing in this dirty courtyard in Afghanistan about five months into his assignment. 'Lord, is this the right one? Is this the right one?' Pleading with the Lord, he cried out, 'This is the one I want!' 'Lord I want her!' Even though those feelings were growing inside him, he held back about those feelings in his emails.

That is...until one day when he called and told her he liked her. "It came out like the worst ever. I sounded like a little kid. I said, 'So, I like you....duh, duh, duh...and she's like, 'I do too'. Wow...OK'!" The only glitch in the plan was the fact that he was in Afghanistan and she was in back in Australia, with no solid plans to reconnect.

The distance wasn't about to stop this young man's heart. He talked with his leader and the response he received was, 'Go for her! You gotta go pursue her!' Jeremy was more than surprised by that reaction. By then, Lauren was back home in Kentucky. "So, I bought a plane ticket that day to go to Kentucky where I had never been before...to her hometown to meet her family. We had never dated. We had that one phone call...and...lots of emails!"

Times of doubt

For Lauren, encased in those long emails were times of doubt, 'I think we just need to be friends. I don't want to mislead you or anything. I...I...just feel like maybe we should just keep it a friendship.'

"At the same time, I felt at peace about him coming to Kentucky if he still wanted to." Now you would think that response might dissuade a typical guy but remember Jeremy isn't exactly typical. He might have thought her comment about staying friends was a little weird, but he still felt like he was still supposed to go visit her.

She said, "It was funny because after that it was like the Lord started working in my heart. There were so many times I had just shut down my heart. If there had even been a slight interest in somebody, I would just turn it off because they weren't called to the mission field or whatever. I had gotten so used to doing that, but the Lord was actually encouraging me by saying, 'Lauren...I want you to start opening up your heart but trust Me to protect you and to guard it.' So, yes, he came to Kentucky in December for ten days."

When he got to Kentucky, he said he wasn't 'feeling it' with Lauren. "Way too much pressure!"

Lauren laughed, "He was trying to say: 'There's no pressure to make a decision'...but there was!"

In his mind he pressed, "I was like...'are we gonna get married? or what?' I'm going back to Afghanistan next month! What do we do about this'?" At one point, he was so desperate and had no one who he thought understood. He called his leader back in Australia, crying: 'This isn't going to work! It's not going to work! This is not going to work!' His boss (and friend) brought to him what Jeremy described as really good perspective and great advice: 'With heightened emotions and being in a place that you are right now with all these weird feelings...don't move! Don't make any big decisions based on what you're feeling right now.' So, once again, they had an airport goodbye with no idea what was ahead for their relationship.

How would you know?

At Christmas, Jeremy was home in Kansas City with his Mom. He and Lauren both laughed as he repeated his Mom's common-sense comment: 'How would you know if you're not around her?'

"Of course! It was so obvious. I felt like I had a green light to make a move to Kentucky for the sake of pursuing her." He called Lauren and told her this wasn't just some desire and they needed to figure out what to do with it. He felt strongly this was what he was supposed to do. Now it seems the pressure had shifted to Lauren!

With eyes and mouth opened wide in shock, Lauren demonstrated what she experienced during that phone call when he said he was heading to Kentucky. She protested, 'No! No! You've got to go back to Afghanistan. People need to hear the Gospel. Why would you come here?' She struggled because she felt like it was such a waste for Jeremy to come to Kentucky. Even though she was puzzled by this proposed move to Kentucky, she soon felt the Lord speaking to her heart confirming the decision. Her answer was 'yes' but she admitted it did make her very nervous!

He even spoke with his three major financial supporters, thinking they would stop their support until he left Kentucky and returned to the mission field. "These three guys said, 'What are you talking about? Consider this a sabbatical! Go after her! We're going to support you through this whole thing'!"

She just shook her head and laughed in disbelief! "Like who does that? Who supports a guy going to pursue a girl? But, Wow...that said a lot to me about what these guys thought of Jeremy."

Know for sure?

They officially started dating at the end of January 2007. They weren't only feeling things out with each other, but they were also doing a lot of praying during the next seven weeks.

That is when the Lord really spoke to Lauren very, very clearly. "At one point, I was having a hard time. My parents were going through some difficulties in their marriage. 'Lord...I always expected to know right away that this was the one, but I don't.' The Lord just kept telling me, 'Take each step. Just keep on moving forward.' God was doing something in my heart in the midst of all that. He was breaking down walls that I didn't even realize I had in my heart."

During this time of uncertainty for Lauren, Jeremy lifted the pressure. He said, 'I'm not praying about this. I'm waiting _for_ you.' Instead of feeling more pressure, Lauren felt the burden lift and a release from pressure.

At the end of the seven weeks, they took some time away individually to fast and pray. "I felt like I was supposed to go to Israel and Jeremy had been in Afghanistan. How does that fit?" There were some fears she needed to break through, but by the end of that day, she had her answer. 'Yes, this is the man I want to spend the rest of my life with.' Now, even though she had her answer, she was nervous at the thought of telling him because she felt almost as if she was the one proposing.

He was hiking in the mountains about an hour away. "I was sleeping in my car and hiking all day long." When she called and asked him to come back, he had no idea what that actually meant. He was a little scared and a little excited. 'Oh, no...this is it?'

When they met, Lauren shared all that led to her answer. The next morning, Jeremy purchased her ring and stopped at her Dad's office to officially get his permission. After seven weeks of dating, they got engaged and after two and a half months, got married. Lauren snapped her fingers as she said, "It all moved fast but it was just right...the timing of the Lord. My family was thrilled because...goodness...my parents thought I was never going to get married!" Laughing, she continued, "But everyone was just so affirming of our relationship. And…I hadn't even met his side of the family…"

He completed her thought, "So, I talked to all of them on the phone before I proposed just to make sure everybody was fine with it." After their engagement, they made a huge road trip for Lauren to finally meet his family.

What magnet did God use?

They both took a minute before answering and then Jeremy slowly began, "Of course, I was attracted to her physically, but I would say it was her passion. She's very passionate." He struggled with words as he continued, "Expressive…emotional. It was like, 'Oh Wow...she's on fire! She loves the Lord!' I would say her heart for the Lord, for sure. It was just abundant...obvious! She wasn't just doing it because it's right or something she wanted to do." His voice cracked, and tears filled his eyes as he tenderly looked at Lauren, "She was doing it for God."

"I loved the way he interacted with people and just how easy going he was. People loved to be with him and hang out with him. I just saw such a humility in him. It was one of the most attractive characteristics...his humility and his teachability. I could see that right away. The way he carried himself. Even just talking about things, I could see his real hunger for the Lord. He wanted more. His commitment." She remembered when talking with him about serving God he said, 'I could be going to Afghanistan for a year or for the rest of my life'. She softly added, "He was just sold out and committed."

Challenges and blessings intertwined

While they were still engaged, they felt God was calling them to Israel. "I had felt that strongly," Lauren said, "but I just didn't know I was going to go married. So just in blind faith and obedience, six weeks after our honeymoon, we moved to Israel. In the midst of the challenges it was extremely foundational and so fruitful. The Lord was bringing us together as a team." She looked lovingly at Jeremy and continued, "It wasn't just you and me...it was us now. Dreaming together."

Their 'I' soon became 'We' as they began their journey of constant adjustments. They moved to be part of a new ministry...lived in a foreign country...were just married and soon found themselves pregnant with their first child, Olivia.

They were away from family and at that time didn't have a mission team in place with them. It meant they spent a lot of time by themselves where they were able to get to know each other better without the constant input of others. Jeremy said, "It was difficult because we didn't have family there, but it was also a blessing."

"It's not for everybody," Jeremy admitted. "Everybody's life is much different, but we were able to do this journey together. It wasn't just me in a job. For us it's been something we have been able to dream together...seek the Lord together...be excited about together...process together...every step of the way. The stability has been our family. We're always together. It's been 12 years and we still prefer to do everything together." They laughed as they said they had only been away from each other for a total of twelve nights.

Less than perfect living conditions

After Israel, they made the move to Central Asia with a one year old! How's that for an adjustment? Add to that the challenge of working with a new ministry team and extremely rugged living conditions.

They prepared themselves as much as they could for living in a third world country. They knew it was going to be hard physically. As far as they knew there had never been any missionaries in that area before, so they understood they were also moving into a spiritually dark place. Jeremy said, "It has been a blessing to be able to see and experience cultures and what God's doing and actually be a part of it but...it's also been probably one of the bigger challenges, too. Dealing with so much transition. It was one of the most challenging times of our life but at the same time, we knew that God had called us and that was so clear. We also knew He was going to walk us through that time."

They looked at each other and laughed as Jeremy described living conditions. "Going to the bathroom in buckets. Electricity...most of the time...because we had a generator. Mud buildings. Everything was always dirty. The roof was leaking...a mud roof. It would just drip into what we thought was a clean room. It was like: Aghhhhh!"

Attacked by the enemy

They also felt what they believed were some very clear attacks from the enemy during that time. "It was very bizarre," Jeremy described, "because Olivia would trip over something and cry like a normal child and then she would lose her breath completely. Her face would go blue and she'd look at me with big eyes and then she'd be out. As a father, it was like I was having my daughter die in front of me. That happened probably a dozen times."

They questioned whether they should go back home to see a doctor or stay and stick it out. Their hearts questioned, 'Is this a big deal or is this an attack?' "We were there less than a year but at the end of that first chunk of time, I remember just walking through this field to go to the market and it was almost like a skip. I had this feeling of, 'We can do this! We can get through this!' It was just like life-giving! It was like a glimpse of the other side. It was difficult, but we were created for this! We LOVE this! We love the pioneering. We love going into places like this."

The decision was made. They were staying!

Preparing the exit

During their time in Central Asia, they were operating on a business visa, running a guest house. In the Spring of 2010, there were two outreach teams, a total of twenty-eight people, at their guest house. During their morning prayer time, the leader and some of the team sensed they were supposed to bring all the neighbors in and present the Gospel clearly. They went out and invited all of their neighbors to a celebration which would take place two weeks later, near Easter.

About sixty to eighty people from the village showed up. For cultural reasons, they split up the men and women, but they all watched the two-hour movie, 'God's

Story', in their local language. Since most of the village were illiterate, as their guests left that night, they received an audio Bible in their local language. Jeremy said, "I remember walking home that night looking up at the moon. It was a peaceful night and I remember thinking, 'Something shifted tonight'."

Lauren said, "So, over the course of that next week there were several people who came...one at a time...asking: 'Would you talk to me...tell me about this book. About the Bible'." Several others came to ask for prayer.

About a week later, one of their native, believing workers came frantically, 'Jeremy, Jeremy...come here! The locals had a meeting today at three o'clock and 100 people gathered and signed a petition to come and riot your property...burn down our property and kill us all.' Jeremy said, "This was a real threat! They signed a petition...it wasn't just rumor!" When the worker left, Jeremy sat there thinking about how he would tell his co-workers. They were families with children. How could he break this news to them?

Jeremy was holding his head as he told us how he prayed for guidance and finally explained to his co-workers and family, 'There are some people that are upset with us in the village. Let's just keep everybody inside tonight.' They locked all of their doors and prayed for safety.

Their relationship with the local commander of their village was a little unusual. He couldn't side with the foreigners, but he also wanted to keep peace. If the village people actually rioted the mission property, there was going to be a major international incident. Jeremy said, "We later found out he told the people, 'Let's give them twenty-four hours to leave on their own.' There were actually six to eight border soldiers standing guard around our property that night in case there were rioters. I never told Lauren the actual death threat part. We just went back and talked about the seriousness of it. So, we had a couple of bags packed that night."

As frightening as it sounded, Lauren said, "I just remember how I felt the peace of the Lord even as we went to sleep that night. It started raining and when it rains there it gets so muddy that nobody goes out. It was just like the Lord's covering and protection...that rain. So, we woke up that next morning and we still didn't know what was going to happen. Our team leader went to go speak with the village governor and commander...just to verify, 'Is this true'? Do we need to get out of here? Basically, they said, 'Yes'! So, he came back and said we had twenty-four hours to leave and that started yesterday...so we just had to book it."

He said, "It was very emotional. A lot of people were crying. Even our workers. Our cook was just weeping...wailing. She had nothing. Her husband died the winter before, so with us she had her own little room with a bed and little mini oven and carpet. These things were extremely valuable to her. In my broken Dari, I said, 'Banapsha...Go get your sons NOW and tell them to get here and start hauling this stuff away because our house is going to get raided in a couple of hours from now. Go get it! It's all yours! You can have all of it'!"

"We had shared so much with our workers," Lauren explained, "including clearly sharing the Gospel."

They had to get everybody to the border into a neighboring country which Jeremy described as 'the fifth most corrupt nation in the world'. The border guards wanted bribes for the almost seventy pieces of luggage filled with belongings of all of the missionaries. Jeremy said, "They shut the door on us. They shut the gate. It's kind of weird because this was a dirt road over the river and these guys got a big gate. He looked Russian with an AK47 and you could tell he was told what to do. So, we were trying to shame the guy. We're holding our kids up with snotty noses in front of them. 'Do you have no heart'?" They both smiled as Jeremy said, "A truck ended up coming through the gate and we RAN through with it. He let us go through!"

The rest of the story

That's only a part of the story! There was still a team of ten students up in the mountains on yaks. They were showing the 'Jesus' film to locals and had no idea about the trouble brewing down the mountain. They had the satellite phone to use in case of an emergency, but the phone was off unless there was a problem. So, no one could contact them to warn them. Jeremy said, "I knew they were going to have some type of satellite reception when they got close to the village, so I texted the leader and said, 'Disperse the backpacks! Destroy the DVDs. You are tourists!' I didn't explain anything. I couldn't!

As the team from the mountains was driving through rivers coming back to the village, the leader turned on the phone to receive the warning. They got interrogated and their pictures taken at our little command post. Border guards beat up our native friend, trying to get things out of him. He's like our hero of this whole story. The next day, they released all of our guys to the border of a neighboring country."

Short but fruitful

They felt their time in Central Asia was cut short and never thought they would actually hear of any fruit from their time there. Later, they heard that about fifty people who had taken all the Bible recordings and buried them outside of our village to be used later. It got so intense after the mission team left that if any foreigners came through, they were going to be killed.

Even later, they heard of one of their former workers who went to another believer in the village and asked how he could become a Christian. The fruit of their work continued to spread as this former worker received the Lord.

No home!

He remembered thinking, 'OK Lord…now what do you want us to do? We don't have a home!' "We were sitting in a hotel room and we didn't have anywhere to go back to." They had nothing to do and no place to go so they prayed for the Lord to show them.

Following their traumatic exit from Central Asia, they were still in a fog as they reeled from the shock of those events. They frequently asked, 'Does anybody know what just happened'? "We were clinging to the Lord and trusting in Him. We felt Him say, 'Go to China and spend six weeks. He gave us four cities to go to."

They were praying. Olivia was sick and was screaming. "We were like, 'What? We're going to go to China and do a six-week scouting trip…right now? We felt so burned out at that point but when we landed in China it was like the grace of the Lord was on us." Lauren shook her head in agreement as Jeremy continued, "As soon as we hit the ground it was like a retreat. It doesn't make sense because...I knew zero Chinese...like zero. We traveled 100 hours on train all the way from Beijing. That would be like going from New York to San Diego but having to get off at all these stops and buy tickets in another language...but, on that journey, the Lord spoke to us so much."

Not a detour

Even though not all plans went as they originally thought they would, they learned every plan was not a detour but a time for God to take them to a place where He would teach them.

Two and a half years in central China learning the culture and language, brought them to a place where their earnest prayer was to partner in ministry with the Chinese. In the search to locate a place where Chinese could be trained and sent out as missionaries, they attended a conference in Thailand. They were invited to be a part of beginning a training base in Thailand and in less than three years, a conference center and training base were completed and opened to students. Weekly sports clubs, a music program and English and Chinese classes are available as well as housing for up to 300 people.

She said, "It's stretched us greatly because we thought we had been dreaming big with God but coming here, we realized God was like: 'You're not dreaming big enough!' We feel like the first seven years of our marriage were really preparing us for this move."

Jeremy shook his head in full agreement as he spoke about their work in Thailand to train Chinese. "It was something so unexpected...something we hadn't even necessarily been wanting on this scale but feeling so challenged and feeling so humbled to be a part of what God is doing here."

What did God do in your marriage?

They both thought quietly for a moment and then Jeremy began, "I would say God Himself has kind of been the centerpiece of everything." They agreed it was not one of them hearing direction from God and following it but they both heard individually and then heard together about any major move they have made.

In the process, they have seen their marriage solidify and strengthen. Lauren confidently spoke about Jeremy's leadership in their lives. "Even before we got married, I knew Jeremy sought the Lord and heard from Him. That was so comforting, especially as his wife to know I have a husband who is seeking God and hears from God...and who's not just going to make these rash decisions."

"Our pursuit of the Lord has definitely brought us together in a greater union and that's what we longed for. It talks in the Word about how the two become one flesh." Even though they believe they are at the beginning of their marriage journey, Lauren said they know this: "This Biblical unity in marriage...is a symbol of Christ and the church. It's the Holy Spirit living inside of us and as we pursue the Lord...we're both hearing from the Lord and that brings the unity in our marriage."

Jeremy has that same confidence in his wife. "I have to trust the Lord inside of her. I know she desires that so much that I know, that I know, that I know she's not going to pick up with her emotions and walk away and say: 'I'm done'. She's grounded in the Lord, even in the midst of her emotions." Laughter filled the space between them when Lauren acknowledged she definitely was emotional.

He said, "That first year of marriage, we didn't really know each other. We knew God had called us to be together, so we held on to that. Over time I am gradually seeing it was like...", he intertwined the fingers of both hands and moved them in front of his body in a figure eight. He demonstrated moving together in union as he said, "One...one...one!"

Unending hope

They both contemplated for a moment before Lauren shared that in their missionary work, there were times they asked, 'Why are we doing this'? But they agreed they never said, 'I can't do this!' Did they have crazy emotions? Sure! But, they never felt like giving up on each other because they were so assured and grounded in what God was asking them to do.

He completed her thought, "Hope has always been there even in the midst of the most difficult times. Even when we are having hard times, arguing or fighting or whatever... there's zero chance that 'This is it...we're done! There's no exit! There's no back door! Tomorrow, she's probably still going to be mad at me, but she's definitely going to be there. I'm definitely not going anywhere, either!"

Passing on advice

Lauren mentioned there were some single girls from China who came to visit. They said, 'You and Jeremy just seem to just be moving as one'. "It sounds so simple but for me to really pursue Jeremy...I need to pursue the Lord. I need God to break in and break through. So, pursue the Lord with all that you are and pursue one another. Be intentional about taking time together. We need to talk about deep issues...listen to each other. Even though he doesn't understand all my crazy emotions...he's there."

Since he works with Chinese students, Jeremy drew a word picture of the difference in the marriage culture. "China's unique in some ways because you don't express yourself...you don't express your feelings. It's a 'you got to be tough' culture. Not vulnerable. Most of the time, their way of encouraging success is to put people down and to say, 'You can do better than that!' It's not actual words of encouragement. It's tearing them down to try to get them to try harder. So, you'll get that in their marriages, too."

The biggest thing he has been telling a recently married Chinese man is to be fighting for his wife. 'Man...you got to bless her. Just go out of your way. You got to tell her you love her'." The response of this young Chinese man was, 'I tell her. I tell her sometimes. She's like ahh...', as he demonstrated her pushing him away with her hand. Jeremy still pressed, 'Look at her in the eyes and tell her'."

His voice cracked, "We're talking about leadership." He put his hands up in form of a tent and said, "Look at a business...with the leader on the top and everyone else falls under that." Now he put his hands together in a V shape with leadership at the bottom. As tears welled up, he said, "Well, Jesus did the opposite (by putting Himself at the bottom)." He struggled to gain composure, but his tears didn't stop just because he willed them to stop. When he was finally able to speak, words came out quietly. "He (Jesus) did the opposite...so ultimately I think the husband should be doing the same thing...just being that servant leader."

Tears streamed down his cheeks, "What does it look like? You know what it is like to even think of your wife's emotions more than this huge division between you, then just make sure priorities are right with the kids. It's my wife first...not my kids. I'm still learning...I am in baby step one..." Lauren's eyes were on him as he completed his sentence, "...but just trusting that the Lord will lead me."

A gift

Lauren said, "Marriage is truly a gift, but I feel like in so much of our personal experience, I'm seeing how Satan hates marriage and he is raging against it. In marriage we can participate in this amazing unity and bond that symbolizes Christ and the church. Satan hates it, so you just have to pursue...be intentional in marriage. Don't let it go! You're just not married. You're usually going forward or backwards in relationships."

Her eyes brightened, "We get excited because we believe that God has so much for our marriage in His heart that we have not even experienced yet. We get so excited to see the years come because we are believing for growth. I am believing that I am going to be a better, supportive wife...meeting his needs next year...more than I am this year. We want to pursue that growth and be intentional and not let it slide."

He shared his insight: "I feel there are a lot of lies out there. 'Make sure you do your ministry before you have kids or before you get married'." They know from years of experience that ministry and family can work in tandem.

"Then, it's these little jabs at the husband: 'Husbands don't listen.' 'Husbands are insensitive.' There are all these things men and women are labeled. 'Women are overly emotional.' 'You're tied with a ball and chain to your wife.' 'She's your master.' That paints a picture of a passive husband and woman that wears the pants and leads the home. That's not God's design. I guess my encouragement to somebody thinking about marriage would be to go to the Word. Find out what the Bible says," his voice wavered with emotion, "and what God says because He's designed marriage."

She agreed, "Let Him define what it is. It's not movies, it's not what we see in social media and junk people think is normal. Divorce...I'm just going to try this out. No! It's a covenant before the living God."

Jeremy intertwined the fingers of both hands, "We can grow in our understanding...being a student of each other. Learning...growing...pursuing each other." They didn't describe anything 'instant' about marriage. Jeremy said, "It's not like we're married and we're one. I believe there's a moving forward in our unity as the years pass. I think that's what I'm excited about."

Not a normal life

Normal? Typical? No! They've lived in strange and foreign surroundings and have even had their lives threatened. English was not always the common language that surrounded them. Travel frequently came in double digit hours; not just a short trip to Grandma's. Their life with their children, Olivia, Micah, Jonathan, Caleb and Sophie may not appear normal to us! However, their normal includes an abundance of love that not only permeates their home, but recently was displayed as they prayed about how to share that love with the people of their neighborhood in Thailand.

One thing Jeremy and Lauren know. In their normal, no matter where they live or what they experience, they need to keep their eyes on Jesus. He has promised to never leave them! They keep that same promise to each other!

Chad & Jenna – It's About WE

MARRIED 8 YEARS

"That is why a man leaves his father and mother and is united to his wife, and they become one flesh." Genesis 2:24

Copyright © Abby Hinz

She lost the bet

He had just come out of a relationship and was hanging out with friends who were in Jenna's circle. He needed a bass player for opening worship service he was conducting and knew she played bass, so… No…he didn't ask her on a date. He asked her to play the bass!

That's not the only thing he asked. He was attending a conference in California and needed an airport shuttle when he returned, so he popped the 'ride question' on Jenna. She brought one of her friends along, to which Chad said, "I was a little bummed because I kind of wanted just that little extra half hour...forty minutes to talk to her." No sparks that time, but it all started when they were painting the church basement in preparation for the new coffee house. He really wanted to get a date, so he made a bet with her. There was this prime area of parking at the university and he bet if there was an open parking spot there, she had to go out for coffee with him.

Jenna smiled, "I had to buy if I lost!"

"I had already seen a spot," Chad smirked, "so I knew I was going to win the bet and would get the date! So, we went out to have coffee. It was supposed to be a 'study' date. Nah...didn't study. Pretty much just talked the whole time." Jenna looked over at him and smiled at the memory.

Her version

According to Jenna, he was still dating another girl when she was asked to play bass with his band. This girl lived across the hall from Jenna and was one of the leaders in her group, so it was difficult to avoid her. Ready or not, there was lots of bumping into each other.

Then, his breakup with the girl down the hall. That's when Chad started hanging out with Jenna's group of friends...only he actually spent time with another girl in the group. Frustrated, Jenna announced, 'Ok God...I'm just over it. I'm not looking for anyone anymore. It's in Your hands.'

Things started to change when she and Chad worked with a team to set up the new coffee house near campus and had what she called 'a couple of 'group adventures'. They got all dressed up for Halloween and went bowling. Prom dress kind of dressed up. She went to a dance over homecoming with another guy, and Chad stole her away. That's when she said they had this 'awkward middle school fake dance' together.

His commented through their laughter, "See the weirdness. It's a good thing!"

"Talk about weird", Jenna said, "I was taking a three-week winter term class. If you miss a day of class, it's like missing a week. I skipped two days to go snowmobiling with him in northern Wisconsin. It was like negative five degrees. We put 500 miles on the machine. I have never been on a snowmobile in my life, but I had to drive it off the lot because it was on my credit card. So, it was just this crazy, weird adventure...one thing after another! I think that's when we kind of finally thought...'There's something here!' We're figuring it out'."

She gleamed as Chad said, "I knew who she was. I loved that she was different...that she played bass and you don't hear of many girls playing bass guitar. She just was straight forward. I had been in some relationships that I kind of felt like I got dragged around or I got lied to and she wasn't that way. Jenna was Jenna. I wasn't getting a sugar-coated version of her." They both laughed as he added, "And she was a little weird like me...which helps."

Will you?

Chad worked two jobs the summer before he proposed. He worked at a church and also part time at a junk yard. "The reason I got the junk yard job was that I wanted to make enough money in the summer to buy the ring. I already thought this through. My parents didn't have a clue. Her parents didn't have a clue. She didn't have a clue."

He made enough money to purchase her ring and actually worked with a local jeweler to design it himself. When he got the ring, he put it in the hands of his best friend, Scrappy. She had been like a sister to him and was part of many of their group adventures. Scrappy lived out on Long Island and had been talking a long time with Chad about doing New Year's Eve in Time Square, so he figured this was the time to take her up on the offer. Chad sent the ring and a bottle of champagne out ahead with her. He asked Jenna's Dad for her hand in marriage and according to his family, it was pretty remarkable my Dad didn't blab about it. Plan A--going well.

They were in Times Square on New Year's Eve but his whole plan was not to do it at midnight. Instead, he planned to propose at sunrise on Long Island, out at the lighthouse. He thought he had the perfect location with the perfect sunrise. (Never mind everybody's exhausted from New Year's Eve!)

Jenna confessed, "It was cloudy. It was cold. I think we got two hours of sleep. 'I don't want to. This is pointless! We'll go another day'!"

Everybody else wouldn't give up. 'Let's get up and go!' Finally, Jenna gave up her fight and they headed to the light house on the very tip of Long Island. Jenna said, "It was miserable. I passed out in the car. The pictures were terrible because I got two hours of sleep and half of that was in a car," they both laughed out loud.

"I have no plan," Chad said. "I am just flying by the seat of my pants."

"We get there, and he flies out of the car! I was like: 'OK...See ya'!" She laughed as she demonstrated her best goodbye wave.

He disappeared to ferret out a huge rock right down by the water and had his sister go to the top of the lighthouse to take photos. Little did Jenna know until she caught up with him and he spun her around and told her how much he loved her. Chad laughed, "I asked her, and I think she said 'Yes' but I had to double check and asked again just to make sure."

They both smiled at each other as Jenna said, "I cried. I don't cry very often. He surprised me. I was not expecting it."

He never had to use Plan B. (Good thing because we don't think he had one!)

Amazing things

Chad looked over at their daughter sitting next to them, "Lilly has definitely been a huge blessing. Just everything with her so far has been amazing because she is such a smart little girl and she is so much a combination of the two of us. It's fun to watch her grow up."

Their plan was to wait a couple of years before starting a family, but, Jenna said, "That obviously didn't happen. Just the way life happened. She was a huge blessing."

They saw God do something amazing through Lilly in a challenging time in Chad's sister's life. Chad said, "We prayed about it a lot and when we were getting ready for Lilly's baptism, we asked Emily to be a Sponsor. She made a bunch of trips down to St Louis to see us and hang out with Lilly."

Emily later told us, "I've always liked kids and always intended on having kids of my own. I more so did not know how to connect with them since I was the youngest in the family…and I never had babysitting experience so never got exposure. Little, little babies…seemed so fragile to me, I was afraid to hold them and do something wrong that might hurt them. I do love Lilly…it was the immediate love I had for her and the love I could feel through her that made her very special to me…and still does."

Tears welled up in Chad's eyes and his voice choked. "That was such a huge thing and even though we really didn't want to have a kid right away. We're weren't ready. You never really are, but it was God's work. He was up to something." They smiled tenderly at each other and at Lilly as they remembered the blessing God gave his sister, Emily, as well as blessing them.

Blessings came with challenges

He was right out of seminary with some church planting experience behind him and an adventurous spirit that enjoyed the challenge of trying new things. "So, I jumped into church planting head-first…ready to roll with it but really not knowing a lot of the mechanics behind it."

In addition to those challenges, his wife was initially not excited about the venture. "I knew that was his passion, but it scared me to death."

"It was not something she envisioned herself doing but she knew it was what I was really passionate about, so she supported me through that. In hindsight, I kind of wish we wouldn't have started planting right off the bat. On the other side, I'm really happy we did."

Through those challenges, Chad admitted, "We learned #1…how to get our marriage through the ups and downs of 'Am I going to have a job tomorrow or not? Are we going to be moving on or not? What are we doing next with the church?' I think it challenged us both to figure out how we were going to live out our faith."

They discovered planting this church wasn't about them. Renew, their church plant in St Louis, was about all the people they would soon meet. They built relationships one by one as they built the church from the ground up. In their own neighborhood, they began to see people out in their yards and started to connect with them on a personal basis.

He knew Jenna didn't want to be up in front of people but through neighborhood get togethers, he discovered she loved to host people. "She's good at it and it made our home a welcome place for people."

After several years into Renew, it became evident the fledgling church plant would need to close. It wasn't just the church that would close down, it was their entire life. Chad said, "In my entire life, it's probably one of the hardest things I have had to do. We had to shut down a bunch of relationships and try to move people on to someone else who could be raising them up (spiritually)."

Even though they were only there for two years, people were disappointed when they were leaving, not just in the church but also in their neighborhood where they had started bringing people together.

As difficult and as painful as it was to leave, Chad said, "I knew...I knew it needed to happen. There was some sort of peace there and we needed to be moving on. So, I just accepted it and trusted that God was going to do something with it. We've grown enough to the point where we both can say we trust God is going to make things happen even if we don't understand when or how. I think we both know that and really, really put our faith in Him, even though it doesn't always make sense."

A place to heal

When Renew closed, they would need to receive a call for him to pastor another church. When that didn't happen immediately, it meant they needed to figure out where they were going to begin their lives all over. In their own words, "That wasn't easy!" They needed to be with people who loved them and would listen to them. They needed a healthy place where they could both heal.

Things happened so quickly and there wasn't much time to process while they were going through those transitions. They found they survived by asking, 'What's the next right thing?' 'OK...the next right thing is to rebuild this bathroom.' 'The next right thing is to pack the truck.' And then on to 'the next right thing'.

"My worst fear." Jenna said, "was having to close Renew because of what I thought it would do to Chad. I didn't see that happen. I don't know if it was because we were so busy or just because of God's crazy peace. I was expecting him to have a mourning period like I did. I knew I had Lily to take care of, but I didn't know if I could take care of him AND the dog AND the move. God's grace was HUGE through all of that and just His presence."

Looking back, she said, "I saw just how God had grace-filled that very difficult situation." Even through pain, disappointment and a move from everything safe and familiar, their faith was strengthened. The stress could have caused their marriage to splinter, but instead they became even stronger partners as they walked through this challenging time together.

What now?

They relocated to Green Bay, Wisconsin, and became a part of Raized, a church where God led them to serve. Chad said, "I still see myself as a church planter...I'm just planting a church at the car dealership where I work as well as working on new things at Raized. The difference is...it's not my baby." They have seen firsthand that this church plant doesn't rest on the shoulders of one or two people. It rests on the entire church community as they serve together.

He began working with US Center for World Missions to become a certified coach, so he can coach other church planters, so they don't make the same mistakes he did. "I especially hope to coach guys who are in a more bi-vocational context because I'm living it out and I'm experiencing it firsthand and I know what it's like."

There is no doubt God is using this time in their lives to be a part of a church where they see people stepping up and unselfishly serving. They have experienced the generosity of this faith community and their impact they have on the local community.

She said, "I think a blessing in disguise was moving here to Green Bay. God's hand was huge and so evident in every single part! As sad as we were leaving St Louis, we knew God was telling us to come to Green Bay. To see what has happened since we have been here with the church plant we are a part of and the relationships we have built, feels like we have been here for years, not six months. God has us in Green Bay for a purpose."

Jenna has made relationships with other young Moms. Chad is developing relationships at work. They are connecting with a school that has a 98% poverty rate. They are coming alongside to mentor a family that has a desire to reach their neighbors. Chad said, "We want to see people change their lives. We are doing things in these little pockets across Green Bay to impact people and we get to do it as a family. We prayed about it and made the decision to move here because we felt this is where we needed to be, and we have seen nothing but fruit from it." A huge challenge turned into an amazing blessing!

Money and time

They are no different than a majority of married couples who list money as their #1 challenge. Chad said, "Money has always been a challenge for us because you never have what you want but we've always had enough. So, there are a lot of dreams we have...we are working towards. We'll continue to figure out that money part as we go."

Chad confessed to being a 'recovering workaholic'. Jenna laughed as he continued, "Moving from just being me into living with Jenna and starting a marriage was like, 'I got to learn how not to be a workaholic.' Jenna does a really good job at helping me take time off. I think that was one of the hardest things when I was working with Renew those first couple of years. I knew I had deadlines. I knew I had to make things happen or Renew wasn't going to continue. I would stress myself out to no end, but Jenna was my peace in the way she would slow me down and keep me focused." Even today, he feels she helps him balance life and ministry at their new church.

Looking back, Jenna said, "When I lost my teaching job at a Christian school...that was really hard. That was my identity. I was a teacher. It is what it is but it just really wracked me. Chad, at one point, used the word 'depressed' for me." She was shocked and surprised at that word, but soon realized he was right. Their lives were left in chaos. They had just signed a contract on a brand-new house they loved. They were just starting Renew church plant and there was not enough coming in to pay Chad a salary as pastor. Jenna's job was their income. Now they had to figure out how to get through that and move on. Jenna said, "I had to learn how to re-identify myself. Who am I then if I'm not teaching?"

"That was tough for me because I'm also a 'fix it' man. I love working on cars. I love that whole fixing thing, but I couldn't fix that situation. I had to learn to just not try to fix it." Chad gave a weak laugh, but pain was still evident in Jenna's face.

When asked how she made it through that time, she said, "I don't know if there's one thing. I think having Chad as a constant...I knew he was there. I knew he was supporting me whatever I did. I ended up being a nanny that next year." Through that job, she was able to stay connected with many of her friends from her former school. "I also just got to a place of forgiveness. I was able to forgive." It was a painful process, but she arrived at a place where she could finally say, "I can move on. There are new things ahead."

Blending together

How do you take two different individuals and blend them together into one united household? They took traditions and family preferences and incorporated them into their lives. They also tried to create their own traditions. Chad said, "My family always gets a live Christmas tree. The big thing was to go out to one of these places and pick out a tree. Jenna's family never really did that, but it was something we both wanted to do. So, taking some of those traditions and making them our own rather than saying, 'This is how MY family always did it and we have to do it that way'."

In-laws

After they married, they lived quite a distance from both of their families, so they made intentional plans for holidays with consideration and fairness to both sides. Chad said, "I love my in-laws! I have a blast with them!" He looked over at Jenna, "I think you love my family, too...but we create balance with that and don't try to one-side it."

"I think our families are so polar opposite," Jenna said. "Pick whatever you want to pick, and they are opposite. My family will welcome anyone into their house...always hosting things. His family just doesn't host things. They are private. His Mom likes things really clean...that's not a trait in my family!", she snickered. "It's been a lot of balance of those things, especially when they come to visit. We've had to blow off a lot of stuff. OK...that's how our parents do it...we don't agree...but that's how they do it and that's OK."

"Jenna and I saw a lot of that as soon as we had Lilly. We have the ways we wanted to raise Lilly and the things we wanted to do. 'Cloth diapering...why would you do that?' When Lilly started eating real food, she just kind of ate whatever we ate, in smaller portions. I remember both of our parents questioning the stuff we were giving her. 'How can she eat that already? I can't believe she's eating with a fork!' Our response: 'She's watching us, and she wants a fork. We're going to let her eat with a fork.' They both smiled, 'Yah...we know. This isn't the way you guys did it or probably the way you want us to do it, but this is the way we're going to do it'."

They recognized when they married, they married into another family. At the same time, they were committed to their own family, making their own decisions. Through this, there has developed a respect for each other and for their families.

You're stuck with me!

When asked if they ever felt like giving up, their answer was quickly, 'No!' According to Jenna, 'It was never an option!" With so many friends going through divorce, Chad said, "You're stuck with me!"

As they began to see people coming to their church, it would be a divorced family, a divorced family, a divorced family-- one after another. Jenna said, "We don't come from divorced families, so we don't know that world. When a family member started going through that, it was the closest we have personally been to a divorce. I guess I have never felt the tension between us. It's always been us against whatever we were facing."

Chad claimed, "We don't fight. People ask us, 'Have you ever had a really good yelling fight?' We haven't." They look at each other and smile, "We never really yell at each other."

Jenna laughed as she said, "My Mom talks about it all the time like when we have little disagreements...'You're fighting! I see it'!" They both laughed out loud at the thought!

"I think we've made it a really good habit that we talk things through", said Chad. "Even if there isn't a resolution to it, we still talk about it." It is evident, they tend to talk it out rather than shout it out.

From Jenna

"Always have your husband's back." She saw that in so many instances as they began the new church plant. "It was his thing and his love, and I was behind him. I wasn't going to be up front, but I was going to be cutting out the ornaments and doing little things. That's the stuff he hates to do. Figuring out how you balance each other is huge. I'm not just that outgoing", she laughed. "I'm like...'Let's go to the self-checkout' and he's like: 'No...Let's go meet someone!' He's the crazy one...I'm a little more rational. I bake and Chad cooks. We figure out how to complement each other and fit it together.

I'm home with Lilly all day so when he comes home, I feel like, 'Here, you get the child!' At the same time, he's been working all day and he wants a break, too. It's figuring that out."

They both smiled in agreement, as she finished, "Being intentional about it and really fighting for it. It's not easy."

From Chad

He advised other couples to never stop talking. "The minute you stop talking is the minute you start fighting."

To which Jenna added, "Listen, too. You can't JUST talk."

She smiled and shook her head in agreement as her husband added, "Go on adventures. We started to see our life as a bunch of different adventures and I think that makes things a whole lot more fun. When we faced a challenge, like moving here to Green Bay...it was going to be our next adventure. We didn't exactly know what it was going to be or how it was going to play out, but we just jumped on it and went for it. I think you grow when you do things that are different and outside of the norm."

Chad's last piece of advice was, "Marriage isn't about you. I've seen a lot of people in relationships where as soon as they get married, everything is about what I need and what I want and how it needs to be for me. When that happens, you totally lose sight of the relationship and you're no longer in a relationship."

Chad & Jenna, Lilly & Adylyn Grace
Copyright © Abby Hinz

Jenna brought up human nature when she said, "And to be real...that's a struggle!"

Chad agreed, "It's got to be us. It's not about you or me! It's about WE!"

Anonymous – No One Knows the Pain

"But the fruit of the Spirit is love, joy, peace, patience, kindness, goodness, faithfulness, gentleness and self-control."
Galatians 5:22-23a

Isn't it just the two of us in this marriage? Aren't we dealing with our two-people problems in our two-focused way? How can life become so complicated by adding children into the marriage mix?

Once our children are adults, their problems don't disappear from our hearts and minds. These parents share their story anonymously, to protect their daughter's privacy.

Our Child – Our Pain

They shared the pain of their youngest daughter and her husband as they traveled the arduous journey of discovering they were pregnant, only to lose the baby a week later. During that very sad time, this couple also discovered their older daughter was leaving her husband...for a woman.

In almost an instant, they were no longer just two people dealing with life. It was now two parents + two daughters in their own pain + two sons-in-law clobbered by life + two grandchildren living in turmoil = compounding pain.

There was no way to prepare for the emotions that surfaced when their daughter announced her gay relationship. No one could anticipate the hurt they would feel! Angry siblings! Confused grandchildren! They didn't know what to do. How should they react? They would often say to each other, 'What would Jesus do?' 'What would Jesus do!' 'WHAT WOULD JESUS DO!'

Drowning in their own pain, they walked alongside their daughter, in spite of her decision with which they didn't agree. They tried to care for their grandchildren through this time of confusion in their lives. They admitted their greatest struggle was showing love even when somebody was acting unloving. Their daughter didn't want to do anything with them, even though they both continued to make every effort to connect with her. It was often through short texts reminding her of their love. No matter what they tried, there was usually no response.

When making a visit to her, they found out you can't make people talk when they don't want to talk. Her Dad said, "Initially, all she would do was cry when we tried to talk to her. She wouldn't converse back with us. I don't know if that was her defense mechanism or if that was her...her way of not having to talk with us or it was just her spirit was so broken. It may have been all of the above."

When they made a visit, her Mom said, "My words to her in that conversation were, 'There's nothing you can do that will make God love you any less. He will always be there. He is ready to forgive, and I love you'." With that, they walked out the door.

Her Dad said, "She does know we are going to love her through this," but, they agreed their daughter needed to hear the truth…and she did…from them.

Too late?

After almost a year, their daughter walked back through the doors of their church. She had a repenting spirit, but by then the damage had already been done to her marriage. They were divorced. She wanted reconciliation. He had moved on. Since her husband remarried, she went back to her previous gay relationship. She told her parents, 'I know how you feel, but this is what I'm doing, and I don't want to talk about it.' Now their struggle was how to stay loving without condoning a lifestyle which was against the principles of their Christian faith. "We're still figuring it out. We don't have the answers except that we try to keep communication open. We go to events for our granddaughters. We support her and love her."

Their prodigal

When they look at the prodigal in Scripture, they see the Father didn't go chase after his son. Her Mom said, "It's finding that balance of letting her have the consequences for what she is doing but letting her know the door is open whenever she wants to walk back through it. We haven't shut the door, but we're not accepting the sinful lifestyle because we know how harmful it is. We know it is ultimately going to lead to more misery and more heartache. We are hoping she knows at any point she wants to turn around, God is there and He's going to be ready with open arms to accept her and forgive her. That's what we want her to see."

United…

Some people in this situation find the cracks and fissures caused by their children, have caused cracks and fissures in their marriage. This couple said they are only stronger together through this. "We talk about it. 'What does this look like? Do we allow this? 'What do we think is the best approach to this'?" They have presented a unified in front to their daughter. They believe it has been possible because they both went to the Word of God to find His truth for this situation. It is through that, they came to agree, "This is sin and we can't condone sin."

They know it might sound trite…'You love the person and hate the sin', but they have gone back to God and asked, 'We don't want it to be empty words. How do we love her, but hate what she's doing?' They trust God will show them how…minute by minute.

Added struggle

Their struggle wasn't only with their daughter, but together they battled with how they should react to her partner. Her Dad was attending a track meet for one of the granddaughters when he saw his daughter's partner. The first 15-20 minutes, he ignored her. "Then, I just felt like God spoke to me and said, 'That's not what I or

My Son would do'. After that, I went over to sit with her and conversed with her just like everything was normal."

God has been teaching them how to love when lines are blurred. He is giving them His love when their own love doesn't seem like enough.

Praying

This Mom and Dad could have turned all of this turmoil inward and become depressed. They could have turned against each other and let it pull them apart. Instead, they chose to pray for their daughter and her partner. "We are praying they will come to know God and find Jesus. Maybe they'll come out of that sin and both repent. That's our prayer. I can't hate the individual that I feel brought my daughter down this road, because it takes two people to go down any road." Prayer was their weapon of choice in this battle for their daughter's heart.

How did she get there?

As they looked back, they saw their daughter and son-in-law had walked away from their church. They were isolated. They didn't have a community of people who would encourage them to make the right choices. Her Mom said, "We can't just be Lone Rangers. Satan used several things in their lives to isolate them and she was lonely. More and more, Satan was able to get a stronghold because she was so lonely." Their daughter even told them, 'I did not express my feelings, so my husband did not know how desperately lonely I was.' That made her a target for an affair.

Her Mom said, "Nobody sets out thinking, 'Oh, I'm going to have this sexual affair.' It usually starts out as an emotional need. We find it being met in somebody other than our spouse. We are definitely not going to God and saying, 'I need You to meet my need'. Satan knows what our weaknesses are and that's where he gets those footholds."

As parents, they tried to deal with the pain and rejection of their daughter's life decisions. Mom had several friends she could be really honest with and who were daily praying for her. She said, "A gift was having those friends I could say, 'You don't make me cry. I'm going to cry anyway. So, either you can sit with me and cry or I'll cry by myself'." These were the people in her life with whom she could be vulnerable. Her heart wants that missing piece for her daughter's life, as well.

Their pain...Our pain

When our children make choices that hurt themselves and others, we as parents often feel the pain of our children as if it was our own pain. The deep pain of loss and rejection could have separated this marriage. For this couple, the pain only made them fall into each other's arms and into the arms of their Savior who would then carry their pain when they no longer had the strength.

These parents don't know the end of their daughter's story, but Jesus does! He's got this! His Hand has never lifted off these two people and their child He loves so unconditionally.

Aaron & Lisa – Didn't Blame Each Other

MARRIED 35 YEARS

Copyright © David Witt

"Even though I walk through the darkest valley, I will fear no evil, for you are with me; your rod and your staff, they comfort me." Psalm 23:4

Notes? Absolutely! They met in college, however…it was the musical kind that brought them together.! How could they know it would be the connection that drew them into a friendship that eventually led to marriage?

College campuses can be daunting by their size! For Aaron and Lisa, it meant even though they attended the same college, they each had a different group of friends so didn't hang out together. After Lisa graduated from college, they ran into each other again.

"My car's all packed and I'm heading to St Louis to teach."

"Oh", Aaron said, "I'm going to be in St Louis at the seminary."

So, she moved there, and he moved there. Lisa had friends at the seminary, so she would go down on weekends to spend time with them. She and Aaron were both part of that group and soon became more than just acquaintances. He invited her to join him in singing with the seminary choir. He bowled on Tuesday nights, so she would wait for him to be done and then they would eat together. (Tuesday night, each seminarian could invite a guest to eat for free. She was definitely a cheap date!) From there, they would head over to choir.

Almost everything was done in a group. They recalled one time they went to a movie with friends. Aaron laughed, "Billy and Michelle sat in the middle and Lisa and I sat on the outside. It was better than splitting them up. They were dating!"

Right before Easter, their choir was practicing on a Saturday for a special performance. After practice, he asked if she wanted to go to a movie. So, she admitted as they walked from the seminary to the theater, she got a little nervous. "We had never really done anything alone together, so I am thinking, 'I don't know if this is a date or not.' I am just going to let him pay first and if he pays my way, then I know it is a date," she laughed. "So, I let him go to the window and he paid for my way, and then I knew it was a date," she laughed even harder.

Aaron was thinking much the same. 'If she lets me pay it's a date.' "So, when she didn't go up to pay, I figured we were on a date," he laughed.

She smiled, "I don't know--it was like 'boom...all of a sudden'...something happened within me as we walked to that movie theater that made me curious enough to wonder if he liked me."

They started seeing each other, but evidently not exclusively. That Easter, Aaron was visiting with another girl he liked. He told her he needed to go out to the airport to pick up Lisa. That didn't exactly fly well with the other girl, but Aaron said, "I remember making a pretty conscious choice to go pick Lisa up." It seems that was when their relationship began to get more serious. When Aaron picked her up from the airport to take her home, Lisa said, "He walked me to the door and just gave me this kiss. I was like 'Awww'," she laughed shyly.

Discovered each other

"She was lively and fun. Like my roommate, Tim, always said, 'Lisa's eyes! You don't have a chance with her eyes. You look at her eyes and then they go blink'." Aaron made hand motions open and closed like eyelids. "That's how he described it and well yah, it was true."

As their casual relationship developed, she discovered he loved sports. She loved sports, too, so the two of them developed a little competitive edge in the football department. An avid Vikings fan, he didn't exactly appreciate the fact that she liked Joe Montana of the San Francisco 49ers!

He looked over at Lisa and added, "One other thing that attracted me was that she could throw a softball like a guy. We could play catch and I could pretty much throw the ball as hard as I wanted to, and she could catch it."

"I also really respected your commitment to be a teacher. I got to know more and more what that meant to you and how you devoted your life to that. It's not just like, 'I'll teach and then have fun with life.' You were devoted to the work you did. You saw it as a calling and the more I saw that, the more impressed I was that you had values that are good for our life together."

She grew up in a small town where most of the time, girls just stayed and married the boy next door. There was a lot of partying going on, which Lisa said she was very good at. However, it was not the way she wanted to live her whole life. She said, "There was just something in me that said, 'I want something different'." As she watched the marriage of her older siblings, she knew there were things she might want to have differently in her own life. "So, I prayed for someone who would respect me and who would want to be married for life and who would love God…someone who would dedicate their life to serving God."

The proposal

When talking about his proposal, Aaron knew he was on the spot. He had shopped for the ring but hadn't picked it up when Lisa came to his dorm room to talk. "I was trying to figure out how to ask her to marry me and I had to be more creative than just, 'will you marry me', you know. So, I asked her if she would be willing to be the mother of our children."

Lisa teasingly rebutted, "You said, 'I want you to be my wife or maybe 'I want you to be the mother of my children' but, you never asked the question, so I didn't have an answer. I finally said, 'Are you going to ask me a question'?"

He asked, and her answer was 'yes'! Two days later he went down to pick up the ring.

Lisa smiled, "I don't think he was planning on asking me that night because he didn't have the ring." She was friends with lots of guys and thought he might have been a little jealous (and perturbed) that she was visiting other guys there in the dorm before coming down to his room. "Maybe he figured he'd better ask me if I was going to keep on visiting the other guys!"

"Maybe that's what it was," he gave a near Cheshire cat grin..

Facing challenges

Aaron said, "I think one challenge that we faced, and still do, is the basic challenge in communication. I…I…get a little bit defensive….very easily so. It's not always easy for her to know what to say or not to say. I think that when I got defensive it would shut her down as far as talking and so we learned some patterns of not talking. I think we have gotten much better in not being short with each other. It can still happen but not nearly like it was.

I think I can express myself, but deep intimate conversation is not necessarily my easiest thing. I don't know all the reasons why. I just don't feel like talking that way all the time. I never liked talking on the phone. She would be in St Louis and I would be in North Dakota during the summer before we got engaged. I am not one who liked to set records and talk an hour. I think there are communication challenges that sometimes made it difficult for us to always feel comfortable like we are pals."

Lisa's challenge centered on the fact her husband was as a pastor and the amount of time he had to be away from her and their family. His reprieve from the stress of work was sports, where he could relax a little and take a breath. Even though she realized playing those sports were relationship building for him; it didn't dull the feeling that between his work and sports, she was often left alone.

"You know...it always to me felt like it's just more time away from me. It was more like he would be working or doing something with someone else. Not that we didn't ever spend time together...but for me, especially, raising the kids...or even sometimes now, it's just a lot of time that it feels like he is not with me. Ok... I could go to ALL the softball games and that kind of stuff. I could go golfing more or go watch him bowl or those kinds of things as well, but I choose not to."

She took a shallow breath and continued, "When the kids were really young, in my perspective, it felt like me doing a lot of it because he would still take time to golf. Then I would hear other husbands who would say, 'I can't golf at this time in our lives because I have kids'. I was like, 'Well that's not my family!' I would get a little bit jealous. Then I would just know, 'This is OUR family, and this is what we look like. We are not any other family'!"

Painful loss

She hesitated a little and then continued, "Probably one of our biggest challenges was being blessed with four children and being able to raise only three of them.

When I found out we were pregnant with our fourth child, I just cried because I didn't think we would be able to handle another child. And then, we thought we had lost him because I started bleeding. When we found out we didn't--that's when I fell in love with Alan."

She took a heavy breath, "There were so many instances...," she paused. "The other kids were four, five and six when he was born, and I would take all the kids to Sam's Club with me. We would have Alan in his little stroller with one of the kids pushing him and I would be pushing the cart and the other two would be holding on to the cart. We would be down one aisle and all of sudden here's the kids and there's no Alan. I would be screaming, 'Well, where is he'?" She laughed, "So, we would have to go and find him. One of the kids got distracted and they weren't pushing him anymore."

Her laugh was a little quieter and a little sadder, "He was always the one left behind. We were camping one time with some friends of ours and somehow, he was locked in our cabin and we didn't have the key. There's poor Alan again! He's in there by himself! The kids would be playing outside with some of their neighborhood friends. I'm a window away from them and all of sudden, here is the neighbor who is a paramedic, holding Alan and saying, 'He was in the middle of the street'."

She had a downcast look as she continued, "--and then it wasn't long after that he ended up in our swimming pool and died. I just felt like the worst parent in the world because it's like 'this is the child...'" Her tears now flowed freely, "I always left him somewhere and it was really hard...because there were so many stories like that where he was there and then he wasn't."

He remembered having the three older children that day and Lisa having Alan with her at a women's meeting. "He was kind of a hit at the whole thing because it was a whole bunch of ladies and Alan. Like 'Duh...they didn't stand a chance," Lisa smiled at the memory.

After a busy day, everyone was back home, and Alan was down for a nap. They were about to go to their small group meeting when Aaron came into the house and heard Alan jabbering, so he got him out of bed. The toddler was following his Dad down the hall but then a phone call came in. While Aaron was on the phone, Lisa was in the kitchen and asked where Alan was.

Aaron spoke slowly, "We started looking all over the house and looked down at the other end, and then we saw the door open to our lanai where the pool was. We always had the pool locked. We had some friends over to swim the night before. We were both gone the next day and we never took time to put the pool fence back up."

Is this really happening?

Their painful story continued as she struggled with words to describe finding him in the pool. "This whole feeling of this blackness just filled my body and it's just like 'it's our life! Is this really happening to us? It always happened to someone else. It was us this time." She jumped in and got him and then Aaron tried to resuscitate. The paramedics were able to get a heartbeat and transport him to the hospital. He was unable to breathe on his own so eventually the tough question would be asked: 'Do we leave him on life support or is it OK to remove it?'

They both had many opportunities to demonstrate to people that they knew Alan was in God's hands and that we as humans don't control everything. However, that didn't mean as parents, they weren't struggling and battling with emotions and doubts. Aaron shared his pain, "I remember driving and just going through in my mind what it might be like for Alan...in the pool and not being able to get his air and wondering, 'Where is Mom and Dad?' That felt like we had abandoned him, and we just didn't do what we should have done."

Lisa shared, "When he was in the hospital we prayed for a miracle. Jesus raised Lazarus from the dead and he could raise Alan if He wanted to. It was kind of scary when they took him off the ventilator the last day of his life because the doctor thought he saw something really hopeful in Alan. They needed to try to remove life support at this point."

They were not allowed to go into the room, but as they waited, they were thinking something would be really positive that day. "When we found out it wasn't, we made the choice to not put him back on life support because he didn't have any brain activity. But...I kept saying it anyway. 'It doesn't mean he <u>has</u> to die. He might <u>but</u>, if God still wanted him to live, even if he's not on those machines, he still could'!" Their pleading prayer was for a miracle.

He was in the hospital for eight days and then he died. Yet, they both knew there was a miracle...the miracle of eternal life. Even through their grief, it brought them great comfort to know Alan was alive with Christ.

Inner struggle

She struggled and admitted almost being embarrassed at explaining how it happened. "How could I have not seen it? No one really knows the perfect thing to say in this situation. It was especially difficult when people would tell us, 'I was vacuuming, and something just told me to turn around and my son was in the pool and I pulled him out'. Lisa agonized, 'Why didn't that happen for us?' I would hear all these stories...and...people thought they were doing a good thing by telling me but to me it was more guilt. Why couldn't I feel that?"

Through tears she went on, "When I was talking to my friends...I will never forget this...one friend said, 'You know...that's not <u>why</u> Alan died. It's <u>how</u> he died.' I don't know...that has always just stuck with me. I know that he's in heaven with Jesus."

Dealing with grief

"I can't imagine", Aaron said, "if one of us would have been alone with the kids and it happened. I am sure other families have faced that challenge. It always comes down to being able to forgive and understand and realize we are not perfect human beings. But...ultimately being able to put it in God's hands and say, 'We're not perfect parents. We're not the ones in charge. 'Alan, you see the hand there...it's Jesus hand.' It's kind of hard to give that up sometimes as a Dad or Mom and say, 'It's not me'."

Aaron was able to talk more about Alan's death because he had public speaking opportunities. She didn't have those times to publicly share her grief, so he eventually came to understand there were different ways to deal with grief. That meant he needed to give his wife room to grieve in her own way. He said, "I think we had compassion for each other in the hurt and loss and were not looking to blame one another for what each should have done differently or better. We tried to recognize the hurt in the other person, which left a desire to help meet that need."

Lisa said everything changed in their lives in those few short days. They then had to try to learn how to live with it. "I think, just knowing that we were...that we were being helped by God and that we were committed to being together. I mean, this is definitely the major, biggest struggle we have gone through." She tried to hold back tears as she breathed out the words, "I know God was with us the whole time and carried us through. I don't know how someone gets through it without their faith!" She could no longer hold the tears back.

Aaron tenderly turned toward Lisa and spoke directly to her and said, "I guess I wanted to say to you, Lisa, that I have seen people grieve who really turn inward towards themselves and will not allow themselves to understand the hurt or talk about how much it hurts. Or just saying, 'It's not fair! It just can't be. It's wrong.' And you didn't do that."

Remember, from earlier in the interview that this husband who normally doesn't like much intimate talk, now struggled with finding the right words to comfort his wife. "You...you kept taking care of and loving, not only the other kids, of course, but me. My needs were still something you considered, and I can see many grieving

Moms not want to consider their husband's needs at that point. You didn't do that. I felt very blessed how you handled the grief as a Mom...and I appreciate that." This very tender moment between them lingered.

Twenty years later...

Now twenty-two years later, he said, "I remember thinking there will be a day when I don't think of him. Well, there are some days we live our lives and I don't meditate on Alan and I don't have to feel we're abandoning him because of that. Alan is in the best hands he can be. Sometimes, I cherish remembering him. I can smell his hair sometimes still. We have a few mementos that we certainly keep and don't hide away. It's a memory that's OK to visit once in a while. Last summer, we were cleaning out the garage. Alan had a couple toys that played music and I remember him pulling the cord down and it would make this doo-doo-doo musical sound as the cord went back. It would stop, and he would pull it down again. We found that toy," he smiled tenderly.

He quietly continued, "It was hard to pull that thing and listen to the music because it was supposed to be Alan pulling it. It's ok to visit those memories sometimes because we don't have to bear the burden of thinking 'it was our fault'...even as much as we could probably prove it was. Life is a gift from God. We're imperfect people and I think we encouraged this whole understanding for one another."

"Alan lived twenty months and that seems like this much," holding up his fingers like an inch. "It's only that much time, compared to the scope of eternity. So, Alan's life was not less. Alan's life was full and still is. So, we know that and trust that and believe that, so we don't have to be responsible as far as questioning, 'Is Alan alive?' because we know he is! We miss that we didn't get to spend more time with him, but we're ok."

Choosing love...

As she watched those around her getting divorced, she said, "I wanted to be committed for life. By God's grace, through every situation we went through in our marriage, I made the choice to love because I don't believe love is a feeling. Even though I feel so much love...I feel love is a choice I would make. God loves me and then I can love others and I can love you," she pointed to Aaron, "but I choose to do that. It's not because I'm feeling all sweaty palmed and stuff like that."

He put his arm around her and spoke rather shyly. "I am blessed you have chosen to love me...especially when I hear you say you 'make a choice'...'you've chosen to love me'. A lot of people would say I'm lucky, but I say, 'Thank you, Lord'!"

We have family

Aaron spoke proudly as a father, "We have family. Not perfect kids but neat kids and gifted kids and fun kids. Creative kids. Kids that love us. We get to go chase our kids around the world." (As of this writing, their adult children are scattered all over the globe. Alissa is working short term missions in Taiwan, Andrew commutes between San Francisco and Denver for his job and Adam lives in Japan. They have the blessing of traveling all over the world to visit their adventurous family!)

"I am also blessed by your commitment, Lisa, and that you're here! It's a blessing that we share a lot of things in life together. You are not afraid of work. Sometimes the intensity of our values even clash a little bit but I'm blessed that you love the Lord and that you know He loves you." He looked tenderly at her and said, "And that is such a blessing for our lives...for my life."

Lisa said, "I appreciate you supporting some things I have been wanting to get involved in like running for President of the LWML (Lutheran Women's Missionary League). Even in church sometimes, it just kind of makes me feel really blessed knowing that you're my husband. I love the way you speak to people and don't just preach at them, the way the people appreciate you and the way that you minister to them and share God's Word. It's just a blessing," they look into each other's eyes, "to know that we're together and that you're my husband. It makes me feel proud! And I appreciate the way--I kind of give things a 'lick and a promise'. You really get it clean," she laughed.

Not about butterflies

Lisa's view began, "Marriage is not about the butterflies in your stomach and the sweaty hands that make you feel like you're in love. Well...that's good to have too," she laughed out loud, "but when those things go away it becomes more about the commitment you have to the marriage. It's about forgiveness. It's about taking your problems to the Lord and talking to each other and not just to other people about your problems. Sometimes couples feel that if my spouse doesn't do that for me, I'm not going to that for them. It's not about what I get...it's about what I give. It's about choosing to love and not making it easy to just give up."

As a pastor, Aaron, said he helps guide many couples through the marriage preparation process. He helps them with principles of communication and encourages them to make sure they give the other person the chance to say what they feel. He encourages them to listen to understand each other and not to find a reason why you think they are wrong. In their own marriage, he said, "If I could listen to understand where she's at and realize that might not be where I'm at...I can disagree 100% but accept that's where she's at."

In talking about expectations, he said, "People have the expectation that this person is going to fulfill my every need and every dream and once that doesn't happen, they find every reason to say, 'There must be somebody different out there'. In a world where the culture says, 'Yes, you should get what you want', it's a lie because it won't satisfy in the way that God designed that you live in a marriage where you learn forgiveness and serving." Aaron believes this is ultimately more fulfilling than trying to find the next person who might make you happy and then never staying and growing through the challenges.

As individuals, they aren't exactly alike and definitely approach things very differently. Lisa laughed, "We've had people over, and he was still vacuuming when the first person gets to the door. That makes me nervous!"

Aaron cracked up with laughter as he looked over at Lisa, "You fill ice in glasses forty-five minutes before people get here and the ice is melted when they get here!"

Looking at us he said, "I just let her do it and shake my head at her." He had his arm around her, and she fell back into his shoulder giggling.

Stronger together

They have lived through unspeakable pain and loss and yet still feel blessed. They didn't blame each other. They choose to love and laugh together. They choose to stay together and grow together. Alone, standing might have felt almost impossible, but together they are stronger!

Rob & Deb – Complement...Not Compete

MARRIED 41 YEARS

"Just as there are many parts to our bodies, so it is with Christ's body. We are all parts of it, and it takes every one of us to make it complete, for we each have different work to do. So, we belong to each other, and each need all the others." (TLB)
Romans 12:4-5

A s if they were spending any summer evening together gliding on their porch swing, they casually shared their story. Rob is a good 'porch swinger' but not much of a talker, so when he said something, we listened.

"We knew each other when we first met up on Main Street where I had my motorcycle," he looked over at Deb, "and you were hanging out on the curb." At that remark, they both threw their heads back in a chorus of laughs.

"Hanging out on the curb?" she said with pretend horror. Then he got the 'look' as she straightened out the facts. "Some of us girls were waiting to go into a movie, if I remember right. He was interested in getting to know me and I wanted nothing to do with him. He was just obnoxious!" (And she <u>meant</u> it!)

"I was a little rough around the edges, but her Mom liked me and wanted her to dump her boyfriend and pick me."

"At that time, I was dating his best friend." After a short pause, she matter-of-factly added, "His best friend ended up in reform school!" At that comment, no one within ear shot could miss the roar!

Rob kept his arms folded across his chest as he laughed at her further description of 'obnoxious'. "I wanted nothing to do with him," she blurted out. "He just kept hangin' around and comin' around and comin' around and...'Oh, I LOVE your shiny hair!' Obnoxious!"

Her voice began to soften, "He was dating another gal that I knew and of course, then we spent time together as two couples. I don't know...it was just like we kind of became friends and the next thing we knew...we were a couple. I don't know how you explain that!"

To put it simply, Rob said, "It just worked." Although he couldn't pinpoint the one thing that attracted him to her, tongue in cheek, Deb suggested it might be her blond hair.

When you wrap it all up in a bow, here it is: She wasn't really interested, and that resistance gave him a little incentive to pursue her...so he did.

They met when Deb was 14 and Rob was a mature 16-year-old. It took about two years for them to realize they were in love and four years later they were married on Christmas Day.

Life together

As with many marriages, their struggles were with finances. Whether they were going to have enough money and who was spending the money. When asked how they met that challenge, Rob didn't hesitate, "I listened to what I was told!" Deb couldn't help but teasingly jab him in the ribs.

Deb said, "I think it took us a while to learn how to manage credit. Once we got a handle on that, we realized with credit cards you don't keep balances. In our marriage, financial things healed very quickly, and they are no longer an issue." They both agreed getting their finances under control resolved potential conflicts, as well as enabled him to cut down on extra hours of work. Their firm commitment: 'Stay out of debt!'

Rob worked in construction and put in extra hours of work, which Deb said created another challenge. She looked over at her husband, "Because then you weren't home much and once we had Theresa, you chose work over being home for your daughter. That created another bone of contention."

How did they work it out? Rob admitted, "You just do."

"You just do", she agreed. "It just didn't matter. When he was home and spent time with her it was good time. It wasn't like he just came home to be disciplinarian. That's not what happened. He was more like her playmate...her best friend."

Rob shyly agreed, "I guess so."

Never packed a bag!

Both Deb and Rob adamantly responded with a, 'NO!' to giving up!

She admitted, "There were times we'd get mad, but I don't think there was ever a time when I would...I have NEVER packed a bag...have you?", she looked over at him and snickered.

"Nope. It's kind of one of them things where you get mad and you walk away...think about what you said or what would you have said. Then you just kind of learn to keep your mouth shut if you want things to work out and not to hurt each other devastatingly." A tender look passed between.

"He did the walk out...but when he came back, we could talk about things and it was different. Him doing the 'walk out' thing created a cooling off."

Rob smiled, "I guess that's anger management."

"I didn't have sense enough to walk away." she chuckled. "And I certainly wasn't going to follow him. I guess if I was someone who was going to be adamant in having my way, I would have followed him and kept at it." One assurance she had was the absolute trust that he would always come back.

Rob teased, "I was like a puppy." A sweet smile crossed the short distance to his wife.

She lobbed back, "Short leash!"

Work it out

When asked if they always worked things out when he came back from the 'cooling down' period, Rob said, "Sometimes. Sometimes we just kind of dropped it and it was however she wanted it or whatever we had to do to get through it."

Deb added, "We have to be really honest about something. We have not had hard times in our marriage."

He agreed, "We haven't had any 'knock-down drag-outs'."

Standing by his wife

Although they loved her, Deb and Rob both felt his Mom could be a challenge. One night, Deb challenged her right back and it didn't take very long before his Mom was on the phone telling him she didn't deserve that kind of treatment from his wife. Rob firmly, but respectfully, stood with his wife and not his mother. The 'two becoming one' was no longer just a phrase, but it became a reality in their marriage.

Sweet blessings

Rob shyly smiled and counted his blessings this way: "Our daughter...grandkids...God...my wife." He moved his eyes over to Deb as he continued, "I think my in-laws...", he looked down to pause "and a few friends we have been fortunate to have."

His wife counted it a blessing to have stability in their marriage, especially since they married so young. "Most of those don't last," she dabbed her eyes with a tissue.

Rob's 'tender' side emerged as he jabbed, "QUIT gettin' sentimental!!!"

To which Deb couldn't even pretend to be serious. "Just for a laugh I should tell you just how sweet he was on Christmas day about 20 years ago. We came home from a family dinner and it was really icy. I fell on the sidewalk. It hurt sooo bad. I am laying there trying to recover myself and he is just looking at me and said, 'Well, for God's sake, get up!' I thought...'You've got to be kidding!' I gathered myself in order to get up." Rob sat with his arms folded and a deadpan look on his face while Deb laughed at the crazy memory of that incident.

We asked, "If she fell now what would you say?"

Rob didn't change his answer. "I would tell her the same thing. 'Get up'!"

Deb couldn't stop giggling at Rob's version of 'tough love'!

"Aww," he fessed up, "I wouldn't be quite that bad. I probably would go help her up."

"I'm going to remember that!"

"Ok," he admitted with a Stan Laurel look on his face, "maybe I would snicker a little bit." He jumped back in the conversation as he rubbed the top of his head, "One time, I did help her. We had Theresa and we had this cheap set of steps on the trailer house and she felt through them."

Deb almost fell out of their swing! She laughed until she cried and reached for a tissue to dab her eyes. "My butt got stuck!", she could barely get out of her mouth before giving an all-out, mouth wide open, boisterous laugh!

"She was holding the baby...so you know...I did go help her then." He stuttered a little before saying, "There's a soft spot somewhere."

"It's hard to find marshmallow under all the crust," she giggled.

Got what we don't deserve

According to Deb, "God has given us jobs we don't deserve. Homes we didn't pay market value for. Talents to build and do our own home. Oh...everything...everything. Friendships and family." She shook her head back and forth in disbelief. "Beyond understanding. God gave us better than we deserve," she added, as tears formed in her eyes and her voice cracked.

Experienced advice

Rob would tell you, "Marry a woman with a soft heart." He jabbed Deb in the ribs with his elbow, to which she responded with a loud chuckle.

"Which takes you to another story because when he finally decided he was going to go have his shoulder fixed. I thought...'This is going to be tough because he's not going to want to behave. He's going to want to go work before it is time and I'm going to be after him all the time. I just need to be able to back off." Rob knew he needed to follow doctor's orders, but she had her doubts. "I did tell him the truth: 'I want you to know I've been praying and not just for your surgery and your healing but for me to have the soft heart towards you when you come home."

He rubbed his chin as he responded with, "And she did!"

She marveled, "It was amazing. He answers prayers like that!"

Rob humbly said, "She's been a lot better to me... than I have been to her."

His advice to other couples continued with, "Think before you jump. Maybe ask questions of somebody who's been there."

Deb added, "I am going to give the advice that I gave at a bridal shower. 'When you're and married and don't have children in the house. Shower together'!" They both laughed. "Conserves water and preserves the love life! Seriously! And to keep your marriage strong, go on vacation but stay out of debt. Make sure you are saving the money to do it."

His suggestion: "Spend time with each other."

"Yes - absolutely! It's important to spend time with each other. Spend time with your kids. Spend time with your grand kids. With your parents. Spend time in church together. Spend time working on the things God has given you to serve in."

Being hands-on and practical, Rob said, "Go put flags out."

Their church puts out flags from all 50 states on several holidays and they both felt it was something that didn't take long and yet, reaped many benefits. They have fun with other people and fun with each other. It's a good relationship builder, as well. Deb said, "When you can work side by side as a couple," her voice broke and tears welled up in her eyes, "it encourages other couples."

Rob jabbed her in the side. "Jeez", as he rolled his eyes and looked over the other way. She jabbed him back in the ribs with her elbow as Rob quipped, "I told you I'm not that nice!"

Tears returned to Deb's eyes as she reminded us, when in a crisis, find something to celebrate. Especially do this for your kids so they know not every tragedy will tear your life apart.

Work hand in hand

She laughed, "I'm probably tougher on the inside than he is. I'm weak on the outside and he's tough on the outside. In this particular home we gutted a bunch of stuff. Some of it he did and some I did. When we came back through to refinish it and do the dry wall, I did all the taping. He did all the texturing. I did all the painting. You just work hand in hand. God has given us opposites gifts and talents. They should always complement...not compete!!!"

In rearview mirror

Looking back to 1977, they saw their faith story in the rearview mirror. They attended a concert at a local church where Deb said, "We accepted Christ at the same time...and then the following December we got married. It was really hard when your other friends are not Christian, and it created conflicts in those relationships. I was still in high school, so that senior year was hard for me as a Christian because it wasn't a cool thing to do. The mockery. So, it was difficult."

They both had a very serious look as she put her finger in the air and wagged it in front of her chest. "God doesn't stop", she smiled.

Rob said, "You just kind of change your friendships with people and I think that's when we just kind of hung out by ourselves and stayed by ourselves.

Faith was part of our lives but still very weak. That changed in 1988, when I finally threw up my hands and said to Rob, 'You either chose a church or I'm going to and you be there.' He chose a church."

They eventually found a church that was Christ centered and felt it changed their lives and their marriage. Deb said, "Faith is definitely uniting and when I think about being an example to our children...", her voice trailed off as tears filled her eyes to overflowing.

He said, "I think faith has made us a lot tighter."

She completed his comment with, "Keeping Christ in the center of your household...before the marriage even begins. Respecting each other."

She still likes me

His proclamation about this period in their marriage, "That she still likes me!"

Deb laughed when she added, "That I'm still willing to take him to the emergency room evidently! Now you can show them your thumb!" Rob held out his bandaged finger; a 'benefit' of his handyman business.

"Today," Deb continued, "we're just comfortable together. I don't know how you describe...."

Rob finished, "We like each other. I mean everybody gets mad at each other..." he shrugged his shoulders, "but we get over it and usually it's for a dumb reason."

They agreed they haven't had insurmountable problems in their marriage, but both also understood you don't have to have something bad in your marriage to make it good! Even good marriages need to work to keep them good.

Deb smiled, "Anytime you have two different personalities..."

"Nothing's easy", Rob added. "It's never going to be easy. Easy is when you have everything handed to you. Being married isn't that way."

Opposites

"She's kind of a funny girl. I don't have much of a personality...to be honest."

"He doesn't smile much either."

"Sometimes she makes me laugh. She has to hit me or something first," he deadpanned. "She can do it once in a while. Sometimes I just think she's nuts!"

"That's right! I live on the outside!"

Rob said, "It's not quite fire and water but..."

"No, he hasn't put out my fire yet!"

Even Rob laughed at that one!

Differences don't divide

The most important thing Rob and Deb taught us was, when opposites are attracted enough to marry each other, their differences don't have to divide them.

Yes, Rob is the strong, silent type.

And, yes. Deb is exuberant and excited about life.

Yet, they have learned how to bring out the best in each other...to complement...not compete!

Dale & Robin - Doubly Good to Us

MARRIED 29 YEARS

"They who wait upon the Lord shall renew their strength. They shall mount up with wings like eagles; they shall run and not be weary; they shall walk and not faint." Isaiah 40:31 (TLB)

Copyright © Hailey Harboer

In true Dale style, he would start their story with a joke. His entire life, anytime he wanted to lighten up the mood, he would crack bad jokes...or even worse...he would start making up songs with 'more than weird' lyrics. He was a Youth Director at a church, so of course, you might think they all got his humor. Most of the time, they just shook their heads like the rest of us and enjoyed being around him because of it. Watch for his unique sense of humor in their story.

Relationship recipe

Start with a group of high school students. Add one Youth Worker (Dale). Drive them up to Minnesota for a week of camp.

Take one college-age camp counselor (Robin). Add a little bit of irritation with youth pastors and youth directors who would come to camp and try to take over.

And...you could be repeating the recipe for a tense beginning to any relationship...and this one in particular!

Back story

Robin grew up at Shetek Lutheran Bible Camp, so to her, being there as a counselor felt as if she was back home again. The 'top of the heap'...'best job ever' for counselors, was to be chosen for the canoe trip down the Minnesota River in Central Minnesota! Finally, her name was drawn!

The camp staff was made up of 18-21 year old college students, so when those pastors and youth leaders came along with their youth on the trip, it could be intimidating, to say the least! This time, Robin and her partner counselor, Pete, were elated to learn there would be NO pastor or youth worker tagging along. That meant they could do whatever they wanted and there was no one older there to tell them what to do. Ah...their dream canoe trip!

That is until they learned, indeed, there <u>would</u> be a youth director named 'Joel' coming with this group of kids. Robin made this disgusted face, rolling her eyes up and almost out of her head! "Already I was just irritated and bitter. 'Here comes another guy. He's going to tell us what to do and tell Pete and I how terrible we are at Bible study. You know you should do this approach with these kids...blah, blah, blah'!" In <u>her</u> book, this was not a good beginning for this 'Joel' guy!

Saturday when the van rolled up to the camp, Dale and his kids walked up to the 'welcome committee'. (OK...maybe they weren't so welcoming!)

Robin looked at Dale and in her best irritated voice said, 'You must be Joel'.

He hesitated, 'No... I'm Dale'.

He laughed, "She didn't have a smile on her face or anything and it's like...Whoaaa! A week with my kids?"

Robin remembered thinking, 'This is going to be a very long week!' At that, she walked away lifting her shoulders and putting on her disgusted look.

He teased, "I guess first impressions were neutral."

"Neutral? You didn't even like me!"

"She was just having a real hard time warming up to the idea of being around me, I guess."

Robin shook her head up and down as together they laughed out loud.

Famous canoe flip

"I was waterfront director...the main lifeguard at the camp," Robin said. "So, I would teach kids how to swamp a canoe, how to flip it back over, stay dry." Her instructions went like this: 'OK...so everybody's got to get into a canoe. Everybody's got to swamp a boat...get it flipped over on their own and this is how you do it.

Nobody swamps <u>my</u> boat! Nobody touches <u>my</u> boat! This is <u>my</u> boat. I don't need to learn how to swamp a boat. You have to swamp yours and I have to see it.'

She rolled her eyes and made a funny face as she said, "Of course, they didn't think that was fair so, obviously you know what happened."

Dale seriously added, "A good leader does everything they ask their followers to do." He barely got the words out of his mouth before he was laughing it up! "I just tipped her boat and it was over! No lecture!"

Robin smirked, "He never told me until after the canoe trip that he had never canoed before."

"I never even passed swim lessons", Dale deadpanned and then couldn't hold back the laugh.

Off to Piggly Wiggly

Cold shoulder and one canoe flip later, they embarked on the trip.

Their first day out on the trip, the girls in Dale's group found out there would be no electricity for their hair dryers and curling irons! Robin snickered, "Like what are you going to do...plug this into a tree?"

Dale laughed, "They were like, 'Daaaale...you didn't tell us!' So...during the trip, we came to a spot where we had to portage the canoes over the road. The girls spotted a Piggly Wiggly grocery store. They just <u>had</u> to go check it out!"

While the girls made their detour, the rest of the team carried all the canoes. Robin came face to face with Dale and said, 'The girls ran off! What are you going to do with them?'

Dale responded nonchalantly, 'I'm not going to do anything! If you gotta yell at them...yell at them. Do whatever you have to do.'

Robin admitted, "I guess that might be the first time," she held up her fingers to measure about an inch, "I was getting a little soft." It was the first time she felt as if she and the other counselor were actually in control of the trip...and not some youth leader along for the ride.

"I guess there was some 'liking' going on." Then in typical Dale fashion, he threw in this quirky comment: "I always took up the back on the canoe trip because the strongest canoer should be in the back. I had never canoed before...but, I had imagined it in my head for a long time!"

They both laughed as Robin finished his sentence with, "There was no YouTube. You couldn't see a video, 'How to Canoe'."

He teased, "You think about football players...they say 90% of it's mental. So, I did the 90% so now I just had to work on the 10."

They weren't in the same canoe, but most of the trip their canoes were side by side. Dale asked Robin questions about what she believed and felt about a variety of topics. At the same time, she quipped, "I had no clue...I was kind of naive back then. My thought was never," she teased with a surprised look, "Oh, he's a guy! or He's cute!?"

He intently looked at Robin, "I wasn't asking questions because I was pursuing you. I was asking questions to find out who you were...your character. As I found out your character, I also found out that I kind of liked that...I like that...I like that.

Then...maybe there's something more. Maybe God brought me here to this place at this time." Another pastor was supposed to make this trip but instead Dale, as the new youth director, was asked to go.

Crazy questions

Dale not only had a habit of making up crazy songs but also enjoyed asking a matching level of crazy questions. Before the trip, he said to one of his youth, 'Hey Roxy, what would you do if I met my wife on this trip?'

Robin crossed her arms, broke out in a huge smile and lifted her eyebrows as he continued. "You know...when you're a Youth Director, you don't always have things to talk about, so you have to make them up. That was what I was doing...making things up."

As canoes were moving down the river, Roxy (who is in a canoe with Robin), yelled across, 'Hey Dale, what would you do if you met your wife on this trip'?"

Un-com-for-ta-ble!

Living the memory, Robin was now shaking her head back and forth as if saying," 'I can't even believe it myself!'

"By mid-week of the canoe trip, after him drilling me with all kinds of questions, I was like, 'OK...this guy's kind of nice.' Of course, the kids on the trip are like all excited: 'He likes you!! 'He likes you!!' My friend, Emily, joined in, 'I think he likes you'!!" There was no running from that cheering section!

He stuttered...God didn't

Their canoes rounded the corner where they would head down the rapids, Dale said, "The kid in front of my boat didn't see this rock just below the surface of the water and we hit it head on coming out of the rapids. Our canoe spilled over and I lost my glasses. That's a big deal because I can't see."

'Ohhh Nooo...how am I going to do this! I'm going to be really depressed about this because it is going to cost me money...which I don't have...to get new glasses. How am I going to get the kids back home because I can't drive without my glasses. God, don't let this ruin the trip'!"

Glasses or no glasses, Dale said, "Lord, I think there's something there with Robin...but unless you give me an opportunity to talk with her about it...I'll assume it's no."

That night Robin and near-sighted Dale walked along the banks of the river. He said, "It didn't feel like at the time that God was saying 'yes' but I didn't hear him say 'No'. Maybe I'm supposed to do something here like actually kind of bring it up. Maybe God's not just going to do it for me.'

As they sat on the bank, he said, 'Hey...tomorrow we are going to be back in camp. Would you mind - you know - if we got together - you know..," he stammered, "to - you know - see each other?"

She reacted with an indifferent attitude and a less than enthusiastic look. 'Ahhh...I don't know...I'm a nursing major and I'm really busy. I guess...if it works out...it works out.'

At the moment she actually said 'yes', God told him she was the one. 'This will be your wife.' "Of course, I'm not going to tell her that because....'I'm not dumb! But...I will always remember back to the day on the shore. I said, 'Anytime I forget, anytime I'm not thinking right...remind me of that moment so I always remember that was what You (God) said'."

How do you know for sure?

Dale said, "In Ray Shorts book, 'Sex, Love or Infatuation'...he talked about 'Nobody can just meet and get married and really know each other. There should be a period of time where you go through it all.' I've always had in my head that you should date at least two and a half to three years before you get married."

She held strong. "I wasn't going to get married before I finished school...that was three years."

When Dale came to the point of wanting to ask her to marry him, he went through thoughts like, 'How do you know for sure? How do you make sure you aren't making a choice you shouldn't be making?'

In the middle of all that doubt, a friend said something to Dale that stuck: 'Love's not a feeling - it's a commitment!' "I was like, 'I get that. I get commitment. I'm all about that'. So, once I understood that, it made the process a lot easier."

The process must have worked because they dated three years. "That first year...luckily he was pretty stubborn and adamant. I liked him. This is kind of neat if this takes us somewhere but at any moment, if he would have said, 'We're done.' I would have been, 'Oh...OK'." She admitted to putting up a wall for that first year, while Dale, by date #3, was thinking she was going to be his wife.

And...his wife she would become!

Becoming one

When asked about early challenges in their marriage, Dale said, "I think becoming one because up until that time, you lived somewhat independently. As a single person 'This is who I am' and now it is 'Who I am' plus another. You don't become one the day you get married. Spiritually you do...but mentally, it is a process."

Robin said, "I don't think 'deep' like he does...that's just not the way I think. For me, it's always been...'once you do something you just do it'. You don't ever back out. I guess I saw our early days like it was just more dating."

She explained more fully, "I was kind of like, 'Here we are. We're married so we just have to do it. It just sort of happened. We got connected in good churches and met good people and that all kind of helped. I honestly didn't think about the whole 'becoming one' thing. I was more like, 'Oh, we're married. We're doing life together. We have that strong bond together of knowing Jesus. So, we did everything because of that and felt this is the right fit. I kind of like the saying: 'There's no perfect person out there for us...but the one we have is perfect for us.'

My parents divorced and that was never going to be an option'. He made it kind of easy to just do life. We just didn't have a lot of conflict."

Many people talk about the first year as the honeymoon. Dale said, "I didn't ever think the first year was very 'honeymoonish'. It just got better. There were a lot of things we did that we liked...that were fun."

Robin smiled, "That's why it almost felt like an extension of dating even though we were married." When they were dating, Robin stayed with friends. She remembered thinking, 'Once we're married, I won't have to go drive back every night to the house of the people who were housing me!' "It was never about sex. It was more like 'so life will be easier'!"

Raising kids

Without a pause, when asked about their greatest challenge, Robin said, "Raising kids!"

They shook their heads as Dale said, "I think raising Godly kids."

She nodded in agreement, "I honestly didn't think it would be this difficult...I admit it. I thought it would be easier."

His eyes softened, "Even after they leave home, there are so many things that have an impact on them that you have no control over. You wish you could do something, but all you can do is love them. Robin and I know that God has called us to love them regardless of their choices."

Letting out a long, deep breath, Robin felt the same.

Had our 'kid' moments!

Softly she spoke, "There have been moments,"

He said, "It put a strain on things."

A smile emerged as Robin spoke about heated reactions between them and their boys during the challenging teen years. "Dale's like: 'OK...wait, wait, wait...we're getting mad at the wrong person. You're angry and you're directing it at us and it's not us. We have always been able to talk it out'."

In retrospect Dale said, "It just feels like the closer we got to God, the more Satan attacked this family. It's trying to figure out how do you get around that. He's going to keep attacking and sometimes you think if you can just always have your head in the spiritual realm...maybe all this will get better. But... it's still hard."

She added, "We knew we needed to be united in how we thought we should raise our sons."

In their experience, and also that their sons are getting older, the relationship with them was also changing. "I can now have conversations with my sons and let them know what I think, but I know in the end the choices they make are their responsibility." As she spoke those words, it was evident some of the emotional burden had been lifted off her shoulders as their sons are maturing into adults.

Dale agreed, "One thing we are proud of is how hard all of our sons work and that they have become independent in their ability to work things out in their lives."

Robin said, "And it's nice they share things with us and want to hear what we have to say about decisions they are making."

He continued, "Our relationships with them have come a long way since those growing up years and we look forward to the years to come."

God is the center

Smiling, Robin said, "29 years later, there are no surprises. It's almost like we're the same people we met, and I'd like to think it is because God is our center. We can go sit at a coffee house and talk for hours or we both look forward to coming home. Our kids used to make fun of us. 'You're boring! You're boring!' But for us, we come home...go for our walks. We don't have to do a lot of things. We still enjoy being together. 'I'm home early. Do you want to go meet for coffee?' It would be like the highlight of our day. We don't have to constantly be on the go."

Dale added, "We don't have a lot of people we hang with."

"We're just kind of simple folks," was Robin's description.

He just couldn't let the opportunity for a joke disappear. "I think the big difference between me now and then is I wear shorts that match the color of my hair."

To that...Robin rolled her eyes!

Financial stress

"I'd have to say finances were a struggle for us until he finally found a steady job. Because of that, we kind of chose to downsize."

Dale continued, "We had the stress of everything going on with the kids and me not being able to find a job for six years and money was always tight." They also had a second home on the market to sell when the market dropped. "It just messed up everything for a long time!"

Robin reminded us, "God always provided."

It was a monumental struggle, but...Dale smiled, "There was always enough at the end of the month,"

Not all challenge

In the middle of challenges, there were many blessings in their lives. Spending time together was always at the top of their list. Robin said, "I think intimacy is also much better than it used to be."

At that, Dale put his head down as if he is embarrassed, to which everyone in the room laughed loudly.

Not deterred, she continued, "Sex is better than it used to be."

He flushed with embarrassment and moaned, "Awww come on!"

Times I didn't like him

"I admit there's times where I didn't like him at all. I admit there was some resentment when he wasn't working. It's just like...I'm tired of working all the time. I'm just tired of having the responsibility for everything. At the same time, it was nice having him home because he was always around and was the one who took the kids to school. It was never to the point where I would think I want a divorce. That was never an option."

She adamantly said, "I truly admit...if I wasn't a Christian, there might be moments where I would have sought that out or thought about it more, but, it's not an option. When I get to those...", she put both hands up like claws and made a hissing sound, "I just blame it on hormones! I kind of back off and just be quiet or irritated or go do something."

Quickly she added, "Definitely Jesus kept me going. That commitment of 'that's not what you do ...you just don't. It's not greener on the other side. There was always that sense of 'we'll get through this.' Usually we never felt like giving up at the same time and that helped a lot."

Dale said, "I don't know that I ever felt like giving up. I may have been angry and certainly would plead with God a lot. 'I don't understand! How do you make this better? Did I do something wrong? Are you mad at me, God?' Kind of the older I get the more desperate for God I get. To hear Him...to find answers...to understand."

Advice to other couples

Dale's marriage advice to other couples kicked in with a humorous, "Kids?.. Get a dog!"

When all of the laughing calmed down, he continued, "I guess I would talk to them...share with them about what I knew from the beginning about love not being a feeling...but a commitment. I would also point them to a relationship with God because I don't think outside of that you can ever find peace."

Robin said she has had that conversation with people at work and they kind of look at her funny when she talks about this advice. "Don't ever be alone with another man...just don't ever, ever do that! It doesn't matter what the circumstances. There have even been times when a co-worker said, ' Hey, do you want to go to happy hour?' I ask, 'Who else is coming with?' I found out it would just be him. 'Nope'! Don't ever get into the mentality, 'I have control. It won't affect me'." She knows anyone can be tempted and she will always put up the barriers to keep their marriage safe.

"Don't put unrealistic expectations on men." She pointed out that women who read romance novels often compare their husbands to all the positive traits portrayed by men in novels. No man can be expected to match those standards all of the time!

As they pointed out, 'affairs don't always begin by expecting to be affairs'. They may start out innocently but progress into more than either individual expected. Robin ended pointedly, "Affair proof your marriage!"

Dale shared, "The years that God has given us together has brought depth to our lives and the lives of those around us. Life can be hard, but God is good. The longer we are together, the more blessing we see and the more in love we grow. That only comes from building our marriage on the foundation of God and His Word.

There is an old song by Amy Grant called 'Doubly Good to You' and these words ring so true in our lives." Here's the chorus:

'You can thank the Father for the things that He has done
And thank Him for the things He's yet to do
And if you find a love that's tender
If you find someone who's true
Thank the Lord...He's been doubly good to you.'

Robin smiled as Dale said what her heart felt, "How true this is. God has been doubly good to us!"

As with many of us, this couple has taken some hard hits and at times have felt beaten and a little battered. Their hearts might have been broken but they are not defeated. They have a faith centered on Jesus, the One Who has strengthened them. The One Who is faithful has also been doubly good to them.

Copyright © Elijah Weerts

_____

Next adventure...

They boldly stepped out and sold their home in Texas and began traveling with Robin's CRNA (Certified Registered Nurse Anesthetist) position. When the leaves began to change color, they arrived at her first assignment in Boston, Massachusetts. That was only one of several places they called home during the next few years. Robin remarked, "We get to see the country!" The bonus "We get to see it <u>together</u>!"

More about the heart of their relationship was heard when Robin honored her husband's sacrifice with these words: "He would do the same for me if roles were reversed."

Rick & Becky – He Can't Remember Their Story...But Remembers Their Love

MARRIED 45 YEARS

"Whom have I in heaven but you? And I desire no one on earth as much as you! My health fails; my spirits droop, yet God remains! He is the strength of my heart; He is mine forever!" Psalms 73:25-26

After Rick completed successful careers in the Air Force and with a major airline, he was diagnosed with Behavioral Variant/Frontal Temporal Dementia (BV/FTD). He can't remember many parts of their life story, so Becky often filled in the details he was missing. It is the same necessary partnership for many other couples dealing with BV/FTD.

She knew something was wrong

Becky knew something was wrong as far back as 2009. Finally, in 2012, as she was recovering from surgery and spending more hours around her husband, she noticed some things that were different about Rick. "He's a mechanic and went to replace the motorcycle tire. He came in and wanted the camera, so he could take pictures, and remember how parts went back. That was not typical. There were a couple of times we were out riding the motorcycle and he would pull over and be confused because he didn't know where he was."

She began to worry if he wasn't home from work on time. "I would sit outside and pray because I was so scared he would be lost somewhere and didn't know how to get home or had an accident." She found hot ashes from the wood stove shoved between an overstuffed chair and the wall. She started finding cat dishes in the cupboards or kitchen knives in the bathroom.

His behavior and personality began to change. "He got pretty angry with me one day and I really thought he was going to hurt me and that's not like him at all!" That's when she began to ask questions and was able to quickly access testing for Rick through the Veteran's Medical Center.

Rick wasn't happy about it, but the changes she was seeing in him were quickly becoming problematic. He was experiencing emotional changes and was spending money they didn't have. He was much more vulnerable and at one point, it became an issue of his safety. He got into a situation but didn't realize the danger he was in. Becky said, "That's part of the FTD...the vulnerability, common sense gone, lack of emotion." This psychological assessment couldn't wait!

It had a name

After two months of testing, it was confirmed he had Behavioral Variant/FTD. They had a name for it. It's not the same as a regular dementia, because it affects executive functioning. Those are the self-regulation skills that enable individuals to plan, focus attention, remember instructions, and juggle multiple tasks successfully.

One day their grandchildren were at their home and were outside playing. Rick was on the side of the house watching the grandkids, when on the other side of the house, Becky tripped and fell. She hit her cheekbone on the cement corner of the patio. "It knocked me out. Rick came around the corner and saw me on the ground and said, 'Oh'...and turned around and went back to the kids. There was no concern. That's the disease...it's not him. He doesn't always know how to respond properly in situations."

Not like him...

It was not at all like Rick to leave Becky lying on the ground. "In his mind, he was thinking, 'I've got to make sure the girls don't run out front.' I had to pull myself up. Get myself inside. Get some ice and go back outside and try to not be concerned."

"We were trimming trees and he would literally throw branches behind him and hit me and knock me over. He did not realize he was hurting me. He's got good days and bad days. There are days when you think absolutely nothing is wrong and then there are other days where he's going to argue with me that the sky's purple." That's when she has learned to ask, 'Is this something that's important or not important.'

Even today, if she tries to correct him, she can be on the receiving end of an angry, ranting reaction where he accuses her of always having to be right, and he always being wrong. This is particularly challenging when he is driving and going the wrong direction. "Even with his protest," Becky said, "I make him turn around and go back. Once he recognizes something familiar, he settles down and it is like the incident never happened."

To those who are not around him very often or for short periods of time, he appears absolutely normal, but Becky has a constant sense of worry. "This morning at church, when we got up to greet everyone at church...all of a sudden, he was gone. Did he go to the bathroom? Is he going to take the car and drive somewhere? Is he going to walk across the back of the church and end up at the lake? I don't know. There are times when we are shopping...he's just gone. I have to stand in one spot and trust that God's going to get him back to me because I don't know where he is."

Rick's reaction

"There's nothing I can do about it. I just got to deal with it and go from day to day. Get up in the morning. Thank the Lord for getting up and then...we have those grandkids."

Becky looked over at him as she smiled tenderly. "We are so much closer. We appreciate life. Every day is special to us. A lot of people don't have that perspective. When we were both working, we didn't appreciate each other the way we do now."

Tears formed in her eyes, "People don't realize that in the middle of the night, if I don't hear him breathing, I put my hand on his chest to make sure he is still alive."

Rick laughed, "Is that why you do that? I thought it was to check to see if I was in bed or not!"

She explained, "I try to make sure he's breathing because I have seen with BV/FTD the spouse can go downhill so quickly and it leads to other issues. There was some testing in December showing the possibility he may be in early stages of ALS (amyotrophic lateral sclerosis - Lou Gehrig's disease), which can be an out-branch of the BV/FTD."

Live each day

She was honest, "There's no point sitting around feeling sorry for yourself. You may as well live each day. God has blessed us with a ministry to our grandchildren and he's blessed me with people in a FTD support group I can love and appreciate."

"God has proven Himself through this disease over and over and over and over. Doctors don't know what to think about Rick because they've never encountered anyone like him. He is supposed to be functioning so low and yet he has areas where he functions so high. We shouldn't have been able to go to Las Vegas on a trip by ourselves, but we did it. We shouldn't have been able to put up a fence by ourselves, but we did it."

Building a fence

Ah yes...that fence! Becky wanted to hire someone to put it up. Rick wanted to put it up themselves because they had always done their own work around the house. Through much prayer and struggling with God, Becky told us, "The Lord said, 'I created the earth in seven days. You think I can't help you and a man with dementia put up a fence?' And, that's all it took. We were putting up the fence. Three to four hours was about all we could do at a time. We had it done in seven days! Oh yes, they were seven 100° days!"

Becky shook her head, "I would measure out everything and then he would look at me and say, 'The measuring's not right. I can eyeball it.' So, that's how we did the whole fence. When we got done, it was up and down...up and down...instead of straight across. A couple of weeks after we got the fence up, one of the girls where he works told him, 'You know, we just love your fence! We love the creativity that it goes up and down'." They both smiled...possibly at God's sense of humor.

That stuff doesn't work on me!

"One of the afternoons putting up the fence, I was getting really frustrated because I'm not mechanical. He's been the mechanical one and now I am forced to be mechanical. So, I started singing 'The joy of the Lord is my strength.' He turned around and said, 'You know...that stuff doesn't work on me! Did you know that?' I looked at him and said, 'It wasn't for you. It was for me!' He said, 'Oh' and that was the end of it!"

On and off switch

At this time, his brain functions much like an on and off switch. When asked if he later remembered things when the switch came back on, he shook his head back and forth and said, "No".

"His short-term memory is gone. So, he might not remember what we made today for lunch. There are times when if I am not going to be home and don't set food out with a note telling him...he wouldn't remember to eat. You constantly have to be thinking. For me, my struggle is the fact that I went from being his wife," tears streamed down her cheeks, "to being his Mom. I don't want him to have to have another Mom. He's got one. I want to be his wife!"

Her voice cracked as she continued, "We've always prayed and made decisions together and I can't do that anymore. If he's having a bad day because his decision-making process is not good, then he's questioning me, thinking I'm wrong. It makes it really difficult. Sometimes, I have to let things go and come back later. I have to only give him two choices at a time. I have to speak slower. I have to make sure he's comprehending because he's losing his speech. He's losing his ability to get words out and to understand words. If we're talking about something, I may have to reword it. I can tell from the glazed look in his eyes if he doesn't understand what I am trying to tell him."

Rick tried to describe how it felt from his end of things. "I don't realize it. I'm popping along on eight cylinders...I'm moving...I'm doing things. Then all of a sudden, it shuts off and I don't realize that either. Sometimes I can tell when I'm not feeling good."

"He has told me," Becky said, " 'I know I'm sick. I know I'm sick'."

Their boys both know about their Dad's illness, but for a long period of time, one son struggled believing his Dad was as bad as they claimed.

They had some testing done to determine if Rick had the hereditary form of FTD. If the test was positive, there was a 75% chance their boys would have it and a 100% chance their grandchildren would have it. They are thankful Rick tested negative for the hereditary form of the disease.

She is very conscious of Rick's idiosyncrasies. "Obsessive-compulsive is a good way to describe it. Laundry has to be done in a certain way. I just let him do it because...I'm never going to be able to do it right!" Rick gave her a big smile and a thumbs up!

She has learned to be observant of his behavior and found there would be a cycle of good days and bad days. That is very typical of individuals with BV/FTD. It would eventually get to the point where the bad days increased, and the good days became fewer and fewer.

A moment's hesitation and she continued, "Structure is important. If he's out of his routine, it's hard. We just can't do crowds. It's overwhelming. I spend my time worrying about where he is and if I'm going to lose him...and how I am going to find him. It's just not worth that effort anymore. At family functions, he usually ends up in a corner by himself and doesn't talk to anybody. Of course, his family thinks he's being unsocial. They don't realize it's the disease."

Again, her voice cracked, "The challenge for me is allowing him to have the dignity and respect he deserves as a man of God yet trying to make those decisions when he's telling me I'm wrong...and I know I'm not."

Disappearing dreams...

Becky's confession brought the admission she had a lot of anger and resentment. "We had worked so hard for the Lord all these years and then all of a sudden, our dreams to travel and to be able to retire and do things together, were gone.

We have had to change those plans. We have been babysitting our grandkids for over six years. It's a challenge many times but," her voice cracked, and tears spilled from her eyes, "we are so blessed. They get to remember their Grandpa and will have those memories forever and ever and ever."

Their financial plans also began to dissolve. "Our finances went from making a decent income to hardly anything. Rick had to retire early, so he lost 1/3 of his pay. Recently, we lost another about..."

Rick finished her sentence, "...about 50% of my retirement." Now, their financial challenges were added to the mounting stress and an entirely new way of life.

Pulling together

Rick readily agreed when his wife said, "It has definitely grown our faith. This man went from somebody who at one time in our lives forbid our oldest son and I to go to church. Now, it's like God's wisdom is coming right out of his mouth."

The doctors in her support group thought she was nuts making a trip with Rick to Las Vegas. "They wanted me to buy a tracking device. 'You're going to lose him. What if he gets hurt? How are you going to handle it?' I just told them...'I've prayed about it and this is what we're supposed to do. I don't feel like now is the time for a tracking device'."

"In preparing for the trip, that is one thing I drove into Rick's head...'You are not leaving me! Do not go anywhere without telling me where you are going!' We stayed together. We held hands. It all worked out. God took care of us."

God days

Becky said, "I've always loved the Lord with my whole heart, but I spend more time on my knees now." She told us previously, their lives were filled with lots of doing things for God. "We volunteered all the time at church and did all those things but that wasn't for God. That was what we thought God wanted us to do. So, this is very different." She explained they now have the ability to spontaneously do something for someone else. "I love those 'God' days. We are running into those more and more and more."

Hilarious beginning

Their 40+ years of marriage has taken some very serious, life-changing turns, but they claimed it had a hilarious beginning! Rick's sister and Becky were best friends in high school. When Rick came home on leave from the military, Becky walked in the door to pick up Debi. That's when she witnessed the whole family, including Rick, 'licking their plates' and flipping them over so they could eat dessert on the bottom! Great impression that made on this young teenage girl!

Not just the plate incident, but she said, "On top of that he wore this ugly long fringed leather jacket all the time and this orange 69 shirt. Then he had these gaudy red, white and blue tennis shoes. Every time I walked by him, I thought: 'I don't want anything to do with him'."

He remembered her from high school but wasn't exactly enamored with her either!

Despite their apparent revulsion, they agreed to double date with Rick's sister because she was scared to be out with a particular guy by herself. Becky bragged,

"Of course, I was a big wig on campus because I was a junior in high school dating a guy that had a brand new 1973 red Dodge Challenger and he was in the Air Force!" She laughed, "I had status for the first time in my entire life!"

They dated almost two years, but they weren't always smooth sailing years. Becky said, "There were definitely a lot of challenges. He cheated on me while we were dating. That was it! Everything was over! He asked if I would please meet him to talk. He was crying and begging and apologized. After that, it was just different. It was like we belonged together. I physically heard a voice and I believe that was God telling me when I met him that this was the person I was supposed to marry. If it hadn't been for that voice...there were many, many times in the entire 45 years of marriage...I would probably have said, 'Nope...done'!"

The unexpected

With the progression of the disease, it was more difficult for Rick to remember details of the past, so Becky filled us in on the specifics of those early years together.

"We were sitting in his parents' living room and I said, 'I'm pregnant.' The next thing out of my mouth was: 'And you're not marrying me! I am not going to trap you into marriage'!"

After they talked, Rick said, 'You're not trapping me. This is something I think I want to do.' "It really wasn't a proposal. It was more like we planned it out together."

What remained was the difficult task of telling their parents about the pregnancy and their decision to get married. She was barely 18, which kept her Dad lividly repeating, 'Too young! Too young! Too young!' "My Mom wouldn't talk to me for three days. His Mom and Dad were not happy either." In spite of their families' shaky acceptance, they were married, packed up the next day and drove to Florida where he would be stationed with the Air Force.

She shared their painful memory that took place three months later, when she went into early labor and their infant son, Jeremy was stillborn at home. "I lived a long time feeling like God had punished us because we had sex before marriage."

Money troubles

Their family of two grew as baby Joshua arrived. Several years later, their oldest son greeted a new baby brother. Jacob was born at 29 weeks and was hospitalized for almost three months. Becky said, "We knew we got ourselves in financial trouble, but the medical bills didn't help. Everything we did...we were charging."

They were living on a somewhat meager salary as a low-ranking enlisted airman. Their son was in a hospital about 40 miles from where they lived. Tanks of gas and meals in the hospital cafeteria were filling up their credit cards. They were eventually left with over $100,000 in medical debt which forced them to file medical bankruptcy.

Becky told us, "The bankruptcy was difficult. We really felt like we were shirking our Christian responsibility, but we just didn't have the money." Walking through that stressful time, they found that God was faithful. When they needed a car and there seemed to be no way they would be able to borrow funds to make that purchase.

Rick called their credit union and was told, even with their bankruptcy on record, 'You don't have any bills. We will lend you the money for the car.' God provided!

He believed most marriages go through money troubles but accepted the fact that his overspending caused many of their financial woes. Becky felt he worked to get many of the 'fun things' he wanted. They have been working their way through that challenge most of their marriage. Counseling has helped them deal with the impact finances had on their relationship.

Absent Dad

Recalling how early in their marriage, Rick's work felt like an excuse for him not to attend the boys' activities. That created a lot of tension in their household. "When he worked nights, I had to carry the entire family because the boys never saw him. He'd get home and be in bed. They'd get up...go to school and by the time they got home from school, he was gone back to work. It was very, very frustrating that he would not be in on the family loop. I would have things in place and the boys would go to their Dad...'Ohhh sure...you can do that!' They knew how to play us off each other."

One thing they believe helped was their involvement in their church where they were leaders of their sons' youth group. Theirs was also the house in the neighborhood where all the kids came. "We always made them feel welcome because we would rather have them at our house and know what our kids were doing than somewhere else and getting in trouble."

Rick teased, "Cuz we had the swimming pool...that's why!"

Opening their hearts and their home to other kids, also provided a way for both of them to spend time with their boys.

Sick child stress

Their youngest, Jacob, had ten operations in his early life, with the last one in 2004. Through their time in and out of hospital, they witnessed the break-up of many other marriages in families dealing with sick kids. Becky said, "I think because we went through the challenge of losing a son and because we moved away from home and had to do things on our own...God better equipped us for Jacob coming along."

That is also when their faith was being built. Becky said, "Without faith first, we would have been in deep, deep trouble. Our Sunday School class pulled together and gave us money for gas. I had a C-section, so they were bringing meals. Women came in every night to give Josh a bath because I wasn't allowed to pick him up. Women were willing to take him during the day, so we could go to the hospital and spend time with Jacob. It was just a lot of Christ putting people together in our path."

Near family - a new challenge

Some years later, Becky lost her Dad to a brain tumor. Exactly one year later, they got a call that Rick's Dad had cancer, too. They made the difficult decision to make the move from Oklahoma to Minnesota to be closer to their families.

Even though they knew without a doubt they needed to be there, Rick said, "Moving was a big challenge because we had been away from family since 1974. I think that is why our marriage survived, because we weren't around family influencing us. We were used to being by ourselves. We were used to supporting each other...not going to family." Sometimes their families' good intentions were like a stumbling block to them.

Becky said their extended families were not used to having them back home either. "They didn't understand the closeness of us four. We had been gone so long, we weren't in any family circles anymore. I'll never forget. We were home the first Christmas and I was so excited that we were going to be here. All my brothers and sisters were going to be there, but they didn't ask us. That's just the way it was because we had always been gone so they would not remember to include us in things."

With a hint of sadness in her voice, she told us when Jake was 21, he had brain surgery. Either she or Rick stayed with Jake 24/7. They never left his side. That was puzzling to their families. Her voice cracked, and tears rippled down her cheeks, "When you are called to protect your children...that's what you do. They didn't understand that when we were with him, he stayed calm, and he needed that calm following his brain surgery."

To their families, it didn't make sense for Rick to take vacation to sit in the hospital with his son. They didn't always understand why they chose to care for their grandkids every day. It seemed everyone had a different perception of how a family should act. They found in setting some healthy boundaries, it helped prevent family issues from becoming detrimental to their marriage or to their family relationships.

Evaluating their marriage

Becky smiled at her husband as he said, "I think we've had a good marriage. We've been all over the United States. Becky's also traveled with me when I had to work on airplanes with my job. The kids have been with us traveling."

She joined in, "We have two boys that love the Lord and they've got wonderful spouses. We've got wonderful grandkids who aren't afraid to talk to Jesus." Their time spent with the grandchildren includes time reading them Bible stories, singing songs and praying with them. Caring for their grandkids isn't a burden to them but a blessing. This is also time for them, as a couple, to be learning and growing in their faith right along with their grandkids.

Grinning, she added another blessing they have seen in their marriage. "I think we've grown. Our marriage definitely is not the same as it was in the beginning." When asked what changed, Becky teased, "We're heavier...and we're grayer!", but we knew they meant a heart change much deeper than surface appearance.

Gained wisdom

Through Rick's illness, they both have learned that God is faithful. Becky said, "When the doctors say I can't...my Spirit rises up and says: 'Who says I can't? And my God always helps me get through'."

When she shares with her FTD support group what God is doing in Rick's life, "It's always so wonderful to watch their faces. I don't mince any bones...my faith is my faith...God is what gets us through. Rick totally amazes the doctors. I tell them straight up: 'This is what God is doing'. They haven't kicked us out yet. It seems to be an inspiration to them and hopefully also for our kids.

I had to learn how to speak up for myself and Rick. With FTD, the person that has the disease doesn't remember a whole lot and so really, they're not hurting. We have to remember that. It's the care giver that has the challenges because they're the ones who have to make the decisions. I'm the one who has to face the arguments when he thinks I'm not doing something right. I have to learn to take time for myself. If I don't take care of myself, I can't take care of him. As our boys let me know," she snickered, "they're not taking care of him!" She laughed out loud as she said, "I think when push comes to shove..."

Rick quickly interjected, "...they would be happy to put me over in the nursing home!" They leaned into each other and laughed over their own bit of humor.

Advice to share

As Rick spoke, Becky looked over at him, "Trust in each other. Be honest with each other. Tell your spouse how you're feeling, because if you don't tell them, they're not going to know how you're feeling."

She shook her head in agreement and said, "I would also say to put Christ first from the very beginning. Pray together. Do devotions together."

What she would do differently

"I look back at our marriage, there was a time he wasn't into doing devotions and he didn't want anything to do with reading the Bible. I wanted family Bible time every night. I didn't insist...and I look back now, and I think if I would have pushed that issue, then it would have happened. I let him off the hook. He was not a good example for our kids, when we were not a priority. He was the priority. I don't know how I could have done that differently, but I think we should have had some conversations.

I kept my mouth shut thinking, 'I want to honor my husband', but honoring your husband also means talking to him about challenges and problems and working that out. It doesn't mean shut up and do what he says. I think if I had asked him to pray with me more; we would have. I would have been more vocal telling him, 'Josh and Jacob need you there. They need you to go to band concerts. They really need you to be at that football game.' If I had been more vocal about that instead of just throwing my hands in the air and going: 'Oh...I'm letting God take care of it.' That can be an excuse, too. So, had I done that, I think our family life would have been different.

I can't fix that now, but I have told both my boys these were the mistakes I made." Becky has also been very proactive with her adult sons and has reminded them to stand up and accept responsibility as a man of God in their own homes.   .

Never leave

She said, "I think you need to not give up so easily. You need to think about the other person. You know...'til death do you part'...is pretty serious."

She revealed there were two occasions in their marriage when she discovered

Rick was secretly spending money. Those were the two times she thought about leaving him. What stopped her? "Prayer and counseling and the fact that I knew that was not what God wanted." She looked into Rick's eyes and continued, "We have been to counseling several times through the years. If you need help...get help! That's important."

Becky related a time in their marriage, when the boys were younger. "Rick and I had just about had it with each other. Our whole family was really feeling the effects of us not being able to get along." Rick came home from work one day and as he came across the kitchen, she pointed her finger in his face and said, 'You're stuck with me no matter what! You get a divorce attorney. I'm still here! I am going to bug you for the rest of your life. Let me tell you...you are stuck with me forever! I AM NOT going anywhere!'

"It totally changed the whole aura of the home because before that he was in fear that I was going to leave. When I told him I wasn't going to leave...it totally changed our relationship." She didn't know it at the time, but now can see it was God who put it on her heart to make that declaration of commitment. "It was just a 'God thing'. He needed to know that he was important, and I was not going to leave him."

"I thought for sure you were going to divorce me."

Laughing, she shot back her response, "Well, I was!"

Her voice got quieter and she said, "You have to be willing to stick through those times and be willing to rely on Christ. You just <u>have</u> to do it. There are marriages that don't make it. Why did ours make it? I think we persevered. You just have to stick to it. It's a decision. Love isn't always ooey-gooey feely stuff...sometimes it's a decision you make." Her voice cracked, and tears filled her eyes. "He's the love of my life."

Get a Corvette!

What an unexpected, unlikely, unbelievable thought...but that is <u>exactly</u> what they believed God wanted them to do! Sell some of Rick's 'toys' and buy a Corvette!

Rick had wanted one since their dating days. During her quiet time one day, the thought came to her to buy a Corvette. She knew how she felt about it! Not something she would choose! 'This is not me! It HAS to be God!'

They looked for three days before finding that perfect Corvette. Becky said, "I was embarrassed at first, especially to go to church in the Corvette. I felt it was kind of like we were flaunting that we had this Corvette. People think we have a lot of money...but we don't. We have a big God!"

At the end of a stressful day, they could get in the Corvette and go. "No one's bothering us. He feels at home in the car. It's like we're normal." Her voice began to soften, and tears slipped down her cheeks. "It's therapy for us. It's our sanctuary. It's a refuge. That's one of the reasons we took the trip to Las Vegas because that had always been his dream to take his car cross country. I am so blessed because the Lord has taken the desires on his bucket list and allowed us to do them. So, when it's his time for him to go 'home'...I know we have done everything God has put on his heart."

The future?

"We are just so blessed," Becky remarked. "We don't know what God has in store, but we do know that the joy of the Lord is our strength. The Lord is the strength of our life."

She smiled softly, "I think when you're diagnosed with a terminal disease, you can either feel sorry for yourself or look at it as an opportunity for God to send you a rainbow in a storm."

Tears trickled down her cheeks, "When he was first diagnosed, I was beside myself. The Lord spoke to me and said, 'You know what...you've been grieving for three days. You get up. You get yourself cleaned up. It's resurrection day! I am starting a brand-new life for you and you need to be grateful.'

She broke into a huge smile and said, "That's all it took. It was a totally different turn around. We went from living with a terminal disease to beginning a new journey with Christ. He surprises us every single day and that's the joy. If we can minister to other people and to our families. If they can look at us and be amazed because we go through challenges and we're still together."

They smiled at each other and with each other as she finished the one thing that holds them together. "We don't know what's going to happen, but we know God's in control, so it doesn't matter."

Rick can't always remember their story, but he never forgets they love each other.

Copyright © The Image Group

"Not by might nor by power, but by my Spirit,' says the LORD Almighty."
Zechariah 4:6a

N o set up. No blind date. No excitement. They were both with friends at a local taco place. Eric said, "It was just by chance we happened to meet each other. By no means were we attracted to each other. There wasn't even that spark between us."

Watching him, Jamie smiled as he continued. "She dated my college roommate while she was still in high school. I honestly used to give him a hard time about it."

As he thought about it, Eric was pretty sure his roommate told Jamie about the snide remarks he made. He figured that probably sparked some of the animosity they felt toward each other in the beginning.

Jamie's view of Eric was colored by the fact that she observed his dating track record and pegged him as a ladies' man. "She thought I was rather loose, and she was extremely conservative. I probably gave her a false impression. Really, at that time in my life, I tried intentionally not to get into very close, solid relationships. I didn't feel I had the time for that kind of thing. I worked, and somewhat struggled with school, so I didn't have spare time. I intentionally kept myself from getting emotionally attached, but I gave the impression that I was more..." Jamie laughed lightly as he searched for the word, "...I was more of a philanderer than I was." Eric was paddling upstream against what was thought to be normal college thinking of dating just to date.

You might think this romance would never take place! But, alas, on Jamie's 19th birthday, she invited a guy she knew and her girlfriends to a dance club. Along with her 'guy friend' came Eric!

No one really seemed to notice the extra guy...until...as Jamie said, "All of sudden that night it was like BOOM!" She noticed!

Jamie agreed, "It was VERY odd! We didn't care for each other. We never talked to each other. That night we sat and talked, and it was like," she waved her hand over her forehead, "Whew...!"

"It was like a switch," Eric said.

With her fingers, Jamie flipped an imaginary switch. "It's like we really didn't see each other until that moment."

Needless to say, it threw some of their mutual friends into a quandary. They weren't sure if they should support this relationship or discourage it. Eric said, "We actually watched friends teeter on both sides, trying to decide which way they were going to go. We had friends who didn't want anything to do with the idea of us being together, and it took quite a while for some of our friends to come over to the idea of us being a couple. It was just that our friends weren't comfortable with it. And then they thought it..."

Jamie finished, "...that it wouldn't last."

They were both surprised by the attraction they felt that night of her birthday and agreed love between them wasn't immediate. Jamie said, "I think because we had so many people standing between us...it did take a few years for us to love each other."

In fact, they had about two years where they walked away from their relationship. Her old boyfriend even wandered into the picture for a short time before she realized it just wouldn't work. Their emotions and their dating rocked back and forth like a seesaw until they were back together again.

It wasn't love at first sight, however, they both broke out into hysterical laughter when we asked what attracted them to each other. Jamie said, "We don't have a clue."

Eric interrupted, "Well, I do..." As if anticipating what he might say, Jamie rolled her eyes. "There were certain things I wanted in a woman. I had a pretty tight list. I didn't want to feel I had to be watching over my shoulder, or worried about what they were doing when I wasn't with them. One of things that very much attracted me to Jamie was that she was NOT a socialite...bouncing between people like a majority of the women did. I certainly dated other girls in college. I just didn't feel that same level of comfort with them when I was home working on weekends, trusting they weren't out having parties and talking to other guys. I didn't have that fear with Jamie."

She said, "...and that's still the truth today. Even when I'm so frustrated with him...the grass never looks greener on the other side."

Eric said there were other people on campus who tried to get a date with Jamie, but she was hard to get! "There were guys certainly better looking than myself, and more socially accomplished. She wanted nothing to do with them. Even the fact that she always treated me with disdain," she smiled as he went on, "I found kind of attractive to me. I even remember the first time I told her I loved her, and that was not early on in our relationship." Jamie held her lips closed tightly as Eric said, "I think she looked at me, and said, 'That's nice'."

He smiled at his wife, "I would rather it be that she was hard to get than she was stolen away from me."

Popped the question...or did he?

Evidently popping the question was quite an event because Jamie started laughing and couldn't stop. Eric hesitantly admitted, "Actually....ah no...it certainly wasn't down on one knee, or anything of that nature. Understand, I was a little bit gun shy after I told her I loved her, and she said, 'That's nice'." Her snickers continued when Eric set the scene of the big proposal outside his mother's home.

He was certain he said, 'Well, maybe some time we can look at...'

She was sure he said, 'When we get married...'

Whatever he said, it immediately sent Jamie into tears!

She was crying, actually bawling, and all Eric could think was, 'Oh great! What did I say now?' About a week later, she finally revealed to him it was tears of joy.

"So, I've had it thrown up to me many times that I didn't do a formal proposal." Jamie made a face like this was the biggest boo-boo of the century, and then laughed as Eric proclaimed, "I plan on our 50th wedding anniversary to go on my knee!"

Jamie silently mouthed, 'I am over it!', but it appears she still likes to tease him as she put her hand up to her ear like, 'Ehh?', implying, 'we'll be so old by then, I won't be able to hear you propose!'

He said, "I knew the statistics of how many marriages fail. I didn't take it lightly. I wanted to date five years before we were married. I wanted to be married five years before we had kids and because of that, we started pretty late. When I look amongst my peers, they are all empty nesters now and I've got a 12 year-old at home. I give some weight to the strength of our marriage when I look back that we had a lot of years together before children."

She agreed, "It would have been hard to go through some of the things we went through early on with children on top of it."

"You could tell it was the Lord's plan," Eric added.

Strengthened by adversity

Right before they were married, they purchased a quaint little home on the river. After a total renovation, they enjoyed their first year of marriage in their home...before it was filled with flood waters. They had rebuilt the home from the bottom up, and now had to rebuild it all over again. In Jamie's words, "It was exhausting!"

Eric said, "It's like the Lord put things in our path to strengthen our relationship." Their flooded home wasn't the only challenge in their young marriage!

Leave your father and mother...

She admitted, "One challenge would be my extremely strong relationship with my parents." They both laughed, "I was enamored with my parents. We lived 45 miles away, so Eric and I would drive to work together. I would drop him off at work and drive all the way across town through traffic to have a cup of coffee with my parents for 15 minutes, and then try to get back to work." She pulled her arms across her chest and smiled, "I was a little...ahhh...clingy."

When her Dad needed help with his business, Eric quit his job in the automotive industry, and went to work for his father-in-law. Jamie said because he worked for her Dad, "We ate, what felt like at times, breakfast, lunch and dinner with my Mom and Dad. Then, we would go to church with them on Sunday. My parents were very wonderfully smothering and domineering at the same time."

The stress of working so closely with her parents made Eric feel that the relationship with his wife was suffering. Being able to lovingly draw boundaries was stressful and difficult for both of them.

Upside down

Life turned upside down when both of her parents developed pancreatic cancer within a couple of years of each other. Her very healthy Dad, could outwork someone much younger, had never smoked, didn't drink and regularly exercised. He died less than a year from his initial diagnosis. Six months after her Dad died, her Mom was diagnosed and lost her life to the same disease. The pain of losing both of her parents was devastating.

In addition, they also were faced with the challenge of taking over the family business. Added to the emotional strain of the deep loss, they now had to work with Jamie's two brothers who became their business partners. Eric said, "It put stress on us. I don't want to paint a picture that I was completely adversarial. I loved her parents, Jim and Marlys, and to this day I love her brothers but when you run a business, by necessity, I had to stand up for things I knew to be right. It created tension, which meant Jamie got to be the person stuck in between both sides."

Then we had kids!

They both laughed as she said, "Then we had kids!" About three months after her Mother's death, their first son, Kain, was born. A year and a half later, Isaiah was born. They got back on that roller coaster of emotions, stress and change! "There was so much. I think I was so tired emotionally from everything that..." she fought back tears as she finished her sentence "...then to have the two little ones, and not have a Mom to call."

Eric was sensitive to his wife's struggle as she continued to fight back tears. "Her siblings were so much older, so she didn't grow up in a household of kids. She really didn't have exposure to a lot of kids, and never really babysat. Her parents were older, and she probably didn't have the modeling you would normally associate with seeing kids reared. It was a whole new thing for her to have kids, and suddenly be responsible for this. I don't want to say 'struggle'...but it wasn't natural for her. I think it was tough for Jamie, and she still wrestles with it today."

As she wiped her tears, Jamie agreed, "Today being a Mom is still a struggle for me." The tears streamed down her cheeks.

He said, "I am by nature, because of the environment I grew up in with a military father, naturally the 'hammer'..."

"Which is a good thing. I really appreciate that because consistently I don't have that in me. I might get control for a little bit, but as a whole, that's what I'm very thankful for in Eric."

"Having four boys...they can really push the limit if I didn't really crack the whip. Jamie's always been one to give." As she wiped tears, he continued, "She will naturally give so much more than she will take, and she finds it easier to do a job than convince somebody else to do it."

In their parenting, it takes two! They have learned how to balance their strengths and weaknesses and, in the process have formed a strong partnership.

Dealing with conflict

Eric confessed, "I'm a pretty selfish individual at times. In my youth, I handled all my confrontations physically, so I'm not quick emotionally to spat or verbally have conflict. My natural response, since I don't like conflicts with females...if she starts getting heated, I kind of just become quiet. I think that burns her worse than..."

Jamie rolled her eyes, "Oh yah!"

He reasoned, "I'm afraid I'll say something that I'll regret so, I try not to add to that verbal battle. So, our battles are pretty short." There was a long pause from both of them when he finally continued, "It's still an issue and I'm kind of torn by it. I've grown to be more comfortable with clamming up when there's a verbal battle, and I see I'm having the kind of effect that I'm winning the argument."

Jamie wiped her nose as he continued, "She's upset because I'm not confronting her so I'm kind of winning the argument without having to confront her. It kind of works in my favor."

She knows that is how her husband deals with conflict but also struggles with the challenge of getting him to talk about it at a later time. We can tell from the expression on her face, as with many of us, she still struggles with how conflict is handled in their marriage. Eric finished with, "It's something we're still working on."

He's done talking

The nature of Eric's job required him to talk with people all day, every day. He said, "I am usually shot by the end of the day. I just do not want to have verbal conversations. I come home, and I find myself watching TV. I kind of shut down when I get home." He does, however recognize her need for adult conversation, and has tried to encourage her to go out, and do something with her friends, or develop a hobby that she might enjoy. She, in turn, is so overwhelmed with all of the activities for the boys, as well as her responsibilities with their business that she doesn't feel she wants to add anything more to her life, even something fun. They have two different needs they recognize might not so easily be filled by each other.

Move or stay?

Eric moved to South Dakota about 35 years ago when his Dad died, and his Mother needed family near. His plan and desire was always to move near the mountains someday. When that hadn't happened, he described this inner struggle as his late mid-life crisis: "I'm feeling that pressure. At my age, I needed to get out of here while I'm still young enough to enjoy the reasons I want to be out of here. We have burned the candle at both ends for so long with our business, jobs and the boys. I'm kind of getting burnt out. A little bit earlier, I started to fantasize about an early retirement." They both laugh at that prospect because with two younger boys still at home, that dream doesn't appear to be an option in the near future. His desire to move, and her desire to stay have presented some unresolved issues between them. Unresolved issues much like theirs, are not all that unusual in normal marriages. They are painstakingly working their way through this conflict of their individual desires and long-term plans.

Pedaling fast...going nowhere

Jamie guessed everyone might feel like giving up for a month or so, "But for me it was never a 'give up' because there might be a person out there who is so much better." A tired look appeared on her face, as she told us how the past year had been a huge challenge for her. "You know how you emotionally kind of quit. It's not that you're quitting and getting a divorce but you just kind of quit." She put her hands on her chest, "I feel like he didn't hear me when I said, 'I love my job but I'm dying. I don't feel like I can keep this up emotionally'."

They needed to sell their current home, which was appraising for about what they paid for it. They needed to clean out thousands of square feet of storage in a business complex they were planning to sell. She described her life like someone pedaling as fast as they could on a little child's tricycle. She was pedaling fast and going nowhere. They are extremely thankful for counseling that helped them push through this very difficult time.

She said, "Eric credits me for everything I do and more. So, that was a huge help just by going to counseling. Did we get everything totally healed up? No, but we got through that challenge. Honestly, we should probably go back."

She put her hand up almost to the top of her head, "Just when we thought we were about ready to drown...God came in and rescued us." Against every realtor's advice, they placed a price on their home, and with only six days on the market they had multiple offers very close to their asking price.

Recognize the miracles

Eric said, "We could write a book on the many miracles that happened in our life because it's seems just one after the other came. You get to the point where you really don't worry that much about life anymore, because you've seen how the Lord just produces time after time after time. It may not be exactly what you thought you wanted at the time, but you recognize as soon as it's over...'Wow, I'm glad that worked out that way'!"

She smiled and reminded her husband they have learned (and often have to remind themselves) they don't have to keep paddling to make things happen in their own strength.

He responded, "Honestly. I feel blessed that we had that feeling, and that confidence at the earlier age when we were going through a lot of stuff. It helped us recognize after so many little miracles in our life that are outside of our control...that you really don't have to have full control. Believe in the Lord and it will work out for the best. It's kind of governed the way we decide things now, and how we live life. We've just been blessed!"

Enjoy 'together time'

They have many of the same interests and enjoy being together. Eric said, "Quite often, when we feel like our tank is empty, we just go away to some small town close by and spend one night. We bond and rekindle everything so much in that one evening." Jamie shook her head in agreement as he continued, "We reunify. That gets us through. If we could do that twice a year, that would probably sustain us. We travel more than most people. We see how fortunate we are by noticing how the rest of the world lives. We bring that back and keep that in the back of our minds. During the recession when we could no longer afford to really travel, and it took its toll." They recognize their need to connect with each other away from the normal schedules and stresses of life.

When talking about their similar interests, Eric also noted that some of Jamie's separate interests were a blessing. "She loves to cook. I've seen nights when she makes almost each kid in our house a full course meal, and they are all different." Even though Jamie doesn't really think she does that, Eric continued, "So, we never have simple can of soup...it's always a four-course meal. That's just her passion, but we all benefit from it. She also loves to decorate. We benefit from that." Eric enjoys motorcycle riding in the hills and camping. Jamie comes with him and will sit at the campsite reading while the five guys are out on the motorcycles. They believe their hobbies mesh well.

Even as a family, they enjoy being home with each other. Their oldest son was crowned homecoming king and was varsity quarterback on his high school team. He could have been out every night, but Eric said, "He's content to come home, and be with his family. We're thankful for that." When speaking about their time as a couple, Eric said, "It's kind of funny, on the last cruise we took we really didn't go on shore for excursions, because we were just content to lay around together or be in our room together."

"I do find that's a huge blessing," Jamie added. "I think we can have a good time together going for a walk, or just being alone together. That doesn't bother me at all. I see a lot of couples really have a hard time being alone. Like when we say we travel in the car together, and some people just get this scared look on their faces! 'You have to be in the car?' Yes, we do get on each other's nerves from time to time, but as a whole, we just really do enjoy each other's company."

Letting go of the past - building for the future

They know their upbringing was not an excuse for present day behavior, but they also recognized it inevitably had an effect on their lives and their own marriage.

He said, "We both saw this. Her parents were kind of bitter towards each other. I don't remember them being physical or screaming at each other, but they had built up bitterness between them, and weren't very close emotionally. My parents, from the time I can remember, actually fought physically. 'Call the sheriff' kind of thing. It was pretty violent. We are fortunate we don't have that.

We would also credit our church for that. The Bible studies we had, as well as some of the classes we taught on marriage or child rearing helped us. The thing you get from going to church that you don't see in other places is the mentoring from older people. I know many couples, when their kids leave, and they become empty nesters, look at each other and say, 'Who is this person I now have to share my life with?' We're not going to let that happen to us.

If I can pass on one thing to our four boys, it's got to be that I hold their mother in high regard. Their mother is my priority, and they all understand that. I will also say that we regularly leave them home and go out on date nights to maintain the relationship we have. Our kids can't come between us. That's stuff we were taught in church."

Eye-opener

One of the things Eric called an 'eye opener' was the premarital counseling they received. "I never really had anybody explain to me how differently women think from guys. I learned you have to read past their words, and that kind of stuff."

Jamie smiled as she recalled a small group Bible study they attended as a very young couple. She rolled her eyes, and repeated one of their most asked questions, 'Why do we have to go to this?' They both laughed out loud as they remembered how the group was made up of older couples who were talking about teenage children, and other challenges they just couldn't relate to. Now she admits, "It was the best!" To this day, they feel many of those same couples are still their role models.

Their words to you

In marriage, she said, "You have to be good about forgiveness. I think that's something I didn't even realize until the last couple of years. You just have to forgive. I'm a real 'check' and 'balancer'. I think I always used to keep track of rights and wrongs. You just have to let that go out the window, because it's really pointless, and you make yourself miserable trying to always 'be right'."

Eric shared his view of young adults who in our present culture, grow up where there seems to be a sense of entitlement, and most are not accustomed to working hard. He said, "I think they have a false impression of what marriage is going to be. By peeling themselves out of the household they think was oppressive, they think it's going to be all fine and dandy when they get married. I don't think they are looking at it rationally. Marriage is a lot of work. It doesn't necessarily come easy. It involves sacrifice and giving of yourself...more than you take. I don't think people are adequately prepared for that.

Study and work at your marriage like it's a business. Don't take it like it's there to feed you. Take like it's something you should grow and work at."

Not trying to fool anyone

They were very honest in their interview. They weren't trying to fool anyone. They didn't try to make their marriage look perfect or hide the fact their relationship, like most marriages, sometimes included sharp words and frustrated emotions.

Their marriage isn't broken. It is made up of two normal people walking together through a very busy, crowded, unpredictable life. Occasionally they hit rough waters or flip upside down going over the same rock. That doesn't stop them from wanting to spend time together. They really like each other. Eric and Jamie are also fiercely loyal and committed to each other. They have the solid rock of Jesus to stand on through any raging storm!

Moving when not easy

Remember the move or stay issue?

About a year and a half ago, they decided to make the move to the mountains of Colorado where Eric took a new position. Their two oldest sons did not make the move but chose to stay with their current jobs and the prospect of completing some college classes. As with any Mom's tender heart, Jamie struggled with the separation but has been assured and reminded they are a family no matter how far away they live from each other.

Even though Eric moved many times in his life, this first move of Jamie's entire lifetime meant learning how to blend into a different community, making friends in a new church and adjusting to unfamiliar schools for the two younger boys. This move filled a life-long desire for Eric, but admittedly it has not been free of challenges for their whole family.

This might not be the easiest thing they have ever done...and there are times they might have questioned God's timing or their decision. Like many of us, through this experience they continue the life-long process of learning how to stop paddling like crazy to make things happen in their own strength. Now more than ever, they are being tested to put down those paddles and float in His current. That is where they are finding His rest and the peaceful waters. What a great place to be!

Because? God's Word says, *Not by might nor by power, but by My Spirit,' says the LORD Almighty.*

Todd & Kelly – They Don't Feel Extraordinary

MARRIED 13 YEARS

Copyright © DeAnn McClure Photography

"Now faith is confidence in what we hope for and assurance about what we do not see." Hebrews 11:1

H e's a Dork!" Translation: On the approval scale of 1-10, Todd was about a minus ten! No wonder! He was just a little eighth grade middle schooler and Kelly was a 'much more mature' ninth grader! Her Mom, however, gave him a much higher approval rating! She told Kelly that was the guy she was going to marry! 'Right, Mom!'

They lived in different towns, so their friendship most often consisted of phone conversations. Todd invited her to his prom, but Kelly moaned, "We maybe danced one song and then we just sat and looked at each other." Good thing they had previously decided they were just going to remain friends because prom was not exactly a hit in the romance department!

When Todd graduated from high school, he made a move, so they at least now lived in the same city. They dated off and on and developed a very close friendship…in fact, became best friends. Kelly's greatest appreciation for their friendship was the fact she could talk to Todd about anything and she could rely on him to always be there if she needed anything.

He hesitated a moment in describing what attracted him to Kelly. He finally said, "You have your friends, but your friends know you so well. It was like they would judge you because they knew your past or what you had done. Kelly didn't."

When it began to look as if they could be more than friends, she told him, 'If we're going to have anything, you're going to have to open up and communicate and express yourself!' (Translation: 'No more of this sitting and looking at each other all night like we did at your prom!')

He's my Dork!

In 2003, Todd was deployed with the Army Guard to Iraq and that was when she knew he was the one. He returned in March of 2005 and when they got married in November, she could tease, "He's my Dork!"

First year challenges

She reported, "That first year was a really tough year of our marriage." They were not only newlyweds just trying to get to know each other and be accepted by both sides of the family; they were also dealing with a soldier returning home from a war zone. She knew very little about what he had been through even though she tried to read between the lines with their phone calls and emails while he was gone. Much of her information was what she heard from other people about adjusting to life after deployment.

In addition, Kelly said, "We knew we wanted to start a family young. We wanted to start shortly after we got married."

About a year and a half after he got home from that first deployment, they discovered they were dealing with infertility issues. Kelly's heart was broken. "It hit me hard. You just kind of shut down to the world because you don't know how to deal with it. You see everybody else with children and you know you want them, too. That was one of our biggest challenges we worked through."

"Women always want kids...not saying that guys don't...but me personally, it didn't matter if I had my own, as long as you have kids. I knew there was adoption. There were other choices. So, it disturbed me a little, but...I wasn't 100% upset. We didn't think adoption, and just kept trying. Obviously, it bugged her more than it did me."

She shuddered with the memory, "Yup...I had to do shots. They had me on meds to the point where nobody wanted to be around me. I didn't even want to be around myself. I would get wicked migraines and mood swings would happen within just seconds from getting the hormone injections. It didn't work, and I finally told them I was just done. 'If it's meant to be...it's meant to be.' I couldn't put my body through it again and I couldn't put him through it anymore. It was a roller coaster because you didn't know which Kelly was going to show up that day."

Took a break

Weary from the stress, they took a break from any kind of infertility treatment. Kelly started doing 'in-home' daycare so eventually she could be home with their own children.

Todd said, "We didn't really focus on adoption at the time either."

She said, "I should say, 'I didn't'."

Eventually, Todd initiated obtaining information about adoption. Kelly was surprised when, "All of a sudden, we get a package in the mail from an adoption agency. He brought it to me and that was hard because as a woman, I failed because I couldn't give him a child of his own. There's so much that goes through your mind. But, then...we prayed about it." That's when they decided to take a look at adoption and see where it went from there.

They did all the paperwork, classes, fingerprinting, background checks and home study. Most adoptive parents wait one to two and a half years before they get a child. Todd would be deploying in September again, this time to Afghanistan, so his return home from this deployment would be about one and a half years from the date they turned in their paperwork. Perfect timing...or so they thought!

Within a month, they were getting calls from the agency. One call was from a birth Mom in their local area who wanted to interview them. The next surprise? The Mom was pregnant with twins!

Kelly shared their shock, "We were just kind of like, 'Is this real?' Then we met with the Mom and just hit it off. The thing she said that really drew her to us was that Todd was in the Guards. Her Dad was in Viet Nam and was a Veteran also and that was what brought her to us."

They were chosen to be the adoptive parents of these twins, but they now needed to make their decision. She said, "Once again, as a couple, we had to stand strong because we had family on both sides telling us, 'Just because you want to be parents...it's not the right time. He's going to miss the first year'."

Not normal

Adoptions just don't normally move through that quickly, so Kelly said they both felt, "There was a reason why we were chosen this quickly. Obviously, we chose to accept it." On September 11th twins, Arial and Lily, were born and Todd deployed September 18th.

Kelly remarked confidently, "The first year...we wouldn't change anything because it prepared us for the journey ahead. We're very thankful for the kind of technology out there because he did get to see them take their first steps on Skype." They both smiled as she said, "The girls knew what a computer and a cell phone were before they were one, because that's how we communicated with Todd the whole time."

Major adjustments

She whirled her head around a little as she said, "While he was gone, I was so busy with them, I couldn't tell you anything about that first year! I think it really helped distract me from what was going on overseas. If I didn't have the distraction here, all I would do was sit and worry."

When Todd finally returned home, they again had some major adjustments. she was used to doing everything her way. All of sudden, there was another adult with other ideas in their home. She had to make a concerted effort to include him in decision making as well as letting go of the way she had always done things while he was gone.

He honestly didn't think his deployment had any effect on him until family members started pointing out some issues they noticed. "Subtle things...like loud noises. There were a couple of times when the girls would start screaming in the middle of the night, I would jump up out of bed. That was a shock to me. I startled Kelly a couple of times."

Like many Veterans and their families experience, Kelly said, "The short temper. Ever since the deployment his temper has been the most challenging." These were all possible signs of PTSD, but no one ever told them that might be what Todd was struggling with.

"It was also a different routine. Overseas, you sort of just did your own thing. You got to things whenever you got to them. Over there, it didn't matter when you ate. When you come home you are thrown into everyday life back here. Now you had kids that had to eat every couple of hours."

They both smiled at the thought of the chaos of her schedule and his non-schedule meshing together!

Second time around

Life returned to a new normal and they began thinking about adopting a second time. They started the process and decided they were going to be a little more selective and ask for a boy this time around. They got their profile book completed and turned in. Now for the wait!

They didn't have to hang around long. The next night they were asked to take their profile book to be viewed by a young woman in a nearby town.

While thinking of adoption...out of the blue, one of Kelly's friends called. During the conversation, she asked if they had ever heard about IUI (intrauterine insemination). It piqued their interest, but they still delivered their profile book to the prospective birth mother, just in case.

When they weren't chosen by the birth mother, Kelly said, "That for us was a sign to try the IUI." They met with the specialist and he wanted to start up the injections and medications all over again. She firmly pushed back, 'Nope...done that...don't want to do that again. I'm ready to jump in and do this IUI if we can!'

They could, and they did! On October 1st of 2011, Todd was in a wedding out of town but came home after rehearsal dinner, so they could go in and do the IUI. As soon as it was done, he hopped in the car and headed back to be in the wedding.

"We had to wait two weeks exactly before I could take a pregnancy test. I took it and the IUI took the first time. Doctors said, 'Don't get your hopes up too much because you want to make sure levels, and everything are ok. From there we went in for appointments...got levels checked...had ultrasounds."

Hick-up turned major

They reached the 20-week mark and were 'over the top' with the news they were having a boy. A minor hick-up happened when an ultrasound revealed what they thought was a cyst that could be drained with a stent. At 26 weeks, an MRI discovered their son didn't have a simple cyst but holoprosencephaly(HP), a major brain malformation.

She sobered, "We were faced with termination of the pregnancy several times because they told us he wouldn't have any quality of life." They held their tongues until finally the third time, termination was offered they said, 'You mention it again and we're switching doctors!'

"We took the leap of faith to try the IUI and it took. We chose to go down this path and now we are pregnant and it's in God's hands. He has blessed us to be able to have our own child. Termination is NOT even an option or a thought in our minds."

The expression on Todd's face indicated his full support as she continued. They didn't think they would get the results of the MRI that day, so Kelly went to the appointment alone. "It was a roller coaster ride! After that second MRI, I was told, the brain had just completely stopped forming."

He remembered, "She called me at work, and she was crying. I knew she had a doctor's appointment, but I didn't know why she was crying."

She got the results right away and said, "It was the most devastating thing ever, having to call and tell him, 'You need to come home. At some point, we are going to lose him.'"

Google it

"They tell you not to do that, but the first thing I did was Google it," Todd said. "I did a bunch of research on it and kind of found out what holoprosencephaly was."

She said, "For parents that are just finding out and you go on the internet...the pictures are pretty graphic." There are often facial deformities as well as other major physical problems.

In his internet search, amongst disturbing pictures, Todd also found 'Families for Hope', an on-line community encouraging affected families to never lose hope. He talked with someone for about 45 minutes and discovered HP is very rare, occurring in about 1 in 10,000 live births.

He asked if there was anyone in South Dakota with this rare condition. He was shocked to find there was a nine-year old boy living only 15 minutes away from them. That gave Todd a little more hope as he remembered thinking, 'OK...maybe this isn't as bad as what the doctors are saying or what you read on the internet.'

You're a stubborn one!

"There was one time I hadn't felt him move for 24 hours. I sat on the side of the bed and just cried. We both cried together. We went in and they hooked up the monitors. They found the heart rate and then he gave a kick." She thought, 'You're going to be a stubborn one.'

At 39 weeks they induced delivery, with so many people crowded into the room there was not much wiggle room for anyone. The crowd might have been overwhelming, but Kelly said, "The face of our doctor delivering him was priceless! She was set in her mind that you could look at him and tell there was something wrong. She held him out there looking...turning him over and back. 'Ok...where is this thing that's wrong'?" They both smiled as Kelly joyfully recalled, "You couldn't tell."

They told us that facial deformities were very common. A lot of kids have either close set eyes or cleft palate or lip. Their little Ryker had none of those.

The delivery room was crowded with specialists they were certain this baby would need when he made his appearance. After they cleaned him up, he started crying. Apgar scores are used to test the overall physical condition of all newborns, and his scores were high. Even though there was no medical necessity, he was admitted to Intensive Care Nursery...just in case something happened.

After being in NICU for 24 hours, he wasn't on a ventilator or IVs. He wasn't hooked up to anything, so he went back to the regular nursery, where medical personnel were shocked when they saw him nursing. They couldn't believe he was actually able to breathe, eat and swallow all at the same time. A physician said, "I commend you because most families would have terminated life and walked away from it whereas you guys have held strong.'

Even the doctor that delivered him said, 'We wish we had families that had faith like you did to be able to walk that unknown.' Kelly smiled, "Doctors are great, but they don't know everything!

We were not prepared when he was born because they told us <u>not</u> to bring the car seat. That is what they put into our heads...that he wouldn't live past birth or if he did, it would be a few hours." What a surprise he gave his Mom and Dad!

Constant medical care

Ryker is now seven years old, but they both admit his first year was a blur. Kelly said, "It was really trial and error. For the first nine month, we walked around in his throw up. We couldn't figure it out. Doctors weren't sure what was going on. Around here, they don't know much about HP, so they were learning with us."

At nine months old, swallow tests were done, and they found he was aspirating everything. They were surprised he wasn't sick or in the hospital before that. He had a feeding tube (mini-button) inserted. Kelly said, "Now we know he'll always be hydrated rather than dehydrated. So that was honestly, truly...for me...was one of the very scariest moments because we were just thrown so quickly and so suddenly into it...we didn't even have time to process it."

Down the road, it was recommended Ryker have a tracheotomy. They were hesitant, "But," Kelly said, "we had a lot more time to process and really talk about the trach. We wish we'd had a before and after just to help other families. We see the difference it has made in him. The sound of his breathing...his increased growth."

Todd said, "Before the trach, he was using up so many calories just to breathe. I remember taking him to one of his appointments about six months after the trach. The doctor was showing me on a scale his first one and a half years. He was on his own little 'Ryker' chart. He was following the curve and all of a sudden you get to 15 months which is where he had the trach. You could see it all of a sudden...it literally goes vertical. He went from the 40th percentile to the 80th or 90th percentile." Hesitant at first, they felt making the decision to have the trach inserted was a huge boost to Ryker's overall health and well-being.

Helping us live our normal

The doctors familiar with Ryker's needs do everything they can to help his parents handle as much as they can at home without having to bring him in. The now have night nurses caring for Ryker so they are able to get some sleep before beginning their fulltime jobs the next morning. In the beginning, they found it difficult to allow strangers into their home and trust them with their child while they slept. Now they deeply appreciate how those care givers allow them to rest and for Ryker to receive the best medical care.

Kelly beamed, "Ryker now rides the bus to school and is loving it! I feel like God has given me peace. Having him in my care for a solid three years and then suddenly turning him over... We couldn't ask for a better group of people we can turn him over to for the day. They are amazing!"

1000 words

Her own eyes lit up as she said, "One thing we do know with HP kiddos is that their eyes will speak 1000 words. All of the eyes of these kids are just big beautiful, sparkling eyes. Someone said, 'Their eyes are their vocabulary'." That definitely describes Ryker! He doesn't need to use words to speak!

Depression...or?

After traveling down to Texas for a national HP (Holoprosencephaly) conference, Kelly said, "...I felt like depression was hitting me again. About a year prior to that I hit a pretty good depression and I was really good at covering it up. I thought, I just have to go in because there are signs again that I'm just not me.

I went in and my doctor was going to give me meds, so she asked, 'Could you be pregnant?' I said, 'No, not a chance! Well...there could be a chance, but we've been told for almost ten years that is isn't possible without any help.' But, we always said, 'If we were meant to have one more, it will be in God's time and not ours'." Just to be cautious, her doctor decided to do a pregnancy test.

As she was backing out of the driveway to head to the pharmacy to get the meds for depression, she got a call. 'Kelly? I just wanted to know your test is positive.'

'What?'

'You're pregnant.'

'No, I'm not. No, I'm not!" she argued. 'Are you sure you have my chart?
'Yes...it has Kelly Jo on it."

"I just kind of took a deep breath and starting crying. My best friend, Katie, was with me and she knew. 'You're pregnant, aren't you?' I looked at her and said, 'Be quiet. I love you dearly, but I really wish you weren't here right now'!"

"When I got home, I put the car in park...got off the phone...and gathered myself and went in the house. Todd was sitting with Ryker and like normal, he looked over the couch to kind of peek at me. I said, 'Are you ready, Todd'?"

'Ready for what? Where am I going?'

'Well, you aren't going anywhere but are you ready?'

'For what?'

'Ummm...I'm pregnant!'

'No, you're not!'

She giggled at the memory of Todd's response. "He looked at the kids and he looked at me and looked at the kids and looked at me and looked at the kids and looked at me. We still joke to this day...'Well, there's part of your face on the floor.' because it was just something we never thought possible...never! We may not have been ready for it but apparently God thought we were."

After announcing their pregnancy, they heard a common response from numerous family and friends, 'Well, don't you have enough on your plate?' Todd energetically chimed in, "We had room for dessert!!" That's when the laughing in the room got just a little bit louder!

What got you through?

"For me, it was truly my faith and having Todd to walk beside me. I couldn't imagine not having faith and walking through this!" She said faith was something she always wanted for her family. Todd grew up not going to church or having faith be a part of his life, but he was willing to open that door. "Just to see how much he has grown in his faith! Now we can walk it together. We do small groups...because he initiated it.

If we didn't have faith, I don't know where we'd be. I don't think we would still be together. I think we would have said, 'Forget it' and shut the doors and walked away from each other."

Not quitters

Give up on their marriage? In unison, they shook their heads sideways in agreement! They told us somedays, they felt discouraged by looking and seeing what was in front of them.

Her challenge came as she tried to keep up with everything at home and the kids. "You just have nothing left. He'd walk in the door at 9pm from work and it was: 'OK, I'm going to bed.' There's nothing left to even talk to him. You're just wiped. When you do get a chance to talk, you have kids around and don't get a chance to have that adult interaction."

As Todd thought about giving up, he said that thought would surface, "When you think you're done and can't take anymore."

She fought tears in the struggle to find the right words that could describe how far down it felt when she struggled to keep going. She barely got the words 'rock bottom' out of her mouth.

Their lives were filled with constant pressures but neither ever wanted to quit!

What they would tell you

Kelly came out loud and clear with one word for you: "Communication!"

Todd included, "Just live each day. Don't worry about what's going to happen tomorrow...just live in today." (They've had plenty of practice at that!)

She quietly added, "Live for who you are and not to look at what others have. Don't let what other people think or say affect you. That can be very hard. Todd works very hard and his hours aren't ideal hours for a family. Sometimes I would like to say, 'Hey, let's go do something or let's just get together'. We don't get that luxury like other people because we only have a couple of people who (because of his medical problems) are comfortable with Ryker, let alone adding three other kids, or that we're comfortable leaving them with."

Her truthful evaluation of her life says, "I am living the life God has chosen for me. That is with my four children and my husband. He has blessed us with these four beautiful kids that we thought we would never have. You just can't get caught up in that jealousy or what others have or what they're doing. You see them going on date nights...well, our date nights are putting the kids to bed and falling asleep ten minutes after they go to bed!" They both laughed at that picture of dead tired parents heading to bed like zombies. "It's not about money either…as long as you're together and hold strong."

Tears caught in the corners of her eyes as she continued, "There is the blessing of seeing us grow with each other in what God has chosen for our path. Seeing how we have overcome so much and been so strong for each other, even in the down times. You would think it would completely tear you apart but that's when you look at each other and say, 'We can get through this together'!"

He's no different

They take all of their kids, including Ryker, everywhere! It doesn't matter if he needs more equipment than all the other kids combined. He goes!

She said, "We treat him like he's no different. Some neighbor girls came while we were loading Ryker in the van. They were asking us why he has this thing on his neck (trach). His older sister, Arial just piped up and said, 'Well, that's just how God made him.' Todd and I looked at each other and said, 'Awesome'. They don't see him any different. They don't see him with a disability. He is doing even more than I, as a parent, thought he would be doing."

There were many times others doubted he would be able to do some of the things he now does. At school, his wheelchair has a button he can push to move his chair down the hall. The therapist has him riding on a special bike he is able to pedal. He has a gait trainer that allows him to take steps down the hallway at school. Each step Ryker takes is a miracle in their eyes and in their hearts.

When we commented we weren't sure we would be that brave or confident if we had faced their challenges as parents, Todd boldly answered, "If you were faced with it and it was your everyday life...you would do it."

She smiled, "...once you learn it...it's your normal."

Our closing thought

They are both humble in their self-appraisal. They actually think they're not doing anything extraordinary, but we have witnessed them loving when the world around them said their child would never be capable of love. We have watched them take life on as an adventure, even when it might mean loading up the car with equipment and kids, so it looked much like all those clowns at the circus loading into a little Volkswagen. They are true partners in caring for their family. In the midst of that, they work to connect with each other to keep their marriage healthy...even if it's one minute at a time.

This couple doesn't have to step into a phone booth to change into superhero costumes. They are heroes every day of their lives. Even if they consider it normal...it's an extraordinary life for two extraordinary people!

Adam & Olivia – Without You
I Was Broken

MARRIED 5 YEARS

"So, they are no longer two, but one flesh." Matthew 19:6a

Copyright © mcg Photography, Corrie McGovern

Sometimes looking back at wedding photos," Olivia reminisced, "it seems like it was forever ago but then other days it seems like yesterday."

It was the Fall of 2008 and it was Olivia's first year at Embry Riddle University. During orientation week, she got some information about a

College and Career group at a local church. That's where she met Debra, who just happened to work at the Financial Aid office at the college. When she heard Olivia needed to come into Financial Aid the following week, she told her to stop by and she would help her.

"So, I get there and I'm waiting in line and it just so happened that Adam was going to be working as a Student Assistant in Financial Aid and Debra was his boss. So that's the first day we laid eyes on each other. We didn't actually meet, but the funny thing is, he remembers what I was wearing. I don't even remember what I was wearing but HE does. I saw him, and he was wearing a Tony Stewart (NASCAR driver) cap. That happened to be the driver I did not like! So, I thought to myself: 'Ugh that poor boy. He just doesn't know'!"

It was a relief to hear first impressions didn't stop her from taking a second look when they officially met at a Bible study. "The first thing I really noticed was his Southern accent. I'm a sucker for Southern accents so that really got me quickly! Then, at future Bible studies, I saw he was playing the guitar." Even on a surface level, those two things were very attractive to her, but the attraction didn't stop there. She remembered in middle school, telling one of her girlfriends: 'You know, one day, I think I would like to date a guy that wears blue jeans and white t-shirts'.

"If you know anything about Adam...he's got a million white t-shirts and blue jeans. He plays guitar and has a Southern accent and works on cars." Olivia didn't actively seek out somebody that met all of those criteria but as she learned more about him, she saw ALL of those things was totally Adam!

From there, they started becoming good friends and started hanging out more. "That's when it was growing in me. I was really liking him more and more. I never in a million years thought I would have a chance with him."

Adam said, "I've actually got a title for my version of the story: It's called 'Truth'." They both laughed as his version began, "Basically, I said, 'Hey let's go out. You're with me now and I'll pick you up at 7:30'."

Olivia laughed, and shook her head, "That's not true!!!"

His 'real' version came with a little background story: "For a long time, I really despised dating, marriage...any of that stuff. It's not that I had a bad home life. My parents have always been together, celebrating 35 years of marriage. Personally, I had a vision...time to pick a college, fly, go to the Air Force and fly fighters. That's what I want to do. I made up my mind then that nobody was getting in the way of that - not friends, not family, not anybody. I was a Christian, but I can't honestly say I had a huge regard what God's vision was for me. This was MY vision. I wanted to go fight for the country and fly fighters and do the Air Force thing and make a career of it."

Just before leaving for school, he was at the home of some good friends from church, who were like second parents to him. "Everybody knows how anti-dating and anti-marriage I am. I was very outspoken and very against it. I didn't have a problem with the idea of marriage or a partner...you know for life. It just wasn't for me. I had set that in my mind early on. I don't need this. I've got this on my own."

There was of bit of joking in the conversation when these friends told him, 'Yah...you're just going to go down there and start surfing, have fun and find you a good girl and bring her home to us.'

"Well, if I have to get a girl, God's going to have to change my desire. I have no desire for it. He'll have to provide the girl and she's got to be OK with the aviation industry and know about it and be OK if I'm not there and support my career."

They were all joking in that conversation, but there is often some truth in joking comments.

Too busy to think

His first year of college in 2007, his typical day began at 4:30am and ended at 2am the next morning. He did that six days a week for months and months. Eventually, that schedule started taking a toll on him...mentally, spiritually, physically. He had to step back and think about what he was doing. That's when some friends invited him to a Bible study.

"They were talking about marriage or a date to find a mate story that night." He let out a loud breath, "I was just like: 'OK whatever'!" He pushed that idea aside and went about his business of doing the same thing he had been doing: Get up for PT, get into the blues, get to class, go do flights, go home, eat, study all night, go to bed for a couple of hours, wash, rinse, repeat. This went on for months.

"I think probably around maybe Spring 2008, I started having the desire to have someone. I didn't really think about it a lot then. I tried to push it off. Those kinds of thoughts are dangerous. They just get in the way of my plans. I can't have that! So, I'd fight it off, fight it off...all through the summer. It was absolutely miserable!"

He remembered a really hot summer night. "Two in the morning...thunderstorms...real hard rain, lightning, thunder. Just having trouble sleeping. Up to this point, I'd been going months fighting this whole thing and fighting it and fighting it and fighting it. I would stay up so late where I got so tired that I wouldn't have to think about it when I went to bed. That was kind of my way of dealing with it. The Lord was kind of slowly working having someone in my life into my mind. I look back and see what I saw the day I left home when I said, 'Well, if I'm going to do this, then the Lord's going to have to provide somebody and He's going to have to change my mind'."

He had a problem

That night, he believes God changed his mind, but he had a problem. He didn't have a woman in his life. "I remember, falling asleep and I had this dream. I was laying in the bed...staring at the wall...watching the reflection of rain fall down the wall. I was just kind of falling asleep to the sound of the rain and the storm and then in my dream I woke up in my same bed. I was lying next to a girl who in my dream was my wife. I don't remember what she looked like. She was beautiful...brown hair. I remember outside of our window lightning hit a tree. It was quite loud. I didn't really startle but I woke up with my head still on the pillow looking at the same wall where she was laying. She wasn't there anymore and that really took a toll on me that night. I laid there and finally I just prayed."

"I prayed for months for the Lord to provide me with somebody. 'I can't do this anymore'!"

It went on for several months. "That hurt...that emptiness was there, and it just wasn't going away. Finally, my prayer was, 'God, I can't do this anymore by myself. It's either...'You take the desire away from me and let me get back to my work or You provide somebody...I CAN NOT do this'!"

That was the day he went into to start work at the Financial Aid Office. "I remember walking in, and I saw a girl standing behind the counter talking to my future employer. It was Olivia. She had on kind of a plum colored sweater with kind of a flowered dress pattern. The thing that really stood out...she's lovely but it was the way she seemed to carry herself. She seemed to have a very modest way about her...the way she carried herself...the way she talked..."

For another month or two they would just see each other in passing but never talked. "Every time I saw her, she just kind of stood out. It wasn't necessarily like love at first sight, but something was different about her and that was just interesting. I had never seen that before."

Olivia and Adam went to the same Bible study and one night a friend finally introduced them. "My mind was like, 'Oh...that's the girl I've been looking at all week'."

After meeting each other formally, they began talking. Adam felt the Lord really started talking to him, but he still wasn't quite sure if the Lord was providing this woman or if this was just something coincidental. They knew they liked each other but when she told him that her Dad owned a helicopter flight school and she had been around aviation most of her life...now he was really paying attention!

When did he know?

Adam answered, "About every day!" They looked at each other and both laughed.

"I'll tell the story," Olivia teased as she leaned into him. "I was attracted to Adam very early on. I just thought he was a great person. I honestly didn't think he'd ever think twice about me beyond just friendship.

When he finally asked me out on a date, we would drive around in his truck for hours and we would just talk and really get to know each other. We really started seeing a bunch of similarities that we had in terms of our thought process and our love for the Lord and what we wanted out of life and what we thought a relationship meant and what we thought marriage meant."

It seemed they were both on the same page, however she began to question where things were going with him. "Yes, we've gone out a few times and that's been great but are we dating...like courting...is that what we're doing or is it just...? I was really intimidated to bring up the idea of courtship and marriage and all of that stuff only knowing each other for a couple of months and going out on a couple of dates. He was only my second official boyfriend, so I didn't have a lot of experience with this," she smiled. "You see from movies or from my girlfriends...if you bring up long term commitment the guy typically runs the other direction. That was my false impression of what might happen, but I figured...we really need to have this conversation."

They were sitting on a dock out on a river where they talked without pause. She was trying to build up the nerve to have this difficult conversation when before she could even say anything, "He beat me to it!"

Adam took the first step, 'I really think we need to have a conversation and talk about where this is heading and what we think. I don't know how you feel but I was brought up and I truly feel that you date to find a mate'.

Smiles surfaced as she said, "And....It....it was all I could do to remain standing because it was like..." She didn't even have to finish her sentence because her smile and excited voice gave away her feelings. 'Oh my gosh! He's bringing this up! He's talking about this!'

"I told him I completely agreed. It doesn't guarantee that we're going to get married, but I don't want to date just to date. I want to date with purpose and really have more of a courtship not like our society uses dating." They continued sitting out on the dock talking for two to three hours until it got too cold and dark. That's when they moved to his truck where at the at the end of that conversation, they talked about what they thought marriage was, what they expected out of marriage and what the Bible says about marriage. They were on the same page about everything!

After that long conversation, she was still wondering where that left them. Were they girlfriend and boyfriend or were they going to wait to get to know each other longer.? "He looked at me and said, 'Well, I don't know...what do you think'?"

Part of their conversation that evening had been that the Bible talked in marriage how the man should be the spiritual head of the household. Olivia told him, 'I would really like to emulate that in a relationship, too. You're probably going to hate me for saying this, but I think that you should make that decision.' She was at the point where she felt ready to enter into the relationship, but she also respected the fact if he thought they should wait, she would trust his decision.

After her comment about leadership, he waited a minute, paused and looked at her and said, 'Let me pray about it. It's not that I don't want to date you because I really do. I really want to make sure that I'm the right guy God has for you.'

Tears welled up in her eyes as she shared how much that touched her. "He really made it all about me." We all laughed as she placed her hand on her forehead like a Southern Belle fainting. "I was swooning!"

It was then she could see he was all the surface things she had been looking for in a man. "That just made me like him even more but, then to see what a Godly man he is and that he wants to be. A week later, he told me he wanted to be my boyfriend. I think that's when I really knew. We didn't tell each other we loved each other until a couple of months into our relationship but I think that's really the point for me that I knew!"

Adam reminded us what he previously thought about marriage and dating and about HIS plans. He admitted to never thinking about God's plans for him. Finally, he prayed and agonized over his decision. "It was something I wanted but at the same time, I just didn't want to jump in."

According to Adam, they spent time getting to know each other better on a personal and spiritual level and their conversations began to be deeper. He prayed and felt he got his answer. "It didn't really come with just words or Scripture. It was more a peace that the Lord gave me over that hurt I was feeling. It was there, it was there, it was there and literally the next day it wasn't there any more and I didn't have to worry about it. I think that taking that pain away...that feeling of hurt or loneliness or emptiness...was God's affirmation of His answer of who I was supposed to be with."

They began dating in November of 2008 and got married five years later. (Just a side note to all of you parents out there. Adam's parents started praying for his future wife the day he was born!)

No challenges?

Challenges? Adam teased, "We're perfect!"

That's when Olivia about fell down laughing and dropped her head on his shoulder! When she finally was able to control herself, she said, "Maybe on the funnier end. One of the things we noticed right away when we got married and were now living together, was that we do laundry VERY differently!" That remark hinted that there may have been a couple of conflicts about how to sort and fold clothes. "Also, for me...painting...I'm very persnickety about painting. Shortly after we got married, we were able to buy the house that we're in now and wanted to do some home improvement. We got into silly arguments that shouldn't have happened...over something so silly like painting. Then, his would be hanging pictures...hanging anything. He can tell if it is 1/16 of an inch off. Where I am just like: 'Eh...good enough.'

I've learned I need to calm down a little when it comes to painting. He's learned, 'OK...she's got a way that she does it. If she wants or needs my help, she'll ask me for it. I'm here to do that...otherwise, I will kind of let her do her own things.' With him hanging pictures, I learned the same thing. If he wants or needs my help, I'm here for him but I'm not going to stand over him and micromanage. He's got a way he wants to do it and that's totally OK."

They agreed finances weren't a big deal in their marriage. They were on the same page when it came to when to save or how to spend their money. They both smiled at each other as she said, "It's just the challenge or the struggles as far as...I'm still in college and we don't make a huge income yet. It's stressful being an adult and paying bills and finding out where that money is going to come from."

Different backgrounds - different responses

"He grew up with a Dad who is very, very handy and can do just about anything. Repairs around the house...electrical work...some plumbing...he's dabbled in a lot of things and he's good at it. So, he's taught Adam a lot of things."

She smiled, "I grew up with my Mom who was single most of my childhood. If something's broken in the house, you call somebody. You call a repairman. My immediate response: 'Oh, let's just call somebody'."

Adam's response: " 'Well, wait a minute...let me look at it and see if I can fix it'. So, that's something we've learned to compromise on. Me trying not to micromanage or to stare over his shoulder and Adam understanding: 'OK, if it's going to take two months to get it fixed, maybe let's just go ahead and call somebody'."

Learning about each other

Adam shared, "When I was younger…I used to have a lot of issues with anger…really severe issues. I would never do anything negative to anybody or take it out on somebody else but there were times when it didn't take a lot to set me off. I had a very, very quick fuse." He eventually came to a point where he realized it wasn't healthy for a marriage or a family. "She doesn't need to see me or anybody else, for that matter, need to see me get that angry." He explained there were days when he came home after a frustrating day and was able to share that frustration. Other times, he might not be able to talk right away and needed time to decompress. He told us he is learning that he can come in and tell her, 'Look Babe, I love you. It's not you. I can promise you I WILL talk to you about it, but I just need some time to myself to calm down cuz I don't want it to spread into our home'.

Same with her. When she comes home and has a bad day…well, I'm the man. I was raised as a fighter, a protector…somebody who's supposed to look after those you love and those that can't stand up for themselves. You need to fix this. You got to protect and that's your job. My thinking automatically goes to, 'Alright…who is it? Go find them out in the parking lot and we're going to take care of this right now!' She doesn't necessarily want me to do that. It may not need fixing. She just may need to get it out and get over it. That was hard for me to overcome. I'm so used to taking care of things and making things happen. By doing nothing and just being quiet and listening to her…I realized quickly that it's doing a lot more than going out and doing something about it." Adam stressed that he was still learning her language in their marriage.

Olivia said, "I am the type of person that if something's wrong or if I'm upset about something or with someone…I tend to shut down and I like to just go sit in a corner by myself. I don't want to talk to anybody. That's been something I've had to learn that I need to give a little in that area. He's trying to help so I need to be able to open up and talk with him, especially if there's instances where if I'm upset with him. It doesn't do either of us any good for me to just be quiet and go stew about it somewhere. He's the type of person that's very much — 'Let's get it solved right now. I don't want to go another minute with this between us.' He's definitely doesn't want to go to bed angry. He's really been an example for me."

She has also learned to ask Adam for a little bit of time to think it over and then talk about it. They have both learned to compromise.

Handling differences

They recognize the fact they are different! "Olivia is very much all Disney movies and radio. I'm pretty much scary movies and rock and roll and going fast. Some things I don't think will ever change but a lot of things do change…and it's not because I said, 'I'm the man of the house, you're going to do what I say.' It was never like that. The Bible says: 'wives submit to your husbands'. That doesn't mean the man's the man of the house and he says jump and you say how high. That's not what it's talking about. You submit to him out of reverence for his anointing from the Lord as the head of your house. At the same time the Bible also says: 'husbands, love your wives and show them respect'. My job is to love her and protect her, in all cases." When they were dating, they talked about patterning their marriage where Christ would be the center of their home.

Example of the cross

At their wedding, they had a unity cross which has two pieces. It's got a very beautiful, intricate piece in the middle that connects and is surrounded by a very strong piece around it...a frame. The frame by itself is very strong, however, alone it's empty. There's nothing in it. By itself, the delicate, intricate, beautiful piece in the inside has nothing protecting it. The frame is what strengthens the delicate piece and that delicate piece is what shows the grace and beauty of the entire cross. This cross reminded them how different they are but also how they complete each other.

"She's filled that gap I couldn't have filled any other way. I think that's where the Lord has really blessed our similarities with our differences."

Blessings come in many forms

Olivia said, "There's blessings in overcoming some of these challenges. When we were dating, Adam shared something he learned a long time ago about marriage and how it is like holding hands and intertwining your fingers. Your knuckle is the stronger part of your hand and then in between in the grooves of the fingers is weaker."

He continued, "When you put hands together, your weaknesses are covered by my strengths and my weaknesses are covered by your strengths."

She wrinkled up her nose, "I think about that often. There are times we go through a situation and I think back: 'Wow, I really had a negative attitude, or I handled that so poorly'. Then I look at how he responded to me and handled it in such a way that I certainly didn't deserve. He took the high road and helped both of us because he was strong through the situation. He's taught me how to have a thicker skin in some situations and not take things so personally. I've always had many self-confidence issues and he's been patient with me because that's not something you can change overnight."

She came to realize he could figure things out about her that she didn't even realize herself. That made her feel cared for and treasured. "I think my predominant love language is acts of service, so if I come home and he's done the dishes, or he's taken care of a bill...that's really a blessing for me."

"Beyond just him...it's been a blessing to be a part of his family. And they're so sweet to me and it's authentic and it's genuine and it has been from the very beginning. I've always felt welcomed and a part of their family so that's been an added blessing that he's brought to me as a result of getting married." It was easy to see the blessing of family doubled when referring to her Dad and Adam's Dad, she proudly said, "They could both be Dad of the universe!"

Breeze vs hurricane

"She's really been that soft, gentle breeze and I typically tend to be more like a hurricane. Sometimes I kind of give her a hard time. I'm not always the easiest guy to get along with at work...in the cockpit. It's not that I'm mean or have a bad attitude necessarily...but when I'm there, if I say do something, I expect it to be done. I've always been: 'There's a time to work, there's a time to play. When it's time to work, show up ready and work'!

Sometimes, I've kind of taken that mentality too far. She's really helped me to calm down and see the sunny side of life on those days when it's just work, work, work, work. When I come home, I'm still in that mind set, she helps me chill out and manage that hard worker in me with the one that doesn't take any lip off anybody." He knows she is a good balance for his driven personality.

He described himself as self-confident and always knowing where he stands. He also admitted that could surface in an attitude of: 'You take me as I am, or you leave me...but I'm not changing for you and you're not changing for me'. "I was very narrow minded...'it's my way or the highway and that's how we're going to roll with it'. Olivia has helped me learn how to give more instead of taking."

She said, "I'm much more of an introvert. I enjoy getting out and socializing with people but it's hard for me to carry on a conversation. I always tend to fall into those awkward moments of silence where nobody knows what to say and he never has that problem. He hardly ever meets a stranger so it's a huge relief whenever he's with me. He's much more of a people person. He can talk to anybody about anything. That's been a small comforting thing."

To Adam and Olivia, different doesn't mean wrong. It only means they might approach things differently but with the same goals in mind.

Advice from Dad

"One thing my Daddy always told me when I was younger: 'You need to find you a girl that loves Jesus more than she loves you. You need to be the same way to her. It's not saying you won't ever have problems...but Jesus provides a way out. You'll be able to handle those issues'."

Here's to you...

Adam began with this tender advice to you, "You can never overuse 'I love you'. She just likes to hear it sometimes. You don't say it flippantly. You mean it. Like the Bible says: 'Never go to bed angry'. If you've got to stay up till two or three o'clock in the morning to deal with it...well, stay up late and deal with it. You're going to miss out on some sleep now but you're going to save yourself some issues in your marriage later on down the road."

Olivia said, "I would definitely tell them to take marriage seriously. I think in our society, unfortunately, it's so easy for people to think they have a back door when it comes to marriage. 'Oh yeah...I'm in love and I'm happy...those endorphins are going...the butterflies are there'. Those are great but you kind of get into this thought process: 'Oh, nothing bad is going to happen in our marriage. We're never going to fight about anything. Or if we are...it's just going to be silly little things. It's going to be great. We're going to have this feeling always and forever. If it doesn't work out...Hmmm, well...there's always divorce'. We talked from the very beginning that we never wanted divorce to be an option...EVER! We agreed that's not even something we're just going to half-heartedly throw out there."

"Not even a thought!" added Adam.

She quickly added, "...people tell you all the time that marriage is for better for worse, for richer, for poorer, in sickness and in health. So many times, we just think about the 'for better' part or the 'for richer' part or the 'in health' part and we don't even think that those other things are going to come. We haven't had huge, big deals in our marriage yet...and I hope we don't...but odds are we probably will. Marriage is very much a commitment and a contract that should be taken completely seriously. Just because those times may come doesn't mean that person wasn't the right one for you."

Adam said, "People are married five, six or seven months or even less and then, 'Well, that didn't last long!'. The first little hiccup or bump in the road that comes, your whole foundation collapses. My question would be: 'What was your foundation built on? Was it built correctly?' The biggest thing I can offer: 'Keep Christ first in your marriage'. We're not saying you won't have problems, but your foundation will stay strong."

They both were shaking their heads in agreement while they admitted it was a difficult thing to do but the most important thing for a marriage. They looked at each other with endearing smiles as he reminded us marriage was given by the Lord, so we could learn more about Him. Adam said, "Marriage is a wonderful thing but at the same time, it's tough...it's real life!"

Their strength

He knew they could go through things together they could never survive alone. "There's a song I used to listen to. 'Without you I was broken. But, I would rather be broken down with you by my side'." (Lyrics by Jack Jody Johnson)

In marriage, and as they have welcomed little Shepherd into their lives, it isn't just Adam and Olivia standing side by side in a perfect, flawless relationship. They experience real life with real problems, but they would rather be broken down together...with Jesus by their side!

Ed & Rose - Give Each Other Space and a Lot of Grace

MARRIED 32 YEARS

"Love is patient, love is kind...Love never fails..." I Corinthians 13

Copyright © Day Three Studios LLC, Karen Aiello

W e don't know if it was actually love at first glance, but when he walked by her, it was enough to make his head snap back and take a second look!

Ed was stationed at Mountain Home Air Force Base, Idaho, where they held an annual Air Force Appreciation Day event. He had been walking around the park most of the day, when he walked by her booth. "That's when I did the old head snap! 'Did I just see what I thought I saw'?"

His friend, Marie, was working at the same booth, so at least he found out the name of his whiplash was Rose Marie. His couldn't, however, convince Marie to ask Rose if she might be interested in going out with him. "She really didn't want anything to do with it,"

Rose laughed, "She was a smart lady!"

Ed didn't give up that easily. One of the booths at the event was a portable jail. He paid money to have Marie locked up. He told her he was going to leave her in there and continue to pay money until she agreed to ask Rose if she would go out with him. "She held out about half an hour and finally said, 'OK, I'll do it!' So, that's kind of how we met."

Wouldn't take 'no' for an answer

Marie finally called Rose and related not just the 'jail story' but the story about him as, 'I know this guy and he's really nice and I know him from the base chapel and he wants to know if maybe you would go out with him.' Rose said, "Last thing I wanted to do was be set up on a blind date with somebody. 'No Marie...not interested. Thank you but no thank you'."

Marie wouldn't take 'no' for an answer.

'OK Marie, you've got three daughters. If he is such a nice guy, if your daughters were old enough, would you let your daughters go out with him?'

'As a matter of fact, I would.'

"I said, 'Eh...single gal's gotta eat. So maybe one date'."

"I could tell Marie was in a tight spot. So, one date. One date isn't going to kill me....'So...Yah...he can call me, and I'll probably say, 'yes'."

Just showed up!

Although he normally attended church at the base chapel, that next Sunday he showed up at Roses' church. He came with the probing question, 'Is she married?' He enlisted a 'spy' who checked around and found out she was divorced and had a little girl.

"So, he shows up on church on Sunday night and I knew why he was there. I did everything to kind of avoid him. I talked to everybody. Somebody had a new baby...I checked out the new baby in the back of the church. But, when I came out, he was standing outside...waiting."

"It was September15,1985. It was a cool evening and we were out there probably twenty minutes. She told me, 'Rather than standing out here freezing, would you like to come over to the house for a cup of coffee?' I said, 'Sure!' So, I followed her home and we sat at the kitchen table and probably talked for about two hours. I asked her out on a date the next Saturday night and she accepted."

He just smiled as she talked about the 'special' cup of coffee she made for him. She wasn't a coffee drinker herself so only had a jar of decaf instant that she kept around for her Dad. Rose laughed, "So, that's what I gave the man! That was the only coffee I had, so you would have thought that would have chased him off cuz it's like 'urp'!"

"To this day, I could not tell you anything about the coffee. I really didn't care about the coffee." He laughed, "It was the last thing on my mind!" The one thing on his mind was asking her out on a date. Even though she agreed, he just couldn't seem to wait that long. About midweek, he and Marie's husband, Bill, were both off work, so they arranged to make it a foursome for lunch. On the way to pick them up for lunch, Ed stopped by the florist shop and picked up a heart designed coffee mug filled with candy. "I took it over and put it on her desk. I think I got off to a good start." At lunch, when it came time to eat, he reached across the table and held her hand and prayed.

Rose said, "That got my attention! God got my attention! He's like, 'Pay attention to this one'!"

They had their Saturday night dinner and movie date. Ed said, "I must have done something right on that first date, but it definitely wasn't the movie!" They both laughed hysterically at the memory of an extremely bad movie but an extremely good date.

Exactly what I'm looking for

As we remember from that original head snap, "Her physical beauty initially attracted me and then after I got to know her...it was far beyond the initial beauty because she had a beautiful heart, also. It was that inner beauty. I don't think there are a lot of women out there that have that inner beauty and the outer beauty, so I knew I had a good catch."

Rose had come out of very hurtful marriage and said, "I wasn't looking!" She admitted she had a list of about ten qualities a man would need to have if she ever considered remarrying. She gave that list to God but thinking in the back of her mind, 'There's nobody out there that's going to meet this list!' Here's a glimpse into that famous list: 'He has to love God first and foremost. He can't just be a pew warmer! He can't just be going through the motions. I really need to see that God is first in his life. And then, of course, having a daughter, he is going to have to love her like his own'."

"Over time, God started showing me, 'I've given you everything you've asked Me for in this man.' It wasn't that he was perfect, but it was that he had these characteristics and these qualities I thought would make a Godly husband and a Godly father."

In fact, they both came out of painful marriages and they were cautious. They also saw God was giving them time to intentionally get to know each other and discover where they were spiritually.

"At one point, we had dated for probably two or three months and Ed said, 'You're exactly what I've been looking for in a wife.' I thought, 'You just keep looking...cuz I'm not looking for a husband!' I was really trying to push back, and God just gave him patience and love. He just kept coming back." During the thirteen months they dated, they discovered each other's character and their expectations for the future. And, extremely important to Rose was the fact her parents also got to know Ed and loved him like she did.

She shared a sweet story about her Mom. "It was funny. He had come to church a few times and my Mom had spotted him first. Mom said, 'Who's that guy?' I said, 'Don't know but there's got to be a wife in the picture because he's color coordinated...and I'm not interested.' I think God was just starting to prepare Mom's heart because she just loved Ed like a son, and he was so good to her."

After Rose's divorce, her Dad had been that spiritual leader to her and her daughter. She felt she was back under his spiritual covering and protection when she needed it so badly. Rose smiled as she commented about Ed's arrival into her life, "It was God's timing." Her Dad died a couple of years after they got married. Rose smiled at God's faithfulness, "He knew, not only was I going to need a spiritual leader and a husband and a protector...but my Mom was, too."

The proposal...

Ed was planning dinner at their favorite Chinese restaurant and conspired with Helen, the owner, to have the ring put into a huge fortune cookie. "It was a big engagement ring!" he laughed. When the meal was over, Helen brought the fortune cookie and told Rose she needed to open it because there was something special in there for her.

Did she have a clue? "Yes...I had just taken a trip down to Arizona with Crystal (her daughter) and I was gone two weeks. He said, 'I don't want any more trips without me.' I kind of knew what was coming because we had been pretty open in our discussions. I can say 'yes' to the proposal...but 'I just don't want to get married for a very long time!' I thought I could just stay engaged forever or at least...I can just stay engaged and see how this really goes," she laughed.

According to Rose, it was August and all of a sudden, he didn't think they needed to wait. There was no holding this guy back. He said, "We need to just get married!"

They agreed to a date in October and planned to have just a simple ceremony. It would be her parents as their witnesses and her pastor in his office. A short time later, she was talking to some of the ladies from church. She said, 'Yah...we're going to get married this weekend in Pastor George's office.' That didn't fly with the ladies from church! 'Ohhh no you're not! We've watched this for the last year and you're having a wedding!' "So, in six weeks, we put together a wedding because our church family said, 'We're coming!' Now, I look back and I'm glad we did it because it was such a celebration and so many people had been a part of our story and walked through it with us."

Looking back over their marriage, they could see all the pieces of the story that was made up of people who poured into their lives. Even 32 years later, when they see the woman who served as their wedding coordinator, they are reminded of how God brought people to pray for them and encourage them throughout their marriage. Rose said, "Each of these people came near us to...to just do life together. It is so important to not be alone through hard times and good times. We celebrated the good times with them, and they mourned with us through some of life's events. We're glad we did a wedding after all, even though it was kind of crazy!"

Sure we can blend this family?

Initially, their greatest challenge was walking head-on into a blended family. Rose went from one little four-year old girl to suddenly adding two older children to the mix. "Normally, you have children and you grow with them in their steps and you kind of see it's a gradual change. All of a sudden, that first summer, I had children that were older...a ten-year old boy and a eight year old girl." When she finally figured out what a ten and eight-year old would do, they would leave and come back the next summer a year older with entirely different needs. Every summer they would repeat that same process. Add to that, different expectations and different personalities everybody brought to the table. It meant they spent a lot of time trying to figure out how this family should or could work.

In the military, he had thirty days off each year and Rose had ten days of vacation. "Of course, I had to realize for Ed, this was his only time to see them and, of course, it was his down time and fun time. A lot of times, I would come home after working all day and they had played games all day or went to the water park. Learning how to embrace that and be OK with it and yet, still communicating: 'I need help! I've got five mouths to feed and laundry has more than doubled!' My life was far from any easier in the summer. It was always a lot more challenging and I was learning how to find the balance and still be able to communicate my needs." She struggled with 'What is a need and what is a want? What can I look the other way on and what are things that really drive me crazy?' "That took us several summers to really figure out."

Discipline

Her daughter, Crystal, lived with them year-round, so that alone made her a little easier in the discipline department. In addition, Rose said, "She was very much a pleaser and didn't need a lot of discipline because of her personality and she was thrilled to have Ed in her life. God worked that in her heart, too, because as soon as we were married and came back from the honeymoon--he was Dad. The whole time he was dating me, he was building a relationship with her so that transition was pretty easy."

Ed had this huge smile spread across his face as he said, "We adored each other pretty much from the beginning!"

"He bought her a bear and life was good. It was a little more difficult on the other side. It was his children and they only came part of the time. It felt very awkward for me. I already was the stepmom and had three strikes against me in their eyes, so it was very difficult. In the beginning, I didn't feel like I had that place to really discipline. I had to kind of think some things through and I learned that I could write some things down to say. 'These are the things that I just really need help with, or these are the things that are happening that are really driving me crazy.' It may not seem like big things but when you add ten of them together at the end of a day, they could make me crazy.

I learned that was a better way to do it because being the crazy lady wasn't working so well. It was a growth process. We did a lot of things wrong. I know I did but also by God's grace we did some things right. In today's world, there are some wonderful resources. There weren't books out there about blended families thirty years ago."

At one point when the kids were older, Rose was lamenting to somebody at church about being accepted by the two new children in her life. Their response was, 'Well, it isn't because you're the stepmom. It's because they are a teenager!' Rose then could jump off the hurt merry-go-round and remind herself, 'Don't be so sensitive to this. They treat everybody like this! It isn't just the stepmom!'

"The kids really never called me Stepmom or referred to me as their stepmom. At one point, it became just Mom and Dad. I never said, 'This is my daughter, and these are my stepchildren.' Wherever we went and whatever we did it was, 'These are our children'." Rose recounted a funny incident when Ed's daughter, Trisha, came to live with them during her junior year of high school. People would meet Rose and Trisha and be shocked to find out they were a blended family. "They thought Trisha was mine and Crystal was Ed's. We even have a wedding picture of Crystal and me and Crystal and Ed. People would say: She really looks like her Dad!' That's a God thing. God blended us."

Loving someone else's children

Rose was adopted herself at nine months old and believes her parents taught her well about how to love the children God gives you. "Mom loved me so much and she never looked at me as somebody else's child. I was always her child. I thought...that's what God did with Trisha and Brian. He did that work in my heart. They were my kids. Yes...I knew they had a Mom who loved them, and I always told them that. I could tell Trisha was kind of struggling with that at one point. I told her, 'That is the neat thing about love. You can love me, and you can love your Mom and you don't have any less love for either one of us. There are things you and I share because you're living here...things we experience...that you and your Mom won't experience. The same way, you and your Mom will have life experiences you and I will never have. You just have to remember you have two women that love you and want the very best for you so don't ever feel guilty that you love us both.' I think over the years, that helped."

Both of Ed's children struggled with their parents' divorce. It just looked different for each of them. Trish was more reserved in how she handled the divorce, but they didn't have to guess how Brian was doing. Rose said, "He wanted everybody together. He loved everybody and he was torn between them. That's why he would live here part of the time. He would go to North Dakota part of the time. He would just be back and forth because these were the people he loved."

As much as it hurt, she understood, "He couldn't be mad at Mom or Dad, so it was easier to take some of those feelings and hurts out on the stepmom and the stepsister." Her eyes sparkled as tears started to form in the corner of her eyes, "The last words we heard from him as an adult was, 'I love you'. To other stepparents she said, "Just keep on letting God do His work and build that relationship."

Coping with the pain

Rose said, "Brian was so hurt by the divorce. That's what people a lot of times don't realize. No matter what you do, the children are the ones who hurt in divorce. As adults, we can process...we can understand, and we can look at logic and understand some things. Children don't have that ability. All they know is that the people they love and are supposed to be safe and secure with have caused their world to just fall apart. 'If you stop loving Mommy or Daddy...then you can probably stop loving me at some point, too'."

She would lovingly advise, "Divorce is the last thing you should ever do. You do everything you can to save that marriage. Do the hard work. Go to the counseling. Whatever it takes to save that marriage...that is what you should do. Both of us were in the situation where our exes were in different places and there wasn't anything we could do. So, we had to deal with the aftermath of that."

He sincerely added, "We tried...both of us..."

Concerning the unfaithfulness of her first husband, Rose said, "We tried counseling. We tried taking that time. There was forgiveness. It wasn't, in my case, a one-time fling. This had become habitual. Actions...I realized were going to be ongoing...probably all of our married life. It was a habit. It was a mindset. I was at a point I couldn't live with the unfaithfulness any longer."

First time around

"I probably should have been more sensitive to some of the things that my first wife was telling me." He had a military job that would take him away for three days at a time...and then home a couple of days; a never-ending cycle. "I think that wore on her. She expressed it and I probably should have tried to do my best to get out of that situation. I saw her as being an independent woman, and in some ways, I admired her for that. Now that I look back at it, maybe she didn't like the independence as much as I thought she did. That's what I learned."

"In my first marriage, I was very young," Rose said. "I know a lot of young couples make it, but I just didn't have the skill set when some things started. There were some characteristics I should have been aware of going into the marriage, but I was blinded by that young love. I also did not take into consideration family dynamics on both sides. It's not just the two of you who are getting married. You are both bringing families together. Unfortunately, my ex-husband came from a very dysfunctional family. I'm not saying anything bad against his family, but it was very dysfunctional in that his father was an alcoholic. His Mom was a very devout, Godly woman and she had seven children. It was in that era that no matter what was going on, you stayed in that situation. At the time, my ex-husband often said, 'I don't want to be like my Dad. I'll never do those things'." She was aware that if you don't get help and counseling and do something to change that course, you can become just like that parent whose character and actions you despise.

Rose had older parents who were committed in marriage for over fifty years. She didn't understand how her husband could be influenced to live a life other than that. "So, he fell into a really bad pattern and got in with some people who were used to living very much 'the way of the world'. I was young and naive and by the time I realized the things that were going on...there was so much that had been done. People need to understand they should look beyond the person you are marrying. Don't just stop there. Ask 'what's the baggage?' We all bring baggage in our marriage and what is it that you are bringing in. At 18...19...I just hadn't had the life experience needed to make that really good, firm foundation we needed for a marriage."

'...Strange and hard and different and impossibly irreversible'

Even with all the challenges, their life was full and happy and normal. Then, it happened. Suddenly. Life. Changed.

Rose recalled a Bible study she was doing in her daily quiet time. The question was asked, 'What is the one thing you never want God to ask you to do?' "The first thing that popped in my head was, 'I never want to lose a child!' I couldn't even write the answer down because of the feeling in my heart. I finished the day's home-work and went off to work. When I got home that day, I came around the corner and the sheriff was sitting in front of our house. At the time, I was an elected official so there could have been several reasons why he was there, but I knew before I ever got out of the car, the news he had for us was not good. Our son, Brian had been killed in a car accident." (Brian would have been twenty-five about a week later.)

They were about to begin on the tortuous road of a 'new normal'. She recently repeated a statement from a study she was doing, 'Everything felt strange and hard and different and impossibly irreversible.' That would describe many of the emotions grief introduced into their lives.

Her words came out quietly, "I was trying to meet everybody's needs. Having older parents, I had dealt a lot with funerals, so thankfully I had a lot of coping skills and life experience with it. So, I was trying to care for everybody while I watched others grieve...and then to grieve my own... Every day...." Tears formed in her eyes and then began to flow, "I cried going to work. Then, after months of crying, all of a sudden, it hit me one day, 'I didn't cry today.' That's when I began feeling so helpless knowing the people around me that I love were hurting and I couldn't fix them. I couldn't take their hurt away either."

She wiped tears as they continued to flow. "I would try to think, 'What can I do today to brighten our day?' I remember trying to give them permission to grieve. I would talk to my daughters and say, 'Don't judge one another. That's what we had to give each other the space to grieve a little bit differently. For some of us it will be very visible and for some of us it will be very internal. Some of us are going to be angry while the other one is in denial while the other one is starting to move on."

She knew Ed was aching and there was nothing she could do. "Not that you get over it in time but as time goes on the pain isn't as acute. It lessens. You go through that grief cycle and that circle gets wider and wider. In the beginning, you want to speed that clock up. You want the world to stop because your world has just fallen apart." She related that just knowing it is a process allows you to be there and make sure we don't shove each other out. "None of us are on our own."

Ed recalled the next February, at a medical appointment, the doctor asked if he recently had a heart attack. He knew he hadn't, but his heart rate was very low. "That was about a year after Brian died and you know, I thought...'Did my heart do something when I heard Brian died and is that why I have the heart condition I have today. Was it from a broken heart?' I don't know for sure, but I wouldn't be surprised." Rose was sitting next to him with tears flowing down her face.

Healing comes with each choice

Remembering Brian's fun personality often helped them to be able to laugh together. Rose said, "We were having Easter dinner and having mashed potatoes. The Thanksgiving before there had been this joke that the mashed potatoes were so dry that Brian kept going back for the gravy. Now it was Easter, and something was finally said about the gravy and the mashed potatoes and we were able to laugh. I could just feel the healing. We have to be able to talk about Brian. That's why I have always loved pictures of him. I hope until the day I die," she said through tears, "there will be a picture somewhere in our home of Brian. He is as much a part of us... I was thinking the other day", her voice cracked, "we're going to have a baby in the family, and he would have been such a fun uncle."

Ed grinned, "If Brian was with us...I'm sure, we would probably have three or four more grandchildren, at least!"

Rose spoke of her personal grief story, "It's allowing God to write the rest of the story. I had a choice. A box of bitterness or a box of grace. I could be bitter because I would never have grandchildren with his eyes or smile or I could rejoice that he could bring a room to life with his smile. I could wonder why he would never take flowers to my Mom again or I could think of how happy Mom had been when he would show up with a bouquet of flowers he had arranged just for her. I could ask why there would be no more Christmases with him or be thankful for the Christmas just passed where he had wanted to get his sisters both something special even though he had a limited budget. I could avoid the color orange since it was his favorite, along with Gerbera daisies, or I could choose to buy an orange Gerbera daisy every Spring and celebrate." The healing continues with each choice.

Sensitive to each other

"We were really fortunate," she said. "I was aware that so many marriages struggle during that time of a death. I felt like we were pretty sensitive to each other." Ed shook his head in agreement as she continued. "Just knowing that was like...we're not going to push each other away. We're both hurting, and it may look different. I'm not going to assume you're not hurting because you're not saying anything. I think we gave each other that grace to know we were all grieving."

Facing another challenge

When she was just over a year old, their granddaughter was diagnosed with hydrocephalus caused by a cyst on her brain. Rose said, "She hadn't walked at eighteen months, and it was like: 'We'll get the cyst out of there and then she should catch up.' So, we went through that time period, but things really didn't change." Doctors finally decided a year later, to check to see what was going on. One side of her brain had a membrane over it and her brain wasn't growing. They would have to go in and snip the membrane and when they did, it immediately expanded to 97% normal size. With that rapid trauma, she didn't have a stroke, but had the appearance and symptoms of a stroke.

Ed said, "Anytime you do invasive brain surgery on anybody, the trauma from the surgery causes other issues. She lost all of her words. Everything she had gained to that point at age two and a half, she lost." With all of that trauma to her brain, she never took steps on her own, until she was almost five and a half. She is now nine and a half and has been in braces and experienced numerous surgical procedures in her short life.

Gently she said, "God has given her a beautiful spirit. That's the thing she has taught us. I remember at two and a half, she had a blood clot and there was a 48 hour period we knew we could lose her. Just making us slow down and appreciate life and what it looks like, rather than saying, 'when she walks' or 'when she does this'. For her, 'meltdowns' would be a common occurrence, resulting from frustration or not being able to express herself. They still decided, 'You know...we're taking the family vacation anyway. We're going to push her in the stroller.' We would get critical comments (about pushing a much older child in a stroller), but it has made us much more aware of other people with disabilities and encouraging those people."

Ed smiled widely, "Whenever our heart aches, as far as our granddaughter with special needs, it is also a very big blessing in our lives, as far as her spirit. It has given us both a new empathy for special needs children because we now have one in our own lives. I know God has a way of doing that with people, like giving you something in order to touch your heart to minister to others. It might be a heart ache but it's also a blessing."

Challenges didn't end...

Unfortunately, their oldest daughter and son in law, after being married fifteen years, divorced. There was a lot of stress of raising a special needs child. Rose said, "We tried as hard as we knew as grandparents to be inclusive and do everything we could to help." It was often hard for them to watch their adult children struggle in their marriage. There were things they wanted to fix but knew the only action they could take was prayer. It was having to accept that their adult children make their own choices; then live with the consequences.

Rose said, "That hurts. But it was also having to say, 'I've done the best I can do' and having those open conversations. We are not perfect, but we have tried to love and support and encourage them in their walk with the Lord and in their marriage." Every year, they gave their married children the gift of a marriage retreat or family vacation. They didn't give them things but tried to help them build in their relationship and their marriage and in their family.

In addition to supporting their adult children and grandchildren, they were also a part of the 'sandwich generation', while assisting Rose's Mom, who had many physical needs. Instead of feeling the squeeze of the 'sandwich', they learned to work together as a family to care for her Mom and in the process, found a balance in their lives and in their marriage.

Somebody to do life with

They looked at each other with huge smiles and laughter. Rose began her greatest blessing in their marriage, "Having somebody to do life with."

Ed couldn't seem to take his eyes off her as she continued, "Just the blessing of the little joys of celebrating just ordinary days together or what God's doing in your life or having that person that is always there. I hope he knows I am his biggest cheerleader and his biggest fan, and I've always felt like he was mine. When you hit those tough moments, even though we may not always agree, or you have those little memories and inside jokes that can cause raucous laughter to come out of nowhere."

She added this blessing, "Our kids and when we see them succeed. When we see them enjoy life and being believers. Watching our kids being baptized and walk with the Lord and serve the Lord and go through school and become productive adults and loving what they're doing. Our joys were watching our girls get married and finding Godly spouses and having grandchildren and getting to spend time with them and influence them. Now retirement together," they both smiled. "Making somebody oatmeal and coffee!" she laughed.

Ed grinned, "Growing old together. I wouldn't want to grow old with anybody else!"

Team Us!

Rose said, "Keep working at it. Like anything in life, it takes effort. Whatever you want to be good at...whether it's your job, a hobby or being physically fit...and marriage is no different. I don't know where we got this idea that a good marriage just happens. It's worth all the effort. Find those things. Read those books. Continually find that thing to keep the spark and to keep growing together," she smiled mischievously at Ed.

"Just like our walk with the Lord...if we're not working at growing in our walk with the Lord, it's going to become stagnant and you're going to go the other direction. It's the same thing with marriage. Keep finding those things you both enjoy doing.

Usually God puts two very different people together, so you need to do those things that also still make you 'you'." She emphasized that you don't lose yourself when you get married, but you really become one. They attended an event that talked about 'Team Us'. That really sums it up. If you're doing something and you're winning...then neither one of you are winning. It's not about 'I win' or 'he wins'...it's about 'we win'. It's about us." She told us they tend to look at everyday life and ask, 'How does this build Team Us?' They just put it in such simple terms, painting such a great picture. That's what we've been striving to do for 32 years. How do we work better together... complement each other?

He bowled for a long time on Monday nights. It gave me the space I needed. Our ministries look a little different. You have an introvert (Rose) and an extravert (Ed)...so it is giving each other grace to go do that."

Rose can say to Ed, 'Go, go...go volunteer over here and meet these 30 people. Let me have my one or two people that I'm going to get very intimate with and know a whole lot more about than most people are ever going to know.' It's OK. It looks different, but we give each other that space to say, 'This is who you are. Enjoy that.' "We also have common ground of serving together and growing together and doing life together."

"When she talks about giving each other space…that's why I have a man cave upstairs and she has the downstairs." They both laughed, "So, we're together in the man cave part of the day but we also have our own time alone and I think that works well for us."

Rose said they might not always agree but at least they listen so they know where their spouse is coming from. They accept the differences because as she says frequently, "Different is not wrong."

"She often works on a project," Ed said laughing, "and if she needs me, she'll let me know and I'll come hold something for her.

"Rather than thinking, 'This is your role or that is your role...or if you were the right kind of wife, you would do this or if you were the right kind of husband, you would have that...because my Dad always did that, or my Mom always did that'."

Ed grinned, "She learned really fast that I was NOT her Dad when it came to fixing things!"

She shook her head up and down and teased with the truth, "That's why my Dad

taught me how. I'm the one with the toolbox!"

Doing life together

It is easy to see Ed and Rose don't expect their marriage to get better by doing nothing. They work at being 'one' and intentionally plan times together to enjoy life and each other. Most of all, they have learned to give each other space...and a lot of grace!

Lew & Sandy – Jesus is Always Their Number One

MARRIED 55 YEARS

"His Master replied, 'Well done, good and faithful servant! You have been faithful with a few things; I will put you in charge of many things. Come and share your master's happiness'!" Matthew 25:21

A kiss tells it all!

Lew's expression of love is kissing your hand. It doesn't really matter if you are a man or a woman, young or old...you get his tender kiss on your hand.

As you join us on their journey, you will find his trademark kiss and ever-present smile express more than his ability to speak allows. You see, Lew suffered a massive stroke at the age of 49. Over a period of years, he has experienced numerous hospitalizations, often with life threatening complications. Gradually his speech deteriorated until now it is even difficult for his wife to understand many of his words. His body has been weakened so he is unable to stand or walk on his own. However, the years weakening his body have never been able to weaken his love for Jesus and for others!

Sandy's devotion to him is seen in her gentle touch on his arm. She leaned into him and listened intently for his words, so she could share them with us. His words may have been few, but they were never empty chatter. Listen closely, not only to Lew and Sandy's story, but listen for their hearts.

Their story began...

He was a senior at Otterbein College in Westerville, Ohio, and she was a freshman. Lew gave his thumbs up and an excited, "Whooooo!"

As Lew laughed, Sandy said, "I'll make this short. He looked really old to me when I met him. He was a senior, and he was dressed up in an ROTC uniform that day. He looked old, but yet so handsome." Lew laughed out loud and put his hands over his eyes in embarrassment. "I was really drawn to him. My friend who was with me said, 'If you ever need anything, he's the guy to go to." Since Sandy didn't have any immediate needs or problems, she stored that information away in case she would need it later.

"Then, one night, they had a freshman dance at the Student Union, ONLY for freshman. No one else was supposed to come. I had been dancing, and I was tired, so I sat down. All of a sudden, Lew came in the room and came over to me and said, 'I want to dance with you.' So, I got up and he said, 'I just came here tonight to dance with you.' He swirled me like this," making a circle with her hand, "over to the door that was the exit, and he left." If he could have rolled over in laughter, Lew would have! All Sandy could do was smile.

"I don't know if God had any part in that, but it did something to me." Lew was laughing out loud and she added, "My heart just went flip-flop, and from then on, it just grew. So, Lew was dating about 35,000 other people at the time..." There was a pause as Lew and Sandy looked at each other and couldn't hold back the laughter. When she caught her breath, she said, "Then finally, at the end of his senior year, and my freshman year, the military sent him to Rhein Main, Germany. We were dating, but Lew still wasn't convinced. I was! We said 'goodbye' and wrote each other for a year. Finally. Finally. He asked me to marry him."

Lew gave a huge fist pump into the air, 'Yeah!'

"One little cute thing. I was so impressed, because what I got in the mail were telegrams that said, 'WILL YOU BE MY FIANCE?' 'WILL YOU MARRY ME?' I think I got three of those...'Will you'? I was so impressed. I showed everyone in the dorm. Look at this! He even sent me a telegram!' When I got to Germany, I went to the post office, and I found out you could pick out a phrase for fifty cents.

So, he actually spent a dollar and a half." Lew's shoulders were shaking as he laughed uncontrollably!

The big attraction

Sandy looked admiringly at her husband, "He was very handsome...that's for sure! He was so kind and caring. Lew had a lot of positions in college, and he could have acted very hoity-toity. (Does that show my age?) But, he didn't. He loved everybody. He smiled at everybody. He would help anybody. That's what attracted me."

Even though it was difficult to understand Lew, this statement came out pretty clearly: "She had a neat body!" That started his laughing all over again.

She looked embarrassed as she said, "Gosh! If you were that attracted to me, why did it take all those years?"

Lew grinned as he kissed her hand and indicated to her, he just wanted to make sure.

According to Sandy, even though they were dating pretty exclusively, he had a lot of friendships with other girls. It seemed since his parents were stationed in England, it then guaranteed he had places to go on Thanksgiving and Christmas!

Lew shook his head in agreement as he admitted the truth of Sandy's statement, "Good food to eat plus they were really pretty, too."

Biggest challenge

He struggled with a few words when Sandy assisted him, "He's not going to say anything bad about me. He's just not, but he could. I would say that the biggest challenge for us was not knowing Jesus. For 13 years, we didn't consider divorce, because it just wasn't done in our family, but we argued a lot...especially when kids came along. I thought I was the leader. He tried to be the leader, but I pretty well squelched that." Lew shook his head in agreement.

Sandy did a Bible study with a friend and then came home and pushed her husband to go to a couples' Bible study. She said, "After about three months he found Jesus, and when he found Him...Oh boy," she gave a little whistle, "did our life change!" That made Lew snicker!

She added, "After giving our lives to Jesus, our marriage wasn't problem free! We truly believe Ephesians where it says the man is supposed to be the leader, and the wife is submissive. What submissive means to me is that I'm a counselor, a prayer partner, pray for him to hear the Lord on decisions. With our children, we both pray together. It was joyful, but it was tough because it changed our whole lifestyle." They would learn a new way to live.

Life changed again

When Lew was 49 and Sandy was 46, he suffered a massive stroke. Sandy said, "We were very young, so we were very surprised."

Prior to the stroke, he called Sandy into his office one day. He said, 'Sandy, I want you to sit down and I want to tell you something the Lord has put on my heart. If anything would ever happen to me, here's what I want....'

'Oh, Lew'…she pushed the thought away. "You know how we wives are sometimes. We don't want to hear that."

"He said...'Just listen. Here's what I want you to do. I want you to get our oldest son and I want you two plus David and Tim (their other two sons) to pray about what to do. If anything would ever happen...call them all together.' So, when his stroke happened, it wasn't like: 'What do I do?' because my leader can't talk or do anything. I knew what to do. I always thank God for that!"

Some years prior, Lew and his partner, Ted, had formed Son Shine Ministries, an international Christian ministry. Lew and Sandy, along with Ted and his wife, Barbara, had been the main team going out and presenting seminars all across the country and in numerous overseas locations. It was, however, no longer a little ministry. A discipleship training program had been operating and the size of the support staff had increased. Sandy said, "The stroke changed our lives from the standpoint of ministry. Everybody was very concerned about the ministry but Ted, our son, David and the Staff just came together. I actually think it was a drawing together that maybe hadn't been going on before."

The stroke happened while they were out in Virginia on a mission trip. Forty days after the stroke, they flew back to Dallas Rehab where Lew spent the next six months. Following extensive rehab, he was able to talk, drive a car and walk with a cane. Even though they could no longer do their signature two-day seminars, they were able to share 'The Joy of Agony' (a presentation about his stroke) for an hour or two.

His deep love for people, caused Lew to go out several days a week to a local water park where he would write books and letters. He would also minister to people all over the waterpark with his wonderful smile, and ability to listen and listen and listen before speaking.

Sandy said, "So, the ministry and our lives just changed. It didn't take our focus off Jesus. We needed Him even more than ever."

Blessed with each other

"We are so different from each other but that's what keeps it exciting!" She wanted us to remember that marriage isn't all hard. It's also fun and brings companionship.

When asked about blessings, Lew's eyes lit up and he gently touched Sandy's arm, "My wife."

"Well, thank you, Lew.' How about your relationship with Jesus? Did that stop with your stroke? Do you still pray?"

Lew said a resounding, "Oh, yes!"

"Do you get answers?"

"Oh, Yes!"

Sandy then asked if he could read the Bible. His words were garbled but his expression said he couldn't read anymore. "So, what do we do in the mornings together?" He smiled and laughed, and Sandy translated, "We read the Bible together. We pray together. People who Lew has told to write books...we get their books in the mail. So, we read a little bit of that. We go back and read some of the books that

Lew has written. We are on 'Parents' Victory Kit' right now and it is just hilarious. We have good laughs over our parenting skills," she crossed her eyes and smiled, "and what God did, in spite of us."

'Give up' in your vocabulary?

Lew's eyes sparkled when he said, "Oh no...never...never!"

She asked, "You never felt like giving up?"

To which his response was, "No...never."

"Lew, did you ever get depressed?"

"Oh yes...sure. But never give up!"

Sandy said, "I don't think I've ever wanted to give up. I think both of us get tired, but I don't think we've ever wanted to give up."

Lew's voice stressed, "Oh, no...never!"

She reminded us, "Every day there is either an up or a down. That's how it is with a stroke. They told us that." Lew gave a little laugh of agreement as she continued. "Sometimes when I get tired, I have to watch...getting tired and our relationship when I am tired. Lew puts up with me."

He lightly rubbed her arm, and said, "No..."

Sandy had a sad look on her face as she said, "No, you do. I know I hurt you sometimes when I get grouchy. So then, usually one of our boys will come, like Tim, and make Lew laugh and just have a great time. It gets us back on track a little bit. It's never like giving up. I would never want it any different than it is right now, because I know that I love Lew and I want to help him. That's something God puts in us women."

He shook his fist in the air in victory, "Right! Right!"

"When Lew does get depressed, he always has told me, even before his stroke...'Sandy, you really can't help me. This is between Jesus and me, and He'll bring me up'."

"Yay!!!!" came from Lew's lips.

From personal relationships they made, Sandy shared about spouses of those with strokes, especially the wives, because she dealt with them more often. "I would say that so many of the women whose husbands had a brain injury of some kind just said, 'I can't do it. I'm leaving'!"

Lew was looking down and shaking his head side to side as she continued, "They would often be counseled, 'You know your husband is going to be completely different. He is not going to be the same man'. That's what they told me about Lew, and I told them, 'He is the same man. He has the same heart. Yes, his actions and maybe speech are going to be different, but he is the same man'." She was not giving up on Lew!

Sharing hope

Together, through this dramatic change in their own lives, they have had a great opportunity to minister to people from all walks of life. In the process of sharing with others, Sandy felt she was also strengthened. "You know how that works when you're talking about Jesus." Without hesitating, Sandy said, "People shouldn't give up. They're missing life and the miracles that God wants to do.

Another patient in rehab could only say 'OK', so we called him 'OK, Ben'." Sandy said Ben and his wife were also counseled by medical staff to divorce. Through much encouragement from Lew and Sandy, this couple stayed together.

Honest appreciation

When asked what they appreciated about each other, they looked at each other and they couldn't hold a straight face! Sandy teased a warning, "Lew, you're on video!" He was laughing out loud and could hardly contain himself. She looked over at us and giggled, "You can cut this out of the interview. I don't know how this came up with our son...I think it was about going to get a massage. I never had one and my birthday was coming up. I said, 'I really don't want one.' Finally, I said, 'Dad and I give massages to each other every night'. Our son, David, waved his arms in front of him like an umpire, and said, 'NO MORE...NO MORE'!" We were all roaring as she finished her thought, "Oh brother! I think that's another thing your kids and everybody else assume is that your physical life with your husband is over, and it's not. It's just different."

Lew laughed, "Gosh no...Gosh no..."

As she struggled to gain composure, she said, "Now I forgot the question!"

Finally, as she pulled it together, she said what she appreciated about Lew was: "His enduring love for me that just continues when I'm out of sorts...when I'm tired. Kindness." She also recounted a day when she was making a doctor's visit. Somebody was coming down the hall when all of a sudden, Lew just glowed. "I mean, honestly, that smile. He reached out and kissed the hand of whoever was passing by. I would like to be more like that. It just shows on his face. That love! That's what I appreciate. I told him the other day he was my greatest witness as far as the love of Christ. God planned it that way."

He smiled and shook his head back and forth in humble disagreement.

When it came time for Lew to share what he appreciated about Sandy, he struggled a little with words as Sandy tenderly touched the side of his head, and said, "Do you want me to make up things?" Lew gave a sweet grin and worked to form the right words. Sandy had to ask him to repeat it several times and even though he was very frustrated, she continued to patiently ask him to say the words. He said, "She's...my...wife. She is always my wife."

Sandy smiled back, "Thank you. You're stuck with me, Kid!"

To that, Lew gave a thumbs up!

Life is a little harder

They have both had to make life adjustments over the years. Sandy said, "We have learned some methods now. Lew always wants to talk at night, and we've learned that is the very worst time to try to communicate, because every muscle in him is so tired. He has patiently learned not to do that." She looked over at Lew, "The reason I think you told me you want to get it out is you're afraid you'll forget it." Lew shook his head 'yes'. "He can't write things down like he used to in order to remember them. Not trying to talk when he is tired is one thing we both had to learn, because I really wanted to know what he says, too. It takes patience on both of our parts. He does get frustrated that he can't get the words out.

You aren't an angel all the time, are you, Lew?"

He faked a shocked look on his face and when they couldn't contain it, they both burst out laughing.

Reaching out

Lew packs up that engaging smile of his and is still excited about reaching out to others at every opportunity God gives him. They go to Chicken Express, a local fast food restaurant, four times a week. She said, "We worked up to that. We take 'Reach Out Your Hand' books (stories compiled by Lew and Sandy), and we've given away about 7000. Sometimes people come and talk to us, and we can pray for them. God has also called Lew to go to churches and encourage pastors. Every Sunday we usually go to a different church. It's really amazing. He encourages the pastors, and now we know almost all of them.

We're happy to do anything. And Lew, what do you do? You encourage pastors. You write a million letters. Honestly, I was counting letters...how many stamps at 49 cents apiece'!" they both laughed. "No discount for bulk! He writes, I would say at least 7-10 letters a day." It is evident that it requires extreme amounts of physical and mental effort for him to write those letters. Sandy said, "He's a witness to me from the standpoint that he's so committed to doing what God has him do."

Lew pumped his fist in the air. "Horraay!"

However, going where God wants them to go isn't always without challenges. Mobility for Lew requires, most often Sandy, to lift him for transfers, as well as lifting his wheelchair to load and unload any time they get out for a drive. Embarking and disembarking a plane with a narrow aisle wheelchair has resulted more than once in torn and bruised skin. Barriers to many are not barriers to Lew and Sandy. They are not deterred from being out with people...where they believe God wants them to be!

Jesus is #1

Lew spoke very slowly, even with great difficulty to say, "Jesus...Jesus!" He held up his thumb, "Jesus is number one! Jesus is number one!"

She added, "You learn every day how He can be trusted more."

Doesn't need words

"Lew doesn't always believe me when I tell him that his look and actions often speak louder than words. He thinks I am just trying to pep him up, but I see it!"

We also couldn't help but notice Lew holding Sandy's hand throughout the entire interview. Most of the time, they weren't looking at the camera or us, but at each other while they spoke. As they gazed into each other's eyes, their love, devotion and commitment to each other spoke even louder than their words!

Going Home

On July 10, 2018, Lew went home to be with his Jesus. It is there he will run with abandon and praise God once again with a clear, booming voice.

For his 80 years here on earth, he had a heart that loved people more than his head feared rejection. There were no barriers his smile couldn't cross. He and his wife, Sandy, together lived every day knowing 'Jesus is the Answer' to every question they would face!

Mike & Connie – Our Marriage was Dead...Just not Buried!

MARRIED 49 YEARS

Copyright © 2018 Kyla Briney Photography

"And the God of all grace, who called you to His eternal glory in Christ, after you have suffered a little while, will Himself restore you and make you strong, firm and steadfast." I Peter 5:10

As a woman, I became very adept at putting on my plastic face, especially at church. I didn't want anyone to see anything but a great marriage. I did all the right things, smiled at all the right times and served in all the right places.

I put up a fake front for everyone to see and from comments I heard, plenty of people were fooled into thinking we had that perfect marriage. Perfect didn't mean I was always happy. It just meant I learned how to make myself look the part.

I wasn't a loud, bossy wife or Mom. I was more of a manipulator than a pusher. If Mike or our son, Matt, was on the phone, I was standing right there beside them coaching on what to say or what they forgot to say. On more than one occasion, Mike pushed the phone toward me and said in a voice loud enough for the caller to hear, 'Here Connie. Do you want to tell them?' I was embarrassed, to say the least…but that didn't stop me from trying to control the two men in my life. I felt as if what they did, how they dressed or what they said would reflect on me and be an extension of my own image. I wanted them to be perfect so that I would appear perfect. The result: I don't think my son and my husband ever felt they were good enough and eventually when my mouth opened, they learned to plug their ears."

A few months to fix them

"My attempts at 'faking it' could continue only so long before someone would eventually see through the façade. The unveiling happened when we were married about 15 years. We moved to Texas where we were to train with SonShine Ministries, a Christian ministry focusing on families. Panic!! We only had a few months to get ready and I needed to have my husband and son 'fixed' before we reported for our classes.

When we worked, traveled and lived side by side with our ministry teammates, I quickly learned nothing was a secret. As far as I was concerned, everyone saw the real us and we failed at 'perfect'. My worst nightmare!"

"As a guy, I was job focused - position focused. I was in the top three rank of non-commissioned officers in the Air Force. In the later years of my career, I was being courted for a job with a large aircraft manufacturing company. I was knowledgeable and secure in my job and felt I was 'good' at what I did. I was President of the Protestant Parish Council at the base chapel, so I felt significant in the rest of my life as well. Sure, there were issues at home, but nothing serious. Besides, everybody has issues. Nobody's marriage is perfect."

Oh, it's you!

Our story didn't exactly start out perfect either. It began with the 'dreaded' blind date arranged by our best friends from high school. A blind date usually meant, 'some poor, undesirable person needed a relationship rescue'!! However, not in this case…

When this tall, handsome guy arrived for the date, he walked into the front entry of her home and saw an open door to the living area. Very welcoming…except there was no one coming to the door when he knocked and knocked again even louder. Still no one answered.

Here he is. Guy on a blind date. No idea what this 'dream date' even looked like! "I heard some movement in the house so I kind of stuck my head in the open door to see if anyone was coming. This girl came down the stairs…and when she saw me, she said, 'Oh…it's you!' and turned around and walked back upstairs. I was standing there thinking, 'What in the world was that?' Later, I learned it was Connie's younger sister, Nancy, who was waiting for her own date to arrive. Then, Connie came walking down the stairs and I liked what I saw." Nothing 'blind' about this date!

Like an old shoe

Mike admitted his dating history was not all that successful, but this night was different! "In the past, if there were any lulls in the conversation, I felt totally uncomfortable. With Connie, when there was nothing being said between the two of us, I still felt extremely comfortable."

We laughed because we both knew what Connie's normal come-back to Mike's 'comfortable' comment would be. "Yah...comfortable...like an old shoe!"

"As much as I hated to admit it...I was also attracted to him because he was comfortable! Not like an old shoe but he was so easy to talk with."

"I knew when I took Connie home at the end of that first night...I wanted to marry her."

He got the look, "If you would have said that out loud, Mike, I would have run away as fast as I could. I never would have gone on a second or third or fourth date!"

"But I didn't kiss you until the third date."

"No...and after the second date, I was thinking...'he didn't even kiss me. Maybe he doesn't like me.' So, why didn't you kiss me? Was it normal for you to wait?"

Without hesitation, "Nope! I waited because I respected you."

"Good! I thought maybe I had bad breath or something."

How much time??

Even though we knew each other for about two years...military assignments (including Viet Nam) allowed us to spend a total of around 30 days in the same location. We entered marriage knowing much of what we did from very limited phone calls and letters. (Remember...no internet or Skype back then!) Our early days were more apart than together!

We looked at each other and couldn't help breaking into spasmodic laughter. We both knew our story well. "On our wedding day, I was walking down the aisle toward Mike thinking, 'What am I doing!! For all I know this guy could be an ax murderer'! However, I kept walking to the altar! Crazy!"

Immediate departure

As soon as the ink was dry on the marriage license, we headed to our first Air Force duty station in Louisiana. We were a long way from home and had no money to make long-distance phone calls. No calling Mom or Dad to get advice or to complain. We had to figure out how to solve our problems together.

Immediately, Air Force Mike worked 12 hours a day - six days a week. Nurse Connie worked rotating shifts in the hospital. We often kid each other that we never had a fight that first year of marriage...because you can't fight if you don't see each other. (More true than you think!)

Different as night and day

'Peas in a pod'? Nope! Throughout our marriage, we found we were 'as different as night and day'. Take a look at this list:

Mike	Connie
* Logical and factual	* Relational/emotional
* Organized (roll up the hose ...<u>every</u> time)	* Tosser (throw it in - untangle later)
* Reserved - draws back in crowds	* Outgoing - energized by people
* Laid back (type Z)	* Go-go-go (Type A)
* Think it out - (talk later)	* Talk it out (now!)
* Adventurous	* Scaredy-cat

Our differences probably drew us together in the first place, but in all reality, doesn't that list look like a KABOOM just waiting to happen??

It definitely was lurking around the corner in our marriage. We wish we could tell you we've found the 'perfect' balance between our differences - but that would be a stretching the truth...just a bit!. The truth is, when one of us wants to hang around after church to talk (guess who), you might find the other one sitting in the car, more than ready to head home. Go-go-go lady finds hanging out in the 'snooze zone' in the afternoon of a sunny day, less than desirable, whereas, the guy who needs some down time isn't always looking for the next great adventure outside of his recliner.

Stop the interview - I want to get off!

To be honest, right smack, dab in the middle of our own video interview for this book, we had to stop the camera. We started talking about our differences and one of those differences jumped out and caused some jaw tightening and smile removing.

We took a breather (about 48 hours worth) and finally joined hands a couple days later to pray at our breakfast table. It was then we were reminded just how different we are and yet how wonderfully we balance each other because of those differences. Our conclusion: Different isn't a bad thing...it's just...well...different! There is no 'perfect' balance. No 50/50 solution (equal time for each spouse to do it their way). Surprise - one of us can't control everything we do either!

As we prayed that day at the breakfast table, God reminded us of how the differences that drew us together, have also formed us into who we are today. He humbled both of our hearts, pointing out our need to put each other first and see the other persons' needs as well as our own. (It's not like we never heard that before...but we're still working on 'putting it into practice'.)

Have moving van will travel

As a career military family, we made the move to a new location every three years almost like clockwork. Definitely, it was something that pulled us

(OK…yanked us) out of our comfort zone. We had to jump right in and meet people because we knew in three years we were gone again. The bonus: we still have close friends from those military years, all over the country!

Being forced to make adjustments to change on such a regular basis, also pushed our little family toward each other. We never dreaded change but got excited about every move to a new location. We would head to the library (an ancient version of the internet) and check out all kinds of materials about the new city we would soon call home.

Our son, Matt, thought moving was absolutely normal and during preparation for one of those moves, we asked him if he was going to miss his friends. He said, 'No, I'm moving. They're 'sposed to miss me, Mom!'

When we moved to Germany, he attended a local middle school, where naturally, only German was spoken in the classroom. He astounded us with his ability to adapt and learn in a foreign culture and foreign language. That move wasn't easy, but change became our family's normal and Matt was often our example of how to do that well!

Never enough money

In our early years of marriage, military enlisted pay and (believe it or not) a nurse's salary were both low on the pay scale. The only thing high was our lack of management of those funds, which made it even more challenging. We bought stuff we didn't need and paid for it long after it wore out.

We weren't on the same page with our finances either. "Mike was more of a spender. I could pinch a penny until it squeaked! Eventually, 'budget' meant we spent until there was no more left in the bank each month."

When we started going back to church, our friends had much more money than we did and bigger and more beautiful homes. Pile envy on to limited funds and it created a very real temptation for dissatisfaction and getting deeper in debt!

"I would stress and cry each month as I paid the bills. (My Mom paid the bills, so I thought I was supposed to do that, too!) On the other side of our marriage, Mike had no idea where all the money was going.

It eventually became less of a challenge when we sat down together to pay the bills. At first, Mike put the checks in the envelopes and eventually he started writing the checks. It didn't take long until he took over paying the bills! We found he was a much better 'accountant' than I was. We both know where the money goes but I don't have to be the 'worrier' each month!"

When we finally let God take care of our money, we started giving to Him first. That's when the stress started to lift off us financially...AND we were finally able to get out of debt and live within our financial means! We always had 'just enough'! That one thing alone lifted tons of stress off of our marriage!

Not just scrambled' eggs

Although back in church and living in a new-found relationship with Jesus, we did a great job of scrambling more than eggs! The more we served God, the more we mixed up our priorities! We lost sight of putting Him first, our marriage second, our family next. Last on the priority list should have been jobs, church, hobbies and whatever else begged for our time. Our mistake was often putting everything and everybody before our marriage and family. It took a toll on our relationship with each other and with our son, who soon saw us take time away from him to do 'church stuff' and 'people time'.

We made a lot of stumbles. Even our church friends didn't seem to have all the answers about how to do marriage right. We were on the road to learn by trial and error…and mostly error!

When we were called into full time Christian service as missionaries, our priority troubles seemed to get more pronounced. Now we had school, full time staff positions and travel on mission teams all thrown into the mix all at the same time. Busyness became an enemy of our marriage. Even though we were teaching others how to have a strong marriage and family, we forgot to take time to strengthen the weak areas in our own family.

The walls came tumbling down

We don't know exactly when or how it happened but about 16 years into our marriage, those outwardly strong, impenetrable walls began crumbling.

"From my side, it started with me comparing Mike to all the other men we knew. I looked at all their best qualities and put them together into one 'ideal' man. There was no way Mike could compete with that model guy!

The comparing soon turned to complaining (not always out loud but more frequently a silent complaining to God in my heart). Discontent became aggravation and eventually turned into seething anger. We weren't screamers, so there was a silent undercurrent of anger in our home. Pretty soon, anger wears you out. You can only hate for so long before you give up and just really don't care anymore. I soon quit feeling. I could look at my husband and I had about as much emotion as if I was looking at a concrete wall.

We didn't believe in divorce, but I prayed a truck would hit him. Then I would be the poor widow and God would have rescued me from a horrible situation and a dead marriage. I would never have left him, but I prayed God would kill him."

Mike teased, "Take me out!"

Memories of that time in horrible time in our marriage flooded back into our hearts and minds.

"Oh yeah! I knew as a husband I was in trouble, but I was just overwhelmed with my job and everything else going on in our lives! I didn't know what to do to fix it."

"At that time, our ministry travel schedule was packed as we now presented programs all across Europe. In addition, I was tasked with meeting all of the military chaplains in Europe." (It was in the 100s…a seemingly impossible task!)

"I struggled with feeling inadequate to fulfill the call God had on my life to minister, teach and preach. At the end of the first year out in the mission field, I was disappointed when for our second year of service, I was moved from being co-director to working under a new director of the office. I felt so down it was just a struggle to survive."

"In the middle of Mike's struggles, I was feeling discontented and dissatisfied with him and everything he did. I remember a conversation I had with a mentor of mine. I complained. She listened. When I was done, she said, 'All I've heard you say is what Mike isn't doing. Where is Jesus in all of this?' I thought, 'Well if Jesus was here, he would fix Mike! I kept looking at <u>him</u> because I thought he was the only one who needed to change. I never verbally attacked him, but I withdrew my support and confidence in him. I don't think he could miss my hopelessness when he looked into my eyes."

"I'm not sure why but being in full time Christian service seemed to make it worse for Connie and me, but our relationship was going downhill, and we were only going through the motions. Our marriage looked good on the outside, but it was very broken on the inside."

"Mike and I worked really hard at doing God's work and got exhausted. Then we didn't have the time or energy for our marriage."

"The dichotomy is that Connie and I were presenting family seminars...focused on Jesus...and yet what we were teaching and what we were living wasn't matching up. What a major disconnect!"

About face

If there could be an 'about face' of a heart and mind, we saw it!

"When my mentor was coaching me, she said I needed to encourage my husband, I remember thinking, 'I'll encourage him when he does something right!' Every time I tried to make a list of what he did right, my paper was always blank. I wasn't only sparing in my use of encouragement. I left that word completely out of my vocabulary.

It was then God spoke into my heart, 'If you ask Me how to encourage Mike, you will never have to lie. I will always tell you something he does right.' It was absolutely true. God showed me many men leave...but my husband was still here. There are men who don't provide for their families, but my husband always worked to provide for our family. When I allowed, God always helped me to encourage Mike with my words."

"That little bit of encouragement from Connie softened my heart...and it was just a small part of us getting better."

"It's wasn't just 'boom' and all of a sudden I was in love with him again...but it was over a period of days and weeks and months and years that God began reigniting my love for Mike and our love for each other. We began to see each other with different eyes and hearts. We had both been hurt and we had both done the hurting, so we both needed healing."

Better forgivers

We have learned to become much better forgivers. Through many years of our marriage, disagreements were followed by long periods of silence with no real resolution.

"He clammed up! I hated silence! I hated waiting to resolve conflict! He wanted to leave the room....and I was chasing after him trying to force him to talk so we could get this resolved...NOW!"

"Connie was faster at processing than I was. I needed time to go away and think."

"The silence would last until Mike started talking to me and acting nicer and then I would know everything was OK again. I just never knew how long it would take. Needless to say, we had an unhealthy way of handling conflict. I needed to learn to give Mike some space to work it out..."

"...I didn't even realize that I eventually got it all worked through in my head but never went back to Connie to talk with her about it."

"Now it takes so much less time for Mike to process and me to wait for Mike to want to talk about it. We have also learned that forgiveness is the key to the 'about face' in our relationship."

Becoming a team

When the spark of restoration began, there was still plenty lacking in our relationship. We lived our lives almost independently from each other. We were both strong willed, made many decisions on our own and got a D+ in the teamwork department.

Teamwork? It didn't happen in the way you might think. Not through attending a seminar or retreat. Not through any great awakening. We started to become a team by digging in the mud! Really! Digging in the mud!

After our first year in the mission field in Germany, our partners left. The same thing happened the next year when our second teammates made the same decision. Mike felt undercurrents that he was one of the primary reasons those staff members left. It was deflating and discouraging for him

Without the other half of our team, our office in Germany was closed and we were returned to ministry headquarters in Texas. When meeting with leadership, Mike felt he heard God telling him not to say anything but to accept whatever decision was made and to work hard at whatever the assignment.

For Mike and I, "It was a turning point for our relationship. We had been working on leadership and speaking teams overseas and were now working in maintenance of the ministry property. Even though meant to help us, our new position often felt like a demotion from speaking and leading- to mowing, trimming, cleaning ditches or fixing whatever was broken."

"The thing that strengthened Connie and I the most was a water leak! A main line on the ministry property had been leaking for a while, so it was a really messy area. As we tried to dig up the water line to find the break...it was almost impossible with a regular shovel. We ended up on our hands and knees in the mud using big serving spoons..."

"...that we 'requisitioned' from the retreat kitchen!" (That's when a lot of loud laughter ensued in the middle of our story-telling!)

"We were covered in mud... It was a lot of hard work, but we got the job done."

"And...maybe for the first time in a long time, Mike and I worked <u>with</u> each other...not against each other."

"Side by side in the muck, God began to change our attitudes toward each other and my heart toward Connie. That's when we started on the road to being partners! (Us against the mud!)"

As difficult as that time was, we can now laugh at the thought of those two big spoons! God used that incident to bond us together and prepare us for the future when we would be working even more closely together than that day working side by side in the mud.

"I think what blessed me was to see Mike's faithfulness. He never complained about digging a ditch or fixing pipes or any other messy work. I watched him over the next few years, as he was eventually promoted to Director of Mission Operations, Director of the Discipleship School and then to Chief of Staff."

Our eyes locked on each other, "When some other men might have left or would have given up or been angry...I watched your faithfulness...and God rewarded your faithfulness."

Marriage remodel

We had been following Christ and serving Him for many years, but the real challenge was being confronted with the Biblical standard for the Christian home. We were operating on our own understanding mainly from what we saw our parents do. (Why wreck a good thing?)

We saw in God's Word where it said the husband was to be the leader and the wife to be the helpmate. We were both laughing at the thought of our early years of trying to grasp <u>that</u> God-concept!

"You didn't want to be the leader and I didn't want to be the helper!!! We fumbled, struggled and fought our way through because neither of us knew how to go home and live what the Bible said. Truthfully, I thought I could lead much better than I could help!".

"And I knew how to lead. The military taught me how to be a supervisor. I was in charge of a shop with eight other guys and they did what I told them to do. But...when I got done at the end of a ten-hour day, the last thing I wanted to do was go home and lead again."

We were a mess! So, we struggled and battled each other...and God!

"For Mike and me, our marriage began to feel like a pendulum. It would swing wide one direction and then swoop down wider another direction. 'I wanna lead! No, I don't wanna lead.' 'I will follow! Fat chance I'll follow!' We could almost imagine we were going to fly off the end of the pendulum because it was swinging so wide and so fast. When you think of a pendulum, it eventually comes to the middle and there's a steady, even pace. That's what happened to our marriage, but it took commitment to hang on tight while it was swinging. By the way, it doesn't mean we do it perfectly now..."

"No, we don't!", Mike teased.

"Sometimes, we still struggle but we know what God wants us to do and we know His way is always the best way."

Much like a home with never ending projects, our marriage continues in an ongoing restoration and remodel. Through that, we continue to see our relationship growing much stronger.

Back to the frigid WHAT???

We can usually tell when something is our idea or when it is God's idea. Our ideas might sound like this: 'Beach ministry in Hawaii!' 'Put your feet up and retire!' God's ideas have more of a commitment and challenge ring to them. 'When you finish your seven-year commitment as missionaries, go back to South Dakota and start your own ministry.'

WAIT A MINUTE! WHAT???? Go back to South Dakota???

From Mike's perspective, "Quite frankly, I hated South Dakota! That's why I went into the military for 20 years and seven years as a missionary. Moving back home was the last thing in my mind. Yet, every time, I walked into the ministry office where I worked, my heart would be drawn back to the map of the Midwest."

"The blessing to me was that Mike also felt a call to go back home not only to start a ministry but also to help care for my Mom. She was the only living parent, so his desire to help care for her blessed me beyond measure. (And you can learn to live like an Eskimo, if you try hard enough!)"

Good for each other

"Mike...number 1, I appreciate your gift of giving. You are very generous in giving of our resources and on top of that, you're a good money manager. I tend to round off numbers and you will work to balance everything to the last penny. Yay, Mr. Accountant!!"

"One of the things I appreciate about Connie is her servant's heart and her desire to care for other people...do things for other people."

"Because of you, Mike, I've learned to try new things. Before we got married, I was afraid I might get hurt or something bad would happen. It almost paralyzed me but, you gave me courage. When you got a motorcycle...I got a motorcycle. (I didn't know what a clutch was...so, it was obvious I didn't know how to ride it either!). I could have killed myself, but I felt safe with you next to me, teaching me. When you learned how to scuba dive, you taught me how to snorkel. When Matt was just a little guy, he and I would go snorkeling so we could be near you. I never would have attempted something like that without you to give me the courage and confidence...as well as great instruction! You pushed me beyond my 'comfortable' into the 'fun zone'. Oh and...you have helped me be more spontaneous and not so schedule driven!"

Got it all together?

We knew God saved our marriage and He was calling us to give that same hope to other couples. If you think we started teaching about marriage because we had it all together, you would be wrong!

When we sat down to look at what we would teach, we discovered the four potential topics: partnership, conflict resolution, communication and rebuilding trust, were the same four hot buttons in our own marriage. We can now see how God taught us (and was still teaching us) so we could teach others.

Learning through aging

This is so laughable! When our ears were younger, we could hear a conversation from another room and not miss a word. Now a 'few' years older (and a little 'deafer'), we can no longer hear through walls. That one thing alone can be an irritant in our marriage and can cause our voices to raise out of frustration.

We are realizing what we learned about communication is still built on solid principles, but we always need to keep learning how to communicate through all stages of life. The same is true of the other three topics we taught. The circumstances might have changed, but those same principles hold true...and...we are never too old to grow and learn!

Don't give up!

So many couples give up...sometimes before their first anniversary. Others hang on until the inevitable seven-year itch or when their nest is empty. If we had given up when our marriage was barely gasping...we would have missed all that we have now. We would have missed the blessings and all God has given us in each other and the life we now share. Life today is way more wonderful than we could have imagined.

Perfect? No...we still know how to push each other's buttons and our strong personalities sometimes clash...so our life is not perfect...<u>but</u> it is wonderful!

Advice from two old gray hairs!

Yes, these gray hairs indicate we might have a few years of experience under our belts.

Mike would say to you - "Before marriage, don't rush the relationship. Spend a lot of time talking, communicating your feelings, dreams and goals. If there's a major mismatch in matters of faith, walk very carefully. People say faith isn't that important but it's probably the most important leg of the tripod in a marriage. When you are dating, ask if you are on the same page spiritually. That issue needs to be resolved and if you can't, you need to walk away from it."

Connie would tell you - "Find ways to stay close to each other. It's so easy to get comfortable. Go to work, come home, sit down and watch TV while falling asleep in your chair. A few years ago, we did 12 Great Dates, where in one year we did 12 things we had never done before. It was a fun challenge to find new and different things to do together. It also helped infuse some new fun things into our lives."

"Have goals. As I look back at my relationship with Connie, the only goals I had were to get married, have a home, have a child or two, a car, a boat and dog, nice house...at least 20 years in the military with a goal to be in upper level management. I never thought about any spiritual goals. We can both be pretty serious so laugh together and laugh often!"

"And...remember...It's not as if you learn it once and 'presto' you do everything right. Every day we have to <u>work</u> at forgiving. Every day we have to <u>work</u> at serving each other. Every day we have to give up our will to do God's will. Believe us when we say, 'It doesn't come naturally!'

Copyright © 2018 Kyla Briney Photography

God has taught me how to look for the things that are right in my husband instead of all the things that are wrong. I am a perfectionist (danger to everyone near me!!) It's a huge blessing for me to have learned to look at all God has done instead of what still needs to be fixed in my husband (or in anyone else, for that matter!)"

Our Answer

There were so many times we both questioned, not only our sanity for staying together, but questioned why Jesus didn't do something to change the other one!

Our marriage was dead…just not buried. Our love for each other was cold. We were beyond arguing because that required emotion. We didn't know a way out and couldn't figure out how to stay in and survive. Tough case? No…Nothing was too hard for Him…even our marriage!

We're so thankful we failed at having the 'perfect marriage'. It was much better for the truth to come out, so we could see just how broken we were. When we quit fighting Him (and each other) we began to see Jesus was the answer to every repair our marriage needed.

It began when He stepped into our broken lives and began a restoration project that gave us brand new hearts for each other. The result: We LOVE each other more than we ever have before. (Really…who would be crazy enough to hop in the car and drive thousands of miles together if they didn't love each other!)

Our marriage is better than it has ever been! Together, we have more fun having fun! God's reconstruction and restoration project has been, and continues to be, a blessing to us!

If you have ever watched one of those renovation shows on TV, you know ometimes you have to tear it down all the way to the studs before it can be built back up! So it was with our marriage!

I've got what??

The past six months have been a roller coaster of emotions as Mike's health took a nosedive. Diagnoses ran everywhere from lymphoma to infection to an autoimmune disease. We saw specialist after specialist searching for the illness with no name! More than once, Mike said, 'I've got what?', only to have it change its name with results from the next test.

During those initial days of uncertainty, we held on even tighter to each other. All of a sudden, projects to install new flooring or reface our fireplace became far less important. We were focused on helping each other through the uncertain days ahead.

Most of the time, while we waited for answers, we held on to each other for dear life...praying and choosing to trust God with the results. To be honest, there were also a few times we were hanging on to each other like a couple of prickly cacti. That's when tensions were high, and it was easy to snap at each other. (If you ask most married couples, that's pretty normal!)

When Mike was finally diagnosed with a rare autoimmune disease, we were relieved. It had a name and we finally had a treatment. He is currently in the process of receiving chemotherapy infusions. The disease is treatable but not curable, so remission is a new word in our vocabulary.

Mike said, "Through all of this, I know one thing for sure: I'm following and trusting (in military jargon), my Lead Scout - Jesus Christ! He has been and continues to be my Hope and my Strength. Connie has been so totally awesome through all of this. The care, comfort and support has been a blessing! She has grown stronger...we both have...knowing that we are in the hands of a great and mighty God. He is Large and in Charge and still sits on the throne in Heaven above! His love and care is sufficient for me!"

We are committed to each other just like our wedding vows said, 'In sickness and in health!'

Many years ago, when our marriage fell apart, sitting in the rubble didn't feel all that great. Now we are both thankful it happened because when there was nothing left, God rebuilt our relationship from the ground up. It made us much stronger so we could withstand any challenge when we stood together!

He knew we would need that today!

Dear Friends…

All of the stories you just read were told by normal people…like you. They didn't try to dress up the 'ugly' but tried to be honest about what you might see when searching below the public smiles on their faces.

As we personally heard their stories, we laughed and cried along with them. We saw God touch hearts and witnessed relationships healed right before our eyes. The bonus - our lives were also changed through these stories. We pray yours will be, too.

Be brave and tell someone your story. Be honest and open. They will love you more for being 'real' than for cleaning and disinfecting it before posting it on social media. Your story isn't like any other story, but like the stories in this book, allow the heart of <u>your</u> marriage to be a story of hope...hope found in Jesus!

Part of a verse in the song, 'God's Not Done with You.', by Tauren Wells, goes like this:

> He's got a plan, this is part of it.
> He's gonna finish what He started.
> He's not done.
> God's not done writing your story.
> No. He's not done.
> He's not done with you!!

If you are in the middle of a 'messy' chapter in your life, let the words of this song speak to your heart. God's not done writing <u>your</u> story. He was there in the beginning glow and remains with you in the middle of your chaos. He will never walk away. He knows how your story ends. Let Him hold the pen.

Remember, you are not alone. We might not be able to run over for a cup of coffee or share laughs over dinner, but we are on your side. We are rooting for you! We are cheering you on! We are praying for your marriage to not just last, but for the heart of your marriage to be overflowing with blessings. He saved our marriage. He can save yours, too!

Mike and Connie

If you want to tell us a little of your story or if you would like to pass on a message to one of the couples in this book, please email us at:
greatplainsministry@sio.midco.net